# ARNOLD SCHWARZENEGGER

## THE LIFE OF A LEGEND

### FIAZ RAFIQ

This edition first published in Great Britain in 2021 by

ARENA SPORT
An imprint of Birlinn Limited
West Newington House
10 Newington Road
Edinburgh
EH9 1QS

www.arenasportbooks.co.uk

First published in 2011 as *Arnold Schwarzenegger: Conversations* by HNL Publishing

ISBN: 9781909715974
eBook ISBN: 9781788853316

British Library Cataloguing-in-Publication Data
A catalogue record for this book is available on request from the British Library.

Designed and typeset by Polaris Publishing, Edinburgh
www.polarispublishing.com

Printed and bound in Great Britain by Bell and Bain Ltd, Glasgow

# CONTENTS

# ACKNOWLEDGMENTS

A big thank you to the staff of *M.A.I.* and *Impact* magazines: Moira, Martin, Neal, John, Roy and especially editor Bob Sykes for giving me the opportunity and embracing me earlier on my writing career. The fifteen years working relationship was fun. To all my editors at the magazines and national newspapers whose help and support have contributed to my success in my professional writing career. Also, I would like to thank the personalities I have interviewed over the years from the sports and entertainment worlds – you are an integral part of the reason behind my success.

I would like to thank my long-time friends Diana Lee Inosanto; Royce Gracie; Rasheda Ali; Ron Balicki; Bob Sykes; Ronnie Green; Lance Lewis; Seyfi Shevket and Peter Consterdine for their countless years of support and encouragement. Special thank you to Alex Ben Block of Alex Ben Block Consulting (www.blockandtackle. biz) for his support.

I would also like to thank Muhammad Ali's brother, Rahaman, who gave me the opportunity to make history. I would like to thank my agent Charlie Brotherstone.

Thank you to Joel Snape for editing the manuscript. A special thank you must go to Neville Moir and my editor Pete Burns at my publishers, Arena, for believing in me and for all their hard work.

I would like to thank my friends in the industry, both in the USA and United Kingdom, who have enriched my life and supported me.

Being a private person, I never really mention my family and certain friends when it comes to acknowledgments. This doesn't mean I've forgotten them or don't appreciate them. Work, for me, is a passion and a profession, as much as I made it an obsession in my life, family and close friends are the heart and soul, so is my religion – nothing is worth living for if these three integral elements are absent.

In life we strive to elevate ourselves and reach a higher plane. Some of us take our passion to the extreme and become totally consumed by it. Of course, to succeed and realize our dreams we must endeavor to pursue our passion wholeheartedly and be dedicated. Achievements and accolades and acclaim are all great, of course, but sooner or later we may, or should, realize that the core happiness and meaning of life lies not in merely fulfilling our ambitions and achievements, but by cherishing those who are close to us and appreciating the normal things in life and be content.

# FOREWORD

## THE TRUTH AND THE LIES

There have been a couple dozen books by or about Arnold Schwarzenegger, on his life, bodybuilding, movies, politics and more. They have covered his improbable rise from obscurity in Austria to his reign as a champion bodybuilder, to his unlikely movie career and subsequent superstardom, to his political career as the 'Governator' of California.

However, few can deliver the details and perspective that Fiaz Rafiq achieves in his exhaustive oral history covering all aspects of Schwarzenegger's epic life and career. It is presented for the most part with a gentle hand, but not without mentioning Schwarzenegger's controversies, especially the stories about his alleged sexual harassment of women and fathering a child out of wedlock with his house maid.

Mostly, however, this is a loving, warm, friendly tribute to Schwarzenegger that provides a lot of insights. It was done without any interviews with Schwarzenegger himself, although Fiaz says they did meet at least once.

My own connection to Fiaz is through our common interest in the late kung fu movie star Bruce Lee. I wrote the first serious book about Lee after his death *The Legend of Bruce Lee* (1974), and Fiaz has written two oral histories – of Bruce Lee and Muhammad Ali – using his same style.

In this book, the extensive interviews are roughly in chronological order with smart narratives that set up the interviews and fill in gaps. Mostly this is the hard work of a dogged professional journalist who interviewed people who know, worked with, worked around or covered Schwarzenegger for both trade and general media.

As a contributing writer for the tabloid newspaper *The Sun* and other prominent newspapers, and as a former regular columnist and contributor to martial arts, action movie and fitness and lifestyle magazines, from *Martial Arts Illustrated* to the MMA publication *Fighters Only*, he learned his trade and shows it here.

What makes this special for the action stars' aficionados is that this covers it all: his early years, his bodybuilding achievements (in great details), his early efforts to get into the movies, his rise to superstardom in the 1980s and 1990s, and his surprise move into politics as Governor of California for over a decade.

The tone is always respectful, sometimes fawning and more often just good solid reporting. People are allowed to speak in their own voice, and freely share memories.

"This man born in a small town in Austria," writes Fiaz, "epitomizes the American Dream perhaps better than anyone else – a ferociously hard worker who moved to the country in his youth, he grabbed every opportunity it offered and now encourages others to do the same."

In an interview with Schwarzenegger's first girlfriend (a relationship that lasted about six years), Barbara Outland Baker, talks about the mountain of muscles she met, how she helped him learn English, and supported his bodybuilding, although it was not of great interest to her.

She also reveals the damaged relationship Schwarzenegger had with his father, who found his son too independent and was not an early believer in his career as a bodybuilder. When she accompanied him on a visit back to Austria for a bodybuilding event at a time he was about 24, Baker recalls Schwarzenegger didn't really want to see his father, but did make a visit out of a sense of duty. She says his father died suddenly not long after that of a heart attack and the wounds between father and son were never really healed.

Actress Tia Carrere, who worked with him on the hit *True Lies*, remembers that Arnold had a great deal of natural curiosity. "He's a perfect example of the American Dream. He has achieved what is possible to achieve in America if you work hard and apply yourself."

At times the Schwarzenegger we all think we know from watching his swaggering, boasting, and self-confidence, masks a deeper brooding inner life.

Mark Lester, who directed him in *Commando*, recalled that, "The night before shooting (began) we had dinner at the hotel . . . Arnold says to me, 'I'm scared to death.' I asked him why. 'The first day of shooting, I'm always scared to death.' I said, 'So am I. Everybody is until we get the first shot, then we're okay.' But I was kind of surprised to hear that."

There are lots of other interesting anecdotes, revealing insights and details about a career that is too amazing even to pass as a movie plot. It was all real to Schwarzenegger. Enjoy this for all the intimate history, color, insights and surprises you will discover about this one-of-a-kind personality. And remember this will not be Schwarzenegger's end. As his famous catch phrase puts it, "I'll be back." And Fiaz will probably write another book about that.

Alex Ben Block
Hollywood showbiz historian and author

# PREFACE

In an age where the word 'superstar' is tossed around lightly, there are still only a few people to whom the title really applies. Of these, there are even fewer personalities who are recognizable around the globe by their face or first name alone, having changed the world and our culture irrevocably: Madonna, Elvis, Pelé . . . and Arnold.

Arnold Schwarzenegger, the greatest bodybuilder in history, icon of machismo, archetype Hollywood action hero and successful politician is a global celebrity and one of the greatest success stories of all time. This man born in a small town in Austria epitomizes the American Dream perhaps better than anyone else – a ferociously hard worker who moved to the country in his youth, he grabbed every opportunity it offered and now encourages others to do the same. From a tough childhood and impoverished youth, he used his considerable talents to pursue first a career in bodybuilding, then films, then politics, and made himself wealthy as he rose to fame. Now, he simply aims to help other people and make the world a better place, paying forward the opportunities he's been given.

Speaking personally, I have always been interested in those legendary and iconic figures – particularly in the sporting and entertainment fields – whose influence on pop culture continues to endure and even grow after they pass their physical prime.

After researching the life and legacy of two of the greatest icons of the century – Bruce Lee and Muhammad Ali – I began to mull over the possibilities of paying homage to another celebrity with global appeal. In a sense, Arnold Schwarzenegger has always been to bodybuilding what Bruce Lee is to martial arts. Lee achieved worldwide fame by coming to America – introducing a whole country to the rigors of a new style of physical discipline – then transmuted that early success into a movie career that changed cinema history. Schwarzenegger did the same, then went on to live a long and happy life, giving us a glimpse of what Lee might have been if not for his untimely death. Like Ali, he was unquestionably the best at his chosen sport – and like Ali, he sought to change the world politically, in an even more direct way than the Greatest of All Time.

Of course, no one lives a blameless life, and controversies surrounded Schwarzenegger during his campaign to become the governor of California. The one-time action hero's past was dredged for details pertaining to his personal life, and his father's views became the subject of popular discussion. He had to contend with his personal life, which had long been a subject of public interest, being freshly dissected in the tabloid press, a situation rarely forgiving for anyone.

Arnold himself would be the first to admit that he has made mistakes. But whatever one's sentiments toward his personal life or political views, his outlook on self-improvement and motivation is harder to criticize. For that reason, I hope that everyone will find something to help them in the next few hundred pages.

This book, of course, is composed of exclusive interviews with his close friends, fellow bodybuilding colleagues and training partners, Hollywood co-stars, directors, executive producers, political personalities and journalists – offering fresh perspectives on a man who has already written two autobiographies. You will discover new details about Arnold's meteoric rise to fame, his ways of training and his early years in Hollywood. You'll also hear about his achievements as 'the Governator' – as well as what was happening behind the scenes during his time holding one of his country's most important offices.

Arnold is an ambitious, intelligent and a profoundly driven individual, a shining example of what monomaniacal drive can accomplish. For me, one of the most striking aspects of this most enthusiastic pursuers of success is his resolute optimism, tenacity, business savvy and insatiable desire to venture beyond the limits – but sometimes, drive is not enough, and one must rely on other people to help. In this book you'll learn just how a scrawny kid from a small European village with an inexplicable thick accent and an unpronounceable name defied the odds to become one of the biggest names in the world.

# INTRODUCTION

According to the people who knew him in his youth, the Austrian Oak's relentless drive was in place when he was little more than a sapling. Born Arnold Alois Schwarzenegger on July 30, 1947, in a small village named Thal in Austria, to Aurelia and Gustav, his immense ambition and restless energy, along with a relentless hunger for new challenges, developed during Arnold's youth. Perhaps part of this was due to his older brother – his parents, Gustav and Aurelia, also had a son called Meinhard, a year older than Arnold, and Gustav – a local police chief who had once served in the army – is rumored to have favored his elder son. With a strict disciplinarian for a father, Arnold grew up a rebel – even if he was able to channel his energy in productive ways.

After taking up bodybuilding in his early teens, to the regular disapproval of his parents, Arnold quickly focused on becoming the best in a sport that was lightly regarded in Austria at the time. His father encouraged him to pursue a 'real' career, but Arnold would have none of it. Inspired by the legendary bodybuilder Reg Park, he began to voraciously read about and follow his idol's methods to build up his body. Soon, Arnold started to compete and a mentor-protégé relationship between the two began, eventually shifting to a friendship that would last until the older man's death in 2007. With the on-screen Hercules' help, the young Schwarzenegger made his own first steps toward stardom, winning several bodybuilding championships in Europe, and fueling his desire to take things to the global stage. "The hunger and the desire, this burning desire inside…to be somebody," Arnold recalled, decades later, "I want to make it and I want to be the best. I think that came from growing up in a little village. I wanted to go out of there and I wanted to be part of something big." And for Arnold, America symbolized that: the American Dream.

He left for America in 1968, invited by the bodybuilding magnate Joe Weider, and quickly made a home for himself in Southern California, the Mecca of bodybuilding and the motion picture industry. As a young man who had dreamed of moving to America since he was ten years old, it didn't take long for Arnold to adapt to his new home. The twenty-one-year-old Arnold arrived with absolutely nothing other than a gym bag, $20 in his pocket, a rudimentary command of English and a grand dream – but he set to work harder than ever, both in and out of the gym.

Unparalleled success in bodybuilding followed, culminating in Arnold winning the Mr. Olympia title – the most prestigious in bodybuilding – seven times. The release of *Pumping Iron* in 1977, which documented his sixth victory, helped to introduce him to the masses – a charismatic, charming young man who trained like an animal and wasn't above using psychological warfare against his competitors. With Hollywood right down the freeway, his next course of action was clear.

Arnold wanted to be the best in whatever he pursued. "I had a lot of motivation and energy and had a very clear vision of what my goals were, and I was going to achieve them, and I went after my dream," Arnold would explain. "I've always thought if you achieve your goals and become the best, then you will achieve notoriety and fame, anyway. It follows naturally."

Despite appearances in a handful of movies in the 1970s, it wasn't until 1982 and the release of *Conan the Barbarian*, that his break came. It was the perfect role to catapult him to stardom – a swords-and-sandals epic that showcased his physique in the role of a Cimmerian warrior who did most of his talking with his blade. In 1984, he made his first appearance in what some would say was the signature role in his acting career, playing the Terminator in the film of the same name. Even though he barely had a dozen lines, Arnold's screen presence as a relentless, near-invincible killing machine, propelled him to superstardom and his reputation as a box-office draw was sealed. Famed for his high-octane action roles and even higher body counts, a string of action movies later saw Arnold became the king of the multiplex. He was already wealthy, having made enough money in real estate to allow him to pick and choose roles rather than jumping at anything that would pay – but by the late 80s, he became the highest paid actor in the world.

The 1980s and early 1990s were the years for testosterone-fueled action movies with tough talking leading men – Sylvester Stallone; Steven Seagal; Bruce Willis; Jean Claude Van Damme; Dolph Lundgren and Arnold – dominating the action genre. Arnold led the way and in 1993 a poll concluded that Arnold was the man most Americans would want to spend time talking to on a long-distance flight (Oprah Winfrey was the only person to outscore him overall). The public had fully embraced this actor who had gone from playing villains and silent muscle-men to action heroes and comic roles.

For Arnold, however, unprecedented success in the motion picture industry did not make him content. He married into American royalty when he tied the knot with Maria Shriver, the niece of President John F. Kennedy, allowing this multi-millionaire to move among the upper echelons of American society. Already, he was contemplating politics. He had fulfilled his childhood dreams – bodybuilding champion and a movie star. Arnold said, "All of a sudden I realized that, *You know, I've done this. I've gotten to the top – the highest paid actor that there ever was in history. Done all of these different things. So I said to myself, I'm tired of the same things, jumping over car hoods three in the morning and then going up to someone and saying, 'I'm back', and blow him away. All of this is great, but eventually it gets old.*"

Though he had a keen interest in politics well before he came to America, he first came to the public's attention as a Republican during a campaign rally for then-vice-president George Bush in 1988. He admired President Ronald Reagan, who himself went from a movie star to venturing out into politics. He knew he could never be President himself, but his own political ambitions took him to office as the Governor of California, where he served from 2003 to 2011. Since then, he's made something of a return to acting, reinvigorating the *Terminator* franchise and appearing in *The Expendables* series alongside a slew of lower-profile roles. He's also become increasingly outspoken on the issues that matter most to him, from climate change to plant-based eating – a dramatic shift in position for a man who once drove a Hummer and ate 200g of animal protein a day.

Arnold's life, ultimately, has been a celebration of self. Many may perceive him as a man with an inflated ego – failing to realize that this self-belief is one of his greatest assets, something, without which he could never have achieved his unprecedented level of success. Other's perception is of a man with a ferocious work ethic and a burning desire for supremacy. Some accuse the former governor of being domineering, while others see a confident, intelligent individual and a businessman who refuses to settle for second best.

Arnold, certainly, is a man of unwavering ambition and self-belief. Thousands every week move to Tinseltown to seek the American Dream and fame and fortune. Most fail. Arnold Schwarzenegger succeeded in not just this arena, but then in the world of politics – and then, when he left that behind, shifted his beliefs as the world continued to change. Whatever you think of the opinions he's held throughout his life, he's undoubtedly a man we can all learn from.

# ONE

---

## BODYBUILDING FRATERNITY

### FRANCO COLUMBU

Franco Columbu, a two-time Mr. Olympia winner and a legend in the bodybuilding world, was Arnold's best friend from the 1960s until his death in 2019. When he first arrived in America, he was one of the strongest men in the world, and indeed competed in the inaugural editions of the World's Strongest Man contest. Arnold and Columbu were regular training partners throughout their bodybuilding careers, and stayed in regular contact for the rest of their lives.

**Q: When did you first meet Arnold, was it in Germany in the 1960s?**
Franco Columbu: In 1965, October 30, we met in Stuttgart in a competition. I competed in a powerlifting competition and I won. I won first place. And Arnold competed in the Junior Mr. Europe. He was only eighteen at that time, and he won first place, too. So, we met on the stage and we received the winners' trophies.

**Q: Did you then pursue to converse with him?**
Franco Columbu: The conversation was very simple. I knew all the

bodybuilders in Germany, and I said to him, "I know all the people here. I've never seen you before. Who are you?" He said, "Oh, I'm not from Germany; I'm from Austria. I'm from Graz." And he said, "I've never heard of you, either." I said, "I'm from Italy. I just moved to Munich." And then we went to a restaurant and talked. We had dinner and beer. I was training in Munich at the time. Then he told me, "I want to come to Munich and train with you." I really didn't believe him because many people, even in Italy, had said to me, "I'm going to come to Germany. I'm going to come to Munich. I'm going to train with you." I forgot about it when he left. Then a couple of months later, he shows up at the gym. And the owner of the gym in Munich made him an instructor. He became a gym instructor. And then we started to train together.

In 1966, Arnold moved to Munich, Germany and started to train and manage the Putzingger Gym, then owned by his lifelong friend Albert Busek, which he bought a year later. Determined to enjoy all the nightlife that Munich had to offer, he started to hang out with rather interesting people – entertainers, hookers and bar owners. He told *OUI* magazine in a 1977 interview that one of his former girlfriends was a stripper. Arnold had grown up in a small farm town, but was learning new lessons in an overwhelming city. In the beginning, he lived in a small room, which was in the vicinity of the gym. Eventually, he was able to get his own apartment, and the young man from a small village settled in rapidly. In those days, weight training was not in vogue – bodybuilders, powerlifters, boxers and wrestlers trained with weights. It wasn't long before Arnold befriended a wrestler and Olympic weightlifter named Harold Sakata, who had played the iconic villain Oddjob in the James Bond film *Goldfinger*.

Often struggling to make ends meet, Arnold refrained from divulging to his parents about his financial troubles. Their understanding was that their young, ambitious son was earning decent money working away from home. They felt he was living his dream. Had Arnold revealed to his parents about the harsh reality of survival in a city, they might have forced him to come home. Arnold was happy where he was, even if not financially stable. Nevertheless, he was making progress in other ways. In 1967, Arnold competed in a stone-lifting contest in Munich, in which a stone weighing 508 German pounds (254 kg/560 pounds) would be lifted between the legs while standing on two foot rests. The young Austrian native won the competition, breaking the existing record in the process. Suddenly Arnold was on his way to becoming a minor star in his own community, often being interviewed and photographed by members of the media. It would be one of his first tastes of fame – but only left him wanting more.

**Q: Would I be right in saying that you introduced Arnold to powerlifting?**
Franco Columbu: Powerlifting at that time was pretty big in Europe, you know, in Prague, in France, in Germany. I told him, "Look, you know, you're the strongest." But he said, "I want to be Mr. Olympia, Mr. Universe." I said, "Let's do both." Then we started training. For bodybuilding parts we always did three main exercises, which included squats and bench press to get stronger. And that really was the principle then. We discovered that by lifting heavy weights it developed bodybuilding, too. It was really, really a good thing that powerlifting helped bodybuilding.

**Q: Can we talk about when you both came to America and stayed together in California in the early days?**
Franco Columbu: When Arnold competed in 1968 in London in the NABBA Mr. Universe, he won and then he was invited to America to compete. He wanted to come to America. Then Joe Weider invited him to come to the United States. And he came to America, around November 1968. Then we kept in contact. And then in June 1969, which was six months later, I sold my car and bought a plane ticket and I went to California. Then we started

training, again, here together and lived together for two, three years in a small apartment. At the time, we would wake up at seven o' clock, have a protein drink and go to the gym for three hours. We trained really heavy. Then at ten o' clock we would go have breakfast, and then we would work part-time in construction.

I got a bricklaying license, and we did that and we made some money. Because at that time we didn't receive much money (from bodybuilding), we only got paid $80 from Joe Weider for taking pictures and writing articles. It was not enough money – $80 each. So we went to work and we made a few hundred bucks working. Then we were able to buy more food and everything, and that really made us become good friends. And the success really started right there. Because then we really started working in construction, and we trained a lot and we started winning like crazy every competition.

Columbu suggested to his Austrian friend they should get into the bricklaying and patio business. Arnold's friend, who had mastered the craft back in Italy and Germany, primarily would lay the bricks and Arnold would mix the cement. Their day job brought in a few dollars, which would help them to make ends meet while they continued to focus on their passion for bodybuilding. The process was simple enough: Arnold's friend went downtown to apply for a license, and the duo placed adverts in a newspaper advertising themselves as the European Brickworks. Business went well, owing to the pair's marketing savvy and an onset of high demand following the 1971 Los Angeles earthquake. It wasn't long before they had a force of sixteen people working for their company. The profits Arnold generated from this business venture would later be pumped into financing a mail-order business pertaining to his bodybuilding products – training booklets and other products. Arnold also had a contingency plan: the profits accumulated from the mail-order business, along with his competition earnings, would allow him to invest in more profitable ventures such as real estate.

**Q: What are your recollections of training with Arnold at Venice Beach?**

Franco Columbu: We trained at Gold's Gym, in the original Gold's Gym in Santa Monica. Then also sometimes we went to Venice to do a second workout in the afternoon, training in the sun and all that stuff. The sessions were, like, things like, we liked to train in public. I remember one time I was doing squats with 500–600 pounds. I could only do three or four reps. And Arnold says, "There are people in the gym from Italy behind you and they're watching you. You cannot do just four reps; you should do eight." When I heard that I did another six, then went up to ten reps. And that shows you how the mind controls the body in doing what you want. That was in Venice. When we trained at Venice, with thousands of people watching, we really, really trained hard, heavy and screamed like hell. So motivation was there and the body responded well. We got in shape and it was incredible.

**Q: What was Arnold's inclination as far as bodybuilding and training principles are concerned?**

Franco Columbu: We trained heavy: do your bench press, get strong in the bench press, deadlift for powerlifting, but let's do the rest and train the entire body, let's train four hours. And the key was to getting strong in every part of the body, the arms . . . everything. It was strength in brutal training.

Arnold developed a philosophical approach to bodybuilding. "You can actually create a vision of what your body will look like. Then you mold your body closer and closer to that vision, and actually you would turn that vision to reality," explains Arnold. "The experience of being much stronger than everybody else, I think that's an unbelievable experience. You feel richer. You feel that sooner or later you can do anything." Also a firm believer in the art of visualization, Arnold often took his mind-power to an elevated level in his training sessions, going on to regularly cite the benefits of the practice to followers. He wrote in Joe Weider's magazine *Muscle Builder/Power*, "Whenever I go into the gym for a workout, it is like a boxer at the height of his fury to deliver a knockout blow. My mind is focused on bombing that workout with ferocious power and with all the mental and physical energy I am capable of generating."

## RICKY WAYNE

Born in St Lucia and raised in the UK, Ricky Wayne won numerous professional bodybuilding titles, including Mr. Universe. He went on to become a prominent bodybuilding journalist and wrote for Joe Weider's *Muscle Builder* and *FLEX*, as well as authoring several books. Wayne and Arnold became good friends and often trained together. In 2007, Wayne was honored as an Officer of the Order of the British Empire.

**Q: When did you meet Arnold and under what circumstances, was it in the 1960s?**
Ricky Wayne: That's correct. Early-1960s or it was in the mid-1960s. He had come to compete in the Amateur Mr. Universe. I was already competing and winning in the States. And I received a message from somebody, a mutual friend, a German friend, who asked me to come to the theater because Arnold wanted to meet me. I went and that's how we met the first time. Shortly after that, the people he was working with in Munich, Arnold called them to bring me over to do a guest posing exhibition in, I think it was either Munich or Dusseldorf. We became very good friends right after that.

**Q: You worked as a bodybuilding journalist writing for the prominent magazines. Did you interview Arnold when he competed in the Amateur Mr. Universe, and what was your impression as far as his body development?**
Ricky Wayne: He was big, but that was about all. He wasn't even tanned. He went up against a guy called Chet Yorton, who was a much experienced American from California. But Arnold made a fantastic impression because he was young, nineteen and big. He didn't win but he made a very good impression. And he, of course, had all the self-confidence that he is known for. He had it back then. In his book *The Education of a Bodybuilder*, he mentions that he asked me what I thought his chances were in the several coming

months. I said I didn't think they were pretty good, yet. And he refers to that in the book. But within a couple of years, Arnold changed totally. If I recall correctly, he won Mr. Universe the next year.

**Q: Arnold stayed with Wag and Dianne Bennett, were you living in England at the time?**
Ricky Wayne: Was I living there? Sure. Wag Bennett was the guy who ran a gym in East London, Stratford, and I trained there. I was a very close friend of the family. When Wag met Arnold at the first Mr. Universe, he befriended him and Arnold became kind of like a son. So whenever he was in London, more often than not he stayed at Wag's house. That's how we all became good friends.

Albert Busek recounts the difficulties the young bodybuilder faced in getting to the 1968 NABBA Mr. Universe contest in London. "A few days before the contest, the owner of our gym presented Arnold with an endorsement contract, which Arnold would not sign because the guy would have owned all sorts of rights for life. The owner owed Arnold 1,000 Deutsche Marks for a guest appearance he had made at the European Championships I had organized in Munich two weeks earlier." Busek remembers that Arnold's refusal to sign the contract forced the owner to hold back and not pay him the 1,000 Deutsche Marks. "Arnold was counting on that money for his flight to London. In front of the owner, my boss, I gave Arnold 500 Deutsche Marks for his plane ticket and risked losing my job."

**Q: In London at the 1970 Mr. Universe competition, several prominent bodybuilders, Reg Park, Frank Zane and Dave Draper, competed. Can you recall this event?**
Ricky Wayne: Yeah. Arnold won. I wrote something about that somewhere. Reg Park was, of course, Arnold's hero. But by then he was getting old. And I don't know why he chose to compete

again, as he had won Mr. Universe many times. Why go up against Arnold, who was just really getting into his prime? So, they were talking in the dressing room, where Reg Park was pumping up. And Reg Park turned around, and said to Arnold, "Look, I gotta go. I can't keep talking to you; I have a contest to compete and prepare for." Arnold said to him, "What contest?" Meaning there was no contest. Of course, Reg was very upset about that. But later on, Arnold publicly apologized for that and made the point that he'd always wished him good luck. Besides, he spent a lot of time at Reg Park's house in South Africa.

**Q: What about Frank Zane?**
Ricky Wayne: Well, yeah. Arnold went to Miami to compete in a contest – I forget what it was called – shortly after the first Mr. Universe. And because, of course, he's huge, Frank is more medium built. When Arnold got there and saw what condition Frank was in – Frank beat him! In fact, that's the one time Arnold said that he would never compete in it again. Because now he was going to start training, and he knows he can beat him this time.

**Q: Can you tell me about training with Arnold in London, what was his English like in those early days – was he able to converse quite easily?**
Ricky Wayne: We trained at the same gym – Wag Bennett's gym. I also trained with him at Gold's Gym in California. He also trained with Dave Draper, Frank Zane – most of the guys – but I think Franco Columbu was his main training partner. The first year, within a year he was making jokes, all kinds of jokes in English. Arnold was a fast learner – very fast learner. He is one of the most fascinating people I have ever known.

**Q: In America you worked for the Weider publications. When you interviewed him for the magazines, what do you remember most about interviewing him?**
Ricky Wayne: We had all kinds of conversations when I was

working for the magazines, whether I was writing in Arnold's name or in my name. We knew each other well. The main thing, and the most important thing, was Arnold had a great self-confidence. And that's what brought me to him. We had conversations. You'd always be with him on a positive note regardless of what it was. Whether it was the movies, whether it was bodybuilding, whether it was a contest, he always believed he was going to be number one. And that's what keeps you alive.

**Q: Would you say that in those days he was cocky, but in a nice way?**
Ricky Wayne: I don't know how you can be cocky in a nice way. Cocky is one thing and confidence is another.

**Q: Joe Weider's ardent propagation of the sport has endured for decades. He was responsible for bringing Arnold over to America. How would you define their relationship?**
Ricky Wayne: It was like a father and son relationship. As a matter of fact, the way he got to the States, right after he had competed in the Mr. Universe contest I wrote to Joe Weider, because I used to write for the Weiders in England. And I wrote to Joe and said try to get this guy on a contract very quickly. And that's how the whole thing started. And eventually, Joe called him over. Joe likes to hype a lot in his main investments. Arnold was one of them. His big thing with Joe was over Sergio Oliva because a lot of people thought there was a lot of racism involved there. But I wrote articles about that. I said, "If you ask, 'Who is the greater bodybuilder?' I might say Sergio. But if you ask, 'Who is the greatest champion?' I would say Arnold." And there's a lot between those two things.

Arnold was a fantastic promoter of bodybuilding. He spoke well. He was very much a personality. He would go to seminars, and he was able to talk to the press better. And he had all those things. Sergio, on the other hand, was a Cuban, came over from political strings attached from Cuba, and so on. Sergio was not nearly the nice guy Arnold was, or supposed to be. Body for body, Sergio probably had the better body, but Arnold certainly was the better champion. Arnold was far more competitive.

**Q: He started a mail-order business where Weider would give him free adverts in the magazines. Then later, Weider started to send him invoices for payment. They had kind of an on-and-off relationship, didn't they?**
Ricky Wayne: Yeah. For Arnold it was good, very lucrative. I think he still does it. It was very lucrative for him.

Now bodybuilding has over 170 national federations spanning every continent – but it was Joe Weider, a Canadian Jew, along with his brother Ben, who transformed this niche, often-mocked pastime bodybuilding into a hugely successful sport embraced globally. Weider's story of self-belief has parallels to the young Arnold's: at age seventeen, he began his bodybuilding and publishing empire with a mere $7, going on to publish his first magazine (*Your Physique*) in 1940. In 2003, his company Weider Publications was sold to American Media for a reported $300 million. In 1974, as Arnold was coming to the end of his competitive career, Arnold told *Sports Illustrated*, "All of these magazines, Weider's, Hoffman's, Lurie's, I call them comic books, circus books!" He exclaimed they all endeavored to expose each other, and he said, "Why wouldn't these get together? I'll tell you why. It is because none of these silly people are really interested in bodybuilding anymore. They are interested only in the money that can be made from it."

He said he asked why Joe printed such junk – all those silly words. Weider allegedly told him that it sold the magazine. By the early 1980s, thanks to Weider's marketing skills and diligent effort in promoting the sport of bodybuilding and propagating the benefits of weight training, health and fitness through weight training, the need for exercise was ingrained in the public consciousness, creating a fitness boom. Today, going to the gym has become the norm.

Arnold recalled in 1997, "I saw the Joe Weider magazines with all these fantasy articles." He had read about how the bodybuilding magnate trained champions, and they were given muscle-building supplements and sent to the so-called Weider Research Clinic. "I thought the clinic was a huge research center somewhere in America connected to the movie industry, and full of guys wanting to be Hercules."

**Q: Arnold competed with Sergio Oliva, Arnold lost to him in the 1969 Mr. Olympia. He may have been rather crude at that point. Did he talk to you about this after the defeat, and was he sentimental in any way?**
Ricky Wayne: What he said was that it won't happen again. I covered most of the Olympias up till 1980.

By this time, Arnold knew that the only way he could beat the giant Cuban was to be in better shape than he might have previously imagined possible. Oliva, it was said, was so good he could beat you in the dressing room before even stepping onto the stage. His shirt would come off and there would be that incredible mass, almost daring you to step on the stage with him. "When it came time to go onstage for the pose down, Sergio took the long apron off and started walking in front of me down the hall," Arnold recalled after the first Olympia. "Then, nonchalantly lifting one of his shoulders, he spread the largest lat muscle I had ever seen. Then he repeated the same movement with the other shoulder." Sergio's back muscles were so huge that he seemed to be literally as wide as the hall. Arnold admitted that doubt clouded his mind and knew that beating the Cuban was not plausible. It would be the only time Arnold would be defeated by the giant. The following year, in 1970, when Arnold took the Olympia title for the first time, Oliva says he had great conviction that he would, again, triumph and take the trophy home. However, the judges saw it differently – leading to the first of seven Sandows Arnold would bring home.

**Q: Sergio Oliva stayed at the Bennett house when competing in England. What was Arnold's and Sergio's relationship like there?**
Ricky Wayne: Arnold was always friendly with Sergio. When they were not, it was usually Sergio's fault. Sergio had this thing in his head that Weider was favoring Arnold because he was white.

**Q: Any social moments you can recall with Arnold?**
Ricky Wayne: Very fun guy, made a lot of jokes, but sometimes his jokes got him in trouble. But that was a time when political correctness was not around yet. So, you know, a lot of people quote him saying he said this and he said that, but they forget that at the time political correctness was not around. Like, whatever he might have said about women. The things we could've said about women back then, if we said them now you would get in trouble.

**Q: He settled in America, which was the beginning of pursuing the American Dream. Arnold once said, "The Mr. Universe title was my ticket to America, the land of opportunity, where I could become a star and get rich." This may have been a myopic vision, but he did pursue it.**
Ricky Wayne: Oh, he loved California. He loved it. California is great for bodybuilding. The weather is fine. There's a lot of competition. There's fun. It's Hollywood. You have a lot of opportunities with the magazines and you can go on TV, and so on. You don't have that in England, especially back then.

To Arnold, the blond bodybuilder Dave Draper represented the epitome of California bodybuilders. The latter was also on another path the Austrian had set for himself, entering the entertainment industry with roles in *Don't Make Waves*, which starred Tony Curtis, and various TV shows. For Arnold, this only confirmed the possibility of opening doors beyond the confines of the bodybuilding circuit. However, his challenge was to compete against the great bodybuilders and defeat them so decisively that his position as the greatest would be unquestionable. Ben Weider had met Arnold for the first time in 1967 at a competition in which Arnold was victorious. The young champion enthusiastically told Weider that he wanted to come to America to compete. Weider reluctantly responded, "If you come the way you are, you're going to lose. You're great as far as the Europeans are concerned, but as far as the Americans are concerned, you won't win." This did not dishearten Arnold by any means, and the very next year Arnold would be invited to America by Ben's brother – the initiation of a long relationship, which would benefit both individuals.

As much as Joe Weider was very passionate about the sport, he was a ruthless businessman. He often took advantage of his new star, which did not go unnoticed by Arnold – but the Austrian knew he was gaining publicity and gaining more knowledge about the marketing and business sides of the sport. Whether it was about making a business deal or promoting, Weider the Master Blaster was the man Arnold would learn much of his business savvy from. There were alternating periods of good and bad fortune and spirits as far as Arnold's relationship with Weider is concerned. Nevertheless, both men had depended on each other to elevate themselves in the past, and, regardless of the past, the friendship endured.

**Q: Monetary rewards were minimal in professional bodybuilding when Arnold was competing. Bodybuilding has changed, would you say this is true?**
Ricky Wayne: Erm, not really. When Arnold won the Olympia, the money was $1,000. It was Arnold who, when he started

promoting, started making the money bigger and pushed for that. Where bodybuilders made some bucks was in personal appearances and endorsements for Weider. Later on, they started doing their own courses, their own postal business. Weider gave them ads and so on. There wasn't really big money in bodybuilding – three or four guys at the top made big money, considering the number of people who were champions.

**Q: How often did Weider cover Arnold in his magazines?**
Ricky Wayne: There was hardly an issue where Arnold wasn't in it. That goes on even now. The other magazines are doing well because Arnold has always been a seller. He has a lot of bodybuilding fans, movies, and even as a politician, it's a good reason to put him on the cover.

**Q: What was his training philosophy?**
Ricky Wayne: Very simple philosophy: train hard and often. That's it. Everybody tries to complicate bodybuilding. How far you go in bodybuilding depends on your genes. Some people have it; some people don't have it. And the discipline, how determined you are. And Arnold had all of those work for him. He was very careful of his eating habits as well, extremely.

**Q: Can you distinguish between the bodybuilding scene in Europe and America back in the 1960s? There was more exposure in America.**
Ricky Wayne: Far more exposure and far more encouragement. That's why a lot of the champions in Europe had to go to the States to be somebody.

**Q: What was Arnold's hardest competition?**
Ricky Wayne: The first one against Sergio, and the last one in Sydney, Australia. He won and after that he did the movies. But everybody booed and there was a lot of trouble over there (Sydney).

**Q: What was the most fascinating thing you saw in Arnold pertaining to training?**
Ricky Wayne: The intensity of his workouts. When he was training, he trained!

**Q: Arnold filtered into the movie business and *Pumping Iron* was an integral chain to his success. Did he talk to you about pursuing the movies, when he was still competing and achieving his bodybuilding goals?**
Ricky Wayne: He went before that. Shortly after he came to the States, he got a break in a movie called *Hercules in New York*, which was crap! Yes, that was his main thing (breaking into the movies). Reg Park and Steve Reeves were his idols and both of them had made movies. Arnold wanted to be like them. So movies were always on his mind. He always wanted to get into the movies, whenever the movies came, it's just that they came along at this time.

# LARRY SCOTT

After winning the inaugural Mr. Olympia in 1965 and defending his title in 1966, Larry Scott – nicknamed 'The Legend' and 'The Golden Boy' – retired as one of the legends of the sport. He popularized many training techniques still in use today, including the combination curl-and-press known as the Scott press. He died in 2014.

**Q: Larry, you, of course, won the first two Mr. Olympias in 1965 and 1966. Arnold went on to win this prestigious title seven times. First of all, can you tell me how did the Weider brothers start this new contest?**

Larry Scott: In 1965, around that time I had just won Mr. America, a year before and Mr. Universe, that was as far as you could go. So Joe Weider, his wife Betty and I were over at a restaurant in California. And Joe says – I can't remember if it was Joe's or Betty's idea – but he said, "We've got to have a contest. We've got to create a contest that will help the bodybuilders to continue because after they win Mr. Universe, they just drop off. They don't do anything. We've got to have something that they continue to get ready for, a contest year after year." And I'm listening, and I say, "That's a good idea." So, Betty gave her input and I gave my input. I thought it was a good idea. I thought it would be nice to continue to compete because you're right: how can you get excited for training if you don't have a contest to compete in? You could always train harder for a contest than you can for everyday fitness.

So, once we agreed that we're going to create a new contest, then Joe said, "What do we call it?" There were a number of options that came up. I'm not sure how we came up with an idea, but anyway, I can't remember what my idea was, but Joe says, "Let's call it Mr. Olympia!" I said, "I don't think that's a good idea because there's Olympia beer. It's like we're selling beer." He says, "No! No! It's like Mount Olympus, like where all the Greek gods were on Mount Olympus." Betty argues with him for a while, but we finally agree with Joe's idea. And we thought, *OK, we'll call it Mr. Olympia.* That's where it came from.

**Q: Can you tell me how much of an impact Steve Reeves had in the 1950s and the 1960s era on bodybuilding, and how much of a part he played promoting bodybuilding before Arnold brought it to the public's consciousness?**

Larry Scott: I don't think Steve ever worked with the muscle magazine owners. And so the impact he had on bodybuilding was the impact of his own physique and his own charisma. He had probably overall the best package anyone has ever had. He had the perfect proportions: his neck, his arms and his calves were all the same size. And he was really good-looking. He was just a wonderful representative of bodybuilding, and we all looked up to him. Just to say that you knew Steve was something. He and George Eiferman were good friends. They would chum together and they would do shows together. I first met Steve and George in Salt Lake City. They came out to do a guest posing for the contest promoter. And Bob Delmonteque, the photographer for Weider at the time, happened to see us. And we saw him at a local health club where we were exercising, getting ready to trying to shape up. You wanted to feel like you had a pump when you went to a physique contest. I mean, you felt much bigger when you went in.

So I trained hard before I went into that physique contest, in which Steve Reeves was going to guest pose, as well as George Ivan Eiferman. Bob Delmonteque offered to take us up to the motel room where Steve and George were staying. He took us and introduced us. That was the first time we had to really chat to Steve Reeves. It was really an honor and inspiring. I could hardly even think of the questions I wanted to ask. Something came out of my mouth, "How do you get big?" He smiled a little bit, but he gave us a few tips for training. They were just resting, waiting for the presentation for the show that night. Anyway, Steve lived in California so he spent a lot of time in Muscle Beach. It had quite an impact on the muscle-building world down in the California area.

**Q: Can you tell me when you first met Arnold? Back then you were a major bodybuilding star, and Arnold was a novice just getting into the sport?**

Larry Scott: Yes. When I went to Europe to do a guest posing show over at Albert Busek's . . . what did he call it? Mr. Austria, I think. It was about the year I won the Olympia the second time. So it was in '65 or '66. I was backstage getting ready to go out to do a posing exhibition when Arnold came backstage and asked for an autograph. And I said to him, "Could you wait till I get done posing because I want to focus on this first?" He told me later that he was put off by me asking him to wait for an autograph. He said, "Now that I've been in the same position, I can understand." Anyway, we got to know each other a little bit there. We didn't know each other; it was first becoming acquaintances. Then a short time after that Arnold came out to California, and he came out to Vince's gym where I was training.

Vince Gironda had a great gym out in the San Fernando Valley, a gym where a lot of the former Mr. Americas were training. We had six training at one time. Arnold came down there to that gym, and he said, "Can you give me some advice on what I should do? Who should I contact?" I said, "Let me tell you something. This is what I would do if I were you. You've got to have three things to be successful. One, you've got to get in the magazines. You've got to have somebody who can help you with your photos, and somebody who could help you with nutrition. If you've got those three things lined up, then you've got a good chance. You've got a good body already, but you need these three things in order to make progress." And then I told him, "These are the three that I'm working with. And I recommend them highly because they're very good." I said, "When you meet Joe Weider, start getting in his magazines because people don't know who you are unless they see you in the magazines." So he went over and he met Joe Weider and became friends with him.

I said, "You also have to meet this other guy, because he's the best nutritionist there is for bodybuilders. He's very good. Thirdly, you've got to find a photographer who will take the photos that will go in the magazines." I recommended a couple of them – one of the ones in the area was Artie Zeller. He was very good, too. He did great photography. There were quite a few others I endorsed, but he was the best photographer. So he lined up with those people I mentioned to him. About that time, I had just got married and I had decided that I knew happiness did not consist of being on the stage, but it required a family life. So I told myself when I won the second Olympia, *If I win this contest tonight I'm retiring.* So, I was fortunate enough to win it the second time, and I announced to the audience this was my last contest.

**Q: Going back to your European visit, what was your impression of the young Arnold when you first met? Was he in the audience or guest posing or competing that day?**
Larry Scott: He was there to compete. I didn't see him in the audience. I saw him when he came backstage. Arnold has always been very forward, and he puts himself forward wherever he needs to. He came backstage to introduce himself. And he was just getting that feeling of what it was like being backstage, and trying to get the 'feel of the ropes', as you might say. He knew he would be soon going into that, so he would ask a few questions and so forth. He was very good at asking questions. I shouldn't say 'good' as much as 'very wise' – going to the people in the know and humbling himself to ask questions. A lot of times people coming up feel a little shy, or don't want to humble themselves to ask questions, but he was smart! He would ask what he needed to do, and where to get the information and evolve from there.

**Q: In America when he came to your gym, did he train occasionally there?**
Larry Scott: He wanted to live near down by the beach in the Santa Monica area, which is right on the beach. He wanted to train down there. There was Gold's Gym down there. Gold's Gym was a good gym. Joe Gold created a few gyms. So, Arnold wanted to train down with the beach crowd. I didn't care for the beach crowd. They

were a little too wild for me. I wanted to train where I lived down in San Fernando Valley, where there was a gym out there, which was owned by Vince Gironda. It was a terrific gym. Vince really knew how to train. He was a great trainer. One of the things Arnold didn't get was a great trainer to guide him. Joe was pretty good. Joe Gold was good. But Vince was the champion of this. He had great ideas in terms of his thoughts were inclined toward esthetics. When you're onstage, you want to look good esthetically as well as just big. And that would have done Arnold some good. Of course, you can't discredit him because he did pretty damn good.

**Q: What was Arnold's relationship like with Joe Gold?**
Larry Scott: They were good friends. Both lived in the same area. He trained in Gold's Gym, and they became good friends and good business partners.

**Q: How would you describe Arnold's physique of the 1960s and how did it evolve?**
Larry Scott: In the '60s, when I first saw him my first impression was he was big and that he had possibilities. But I didn't suddenly say, "Wow, this guy's going to do everything!" When I saw Sergio Oliva for the first time, I thought, *Man, this guy's from a different world! He's not from the same planet as us.* His (Sergio's) genetics were incredible. Arnold was big and he had good size and everything, but he was on his way up. He was naturally big. He took after his father, but he wouldn't knock your eyes off, he was just starting, you know. He learned. He got better and better. Arnold is very quick-witted.

He wants to demean you because it makes him feel bigger and better. Maybe not, maybe that's not the right thing to say. Let me just say that he had a tendency to be a kidder, and he likes to make you a little uneasy. So you have to be quick on the comeback in order to hold your own with him. And Sergio wasn't that kind of a person at all; Sergio was more mild and not so much quick on the comeback. The other thing is that Sergio was so big. Sergio was big that he became so confident, and he became a little bit full of himself. But as far as Arnold and Sergio are concerned, they had completely different personalities. Arnold was very aggressive and sharp and quick to respond to any kind of question.

**Q: Can you further differentiate and elaborate on Arnold and Sergio Oliva's personalities back when they competed together?**
Larry Scott: Well, I can't give you an example of Sergio's personality. When he first came when I first met Sergio he'd just come over from Cuba. Joe Weider brought him backstage. He didn't speak any English at all. So he was understandably a little shy because he hadn't been around the top bodybuilders. Even though he was big and well-esteemed from where he came from, Joe hadn't made a niche for him yet over here in America. He was probably a little bit more withdrawn at that point. Certainly later on, as he grew a prosperity and became well known, he had much more confidence in himself, but he was not as articulate as Arnold. Arnold was very articulate from the get-go.

So, you had two different types of personalities completely. When they were together, there wasn't a lot of interchange. In fact, it was Arnold and Franco, there was a lot of interchange between them. Arnold and Frank Zane, there was a lot of interchange because they were both articulate. And intelligent people can speak well and use this, as you see a lot more interesting conversations and give and take between those types of personalities than you would from someone who is more non-inclined to give and take conversation, or kidding and so forth. That wasn't Sergio's way.

**Q: Frank Zane beat Arnold in Miami when Arnold first came to America.**
Larry Scott: Frank did beat Arnold once. I think he's a totally different person than Arnold. He's very cerebral, methodical, who trains hard, works hard, and he's not one to kid around at all. He's very serious, a very good trainer and very knowledgeable with his nutrition and his training. He still is. He is very heavily into

that. He's not left the bodybuilding field at all. Whereas Arnold moved into the political arena whilst Frank has been involved in bodybuilding and doing his books and training concepts and continues to train regularly. I think Arnold had a hard time to find the time getting away from all these responsibilities to train like, I'm sure, he would like to. But he's not a person you want to consider he's no longer in the program because he's got a lot of innovation and ability to bounce back to get in great shape if he wanted to.

**Q: Can you ruminate on and share with me some anecdotes?**
Larry Scott: Arnold and I have always had a relationship where we're always kidding each other. So, we had a lot of those circumstances in which we're trying to put the other guy down jokingly, looking for some way to put the other guy down, and we continually do. So, we had a lot of those kinds of things. Arnold and Franco Columbu were living down in Santa Monica. I was selling insurance. I called him and I asked Arnold if he needed insurance. He said, "Yes, I do." I said, "Do you need medical insurance?" He said, "Yes, I do. I need medical insurance." So, he said, "Why don't you come to our place this Saturday and we'll have breakfast together and you can tell us about the insurance?" I said OK. So I went to his place and we had a nice breakfast. And before we ate, I said, "Would it be all right if I offer a blessing on the food?" He looked over at Franco, like, *This is unusual.* He said, "Yeah, go ahead. Say the blessing." So I said the prayer on the food and then we ate.

We talked about insurance, and I forgot all about it. It went completely out of my mind. Some years later, we were at the Mr. Olympia contest. After the show they always have a nice dinner. And they have tables and they cord it off so the fans can't get in there, so the competitors get the chance to eat in peace and relax. I was at my table and Arnold came over, and he said, "I have a story to tell you about Larry!" So he starts telling that story when I came over to their place for breakfast. He told it just the way it happened. Then he said, "As soon as we started to eat, Larry says, 'Can I pray on the food?' So he prays and he prays and prays. And I said, 'Larry, stop praying, the food is getting cold!'" He likes to turn it in to humor. I said, "That's not what happened." He says, "Oh, yes, it is." So, he went back to his table. I was thinking about that, *Oh, I've got a way to get back at him.*

So I went to his table and said, "I've got a story you tell you about Arnold!" Arnold said to his table, "Quiet everybody!" I said, "Years ago . . ." I told the same story about how I went to his house to sell insurance, but I changed it a little bit. I said, "When I got done, I asked if I could say a prayer on the food. He said yes. I said a prayer and when I got done Arnold said, 'No, don't stop, Larry, we need more prayers or else you're not leaving . . .'" That's been typical. Arnold will be at his Arnold Classic, and he's going to have a story just like that. I've got one I've made up already, which I will use for a comeback because I know it's going to take place. We only see each other once a year. And we always have that joking way with each other.

## Q: Did you talk about specific bodybuilding training with Arnold?

Larry Scott: I never talked bodybuilding training, or nutrition at all with Arnold. We never seemed to have moved into that direction. With Frank Zane, I always talked bodybuilding. Sergio, well, I don't think so with Sergio, either. Sergio is very weak now. He's not in good health at all whereas Arnold is in good health. One of the things that I do is, I really like bodybuilding, researching better ways to exercise. That's not Arnold's bag; he's more into different things. But that's my bag, and I like to find better ways to train. I like to find better nutrition packages, and I'm always researching like Frank Zane a lot. Sometimes I'll find a really good exercise and I'll tell Arnold about it. He'll listen and he'll say, "That's a great idea." One time he said, "How do you come up with these ideas?" I said to him, "This is where my heart is. Your heart's in moviemaking. My heart is in finding better ways to exercise." Sometime I'll call him and say, "You've got to try this. This is a great exercise, which I've just discovered."

**Q: Arnold envisaged himself becoming the best bodybuilder in the world. The absurdity of Joe Weider's subterfuge pertaining to adverts in his magazines didn't necessarily influence the readers, and he made a star out of Arnold.**

Larry Scott: I'm not sure if he was interested in himself of promoting himself, but rather to become a better bodybuilder. That's Joe Weider – Joe Weider is the promoter. Joe was always promoting you to train hard and had him in the magazines and on the covers. He'd put you on the cover. He would also try to get bodybuilders motivated to train hard because he wants the bodybuilders on the covers of his magazines. And as far as Arnold was concerned, he trained because he loves training. Then, I'm sure he'd like to train now but he's busy. But at that time, he wasn't busy and he trained hard because then it helped him in the movies, *Conan the Barbarian* so forth. So he's got to train and look good for the kind of movies he was doing. Plus the fact he liked to train and enjoyed the training. And it helps to promote the image he was trying to convey and to keep himself in the limelight.

**Q: Some people would say the two body parts Arnold lacked were the legs and calves. How would you assess him in comparison to the other bodybuilders of that era?**

Larry Scott: I would say that his legs were not his best parts, but they certainly were in proportion with the rest of his body. His upper body was very, very good – one of the best upper bodies you'll see in the physique world. His legs weren't quite as good, but he had great thighs, really good thighs. And his calves, I don't think he put enough effort in his calves like he did with his upper body. It's hard to do both. But he was very proportionate and he would never have lost any points in a physique contest because of his calves or his thighs if they're always proportionate to the rest of his body. But it's hard to look at his calves and thighs when he's got such great arms, deltoids, chest – you can't take your eyes off those body parts. You can look at those other parts that are not even at that level and not as outstanding as the rest of his body.

**Q: In the late 1960s and early 1970s, bodybuilders didn't make much money. Did Arnold have to do jobs to support himself? Did he do construction work among other jobs?**

Larry Scott: Yes, he did. He got paid from Joe for some of the things he did. I'm not sure of exactly those initial jobs when he first came over. I do recall him having some work. When he first came over, he was just trying to earn a living and he got some jobs. He started to do some real estate work. He started buying real estate and started making money in that area.

**Q: When Arnold had retired from bodybuilding and was pursuing a movie career, was he accessible to his fellow bodybuilding buddies?**

Larry Scott: When he was working in the movies, this is before he started doing political work, he was more accessible. You could reach him. You could get him on the phone, and you could talk to him about everything. But once he became a governor, then he had a crew of people around him that he kept, and if anybody called you had to make it through them in order to talk to Arnold. It was just too much work to try to get through to him. If you didn't have anything important to say to him, you just tried to stay in touch, it was just too hard to. He was inaccessible for most of us to get through to him because you didn't have a real reason to contact him, other than to keep the friendship alive.

**Q: Interestingly, you were in a movie in the 1960s. How did you get this part, did you have any conversations with Arnold pertaining to movie appearances in those early years?**

Larry Scott: I never did. That took place way before Arnold came over. I was training in Vince's gym one day, and, I guess it wasn't the director but the person who looks for people for the movie, they were going to do a movie called *Muscle Beach Party*. So he came to Vince's gym and asked if we would be interested in being in this movie. And there were several of us. I think it was about ten or twelve of us. We said, "Yeah, we'll do it." They sent us over to a casting at 20th Century Fox. We walked in front of the producers and directors, and they looked at us and they picked out the ones they wanted. That would happen quite a bit because Vince's gym was right next to Universal Studios, which was one of the biggest movie studios in Los Angeles.

They would come over occasionally to that gym and look for people for parts. That's where Clint Eastwood got his start. He was there training with us, and he got his start. He came over occasionally. Clint was a lot of fun to be with. He didn't take himself too seriously. He trained there regularly but didn't train very hard. I remember one time he was doing shoulders, and I said, "Clint, let me tell you something about that exercise, how you can progress with it. I'll show it to you." I showed him how to do it, and he said, "Oh, man, you're making me tired. I'm going home." So he didn't want to do it at all and he left. Most of the people would want to try it, *Yeah, that'll be right,* but he was, like, "Nah, it's too much."

**Q: What are your recollections of some of the more light-hearted moments with Arnold?**

Larry Scott: I remember one. He did a movie called *True Lies.* He's hanging on a helicopter and Jamie Lee Curtis is in a car. And as he flew over, he was yelling to her, "The bridge is out! Reach down and grab my hand!" She was down in a convertible on the freeway, and he's on a helicopter trying to reach her hand. Anyway, several of us were driving to a physique contest, everyone always likes to impersonate Arnold because he's easier to do. So, all through the way when we were driving, we were all saying, "The bridge is out! The bridge is out!" It was just silly what we were doing.

When we got to the Mr. Olympia contest, we were in a group, all gathered together before the show. We had been saying that phrase for so long that when Arnold came behind me and tapped me on the shoulder, he said "Larry, how are you doing?" I turned around and the first thing that came out of my mouth – I didn't even think about it – it just came out (impersonating Arnold's accent), "The bridge is out!" He didn't know what to make of it. There was no comeback or anything. He thought I was putting him down because of it. He says, "Where's your lolly, Larry?" In other words, he meant he made a lot of money out of it, whereas the money I didn't make. So, those are the kinds of things that generally take place when we see each other. I'm sure it's going to happen when we see each other again.

**Q: Arnold has been an influential figure in the sport of bodybuilding. He has truly left his mark on the sport. How do you perceive his place in bodybuilding history?**
Larry Scott: I don't think there's any way you can ever take anything away from Arnold, he's certainly the most well-known bodybuilder in the whole world by far. By virtue of the amount of exposure that he gets, he's a very, very good promoter – the promoter for Arnold – he's very good. The producers want Arnold to do their movies because he worked so hard to promote the movies. So, he is not afraid of work. It's tough to work with him because he works so hard and you get exhausted. He has this incredible stamina and endurance. He's an amazing guy. He's not just a make-believe character; he's really real. He's very dedicated. I saw him one day when he came backstage at one of the contests. He looked very haggard, very drawn-out. He said, "I just got back from doing the promotion for *Twins*." The movie he was in. He said, "I did one hundred and seventeen interviews with the press over in France." And he came right after that to do the physique contest.

I watched him, and what they did, because everyone gets an autograph, they've got two photographers backstage. And they stood on one side, and a person walks up to Arnold, takes a shot with him, and maybe six feet away there is another photographer with another person all ready. And Arnold walks over to take a photo with him. He went back and forth for about two hours. I watched the expression on his face – that's very fatiguing. You can't just take a picture with the people; you have to make them feel good. He was very gracious and he put himself out for each one of them. He made them feel welcomed and pleased in what they saw. He knows how to promote, he does. He puts himself out tremendously.

## ED CORNEY

Ed Corney, born in Hawaii in 1933, is commonly acknowledged as being one of the greatest posers in bodybuilding history. He won countless competitions, including two victories at the Masters Olympia. Arnold met Corney in the 1970s, when both men became close friends and training partners. He died in January 2019.

**Q: You and Arnold became good friends and training partners. When was the first time you met Arnold and sought to train with him?**
Ed Corney: In the early 1970s, because in 1975 I moved down to Los Angeles to live with him. I had heard about him, and I suppose he had heard about me. But I met him at one of the local bodybuilding shows in the Bay area called Mr. San Jose. And, of course, we exchanged greetings, but that was about it. I continued on pursuing my career. One day I get a call, he says, "This is Arnold!" I said, "Hey, Arnold, how are you?!" He said, "I want you to come and live with me in Santa Monica, we'll train together and we can do the movie *Pumping Iron*." So I said, "OK! I'll be there tomorrow." San Jose is about four hundred and fifty miles from Los Angeles. So, I went down to Santa Monica, Los Angeles, and met with Arnold. It was a tremendous experience. On the first day of training, he says, "Eddie, we have two choices: either we train or we train."

I wasn't interested in anything else but training and getting better. Then he says, as we progressed in our training, Arnold said, "You're going to South Africa to compete in the Mr. Olympia." I said, "Oh, my goodness. Now I'm going to compete against my idols, Franco Columbu, Frank Zane, Albert Beckles." I couldn't believe that. But I did. I said OK. Of course, they had the under 200-pound class back then. I was in the under 200-pound class and came second to Columbu. Arnold won the over 200-pound class and then won the overall. Short story.

I was still living with Arnold in Santa Monica. His first investment that he bought was an apartment complex. He lived in the first apartment and rented out the other four. Another time, for taking care of the building, he hired a secretary to take care of everything. That way he could concentrate on bodybuilding. I lived with him and we trained every morning like clockwork. We would eat and rest. We trained in Santa Monica at Gold's (gym). He was unbelievable. I mean, he was very well-focused and trained very hard – very strong. I learned a lot from him. Even though I was older, I still learned a lot from Arnold. And still today, I use those things that I learned from him: you don't make any excuses.

**Q: How did you spend the time away from the confines of the gym?**
Ed Corney: Here's an example. We all went down to Birmingham, Alabama, where we did the movie *Stay Hungry*. Of course, Arnold was the star. The movie stars Sally Field and Jeff Bridges. Then when we came back to Santa Monica, Sally put on a party for all the movie people. We were invited and we drove to her home in Bel-Air. And the socializing didn't begin till late at night. So we left early because he said, "We go home now because we have to train tomorrow." So, his determination and focus was there. So we went home. And another time he said, "Eddie, we don't train today. Let's have a glass of wine and rest," and we did. The next day we were super strong. So, his training was focused and very determined. One time we were on Santa Monica Beach, and there were always women around us. One girl says, "Arnold! Arnold!" He looked up and said, "What is it?" She said, "I can't take my eyes off you." So then he answers her, "I don't blame you."

**Q: Which other event did you compete in with Arnold other than the 1975 Mr. Olympia and the 1980 Mr. Olympia?**
Ed Corney: Those are the only competitions we competed in the same show together. Other than that, there was my career and he had his own career. To make a long story short, I bested Frank Zane and Albert Beckles. Franco Columbu was the only man I had to beat. Of course, I didn't. I came second to him.

**Q: Can you recount the ambience at the time with bodybuilders training at the Santa Monica gym?**

Ed Corney: Everyone was there. Frank Zane, Mike Katz, Bill Grant, everybody training hard, really hard. Ken Waller doing inclined with 150-pound dumbbells. Danny Padilla was there. Up on the wall they had a sign, which stated how many days were left to the Mr. Universe contest, how many days for the Mr. Olympia. It was like a countdown. But you couldn't wait to train. Why? Because everyone was training, that was the atmosphere. People couldn't wait to get into that atmosphere. Everyone trained super hard! And they were very friendly, too. There was no animosity.

One guy would do a pose and the whole gym would look at him. And we would comment on his posing to encourage him, "That's it, you're getting better. That's it, a little bit more. Now you've got it!" He would be doing his training and I'd be watching. He'd be telling me, "You've got to go for more! You've got to do more! You've got to challenge yourself." When he did his set, now it's my turn to do the same, "Challenge yourself. Use heavier weights. Increase your effort, get better." You might say it was the unspeakable force between us, we didn't have to say anything; we just knew about each other and what we both wanted. I had the opportunity to train with the best, and in doing so I became one of the best. Unbelievable.

**Q: Did you go around with Arnold guest posing? Did you discuss posing with Arnold – you're probably known for being the best poser in bodybuilding?**

Ed Corney: We did one guest posing. Because I had a commitment made, to do the San Francisco show as a guest poser. In the meantime, Arnold was in Los Angeles doing *Pumping Iron*. So, the promoter said, "Do you think Arnold will guest pose?" I said, "You'll have to talk to him." In either case, the promoter brought everybody up to guest pose – myself, Ken Waller, Frank Zane, Franco Columbu and Arnold were the main entry to guest pose. We did discuss posing. We also went to ballet. We discussed body movements – how to move the body from one movement to another, movement with your hands and your head. We discussed posing on how to do certain things. One pose in particular with Arnold: hitting a front pose, then he turns around and everybody is following him, he does a back pose. While they're committed to a back pose, he wants to know how he can get to the front pose really quickly. And we worked it out and that was interesting.

**Q: Regarding Frank Zane, was there a competitive edge between him and Arnold?**

Ed Corney: Frank Zane was more on the ripped side. He would get totally ripped, not too much muscular. Arnold had both, muscular and ripped. Friendly! They were competitive as far as competing was concerned, like, *Let's get it over with. Let's get onstage and let them pick the best one. Then let's go have dinner.* No animosity. Arnold was like me: very happy, very happy-go-lucky. And he had this magnetism about him. When he walked into a room everyone noticed him, looked up to him. That was his way of letting people know he was there, not in a cocky way, but it was his presence. I suppose he got that from his parents. But he was very welcomed.

**Q: Did Arnold have any other hobbies, in which he found merriment, besides his passion for bodybuilding?**

Ed Corney: Yes. He and Frank Zane would shoot bow and arrow on Sundays. He also loved guns. He would go to a pistol range and let off some steam, I suppose. He came up to San Francisco. He and I were guest posing in the same show at the Mr. USA. We both went to the gun range and shot for two rounds, and then we saw the movie *Taxi Driver*, which starred Robert De Niro. Great movie. People always told him that he couldn't speak English very well, and he had this accent. But Arnold would tell me, "I'll smile all the way to the bank." And he did not only as an actor but as a director as well.

**Q: Did you continue to see Arnold when he became a star in the mid-1980s, and how did you keep in touch?**

Ed Corney: He came to Fremont to do *The Terminator*. Of course, the movie people were up all night and I'm asleep. And in the day, I'm working and he's asleep. So we missed each other more or less. I never used his fame to further myself. He called me not long ago, "Eddie, it's Arnold, your training partner, 1975, remember?" I said, "Of course I remember." We chatted back and forth. I always go to his Arnold Classic bodybuilding show. And he comes over to my table, we'll shake hands, and he'll say "Eddie, what is this? You're still in shape!" Only because I've kept on training. Then he'll hit a couple of pauses, and I tell him, "If I can help you in anything, let me know." As if I could. Arnold put bodybuilding on the map. His charisma, his focus, his everything, was bodybuilding then. He did quite a bit for bodybuilding, an awful lot. He made people notice bodybuilding.

**Q: In 1972, you went to Baghdad to compete in the Mr. Universe show, did Arnold accompany you?**
Ed Corney: Mr. Universe. Arnold didn't make it to that one. Well, there were three thousand people at the show, and another two thousand couldn't get in. Me being from Hawaii and from an ethnic group, I looked like an Iraqi. Dark skinned. But, you know, there was no music for the competition; you just had to be prepared. Of course, Mike Katz won the tall class and I won the medium class and a kid from Japan won the short class. Then I won the overall. Of course, when I won the overall everyone thought I was God. "Ed Corney! Ed Corney! Ed Corney!" They all wanted to touch me and shake my hand and take pictures and what not. It was tremendous.

**Q: What were Arnold's attributes, his strong points and body parts as a bodybuilder, which inspired the observer to look on with goading awe?**
Ed Corney: His strong points were: learn how to act with people. He was a people person. Of course, he was also a businessman. Shrewdness, I guess you might say he knew how to be a businessman. He knew what he had to do. He came over here from Austria, spoke no English, so what does he do? He takes English-speaking classes. Doesn't know how to act, so what does he do? He takes acting

classes. That was Arnold. His strongest body parts were everything. Tying in with the legs, with the calves, everything tied in. He had no favorite, but you exercise all of them. Your favorite body parts would be all of them. In other words, he would train his calves just as hard as he would train his back. So he had everything together.

**Q: Did you and Arnold do any cardio in those days, and if so what type – running, jogging?**

Ed Corney: Cardio by increasing the reps and the time you rest in between the sets. That was our type of cardio. I started to jog when I moved back to Santa Monica, again living with Danny Padilla. This is interesting, because our diet was, compared to today's standards, it was nothing. We had beef steak, green vegetables, egg whites and tuna. We were just using ourselves as guinea pigs, finding out what is good to eat to get a better physique. Arnold's favorite food was cheesecake. He introduced the cheesecake to me. Once we were up in San Francisco, before the Olympia was coming up, and we're having dinner. And Joe Weider is there and everyone else. Arnold said, "Eddie, order two cheesecakes." I did. Everybody is looking and they're saying, "Hey, they're eating cheesecakes!" Of course, cheesecake's aren't very good for you, but on the day it's got calories, which is good for energy.

He phoned me a while back. Some people wanted to do an interview with me. When Arnold and I spoke, we kept the recording machine on. So when the channel called me about the interview, I said OK. They came here at 6.30 in the morning. I've got pictures on the wall of Arnold and myself. The TV people asked, "Do you know Arnold?" I said yes. I pressed the recording machine and his voice came on. Meanwhile, my daughter is downstairs watching me on a big TV, watching my interview. I've always supported him. I'll always support Arnold regardless of what people say or do, even when everybody's pointing a finger at him. He can't please everyone. He's his own person – that's what I am. I'm my own man I don't mean to step on other people's toes or anything like that. But Ed Corney is Ed Corney because of Ed Corney, not because of anyone else.

## BILL PEARL

William Arnold 'Bill' Pearl is one of the greatest bodybuilders of all time, with five Mr. Universe titles among his list of accomplishments. Well-liked in the bodybuilding community, he was named the WBBA's Best-Built Man of the Century in 1974. A lacto-ovo vegetarian, he currently lives in Phoenix, Oregon.

**Q: Bill, you were a prominent bodybuilding champion and star before Arnold came on the scene. Can you please tell me when you and Arnold met for the first time?**

Bill Pearl: Yes. I met Arnold in Frankfurt, Germany, and I believe he was eighteen years old. I had just entered and competed in the Mr. Universe contest. I don't remember the exact time, it might be 1965. I guess it was. I was giving an exhibition in Frankfurt, and Arnold and Franco Columbu came to watch the exhibition. Well, it wasn't so much the exhibition; it was my impression of Arnold. He could not speak English, but it was obvious by looking at him that he was very enthusiastic in the bodybuilding world. There's no question that Arnold was going to rise to the top as he did, and it was just obvious that he was a young kid who wanted to get ahead. That's all there was to it. And whatever it took to get there, he was willing to do it.

**Q: Arnold has countless times expressed that it was his biggest dream to go over to America and train with the American bodybuilders. California was the Mecca of bodybuilding.**

Bill Pearl: I think Arnold was smart because the magazines – Joe Weider's magazines, *Strength & Health* magazines so on – if he wanted to ever get in them, it meant more publicity. So whatever he could do in Germany or Austria, he probably had to come over to America to do this because that's where the sport was more popular. And if he was going to get any type of notoriety at all, it was about coming and competing in the United States and being with the best we had. This was going to take him where he wanted to go.

**Q: Did you see Arnold in America when he arrived in the late 1960s virtually penniless?**

Bill Pearl: Yes, I remember him very well. I had a health club in Pasadena, California, at the time and Arnold used to drop by. He and Franco Columbu were just like brothers. You couldn't separate the two. He did train at our health club, but he was never a member; he preferred to train down in Santa Monica and be with the guys that trained there. But even back then, Arnold was smart enough to surround himself with the hardcore bodybuilders that we had in the United States at the time. But he was also smarter, and he immediately enrolled in college and continued to advance his education, which I think is the smartest thing he could've done.

**Q: Other than Reg Park, who Arnold wanted to emulate and adulated, which other bodybuilders did he admire?**

Bill Pearl: I think Reg Park was his mentor by far, and he spent time with Reg Park in South Africa after he won the Mr. Universe competition. Reg was a very nice guy, and I'm sure that he, maybe, turned out to be like a father figure to Arnold. I don't know for sure, but I assume this was the case. Arnold went to Santa Monica and trained at Gold's Gym and World Gym. He hung around with the top athletes there who wanted to do exactly what he was attempting to do. He could just go to a health club and say, "If I'm going to get to the top, I'm going to have to beat these guys to have to do that." And that's what he did.

**Q: Competing in 1967 at the NABBA Amateur Mr. Universe, did you actually compete with Arnold and do you have any backstage stories?**

Bill Pearl: OK. That was the 1967 Mr. Universe contest. I won the professional class and I got all the votes. And Arnold won the amateur class and he got all the votes. He and I walked onstage together. Only I was a professional Mr. Universe winner and he was an amateur Mr. Universe winner. I'd rather not get into all that stuff because I want to keep everything . . . Arnold was the type of a person, and he's probably still that type of a person, he's going to win something no matter how he does – that's it, period. So Arnold had an attitude, perhaps still has an attitude, that if you're going to beat him you're going to have to take everything you possibly can to put that guy on the ground – that's all there is to it. He was out to win. There were times backstage where he showed this, but he was never in a position where he did this with me, and I don't know whether he would have done. Maybe out of respect, I don't know.

**Q: Can you tell me in those days what the fans were like who attended physique shows compared to the fans in the modern era?**

Bill Pearl: That's a very good question. Back then everybody who was onstage was a champion. Regardless of if you won the contest or you did not win the contest. If you are on the stage with the caliber of physiques of Arnold Schwarzenegger or Franco Columbu or Frank Zane or Reg Park, whoever it was, if you were onstage competing you, too, were equally a champion. You may not have been a top champion, but you were a champion. Once, for example, I was talking to Larry Scott on the telephone and he had gone to the Mr. Olympia contest in Las Vegas, and I asked Larry Scott, "Larry, other than J. Cutler, can you tell me of the name of one person who was in the contest other than J. Cutler?" Larry Scott said, "No. I cannot." So, the comment I'm making is: where are all the champions? Who's taking all the champions? Who out there now is taking the champions' places? There's nobody, period!

**Q: Arnold mainly trained at Gold's Gym, didn't he?**

Bill Pearl: He trained at Gold's Gym, and he also trained at Vince Gironda's gym. Joe Gold, again, definitely became a father figure to Arnold. He felt very comfortable there. The group that was there was a very close, tight-knit family, nobody could just walk in there and get into that family. You had to be invited into that family. Of course, Arnold was there because of his physique, but also because of his demeanor.

**Q: Arnold had a great sense of humor and joked around a lot, didn't he? Is there anything you would like to share with me?**

Bill Pearl: Nothing I would like to share with you. Arnold could be very, very funny, but he could also be very cruel. When we're talking about anecdotes and so on, Arnold could be extremely funny at times, but he could also be very funny at other people's expense. I'm not doing anything in the world to demean him in any respect, way, shape or form. If you're talking about Arnold as a person, he joked sometimes at other people's expense, which I did not like.

**Q: Did you socialize with Arnold often?**

Bill Pearl: I socialized with Arnold, but it wasn't on a business basis and not on a friend basis. I could never consider Arnold a close friend, and I don't think he could consider me a close friend. We were people in the industry who had respect for one another, but we did not run in the same circles. We never had conversations about business. I never talked to him about my weight training. He never talked to me about his weight training. It was obvious what he was doing was good for him, and it was obvious what I was doing was good for me. There were certain things we did, but there was no sense in discussing them because I wasn't going to change his attitude and he wasn't going to change mine.

**Q: Apart from the 1967 Mr. Universe, did you both compete with each other again?**

Bill Pearl: In 1971, when I won my last Mr. Universe contest, Arnold made a challenge to me in Weider's magazine on several occasions, that people such as myself who were former champions, we were afraid. He wanted to compete against people such as myself in his contest. So he gave a challenge for all of us, anybody, you know. He wants to be top draw – that's it. He wanted to knock everybody off – that was it. So he made a challenge for me to compete against him in the 1971 Mr. Universe contest in London, England. I trained for the contest, and a week before the contest Arnold backed down. He claims that, I'm not saying this isn't true, he did not compete in the contest because he had a contract with Weider. And he was so popular in Weider's magazines and there was so much publicity in the magazines that if I had beaten him in that contest, it would've destroyed Weider's comments he had on Arnold in his magazines. So Weider would not allow Arnold to do that because of the monetary factors more than anything.

You have to remember that when we were at the contests and so on, there was a tremendous amount of people involved. You laid a lot on the line: you're the world champion, the best that there are out there. And in the contest, these guys take this stuff very, very seriously because it's their entire reputation. They're standing out there and putting it on the line. There was a whole lot of ethics going on. There was a common ground because these were those guys whose whole lifetime's work was put onstage there. It was all business.

**Q: The Weiders controlled bodybuilding in America. They did have a competitor, Bob Hoffman. How did you perceive Arnold and Joe Weider's relationship, it seems as though he felt Arnold was beholden to him?**

Bill Pearl: You're talking about two different individuals, but I think in some respects, because Arnold was so powerful, psychologically powerful, that Weider was afraid of him. Hoffman couldn't overcome the Weiders. Hoffman was AAU and Weiders were IFBB. Weider totally controlled bodybuilding in the United States. He totally controlled the sport and Arnold was his top man. Arnold was able to get publicity when probably no other physique star at the time could get publicity. And getting in the movies, *Pumping Iron* and so on, it brought bodybuilding to the mainstream and Arnold Schwarzenegger's name became a household word. So, every time you thought about a bodybuilder, or talked about anybody who was onstage, Arnold Schwarzenegger's name is still in the United States a household name. So, Arnold brought the sport up. Probably from all the bodybuilders combined, Arnold's probably the most responsible for the publicity it got from the late 1970s and early 1980s.

**Q: You were inducted into the Pioneers of Fitness Hall of Fame in 1988. Arnold often was present at such events.**

Bill Pearl: There probably aren't many Hall of Fames in the bodybuilding world which I've not been inducted into at one time or another. It's always nice to know that you are remembered, and giving interviews to such as yourself who is willing to take the time to talk to me, this, too, is much a compliment as getting any achievement where I am. If I could still get people like you ask me questions and so on, that's as big a compliment as any Lifetime Achievement award I've ever received. I'm laughing because every Lifetime Achievement I've ever received, it was given to me by Arnold Schwarzenegger. I've always received it from him. Arnold was always the one passing on the trophy to me.

**Q: Did you bump into Arnold at the height of his movie career?**

Bill Pearl: We did. One time he was doing a movie up in Oregon. I was living in the state of Oregon, just above California. He was shooting here and he was kind enough to invite me to come on the set. But you had to be there on a Saturday, and he told me on a Friday. it was impossible for me to make a trip on short notice. I respect Arnold as much for his movies as his political campaign as I do for his bodybuilding field. He's an extremely well-rounded individual. And his entrepreneurship, I'm probably more impressed with that than any of his bodybuilding titles he ever had. He was an extremely good businessman and still is to this day.

**Q: Bodybuilding era of the 1950s and 1960s, can you differentiate between your generation and the modern-day bodybuilding scene?**

Bill Pearl: I think most people in the 1950s, '60s and '70s involved in the bodybuilding almost took it as if it was a religion, almost as if it was holistic. Today, I think it revolves around drugs and money. I think the 1970s and so on, the modern-day bodybuilding as we know it today, Arnold probably brought more crave and notoriety to the sport of bodybuilding than anybody has in the last thirty, forty or fifty years. Even probably more than Joe Weider's magazines, simply because of his demeanor, and, like I say, Arnold Schwarzenegger is a household name. And I can think of very few people than him who have had the impact he has had. So, all the popularity for bodybuilding to this point, Arnold is probably responsible for a great deal of this.

**Q: When Arnold went into politics, do you feel it was an extension of him to reach further heights?**
Bill Pearl: Yes, I do. And I think he had that plan even before he came to the United States, to tell you the truth. I think this was something he was talking about when he was a nineteen-year-old kid.

**Q: You were scheduled to judge at the 1980 Mr. Olympia in Sydney, and you also did commentary for TV. Arnold was expected to compete, but he then decided he wasn't. But he did compete, even though he had taken a myriad bodybuilding titles and had retired.**
Bill Pearl: I can't tell you anything that he has told me. Everything I tell you is hearsay. I heard from other people that he had no intention of competing, but when he found out who the judges were – there were several of the judges he personally was in business with – then he made his decision to compete. But he did not tell me this, but I'm telling you what other people have said. I'm reiterating what they said.

Arnold had his reasons for competing at the 1980 Mr. Olympia. Later, when he was delving into politics, he reflected back on the controversial event. "I retired from bodybuilding in 1975, and I signed for a series of *Conan* movies," he said. "Here I was. You've got a big studio behind you, a budget of $20 million, which, of course, in those days was the equivalent of $150 million. I was going to Australia to be a judge at the Mr. Olympia competition. Then all of a sudden, I thought I should compete." The other competitors felt very disappointed. They felt that their chances of winning were diminished. Some of these men's ultimate dream of becoming Mr. Olympia was put in jeopardy now. But for Arnold it was something he needed to do. He felt very strongly about a comeback so he decided to compete.

**Q: One of the things surrounding the 1980 Mr. Olympia was there was some talk about changing the weight class. Can you tell me if you were present at the meeting, which took place where fifty other people were present?**

Bill Pearl: That was Arnold's decision (weight class change), he wanted to have it. I'd say he's a very smart man, believe me, the guy's manipulative. I admire him for his tenacity. But he wanted to make some changes in the rules of the contest. But at that particular meeting, I was there. He actually almost had Mike Mentzer in tears! Just because of the comments he had made and so on. Arnold just dominated that meeting, there's no question about it. Arnold was intimidating to the point where he belittled him to the point where Mike was just about ready to start to cry. I think Mike respected Arnold. And he was involved in the meeting. And the comments Arnold made, I can't tell you specifically what they were now because it makes no difference to me, but he hurt Mike Mentzer's feelings to the point that he nearly broke down.

The tension was unbelievable in that room, believe me. It was unbelievable. Boyer Coe is a tough guy, and he stood up to Arnold tooth and nail. Boyer wasn't going to have any part of it at all. He's tough. Well, there's a difference between the height class and weight class. Arnold was making sure whatever he decided and what he wanted done was going to be more beneficial to him, let's put it that way. You've got to understand that Mike Mentzer was the editor of the magazine for Joe Weider, and Joe helped him with his posing. And Joe was telling him he was going to win for his . . . and so on. Mike was a very fragile person psychologically, almost too smart for his own good. He believed all of this pre-release publicity, which he was getting, and when it didn't pan out he was really devastated. He felt his entire bodybuilding career had gone down the tube because he did not win that particular contest. So, everything he had done prior to that really made no difference to him because he did not get the jewel and he did not reach that, and that's what broke the guy's heart.

**Q: Was Joe Weider present at the meeting, did he intervene to placate the situation?**
Bill Pearl: Even though Joe and Ben were there, I don't think Joe probably uttered a word at that meeting at all. Joe was smart enough to keep himself out of that because if there was going to be something that was going to go off, Joe wanted no part of it. So he was smart enough to keep his mouth shut.

**Q: You withdrew from the judging panel because you had trained one of the competitors, Chris Dickerson, is this true?**
Bill Pearl: He trained for the contest up at our house here up in Oregon. I didn't feel it was fair for me to judge him. But all these other guys, Frank Zane, Boyer Coe, and all these guys didn't know Arnold was going to compete. But all of these guys are my friends. I didn't want to look bad for Chris, so I stepped off the judging panel because of that.

**Q: Onstage, some say Arnold wasn't in the best of shape. Which other bodybuilders were there who were in greater shape? Can you tell me about the strategy Arnold utilized onstage? Arnold would go forward, and as soon as the other competitors came forward, he would go back.**
Bill Pearl: If I had placed him in the contest, I would have placed him fifth. Boyer was in really good condition, Chris Dickerson was in very good condition, of course. And all of those guys on the stage, Shamir, were in fabulous condition. Arnold was pushing and shoving on the stage like it was some type of a high school wrestling match. It was ridiculous. To the point where the judges almost lost control because the guys onstage were pushing each other back

and forth like a bunch of little kids. There, again, he was doing everything he possibly could to get the attention that he wanted, not only from the judges but the audience as well. But he did that not just walking in front of somebody, but he would shove them and push them to the side like they meant nothing to anybody. I'm not trying to belittle Arnold. Like I mentioned before, he is . . . and I told him at the end of the contest that he was the most fierce competitor I had ever seen onstage.

**Q: Do you think one of the prime reasons for Arnold to come back to compete at the Mr. Olympia was he was going to start filming a Hollywood movie, and it would elevate his profile?**
Bill Pearl: I think it was ego. Pure ego. I didn't even know the guy was going to be there, to tell you the truth.

**Q: He had told Frank Zane he was coming to Australia to do commentary for NBC. Frank wasn't too happy after the decision. When did Arnold broach that he was going to compete?**
Bill Pearl: That was his reason to go over there, he claimed. But I think he decided to enter the contest the day before, when he saw who the judging panel was. And everybody was upset. In fact, when everybody was done we made a ruling where all of us got together. I was the head judge, but Weider and everything, in fact, there was ruling at the time that you had to let them know or announce if you were going to compete in the contest thirty days prior to the contest taking place. And the guy who was the head of the judging, I can't remember his name now, he's from England, he just let him slide into competing because he was Arnold. So he overruled the judging. Those guys trained so hard for the contest, and they had so much to put on the line. and most of those guys like Frank Zane were making their living from these contests, whereas Arnold wasn't doing this. So their whole reputations were on the line. So it was a very important thing for these guys. Not to have anything going on, that would not make them do what they felt they could possibly do. It's like putting your entire career on the line. That's

what all those guys did, Frank, Chris, all of those guys, Boyer in particular – all of them. Arnold came in as a cold turkey almost taking the whole lot, they just couldn't understand it.

**Q: When the contest was over, it left a lot of people upset. Some fans were even booing after the contest. Critics may have concluded a foul stench permeated Arnold's decision to compete and win when he actually didn't deserve to.**

Bill Pearl: They were booing and actually throwing the programs on the stage. I think when Arnold went up to get his trophy, he may have said something, but I can't recall. But he was virtually talking to an empty house because everybody walked out of there like the contest didn't even take place. Almost all of the competitors that were there were going to boycott the Mr. Olympia contest in 1981. They decided that this was it, there is going to be no more, we're not going to put up with this. A lot of guys who were there at the contest decided there that they were not going to compete in 1981 because of what happened in 1980. After the contest, the following morning, he came up to my table and he made a comment. He said, "I hear you've been saying bad things about me." He came up to me and insulted me. I said, "Arnold, the only thing I've told anybody is you were the most fierce competitor that I've ever seen onstage." And he said, "OK, that's fine." And he walked off and that was it.

**Q: How would you sum up the 1980 Mr. Olympia, which has been the most controversial Mr. Olympia contest to date?**

Bill Pearl: I can sum it up very simply: it was probably one of the poorest decisions Arnold made in his bodybuilding career to compete that night. He actually gained nothing from the contest at all by winning it. He probably had lost more esteem from winning the contest than if he had not competed.

## BILL GRANT

'Man of Steel' Bill Grant, who won Mr. America in 1972 and Mr. World in 1974, had a friendship with Arnold which went beyond the confines of the gym. With a competitive career that ran to more than 40 competitions, he popularized superset-style training and continues to stay in shape as the president and owner of Grant Nutrition, a company based in New Jersey.

**Q: Bill, how and when did you meet Arnold?**
Bill Grant: I met Arnold in 1969. I met him in North Hollywood in Vince's gym, which used to be on Ventura Boulevard. Arnold lived not too far from that gym, maybe a couple of blocks. That was all located in North Hollywood. I'll give you the rundown how that worked. Gold's Gym wasn't the top gym; Vince's gym was the big gym back in the days before World's opened up. All the big bodybuilders like Larry Scott, me and Arnold trained there. All the up-and-coming guys were training at Vince's gym. He was called the 'Guru'. He was the guy. Then some guys moved to Gold's Gym some years after because Vince was a little strange. Vince trained a lot of the movie stars at that gym. I don't think Vince really wanted to deal with a lot of the bodybuilders anymore, so he took some strategically important equipment like the leg equipment, he took that out of the gym. Joe Gold at that time was building Gold's Gym, and everybody started gravitating to Gold's Gym. That's where we ended up going.

I could tell you a good story about Arnold training at Vince's gym in North Hollywood. A good friend of mine, Jerry Brainum – he's also a writer and nutritionist for *Iron Man* magazine – told me this story. And I told this story as well on Fox News. But I had to really confirm that story with Jerry before I told that story. He and Arnold were walking down a Boulevard one night and they were having a conversation. Arnold said, "Jerry, do you know who Steve Reeves is?" Everybody knew who Steve Reeves was. He says, "Jerry, one day they're going to be talking about me in the same light they talk about Steve Reeves." Jerry was kind of taken aback and looked at him. And he says, "Yeah, right. OK." Then Arnold came over with another statement, he said, "Jerry, do you know the most fantastic thing of all? I'm going to be the biggest movie star in Hollywood." This is unbelievable!

Arnold told this story in 1969. I mean, I don't know whether he had a crystal ball in his hands, someone was reading him and telling him what was going to happen and figure out his future. But, anyway, Jerry laughed and said, "Yeah, Arnold, right. With the name Schwarzenegger? You can hardly speak English and you're a bodybuilder. Yeah, right, you're going to be the biggest star in Hollywood!" To this day, Jerry and I still laugh about that story because as we all know, not only was Arnold the biggest bodybuilder in the world, but he's the biggest actor in the world. He married a Kennedy and he became the governor of California. And he's a billionaire. I mean, how much better can you live the American Dream?

**Q: Did you train with Arnold in Vince's gym or later in Santa Monica at Gold's?**
Bill Grant: A little bit later on in Venice, that's where Gold's was originally based at. Arnold trained with quite a few guys. We trained a few times together because we had different programs. Arnold had a different body type. But Arnold would train six days a week, and three of those days would be twice a day. That was pretty common in those days, if your body could handle it. I had such a fantastic metabolism that I really couldn't do it. Arnold would come on those days. On Monday he trained chest and back in the morning. And at night they would come back late, and that was followed the rest of the week. Tuesdays would be shoulders and arms, and Wednesday he would repeat Monday. And on Thursday he would repeat Tuesday and so on. Arnold really was a very, very competitive person.

I can give you a real anecdote, a real story about what happened one time we were working out together. It's a great story. We were squatting this day. We agreed we'd do twelve reps. And that's the way it worked. I did sets and Arnold does his last set of twelve. And when I'm doing mine Arnold's counting. He says, "Ten, eleven, twelve, thirteen," and I put the bar down at thirteen. Arnold looks at me, and in his heavy accent he says, "Bill, what are you doing? You did thirteen reps!" I said, "Yeah." He said, "But we agreed we'd only do twelve reps." I said, "Yeah, but I did thirteen." I mean, he was pissed and he stormed off upstairs. And he said, "You'll never beat me again." I mean, you're talking about a competitive person! You can't even do one more rep with this guy! That's his whole life: Arnold was totally competitive, not only in bodybuilding but in business and in the movie business. Arnold had a drive that I don't think anyone had. He was a real driving force in the gym, and he had a real positive attitude.

He really didn't like it when people had negative things to say. He'd actually tell you to shut up, "I don't want to hear it." But you really had to like Arnold for what he was doing. The guy was motivated. People thought everything was given to Arnold when he came to the United States. They thought Joe Weider gave him everything. That's far from the truth. Joe gave Arnold $100 a week. He paid for the apartment, of course, and a dumpy old Volkswagen to drive around in. That was in 1969. When he first came over, he did not dress well, you know. Arnold went to school at night, he had a job. He had two jobs. He worked with Franco and he was a carpenter. Arnold really did a lot, that's just the way he was. He was determined. I think he saw the advantages of being in America more than most Americans did, you know. Sometimes you've got to be outside the store to kind of see how good things are inside. And we're inside looking out, so we don't really realize the opportunities that we have around. But Arnold saw that right away. I think Arnold had that plan when he first came. He seemed like a guy who had a lot of plans and he planned way ahead of time, too.

I think he's somewhat of a humanitarian. And he really loves kids. Most people think it was all done for kids with the Special Olympics just to look good, but I can give you a good story about me thinking how genuinely he loves kids. I used to work for United Airlines. I want to make it clear to people: most people thought all of us bodybuilders back in the day didn't have jobs, and that Joe Weider gave us money. No. I had a job. I used to work for United Airlines for ten years. At one point, I took my kids to the gym one day and I had a meeting at United that day. I forgot that I had a meeting and I brought my kids to the gym. It was time to go to the meeting but I couldn't take my kids. I'm looking around the gym and saying to myself, *Oh, my God, who's going to watch my small kids while I go to the meeting?*

I'm looking around the gym. I'm psyching everybody up and I get to Arnold. I kind of sheepishly walk up to Arnold. I said, "Arnold, I've got a meeting at the airport. I can't take my kids. Do you think you can help me out here and watch my kids for a couple of hours?" There were three boys. Wow, Arnold says, "Don't worry about it. I do it." I'm worried shitless! I'm worried! I'm thinking, *Oh, my God, what's my wife going to say if he loses my three kids?* Anyway, fast forward to a long story short. I get back and I say, "How did everything go, Arnold?" My kids say, "Oh, Dad, it was great! Arnold took us to the beach. He took us to McDonalds. We had hamburgers and ice cream. He was great! We had a lot of fun!"

I thought I was going to faint, man. He did a great job with those kids. That right there told me that Arnold really has some kind of feeling for kids. He really played well with those kids. To me, Arnold is a very rounded person. Of course, he's not perfect like everybody else. He can get angry with people, he can get mad, you know, and all those things. But I think all in all Arnold had a plan. Arnold was very interested in getting ahead. He saw the opportunity here and that's just the way it worked.

**Q: Can you relate any anecdotes in the gym?**
Bill Grant: I think for Arnold, that was a great time in his life. I mean, it was the biggest thing that could happen to Arnold. Arnold was very good at playing tricks on people. He was a competitor and that's what competitors do. He had a little boyish, prankish thing

about him as well. There's another story I can tell you. We were at the gym one night and we were finished training, and Ken Waller was there. Ken Waller was the manager of the gym at the time. So, a guy walks off the street, obviously, he was all whacked out, whatever he was doing. But he stumbled into the gym. He said he wanted to be a bodybuilder. And this was really funny. Arnold was standing and we were standing. Arnold said, "So, you want to be a bodybuilder, huh?" He says to Ken, "Ken, this guy wants to be a bodybuilder. Go get the oil." He says to the guy, "I'm going to teach you to pose now."

Ken Waller comes back with a can of motor oil. Can you imagine? Ken Waller opens it and Arnold says to the guy, "Open your hands," and tells him to wipe it all over his body. I mean, it was harmless. The oil wasn't going to hurt him. But he came in and he wanted to be a bodybuilder. I don't know why because he couldn't be. He put on the oil and Arnold had him posing and screaming up and down. I was falling on the floor laughing. Arnold was really a jokester. He was very fun to be around. Again, like most professional athletes, you have fun, you have pranks on each other. He'd do all these things that athletes would do. Arnold loved to play jokes on people, and that was one that I just never forgot. It's like I'm still there looking at it as I tell you the story now.

**Q: Can you give me an example of how Arnold treated his friends, did he ever have a mercurial temperament?**
Bill Grant: I left Los Angeles in about 1970 or 1971, then I came back for good in 1972. So there were three years in between when I didn't see Arnold. We met up again in 1972, when we kind of like hung out – that was great. Those were the good times. I was in South Africa in 1975 doing *Pumping Iron*. As you know, in 1975 there was a lot of apartheid going on in South Africa. Arnold, again, stepped up to the plate. It was really weird. I'll tell you that story and I'll tell you my story about me being there. The bodybuilders got on the bus, and they were told that the black guys could not get on the bus with the white guys. Arnold says, "If these guys don't get on the bus, we don't

get on the bus. We're all athletes. We're all friends and competitors together. We all ride on the same bus or we don't go at all." That's the kind of guy Arnold was. He stuck up for the other guys.

As far as I'm concerned, Reg Park, as you might know, was British. He was Hercules. He lived in Johannesburg. I stayed at his house for a week. As you know, if you were a person of color, there was no such thing as you going into a regular restaurant. I can remember Reg Park calling the restaurant owner and telling him that he was coming into the restaurant, but he had an unusual guest with him. He kind of had to let him know who I was. So, I got to the restaurant and it was really a scary feeling, especially for me. I walked into the restaurant and the place just got quiet. I remember it was 1975, apartheid in South Africa and a black man going into a restaurant to eat that was all white. That did not fit well, but the owner graciously said it was OK. The caterers in the restaurant looked and they didn't like it at all. The workers from the kitchen would come out and look at me. People would walk past the window and look at me because we were sitting near the window. And they looked in wondering, *How did this black guy get in to eat when we can't go in there?* I mean, that to me was great.

Reg Park didn't put up with that kind of crap. They even told him he couldn't have blacks working in his gym, but he actually told them, "You're full of crap because this is my business. I'll have whoever I want to work in my business and you can't tell me." Reg Park was totally against it. So, for me going to South Africa with all the other guys as an athlete doing the Mr. Olympia, on the hills of *Pumping Iron*, which everybody thought was going to be a great movie, we didn't know exactly what it was going to do because it hadn't come out yet. But we knew there was something great about it, something great about Arnold. It was a great experience to go over there with the crew and Arnold and experience what we experienced.

**Q: Can you tell me more about the day of the competition?**
Bill Grant: The Mr. Olympia thing was absolutely great. Arnold psyched out Louie quite good. It even showed in the movie, where

Arnold's telling his father and Louie how he had told his mother that he had won the Mr. Olympia even though it hadn't even taken place. And he asked Louie, "What do you think about that, Louie?" And Louie got very nervous. I think it totally freaked him out right away. Arnold, basically behind the scenes, backstage, was kind of quiet. He kept himself to himself and he pumped up. Arnold was a very focused person, he didn't joke a lot backstage and he was very kind of serious. He did all these things he had to do to get ready. He did like to play the mind game stuff. He always would try to trick people with that kind of stuff. But for some reason or another, I was kind of oblivious to that, but it worked. But for Arnold, it's whatever it takes. You know, for athletes it's always a psyche-out game.

You're friends. Arnold would say, "Hey, we're friends in the gym and stuff, but when it comes to competition you're my enemy." It's like the same in football and basketball. You're the enemy now and we're fighting against each other. And Arnold would do anything he could to psyche out his opponents, and he was very successful at that. There's another big story most people probably don't know. Arnold was a commentator at one time after he had retired. I remember Frank Zane winning his third Mr. Olympia. As you know, I told you Arnold didn't like to lose. He really hates to lose, like a lot of athletes. He asked a question to Frank Zane, "How do you feel winning your third Mr. Olympia?" And it was really strange what came out of Frank's mouth. He said, "Well, Arnold, guess what, it felt just as good as when I beat you in the Mr. Universe." Wow! You should have seen Arnold's face. His mouth dropped open, like, you can just hear the words coming out of his mouth if he was going to say 'you asshole!' He didn't say it, though, but if it came out of his mouth that's what he would say.

They broke for a commercial and he was pretty upset. You see, most people didn't know, and you probably didn't know, that Frank Zane beat Arnold in Mr. Universe in Florida. When he first came (to America) Arnold wasn't really the greatest bodybuilder. He was smooth, he was bulky and he was big. Even Vince Gironda, in all honesty, never thought much of him. He used to call him 'German

Sausage' at Vince's gym. He thought Arnold had no chance in the world as a bodybuilder. Let me tell you, most people had that kind of a view about Arnold. They thought he'd never be a great bodybuilder, let alone be a big actor. But Arnold proved everybody wrong, especially when becoming the governor. You don't have to like Arnold, but you have to respect this guy for what he's done in his life.

Literally, I always tell them, being an American, "He took all of our lunches." I mean, here's a guy who came over from another country, didn't know the law of the land, couldn't speak the language, didn't have a top education and look what he did. It only proves, again, that when you do come here the opportunities are here. Arnold saw them and he took advantage of them. Educational opportunities, the work opportunities, Arnold took the opportunity when it was there. Arnold didn't let any opportunity walk past him. He had some great advice from people. I understand he had a great advisor as far as property is concerned – a guy at the World Gym who was working there helped him out. That was great, too. So, the respect is there for me with Arnold. I respect everything he's done. Whether I might disagree with anything else, the respect is there wholeheartedly.

**Q: Another bodybuilder who worked out with Arnold was Dave Draper, who was Joe Weider's top star until Arnold came onto the scene. What can you tell me about Arnold's and Dave's relationship?**

Bill Grant: That's a good question. Dave Draper is from where I'm from. Draper's from New Jersey, he's from Syracuse. He actually worked for Joe Weider in his warehouse in Union City. That's where I met Joe Weider when I was fifteen. It was on 801 Palisade Avenue in Union City. He worked there with Leroy Colbert and Harold Poole. They worked in the warehouse. Leroy Colbert ran the warehouse and Harold Poole and Dave worked with him. Dave Draper was a great bodybuilder. Like Arnold, he was heavy when he started. Have you ever seen before pictures of Dave when he really got good? I remember Joe Weider, I remember at one point he said he was moving to California, and a couple of years they kept saying they were going. But what he did do was he opened up an extension store on Fifth Street in Santa Monica, which was right up the street from the post office. And he sent Dave Draper out to California to run the store. It was just a small store. I still see that store there. It was like a warehouse store and a regular store to sell the products.

Dave Draper, as you know, they called him the 'Blond Bomber'. He was the guy Joe was pushing. Joe always had a few guys. He usually had one guy he really promoted and Dave Draper was that guy. I mean, he was a nice-looking guy, very pleasant to talk to and very pleasant to be around. A great personality but very quiet, though. But Dave Draper became a movie star! He was one of the next big movie stars as far as bodybuilders are concerned. He was in *Don't Make Waves*. He had his own television show. He was in commercials. He was in all the ads Joe had. He was on the cover of all the magazines. He was Mr. America, and, of course, he was Mr. Universe. Then Arnold came.

Dave, I've got to say, was a little bit shy, where Arnold was a little bit more outgoing. I think maybe that was the demise of Dave, why the career went down. Dave wasn't as outgoing, and I don't think Dave really liked all the lights, action and all the publicity you got as a movie star. I think in the beginning he thought it was great, but I think the pressure got to him and it was a little bit too much for him. But Arnold was the exact opposite. Arnold loved the camera. He loved the lights. He loved the attention. And Arnold became the next big star. I mean, he almost, like, took Dave's lunch, too. They used to train together as well. But it wasn't anything malicious that Arnold was doing to him, Arnold was just a little bit hungrier than Dave was and had more insight and foresight of what he wanted to do.

He loved acting. Like I told you, he told that story about how he was going to be the biggest star in Hollywood. That was one of his main focuses. He and Dave trained together. They were very good friends – to this day. I remember when Dave moved from Los Angeles, he opened up a couple of World Gyms in Santa Cruz, and Arnold went up to the grand opening. They got on really well. Arnold just became a bigger star. He was a little bit more aggressive maybe. He had a better plan whereas Dave was a little bit shyer. One thing led to another and Dave was out and Arnold was in, let's put it this way. I don't think there was anything malicious from Joe, that Joe would throw him out. If somebody would say that, then that's not the truth. Dave just kind of faded away, and Arnold was becoming a shining star and Arnold was the guy he pushed. I think Arnold is really the one that boosted those magazines. Let's put it this way: they both helped each other along the way. I think Arnold made the magazine and the magazine made Arnold. So, I think it was a nice marriage between Arnold and Joe Weider.

Dave Draper was great because he actually set a tone for the magazine, and started up and kick-started it and made it a great magazine because he was one of the big players. And other guys came behind. It's like a movie where you have the stars of the movie and you have the cast and characters. Dave was the star and all the other guys surrounded him. It's like Arnold. Arnold was the star and we were the other cast and characters around him throughout the magazine. That's just the way it was. Dave is, to this day, a great guy. I've seen him a couple of years ago. He was down in Los Angeles and we all got the Muscle Beach Hall of Fame award. Hopefully, Arnold is going to accept this year. Those two guys really gelled together, they hung out together. There are a lot of pictures of them training together. They would go eat together. So, I would have to say, to this day, they're still good friends. It's just that Arnold became a bigger star than Dave. That doesn't make Dave anything less, but Arnold just got greater and greater.

**Q: What would be the most intriguing conversation you ever had with Arnold?**
Bill Grant: I had a lot of respect for him and he had for me. But like I said, everybody doesn't agree on everything. Arnold and I had

our bouts. We had a couple of disagreements and stuff, you know, it was all about competition. I was very competitive myself, I've got to say. So that maybe made us mash heads a little. Sometimes when two people are really working on the same thing, something might mash heads and they might disagree on some things. Arnold and I had a couple of disagreements, and we had a falling out for a little bit. But it's OK. Things happen like that, but I have a lot of respect for Arnold and I think he has a lot for me.

I'm always at the Arnold Classic and they treat me like a star when I'm there. I'm always talking to Arnold and he always takes the time. To show you the mutual respect we have for each other, at the Arnold Classic Arnold walks in the hall. He has a lot of security and he has certain areas he walks through. There are a hundred and fifty thousand people that come to this place, and the place is huge. So, I can remember specifically. I have my own supplements company and we were pushing it at the show. Arnold is walking down the aisles. He wasn't slated to stop at my booth, the one I was at. I had a huge cutout, Fiaz, that you could see all over the hall. Arnold is walking down toward it. And all of a sudden, he walks in the booth I'm in. And the security is looking at him, like, *What the hell is he doing?* When he jumps in, he says, "This is fantastic. I saw the cutout yesterday and I've been looking for you, and here you are." I felt so great.

He came in and we had a chat and we talked. The security kind of realized, *Oh, OK, I guess he knows the guy.* You know, speaking of the lights, maybe Dave Draper had a thing about that, but the glare of the lights and the cameras were absolutely incredible! The people that push up on you and take pictures. I mean, the place was like a sun had hit me in the face, with all the light bulbs. Arnold said let's go over there where your section is, so I can give you some publicity to promote yourself. Yeah, every time I see Arnold we get along very well. Backstage, he always takes the time to talk to me and we just talk about things going on. He asked me a lot of times how I'm doing and how my company's doing. I get along with Arnold very well. I mean, I can more than likely pick up the phone anytime I want and give him a call.

I think for me, maybe other guys don't think that, I think Arnold has been the prop for bodybuilding for many years. I think if it hadn't been for Arnold, bodybuilding would almost be dead. I'm serious. I think Arnold was the guy that absolutely kept bodybuilding in the mix. That is what I love. I really respect him for that part because he still loves bodybuilding. You have to understand, when he was the governor they didn't want him to do the show anymore – you might not have heard of this – because he was the governor of California. He told them no. Like he's always told me, "Bodybuilding is what got me here. This is who I am. I'm a bodybuilder." And he never stopped doing those shows. For that, again, I have a lot of respect for him. Maybe a lot of other guys would have bowed down to that pressure if they were in the movie business and the governor. But he didn't listen to one word they said. He continued promoting the Arnold Classic for the whole time he was the governor.

Now that his governorship is over, he'll be promoting it business as usual. So, these are the things you have to respect Arnold for. He never tried to get around who he was; he always let everybody know that he was a bodybuilder first. Lot of guys would never even talk about that if they were doing movies, they would probably want to leave it behind, but not Arnold. That's the reason why he's at where he is today because of bodybuilding. It's true. I mean, all of us who are doing something have gotten there because of the sport of bodybuilding.

**Q: Did he ever talk to you about growing up in Austria, or did he obviate the need for elucidating on this?**
Bill Grant: He never really talked too much about that. He just told me that he trained in the gym with a couple of guys. I don't think Arnold talked to many people about his upbringing in Austria. I don't know much about it, only from what I've read. So I can't really interject on anything I don't know. Arnold really didn't talk to any of us about those things. I know he had a brother. I know his father was a police officer, and his mother, he lived in a small town called Graz. Those are the things I know. Other than that, I know

Albert Busek. When Arnold moved to Germany, Albert Busek was a big friend and supporter of Arnold back then. Other than that, I really don't know. I wish I did but I don't.

**Q: Did you hang out with Arnold and Franco Columbu, who had close fraternal ties, in the 1970s when they were at the peak of their bodybuilding careers?**
Bill Grant: Franco was, yes, a good friend of Arnold's. If you don't know, Arnold is the one who helped to get Franco over here. When he got here, he got Franco to come over. I can remember a scene with me, Arnold and Franco together. I remember one day Arnold asked me what I was doing after the workout. Like I said, I worked for United Airlines, but I happened to be off that day. It was on a Tuesday and I was off. I said, "Nothing, Arnold." He said, "Why don't you hang out. I'm going to do a photo shoot." I said, "OK, that's cool." We were doing some photos and Franco and I were sitting on his back. And I can tell you that that's the best thing that ever happened with me. I mean, Arnold said it was going to be a great photo shoot and it was going to be a great article. They've ran one of those photos of me and Franco sitting on his back for the last thirty-five years – the same photo in various magazines. It's been running back and forth.

When Arnold said it was going to be a great article, he wasn't lying. I mean, anything you get involved in with Arnold, you know, it always goes in the right direction. It seems like Arnold has a rainbow over his head, man, whatever he touches turns to gold. If he says he's going to do something with you, it always works out well. I also did Friday Night Movie of the Week with Franco. It was called *The Hustler of Muscle Beach*. It was great. That was a fun time of working together. As you also know, Franco is a chiropractor practitioner at this point of time. Most of the guys would go to him as patients. Of course, as bodybuilders you get injuries so we would go to see Franco. But Franco was a great guy. Franco was a good cook, by the way, when Arnold and him were living together.

Arnold really helped him to get here. They worked together on the jobs. But they also were partners in work. They kind of took care of each other. Arnold took care of Franco and Franco took care of Arnold. They were real great friends. Today, they're still great friends. Those are the kind of stories that I like. Like, the same with me. I have friends from back in the days that I've known for forty-something years. That's what it's all about, this whole sport, making your relationships. Guys came from everywhere; nobody actually lived in California originally, by the way. Dave Draper and all of us guys came from elsewhere. I mean, I'm from Jersey; Ken Waller was from Kentucky; Arnold was from Austria; Danny Gable was from Iowa; Franco was from Sardinia; Dave Draper was from Jersey; Chris Dickerson was from New York.

So, as you can see, all the guys at Gold's Gym were from somewhere else. If you wanted to be a great bodybuilder, you had to be in California. That's the way it worked at that particular time. In other words, if you wanted to be in the magazine you had to be there. Here's another thing that Arnold did. There's another bodybuilder named Tony Pearson. Now, this is how Arnold wanted to help everybody and make sure everybody got the publicity. Tony Pearson came to the gym, and we introduced Tony to Arnold and told him that he's just come in looking for publicity. You know what Arnold did? He said, "Don't worry about it. You finish the workout, we're going to take you up to Joe and introduce you." He did. He got him publicity in the magazine. Arnold was a better person than what a lot of people think he was. He thought about other people and he loved the sport. As you can see from the last story I told you, about the show with him about not bowing down to the powers who said you shouldn't be doing an event like this bodybuilding when you're the governor.

Arnold did the same. He had a very good feel about bodybuilders and he wanted bodybuilding to grow. And he thought all the guys who worked out hard should deserve some publicity in the magazine. He helped a lot of the guys and it was great. He helped Danny Gable. I remember the parties he had, one of the parties specifically. Because he and I had the most television experience out of the guys in the beginning. He had a party one time at his house, this was in the 1970s. This was when he bought his first house on Twenty-Third Street in Santa Monica. It was an apartment just a couple of blocks around the corner. That was his first investment in property. I was over there several times eating lunch with him. Like I said, we got along real well. For some reason we had the same kind of chemistry.

I was doing something he was doing, especially in the movie business. I was doing Toyota commercials. I was on every television show in Hollywood – *Cher Show* – it was great. I mean, all those things I did on the *Cher Show* were good. I also did a pilot with George Burns and Pat Boone. So Arnold and I were on the same kind of level. He would invite me to his house and we'd talk and have lunch together. He was just a genuine and nice person to be around. I liked talking to him. We'd talk about training, careers, where he wanted to go. After I left California, I came over here (New Jersey) some years ago. I own a nutrition company. That's why Arnold stopped by the booth that time to see me. He wanted to know how the nutrition company was going – Bill Grant Nutrition. There are a lot of things that came out of those relationships. I would like to call Arnold and discuss those things with him, it's great. Because he's always asked me what I'm doing, so I'd like to throw those things at him.

Arnold doesn't owe anybody anything, but I'm sure I can pick up the phone and call Arnold and have a conversation with him, and get some advice on some of the projects I'm doing. All round I get on very well with Arnold. I don't know about the rest of the people. Arnold's a very motivated guy and he's a no-nonsense guy. I can give you another story. When Arnold tells a person something, say you're in the gym, Fiaz, and you want to know about working out. And Arnold sits down and takes the time and he tells you what you need to do. And if you don't do it and you come back and you ask him again, you know what he tells you? "Get lost." Because he already told you, he doesn't like repeating things over and over again. It just bothers him. And it's, like, once he explained it to you once, but you have to keep coming to him then you're not listening to him. He just walks away from it. I mean, it's, like, he doesn't want to keep repeating things over and over.

He's constantly moving forward. I would say Arnold has a five-year plan. He has a plan what he's going to do, then after that he'll move on to another project. Arnold is pretty methodical about what he does. As he continues his life, he's pretty methodical. He's a guy who's held his own in the movie business for over thirty-five years. I can't believe it's that many years that have gone by.

I remember his first movie. You remember his first movie *Hercules in New York*? Well, I had a friend of mine, God rest his soul, who played in that movie also with Arnold. It was a very, very low-budget movie. If I really get a chance to talk to Arnold, I would love to tell Arnold that he should remix that movie, retool it and put it back out. I think a lot of people would love to see Arnold's first movie. I think maybe, I don't want to speak for him, in his mind he thinks it was such a bad movie and it wasn't that great that he doesn't want to show it. But everyone knows he's improved as an actor and he's much better. People would love to see the first film he was in. I think he will sell millions of dollars worth of that film. That's my opinion. I don't know what everybody else thinks of it, but that's my opinion. I think he'd do very well with that film and a lot of people would love to see it.

I remember doing his campaign, you know, he was having a lot of problems with this groping thing. I got a phone call one time at the gym. It was a guy on the phone, and he said, "Hi." I said, "Who is this?" He said, "I'm Arnold's campaign manager." I said, "What can I do for you?" He said, "Well, you know that groping problem Arnold had, Maria told me to call you. You might know what to do." I said, "I don't know what I could do, but I'll step up for him. I mean, I think Arnold's a great guy." I think they knew I had some contacts with the news media. I did. I was friends with Rita Cosby at Fox News. I immediately called her up and I said I'd like to go on.

She always wanted to put me on the show, but she had to have a hook. And that was the biggest hook that she could have. I said, "I'd really like to go on there and stick up for Arnold for all this crap that's going on with him. I'd like to say a few things about him. Why he's running for governor." I got on the air and I talked about that. I basically just talked about his meager beginnings. I wanted to kind of humanize Arnold a little. Wow. It's been a great ride being a bodybuilder, and meeting Arnold was just another plus in my life, I think. I think the guy's doing all the right things, he's really a big backer of bodybuilding and he's never given up on the sport no matter what kind of controversies we have. He's still there. And he's the first one they're going to take a stab at because he's Arnold and the most visible person.

## MIKE KATZ

After a short NFL career ending in injury, Mike Katz went on to become one of Arnold's closest friends and training partners during the 1970s. Both men trained and socialized together, and Katz appeared in the documentary *Pumping Iron*. He competed in many bodybuilding events, including the IFBB Mr. Universe and Mr. Olympia several times. He lives in Connecticut.

**Q: Can you tell me when you first met Arnold?**
Mike Katz: It was either 1969 or 1970. He had just got to Santa Monica from Austria. Weider brought him in. It's interesting that at that time many Americans, including myself, Dave Draper and Sergio Oliva, were kind of heroes of his because of the media coverage we got from Joe Weider. So, when he got to this country, he asked Joe if he could get 'Big' Mike to come to live in California during the summers, when I wasn't teaching in high school, and train with him – which I did for four years. I think it was either 1969 or 1970, through making the movie *Pumping Iron*, which was 1975.

**Q: Training with Arnold, how would you describe your experiences training with him?**
Mike Katz: I feel two of the reasons why Arnold was just enough better to have won as often as he did, and rarely was ever beaten, was because he had great genetics and he had a great will to win and belief in himself. He also knew how to train with the most up-to-date science that was available at that time, in the 1970s. Now, again, things have come quite a bit further, and when you look at the bodies of the 1970s compared to maybe, as an example, Cutler, Cutler isn't better; Cutler is bigger. Flex Wheeler would have been better because he had all the beauty that we had in the 1970s, but was able to take his genetics a little bit further. Even though he was unfortunate that he never had emotionally what it took to win the Olympia five, six or seven times. His symmetry and genetics

were great. He had the science and the nutrition information that somebody in 2000 would have, which we didn't have back in the 1970s.

Arnold took his genetics and he took his will and positive approach, as well as training as perfectly as he could. He was like an artist or a musician that could strike the note and paint with the brush in reference to the way he trained. And those are the things I learned from him in the five years that we trained together. No negative attitude, you know, everybody's got genetic flaws, and we use the most appropriate nutritional and training perfection to perfect whatever weaknesses that we have. So, it was a pleasure. It was extremely difficult training as hard as anybody trains today, but very smart training; not just hard training. Not always heavy; sometimes light. Not always with much rest between sets. I think the things we did back in the 1970s and late '60s, we were able to be at the forefront of what people are doing today.

And as I say to people today, who continue to make the same mistakes, even in 1970 we didn't rest! I mean, there was no sitting around like a powerlifter resting three minutes between sets. It was high-intensity training. It was cardiovascular necessary to almost be like a marathon runner to be able to get through these workouts. Because of the workload and the resistance that we used and the speed that we went from one exercise to another, we were able to get probably a four-hour workout done in an hour and a half.

**Q: What do you remember about the social moments with Arnold and hanging out with him, did he possess a sense of elated attitude?**
Mike Katz: He was just a great, fun-loving guy, and he still is today. Young boys grow up to be young men, who grow up to be older men, who never lose their boyhood. If they ever have such a time in their life, Arnold knows how to have a good time. He enjoys life. He did when we were kids, and I'm sure as an adult with his own children he has that same type of flair. Every time I go to Columbus and judge the Mr. Olympia during his Arnold weekend in Ohio,

he doesn't forget his friends. He's loyal to the people who knew him when he could hardly speak English when he came over. He didn't have any money and was driving around in an old Volkswagen Beetle. And Maria wasn't there; it was just workouts and trying to beat Sergio in Mr. Olympia. And obviously becoming a star with Joe Weider in the magazine. So, when we enjoyed ourselves on the beach, in the restaurants that we went to and in the gym and at the contests, he was a real fun guy to be around. Hopefully, now he doesn't have to worry about being governor or the political office. At present he could even lighten up a little bit and get back to some of his, as he calls it, 'money business' that he enjoyed a lot when he was in private life, as opposed to a sort of public figure being in politics.

**Q: Arnold went to school to further his education when arriving in America. His English was weak. Can you tell me more about him pursuing further education?**

Mike Katz: Yeah. When he first came over here, he knew what he lacked. And it was not only convenient, it kind of was interesting how he became friendly with and developed a relationship with a girl named Barbara. She was a very attractive Southern California surfer-looking girl, who happened to be an English teacher. So he was able to, not only with his romantic involvement, and at the time he, obviously, loved her and, again, this was years before Maria came on the scene. I'm sure that Barbara helped him with his business and helped him with his English, and some of the American ways – Southern California ways. I really don't know about the college and whatever degrees he got. I know he was studying going to business school, whether it was a college or UCLA in Southern California, I'm not sure. I think he could've done it without anybody. Without going to college, without the involvement with the girlfriend, who happened to be an English teacher. I think Arnold was so motivated and so self-disciplined that he would've learned it himself. But whatever help he could get along the way, it was to get him there quicker.

**Q: Barbara wasn't into bodybuilding at all, was she?**
Mike Katz: No, no, no. I don't even know how they met. I just knew that at that time, back in the early 1970s, that she was his girlfriend for a while.

**Q: Did you travel with Arnold to guest pose at bodybuilding shows or events?**
Mike Katz: Yes, we did a lot of different places. We went pretty much, you know, in the movie *Pumping Iron*, that exhibition which was in the beginning of the film was in Helio, Massachusetts, which is outside of Springfield, Massachusetts, which isn't far from Connecticut where I live. And the people who made *Pumping Iron*, Charles Gaines and George Butler, those two fellows did the book. And when Arnold came here, they got that done. They also did a lot of work with still pictures and movie pictures. When they decided to do the film *Pumping Iron*, they came back to Helio and I guest posed with Lou Ferrigno and Franco and Arnold there. I'm sure there has been other places we've posed together. I competed in Mexico and Arnold gave an exhibition there.

Obviously, in South Africa he was in the Olympia and I was in the Mr. Universe. So, we've been on the stage together. But I was never a pro. He retired for the first time in 1975, at the end of *Pumping Iron*. I was still an amateur so I never directly competed against him. But when I won Mr. America, Dave Draper won Mr. World and Arnold won Mr. Olympia in 1970, and that was on the same stage on the same night. It had the World, the America and the Olympia all at the Brooklyn Academy of Music in New York. That was another time we appeared on the same stage.

**Q: What's the most intriguing conversation you had with Arnold that's left an enduring impression on you?**
Mike Katz: I've mentioned this before when I've been interviewed, these are sort of excerpts from my life, my involvement with Arnold. When I had to make a choice to leave my family for a

month or two to train with Arnold, it was difficult. Because my kids were – my son Michael was born in 1970 – and it was difficult to leave Connecticut and go three thousand miles to California. And teaching in school, I wasn't making much money. Now, I leave my wife along with my son. I'm missing my son and I'm missing my wife. And instead of try to work a part-time job in Connecticut, when I wasn't teaching, I had to take summer off. I wasn't making any money so I was writing articles for Joe Weider. But I wasn't getting paid in a timely fashion, and I didn't have enough money to buy my supplements.

I started to get kind of homesick and negative because I just didn't have the money to continue to stay out there without Weider paying me in a timely fashion for the articles I was writing about myself on how I trained. So, Arnold saw this negative attitude in me, which he wasn't going to allow anybody to have around him for very long – to be negative – because you're going to drain him and drain his strength by complaining or acting negative. He doesn't want to be around people like that. That's why he continues to be so successful. So he said to me, "Don't worry about it, Mike. I'll go to the office in Woodland Hills and get you your money." He said, "But I don't want to hear any more whining. I never met a Jew who is a quitter."

Here is a guy whose father was in the Nazi Army in World War II, and he's talking to a guy who's had almost his entire nationality and religious group annihilated by Hitler. And he's telling me the only reason Jewish people have been able to survive is because they didn't quit. They didn't give up regardless of the Holocaust, or anything else you would be reading between the lines of that statement. And that is something, since 1970, I will never forget. When I get down or depressed or negative, I always think about those words Arnold said. He said he's never met a Jewish quitter and I'm not going to tolerate you acting this way. It was sort of, without getting slapped in the face, a verbal wake-up call that has worked well for me for the last forty years.

**Q: Arnold won the Mr. Olympia 1971 in Paris and again in 1972 in Germany. You weren't present at the show, but did he talk to you about these two contests?**

Mike Katz: It's interesting that there is some footage of the show in Essen against Sergio. I have seen it. I just don't know who owns it. I'm sure if I've seen it, thousands of people have seen it. I know that film exists. It was not a fancy film. It was probably 8mm. It was probably filmed by a handheld camera. Like in the movie *Pumping Iron*, I think either (Danny) Padilla or (Ken) Waller had a little handheld camera that they were filming with when Ed Corney was doing his posing routines. So, those little movie cameras existed back in the 1970s. Sergio did a most muscular pose and turned, they were both facing the judges. As I remember, Sergio really believed he was better. I think that if he was better it was simply because Arnold wasn't in the good shape he could've been in. But I think Sergio felt he was going to win the title back.

He turned away from the judges and turned directly to Arnold and hit a most muscular pose at Arnold. It was the first time I've ever seen Arnold not have a comeback, you know, verbally or facially. He had no comeback for that most muscular pose. As if to say, *What can I tell you?* He's in shape. Now, whether Arnold believed he should've won, or gave him credit for being in great shape, what was on Arnold's face was priceless. Because I never saw him so dejected or looked sort of . . . maybe you would interpret the look different than me. Maybe Arnold would say you don't know what you're talking about.

I wasn't there, so from 8mm film I can't tell you who was better because you've got to go through the judging, and it didn't show any of that. It just showed Oliva hitting the most muscular pose totally disrespecting Arnold. And it didn't matter that they were in Essen, which is Arnold's backyard. I mean, obviously, if I wasn't in my best shape and I was looking for any means possible to win, you can't say it's not an advantage to be in my own country. Just like it would be a home game in soccer, or your hometown when you're fighting for the world championship, that the crowds and the officials are kind of going to give you an edge. So, it was a long time ago. My recollections are: Arnold didn't look happy about that most muscular pose that Sergio threw at him.

"People are still talking about Essen 1972," recalled Sergio Oliva years later. "Even Arnold himself said that he didn't win, that it was nothing but politics . . . But they gave it to him. After the contest, Weider put the promoter out of the promotion business." Arnold, meanwhile, has conceded that he sometimes went too far in his quest for triumph – but little more than that. "Of course you were competitive," he explains. "Of course when it came down to the pose-off and when it came down to who brings the best body in on the day of the competition, yeah, I was the most competitive." But since he became wiser and older, Arnold realized that he often went a little overboard. Arnold was so competitive and so dedicated in his craft he felt he had to push the boundaries to stand out from his peers and prevail.

**Q: Sergio retired from competing in the Olympia after that, didn't he?**
Mike Katz: Possibly, he did. I don't know whether he went to another organization with Dan Laurie, or if he just got disgusted saying, "You know what, Weider wants Arnold and that's how he's going to promote his products. And no matter what I do, I'm not going to win. I've served my purpose to Weider before Arnold came." Weider tried to get Draper to beat Sergio, but that wasn't going to happen. Obviously, he looked to see if I would be the one to win. Because if you had at the time, before Arnold was ever Arnold, a guy like Larry Scott, who was 6ft and 250, not 5ft 5 and 190 – if Larry Scott had ever been 6ft 2 and 250, 260, like myself and Arnold, it's interesting that he (Joe Weider) would have had the desire to continue Larry Scott. You wonder if Weider would've had the need to go halfway around the world to find Arnold to try

to beat and compete against Sergio from a marketing standpoint. It's just interesting.

I think anybody would've looked and said, *You know, who can I market my products best with?* And it's not always potentially who the best person is. That's why when you take a look at the covers of the magazines, they're not always the best guys on the cover. It's about the people who would buy your magazine, that's why the covers of the magazines have the people they have on them. So, Scott was too small; Draper wasn't good enough; I wasn't good enough genetically. So he had to go and find someone else. He, obviously, went to Europe. And it was smart for him because he wasn't looking to reincarnate Reg Park, who was already great. Joe couldn't take any credit for building Reg because Reg was Reg, and Bill (Pearl) was too old. He was coming to the end of his career. Chuck Sipes wasn't good enough. So who could've been good enough? There was no Flex Wheeler back then. If America had Flex Wheeler back then, Weider would have gone to Flex Wheeler and Arnold probably wouldn't have ever come here, and who knows where he'd be now.

So, it's all interesting to me. That's something I've not talked about before because as I get older, sometimes I think of things when you ask questions, you know. And, again, it's 'would've, could've, should've'. In America they call it a 'Monday morning quarterback', which means: if the game was on Sunday, you could talk all you want about Monday. Arnold got married. He was the governor and he's a billionaire, and God bless him. It's just funny how the history is and the opportunities one has, and Arnold got the opportunities. And Flex got the opportunity, but Flex never cashed in on an opportunity to be seven, eight or nine times Mr. Olympia because he just didn't have what Arnold had. So you've got to even commend Arnold more because it wasn't that Arnold was the best; he made himself to be the best. He did whatever he needed to do to make sure he continued to be on top. You've got to admire that. I do, anyway. I admire the 'I'm not going to lose' attitude. Everybody in the world could be just a little bit better if they believed a little bit more like Arnold.

**Q: Did Arnold talk to you about growing up as a youngster, what was life in Austria like for him?**

Mike Katz: I'm sure that from what I read – I'm sure you read the same stories – he never talked to me and I never really got involved in psychologically wanting to know about the treatment of his father, mother and brother. I never got into that. I know that, whether it's true or not, I heard that he was kind of a hellion, which isn't bad, you know. I'm sure Switzerland and Austria are pretty conservative places, and you've got a teenager like Arnold. In Southern California it's perfect, but I don't know if it's perfect in Zurich or in Munich or Essen or Graz, where things are more conservative and people are much quieter. I mean, Arnold's personality, it's a good thing he came to Southern California because I thought many times that if he went to New York who knows. I mean, he could've got shot! Going to Southern California, everybody was doing their own thing and there were different religions on every street corner. It was love and peace, the Vietnam anti-war movement and different cultures.

Southern California was like a great place for a free-spirited person. I remember once when we were in a supermarket in Santa Monica, he didn't want to wait in line. Obviously, at the time he was pretty brash. We had a 15-pound roast from the butcher, and he shot-putted the 15-pound over the top of about six people's heads and it splattered down on the cash register, where you get checked out at the supermarket. There were about six to eight people in line. Arnold wasn't going to wait because he was hungry. He wanted to go home and cook the food. And the people said that's cool, no problem. Because they saw how big he was. He had the Austrian accent – the German accent – nobody was going to screw around with him. In New York if he did that he probably would've got shot. But in Southern California everybody was cool about it. It was one humorous story after another.

**Q: Can you tell me more about hanging out with Arnold in the 1970s?**

Mike Katz: We were so tired because we'd train twice a day. Believe me, we were so exhausted. One of the stories is that he never believed that my chest was as big as it was. He always made fun of me. Like, I have to relax, he would say, "You have to relax, Mike. Big Mike, relax." He would tell Franco, "Mike never relaxes. His chest is always sticking out of his clothes. He was always worried that the buttons on my shirt would pop his eye out. So whenever he came near me and saw my chest, he would always put his hands up to his eyes to make sure the button did not pop off and blind him. We were so tired from a morning workout. Arnold and Franco lived together, we had lunch and then we took a nap. I found out later that he came over with Franco because they wanted to see if my chest would really go down if the buttons holding my shirt together would really relax. And they didn't! So he knew I wasn't holding my breath trying to make my chest look bigger because when I was sleeping, it was the same size. He said, "It's so much safer when you wear a tie." Because when I have a shirt and a tie, the buttons won't deflect off the tie and hit him on the eye. He was a character.

**Q: After Arnold initially pursued the movie industry, you kept up your friendship. Did he talk about the fame he was finally achieving beyond the confines of the bodybuilding world?**
Mike Katz: He was in a movie called *Stay Hungry*. It only lasted about a week in the movie theaters. It was with Sally Field and Jeff Bridges. And Sally Field at that time was in a television show called *The Flying Nun*. Like a Nun in a Catholic church. It was kind of a goofy thing. The Nuns would wear something and she could fly. It was a cute show on television for years. But Sally Field, who has become an Academy award-winning actress, wanted to break out of the *Flying Nun* television character and become a movie star. And the first movie she made was with the famous Jeff Bridges, who later made *True Grit*, which was the John Wayne movie. John Wayne made that movie years ago and Jeff Bridges has recreated the film. So, he was a famous actor. There was a bodybuilding scene in the movie, and Arnold got his best friends to come down to

Birmingham in Alabama for a week and film with him in the movie. So, he sure didn't forget us as his friends and hasn't forgotten us today as well. I got a card from him and Maria during the holidays.

**Q: Did you talk about religion and was he religious in any way, shape or form?**
Mike Katz: No. No. I don't know if anything's ever been written about religion and Arnold, or a conversation he had about religion.

**Q: What do you remember when Arnold was on the brink of fame in Hollywood?**
Mike Katz: I definitely remember when he did *Conan*. I guest posed at a contest in Canada in Victoria. It was a famous show and I think they still have it. Arnold was a guest poser and I was a guest poser. I can remember working out with Arnold and he was practicing the sword. In *Conan* he had to wield this big, heavy, gladiator-type sword when he was fighting. He was doing a lot of choreography work with this big sword when we were training. That film, *Conan the Barbarian*, at that time I was coming to the end of my career, in probably 1981 or '82. I guess it was 1982. Waller placed lower and I placed just a little bit higher than him. But I went in the contest and I had been drug tested to prove that I was drug free, and that I could compete against the athletes who were not tested. And that was my motivation. I beat Waller and I got him back for the t-shirt incident in *Pumping Iron*. I retired in 1982. My son was twelve years old. I had had enough of going around the world being away from my kids.

**Q: Having been a friend of Arnold's, what are some of the most significant memories that come to mind?**
Mike Katz: I think anybody who is successful, I mean, who has been really successful in life, whether it's a teacher or doctor, an attorney or an athlete, success can come in many different forms. But what he possessed, which I've tried to possess – and why I think I've been somewhat successful – is I don't let negative feelings get

the best of me and enter into me. I've got blinders like a racehorse. I've got tunnel vision and blinders on. And I'm focusing on what is important to me to attain. And whether one day I wanted to be an actor or a politician or a millionaire, billionaire, I've accomplished everything in my life that I wanted to accomplish. It's not, like, I'm ready to die, I've got grandchildren that I'd like to see grow up – three little granddaughters. But I rest easy in reference to what I've attained and what I've achieved and to thank Arnold for it. Again, I had some of the qualities because I played football professionally before I met Arnold. So, I couldn't have become a professional football player at the highest level if I wasn't positive and not coachable and if I did not have a good attitude.

So, I had that at the beginning and Arnold helped to support me. And how I knew I could continue to stay successful and be able to achieve the dreams I had in my life. So, if people look at Arnold for those reasons, sort of like: he came in with no education, couldn't speak the language, and here he becomes world famous like Muhammad Ali, like the Pope or like any famous president. And the question here is: if he did it, then what's your excuse? Why aren't you doing it to some reasonable level? You're not going to be a billionaire. You won't marry a Kennedy. You may not make movies for $30 million a movie, or be a governor. But in your own way, you can be a better parent; you could be a better husband; you could be a better person in your workplace, if you have the qualities Arnold and successful people, I think, like us have got. That makes the whole world better, if people would just believe in that and listen to that.

# AL SATTERWHITE

Al Satterwhite is a professional photographer and cinematographer who has shot for *Newsweek*, *Life*, *Time* and *Sports Illustrated*. He photographed Arnold on numerous occasions. He is the author of several books and lives in Los Angeles.

**Q: You photographed for some prominent magazines, including *Life*. How did you get the opportunity to shoot Arnold back in the 1970s?**

Al Satterwhite: I met him in 1974. I think it was probably around June. I'm not sure of the exact month. I had an assignment, I think, from a European magazine, to photograph him at Gold's Gym – in the original Gold's Gym. I went and met him and took a few pictures. It kind of expanded over a few weeks that I spent with him. I didn't know much about bodybuilding, anything at all, really. So it was new and different and really interesting for me. And I didn't know anything about Arnold at all, either. He hadn't done any films yet, so he wasn't very well known, didn't attract much attention anywhere he went other than he looked pretty much awesome.

But he was really nice and a gentle personable person. He was fun to be around. He had a good sense of humor and didn't take himself too seriously. It was a delight to be around him and photograph him. I would spend a day or two with him, then some time with the labs, and then two or three more days with him. It was over a period of three or four weeks. Usually, you might shoot the same person for three or four different magazines, three or four or five different times. *Time* or *Life* magazine, they would call up, or through my agent, and assign me to shoot. So it was pretty much always assignments.

**Q: Did you photograph him on the Santa Monica Mountains?**

Al Satterwhite: Yeah. I think it was up in the mountains, we went skeet shooting. One day, with him and a friend of his, whose name was Roger, he was Mr. USA, we went up there to do some skeet and maybe trap shooting also. Arnold had obviously done it before because he knew the people. They just had the best time. I think you can tell from the photographs, they're joking with each other – missed shots and the shots that they didn't make. It was kind of a fun afternoon.

**Q: When shooting Arnold, did you detect anything that reflected the way he posed for the camera – did he have specific posing routines?**
Al Satterwhite: I don't think so. When he was working at Gold's, he had whatever methods he used. He went from one machine to the next machine, and actually helped a few other people who were working out at the time, helped correct their form, or held the weights for them. And he would, obviously, look in the mirror and check his own posing. Then he would go back to working out again.

**Q: Can you recall the atmosphere when photographing him on Muscle Beach?**
Al Satterwhite: Yeah. Down in Venice at the boardwalk, where Muscle Beach is, they have a weights gym where the bodybuilders work out. And it's pretty open. Some people would stop by and watch. A lot of people, to them it was new and different. Depending on who was there and what they were doing, they would sit down and watch. One day, when we were out there – Arnold and I – he was working out on one of the pieces of equipment there, and another photographer was shooting pictures of him also. So Arnold kind of stopped what he was doing with me, and he sort of posed for the other guy, gave him a couple of different poses and then went back to working out where I was photographing him. And the other photographer stayed around.

Arnold asked him to leave, but the guy kept shooting pictures. So he turned to him, and in his thick Austrian accent he said, "Do you want me to stick that camera up your ass?" So the guy turned around and left, and we kind of laughed about it and went back to working out and taking pictures. I mean, Arnold looked, at that time, certainly intimidating, but he was kind of like a pussycat. He wasn't really going to do anything to this guy; it was kind of a joke. Then probably an hour later, he was working out on another piece of equipment and this little girl came up to him. I don't remember what she said, but he stopped what he was doing because he just loves kids. He went over and he talked to her, and he flexed a muscle for her. And they had a conversation together, couple of moments in between working out.

**Q: When you were shooting at Gold's Gym, did the gym attract people such as Hollywood personalities back in the days like it does today?**
Al Satterwhite: No. I don't think so because it was kind of removed from the Hollywood area. And down in the Venice area, I never really saw any Hollywood types there – mostly people who were very serious about bodybuilding. They would support each other and help each other out with different pieces of equipment, and whatever muscle groups they were working on at the time. I remember Roger Collard, who was Mr. USA, he and Arnold were pretty good friends at the time and palled around together.

**Q: What was Arnold like on a social level, did you spend time hanging out?**
Al Satterwhite: Yeah, sometimes after he worked out in the morning we would go to this Mexican restaurant, which was nearby. And he would have either a late breakfast or an early lunch, and we kind of would sit there and talk. I remember I was asking him about bodybuilding because I didn't really know anything about it. I don't really remember much in way of conversation, but it was pretty pleasant and easygoing. I went over to his apartment once. He had a business where, I guess, he was advertising courses in the back of some of the bodybuilding magazines about how to work different parts of your body and different muscle groups. I don't remember

how many different ones there were and whatever amounts he was asking for them.

He had a secretary who would come in and open up all the envelopes and then deposit all the money and send all the pamphlets out. So he was making money. And at the same time, he was investing it in real estate. When I met him, I think he owned one or two apartment buildings in Santa Monica. So, I got the idea very quick that Arnold was pretty smart, especially in business. He was not your average person, surely not your average bodybuilder. I guess most people think of bodybuilders as all muscle and no brain. He was pretty smart and you could see that right away.

**Q: What do you think were the misconceptions behind bodybuilding in the 1970s, it wasn't a widely exposed nor embraced sport?**
Al Satterwhite: I don't think many people knew about it at all. If they saw somebody who was built like Arnold, I mean, it was pretty impressive. I mean, I asked him once where he got his clothes from. And he said he had to have them made because he couldn't fit into normal ones. His arms and legs were just huge! Most people, and I was among them, didn't know anything about bodybuilding. I didn't see any negativity at the time, and the movie (*Pumping Iron*), which I saw later, certainly helped up the bodybuilding. I mean, it showed, particularly on backstage, that one Arnold had a great sense of humor, and two a great ability to be able to psyche out his competition. He was brilliant at doing stuff like that.

**Q: What were his best qualities as a person, human being and a driven person?**
Al Satterwhite: I got the feeling he knew what he was doing, and he had a goal in mind and he was not just going to sit back and let nothing happen. He was very exceptional in that, just like (Muhammad) Ali. They both had a total awareness of their abilities and they could push it much further than anybody else and go beyond just being a bodybuilder, but being a humanitarian and a

person capable of doing other things, which they both pretty much proved. Arnold still has time to prove even more yet.

**Q: How would you sum up his personality overall?**
Al Satterwhite: At that time, he had a great personality. He was fun to be with. He could carry on a conversation on pretty much any topic – just an all-around guy. A lot more than you would expect. He had a pretty thick Austrian accent then, but he was certainly able to get ideas across and communicate in a great way. I think that's why he has got as far as he has, even in politics, which was kind of a difficult field.

**Q: What is the most fascinating thing you ever saw him do?**
Al Satterwhite: Obviously, it was impressive to watch him work out and lift weights because I'm a guy who weighs 150 pounds, he could probably lift me easily. I think the thing that really got me about Arnold was his inter-play with other people, especially kids. He had an ability to touch anybody. He could talk to a guy in a suit, or he could talk to a little girl who just didn't know what he was all about. And that's kind of why everyone liked him. He was such an easy-going guy, who had a great sense of humor, a great sense of humanity. He never seemed to have any of this, *I'm the greatest, or I've won Mr. Olympia many times therefore I'm really somebody big*. That never ever came into any kind of play.

## BILL DOBBINS

One of the most prominent bodybuilding journalists and the former editor of *FLEX*, Bill Dobbins worked closely with Arnold on several projects in the 1970s and 1980s, collaborating together on Arnold's *Bodybuilding for Men* and *The New Encyclopedia of Modern Bodybuilding*. He's well known for his work photographing female bodybuilders, and has published two books on the subject. He lives in Los Angeles.

**Q: How did you get involved with Arnold?**
Bill Dobbins: Well, I've known Arnold since 1975. I used to work out at the original Gold's Gym, the one which was in *Pumping Iron*. It was a very small place, and there were a lot of really famous bodybuilders there. I felt sometimes, like, if you've ever seen the cartoons, little creatures staring around the forest trying to avoid being stepped on by the dinosaurs. That's how I felt. Because there wasn't much room there, and I had to stay out of these guys' way because they would've kicked me out. But Arnold trained there, that's how I first got to know him. Later, I became the founding editor of *FLEX* magazine, and Arnold was looking for someone to do a book with him who knew something about training. Because his biographer, who was a very good writer, tried to do an exercise book with him, but didn't really know much about training. So Joe Weider recommended me and Arnold and I got together and did *Bodybuilding for Men*.

**Q: What were you both aiming at with this venture – commercial or highlight the confounding factors surrounding the sport – because bodybuilding wasn't as widely accepted as it is today?**
Bill Dobbins: The principles of bodybuilding are the principles of bodybuilding, whether or not there's an audience of a thousand or a million. When we did *Bodybuilding for Men*, it was meant to be a general interest book. Something that was accessible to anyone who wanted to work out. But then Arnold decided that what he wanted to do was the definitive book for someone going to the gym. He

described it to me: he wanted anybody from somebody going into the gym for the first time to the Mr. Olympia competitor to be able to look in the book and learn something. So, it was about a thousand pages of comprehensive information. There are two versions. The first version was really an attempt to create something that was really an encyclopedia. There was a book at the time out by Bill Pearl, which was the biggest book in bodybuilding that existed – it was more of a catalog. It was a catalog of training exercises; it didn't really explain very much. Arnold wanted something that was more comprehensive that explained more, and he used his own personal experience to illustrate what was in the book.

Arnold believes that he made the sport more acceptable with his relentless promotion of bodybuilding in the mid-1970s, even if he occasionally came across as the bad boy of this once misunderstood sport. "I didn't say the kind of things that put people off," he told *Playboy*. In the pre-Arnold era, it wasn't out of the ordinary to hear bodybuilders bragging about eating a couple of pounds of meat and over two dozen eggs a day. There was further misconception: bodybuilders had to sleep for twelve hours a day and abstain from sex. Arnold said to himself, "Who the fuck wants to be part of that kind of *sport*? He added, "First of all, it was not accurate. And second of all, if you want to make people join a particular activity, you have to make it pleasant-sounding." For his part, Arnold realized promoting bodybuilding was just like promoting any other product or service. The secret lay in making the experience fun. To this end, Arnold broached the subject and talked about the need for a strict diet, but he said he ate dessert as well. He said that it was perfectly fine to stay out at night and have sex and live a fun-loving life. As long as one didn't deviate, Arnold said that one could train three times a week for forty-five minutes to an hour – taking into account that he was publicizing bodybuilding to a broader audience now. It didn't take Arnold long to grasp the American shrewdness for promotion and marketing, skills he came to be famous for.

**Q: Can you shed light on some of the photo shoots you did with Arnold?**

Bill Dobbins: Honestly, although I've shot all the top male and female bodybuilders over twenty-five years, rarely ever did I shoot Arnold. When I got really active with the magazine, he had retired competing. So I wasn't shooting him competing. When we were putting the photos together for the book, mostly he used the pictures that had already been shot that were in file. And when he did do photo shoots, he didn't want me shooting; he wanted me writing. Because a thousand-page book is quite a lot of work. Of course, we did it twice. So, I actually only shot on rare occasions. Although I observed many photo shoots. Arnold was a highly experienced guy doing photos. And if the photographer knew what he was doing, he'd have a great time shooting Arnold. If he didn't know what he was doing, Arnold would straighten him out.

**Q: Arnold learned a lot from Joe Weider pertaining to business and utilized his shrewdness in this area. Emboldened by his mentor's business approach, Arnold ventured into mail order. Can we talk about the mail order business that Arnold ventured into?**

Bill Dobbins: Joe and Arnold were sort of collaborators, to help and make each other very successful. I would have to say that there's a talent for business, just like there's a talent for bodybuilding. It's almost generic. I don't think anybody ever taught Arnold how to be a businessman as much as they just gave him examples to learn from. I'm sure that seeing how Joe Weider was able to use, for example, mail order in order to sell products, influenced Arnold. Because I remember going up to his office quite late in his career, when he was already a famous movie star, and there was a section of a room set aside for mail ordering – his t-shirts and other things he was selling.

So, even when he was making millions as a movie star, he would continue to sell products because that was part of his business. I think Arnold's always kind of moved on to be famous, but not abandon the things that he already had going. In the same way, when he became a movie star he didn't abandon bodybuilding. He still had the Arnold Classic and still contributed to the magazines. So, one thing I point out to people all the time is: if you have something successful going and you want to move on to something else, that doesn't mean you have to abandon what you already have going for you. You simply expand and include the old with the new.

**Q: Arnold and Joe's relationship included Arnold contributing to the magazines, what kind of a relationship would you say they had?**
Bill Dobbins: Joe and Arnold had a very long relationship. It's taken up many, many different forms. I'm sure they had all sorts of trade agreements. I'm not aware of the exact deals that they made, but certainly there had been trade deals like that done. I'm sure there were other types of deals done. Joe had a very complex business, and Arnold grew into a very successful man. So, I'm sure their relationship was multifaceted.

**Q: Did you accompany Arnold to book signings and meeting the fans in the early days, when your first book came out?**
Bill Dobbins: On our books, Arnold did very little on that. Arnold had a national audience through the TV talk shows. So Arnold wasn't a person to sit at the desk and sign his name. But he did go out and promote the book on television quite a lot. He's always been someone who could get on whatever television show he wanted to. And that's where the real mass audience is.

**Q: Any social moments that surface at Venice after training at the gym?**
Bill Dobbins: There were times I traveled with Arnold, both on commercial aircraft and also I've flown on his private jet. The thing about Arnold is, whenever you go with Arnold it's always about Arnold, as you would expect. I think if you were dealing with any major star, everything centers around that person. I've

sat with Arnold at his house and we've just talked about sports, or about anything else, just like regular people. But once you get out in any situation, Arnold is so much the center of attention. That sort of becomes what the whole thing's about. It's very difficult for Arnold to be in public to go through an airport, to be in a restaurant without attracting a great deal of attention. I've noticed that he's learned to walk through a crowd, walk through an airport and focus on where he's going and not paying any attention to people asking him things, or want things from him, or trying to talk to him. Because if he did, he would never get anywhere. And Arnold is a very practical guy.

He learned early on that the only way to go somewhere in public is to just go. And I've seen other celebrities who have more problems with that. For example, Lenda Murray, who is eight-times Ms. Olympia, there's been a few times I was going with her at a contest and I would be in a hotel lobby and it would take her forty minutes to get across the hotel lobby because people keep wanting to talk to her. And I just had to accept the fact that Lenda's nature is she doesn't like to say no to anybody. And so I would just have to stand around waiting till she finally got clear, so we could go wherever we were supposed to go. But that didn't happen with Arnold. In the old days, he would just go. And nowadays he has a lot of security people who make sure he goes. Otherwise Arnold would never get anything done.

**Q: You've mentioned you've sat with Arnold at his house. What kind of atmosphere was there in his private surroundings behind closed doors away from the public persona?**
Bill Dobbins: I've known Arnold for a very long time, and he's gone through sort of major changes, sort of what he's like. When I first met him, he was kind of a brash young bodybuilder. He liked to shock people and liked to play practical jokes. He was very playful and outgoing. Then he became a major movie star. And as that went on for twenty years, he became more and more, how would you say, surrounded by that kind of a thing. He evolved, as

everybody does. He got older, for one thing. I mean, we're talking about a long period of time. But when he was a major movie star, he was much more formal and not interested in as much shocking people and playing jokes and things like that. Now when he became a politician, he's also a father to teenage children. I just find it has mellowed him out tremendously. I find him easier to deal with now than ever before. As I say, he's matured. He's experienced and he's also been in a job where not everybody he's dealing with is trying to kiss his ass.

Remember Arnold has always been the most famous guy in the room and everybody catering to him. When you are the governor of California, you've got a lot of people who are not trying to kiss your ass; they are opposed to what you are doing. I think because Arnold is so good at learning new things, and he is, of course, older and he has teenage children and all of those things, I think he's kind of become a much more mellow personality. He's, perhaps, more aware of other people and other people's feelings and much better at dealing with them. As I say, Arnold learns things and he's learned to do this. I actually like him better now. I think having done his incredibly difficult job, being the governor of California, has allowed him to grow that much more.

## Q: What's the most compelling conversation Arnold had with you?

Bill Dobbins: I wrote an article called How Arnold Thinks for *FLEX* magazine, and I didn't show it to Arnold first – I just wrote it. A few months after that there was an event in Northern California, with Clint Eastwood, where Joe Weider and some other people were donating equipment to gyms that Clint Eastwood was putting together for young people. I went up for that and Arnold was there. And he came over to me, and he said, "I really liked that article you wrote. As a matter of fact, I sent it to Germany to be translated for the German magazines." He seemed to feel that I understood him pretty well. The things that I wrote in that were, for one thing, that as big an ego as Arnold might seem to have, he's one of those people who thinks about himself all the time, but he's very confident in himself and he pays attention to other things. He's very effective because he's paying attention to who people are, what they're like and what they want.

He's extremely good at deciding what he wants and then taking the steps to get what he wants. He's very practical and very realistic about that. As I say, he pays a lot of attention to who he is dealing with. He's very aware of what the circumstances and realities are, what's possible and what isn't. When he was a competitive bodybuilder, he would come in backstage. All these other bodybuilders were wrapped up into themselves. Arnold was looking around to see what was going on and how he could benefit from the situation. He had the confidence not to pay that much attention to what he's thinking and feeling, but looking to see what other people are thinking. As a result he was able to respond to a situation better and faster than the other bodybuilders because they were all wrapped up in themselves.

Also, what Arnold has always done, since I've known him, is made a pretty good amount of money. In the early days, when I dealt with him when he was making a lot of money, he just rented a place. He had a very nice car but it was an old Mercedes. He didn't spend a lot of money on himself. He's not really materialistic that way. He put his money into fine art, which is, by the way, one of the things he directly learned from Joe Weider – to invest in fine art. That's specifically something he learned from Joe. But he was also buying apartment buildings and shopping malls and things like that. Afterward he made so much money as a movie star that he was able to buy pretty much anything he wanted to, but he wasn't really ruled by these things. Arnold's not the sort of person who measures success by what he owns. He's not like Elton John, who just seems to like buying things. He buys what he wants but he's not ruled by it. He's not dominated by that.

So the other thing is, Arnold is like many really great athletes. He is highly intelligent without being terribly intellectual. Somebody once talked about Michael Schumacher, the Formula One champion, saying that he was smarter than anyone, but he wasn't lost in his own thoughts. He was feeling the reality of driving a Formula One race car. Arnold applies his intelligence to achieving whatever his goals are, he's not interested that much in thinking about thinking. He's not that interested in the kind of things I do – that sort of creative things such as writing and photography, whatever. He's got a more practical businessman's approach, or an athlete's approach. His attitude is: if he needs something like that he'll hire the right person to do it, which is why he hired me to write his books. He loves working with James Cameron. He used to talk about James Cameron all the time, as an example of someone he approved of because James Cameron, apparently, is just an incredible person who sets a goal and then goes on achieving it. That's, of course, what Arnold's like. So, not only did Arnold get to do *The Terminator* with Cameron, which he was very happy with, but he approved of him as an individual. Apparently he and Cameron have a lot in common.

**Q: Did you ever go to any of the movie sets to shoot pictures of Arnold?**
Bill Dobbins: I think once or twice – not very much. One thing Arnold is very good at is compartmentalizing. I noticed when I would go over to his house or office for a writing session, when he was involved in something, whatever it was, he'd have some materials, documents or whatever, and he would very carefully put everything away. Put them in the folder, put them in the files and he would clear his desk. Then he would work with me. I noticed when I first met him, he would be in the gym and he would work out and he would totally focus on working out. Then when he left the gym and went somewhere else to do business, he would then turn his mind totally to that. A lot of the bodybuilders like thinking about bodybuilding twenty-four hours a day. It's kind of always on their minds. Arnold would think about what he was doing now, and then he would move on and concentrate on the next thing.

When Arnold was working with me on books, I did a lot of writing with him for the magazines, occasionally I did photography.

Each of these things, he would focus on. I never socialized with Arnold a great deal. That wasn't our relationship. But I was invited to his bachelor's party before he got married. So there have been some social occasions. But basically when he was working with me, he was focused on books. When he was making movies, he was focused on the movies. So, I would not automatically be included in that unless he wanted me to do some work on a movie set or some other place. And he would call me up and say, "I need you to come over and spend two hours." But it was work-related. I didn't hang out with Arnold. I was never entourage.

**Q: Arnold became an icon that most bodybuilders would aspire toward. Can you tell me about the fan mail he received at the pinnacle of his bodybuilding career?**
Bill Dobbins: I really have no particular opinion on that. It was a long time ago and I don't remember any discussions on that. As I say, when Arnold was dealing with me we focused on what we were doing. I just observed. And he did get a lot of fan mail and he did do a lot of mail order. But I can't tell you exactly what his reaction to it was. Occasionally, things would come up. For example, it didn't have to do with fan mail but his opinions on things. A few years ago, *Sports Illustrated* published a very derogatory article, and really bogus, about the fact that some bodybuilders had been involved in murder, specifically Bertil Fox. Of course, Bertil hadn't competed in twenty, twenty-five years when he committed murder. So it wasn't like he was active in bodybuilding. But this woman wrote an article in which she locked together two or three different situations in which bodybuilders had been involved in killings.

You're talking thousands of bodybuilders in a period of over forty years, and they came up with two or three examples. I think if you were to survey British football, you'll find more people guilty of crimes than that. Arnold pointed out that if he was running bodybuilding, he would have public relations – he had publicists, he knew how that worked. He said he would have found out that *Sports Illustrated* was going to run that article. He would have had somebody putting pressure on them to keep it honest and make sure that the material was accurate. And he would have had counter articles and interviews done to protect the reputation of bodybuilding because that was really distorted kind of accusations. Again, it's another example of Arnold being aware of what's going on in the world and having a very practical approach to how he would handle it. But, of course, he wasn't running bodybuilding. He was very dismissive of the fact that bodybuilding, on most levels, does not have the same sort of public relations that almost every other sport does. And to this day, they still don't. So, he is aware of those things. But the fan letters, I can't tell you about.

**Q: What is your opinion on when Arnold pursued the movie industry, it helped put bodybuilding on the map attracting the attention of people in droves as well as putting the sport on a wider mainstream and global stage?**

Bill Dobbins: It certainly publicized bodybuilding. I don't know how many tickets sold in the bodybuilding contests, but in terms of public awareness of bodybuilding, absolutely. I mean, if you look at every sport, when there has been a major superstar it's promoted the sport. Going back to Arnold Palmer, Billie Jean King, Bruce Lee in the martial arts. Bruce Lee is a perfect example. Bruce Lee was to this day the only major martial artist to universally become famous. Bruce Lee was famous in the 1970s, still is famous today. He's a total icon. And Arnold's the same way. Tiger Woods was doing that for golf until he ran into marital problems. The point is: an awful lot of kids have got into bodybuilding because of Arnold. I hear all the time that as soon as they got into bodybuilding, they bought *The Encyclopedia of Bodybuilding* and that was their bible.

When I was the editor of *FLEX*, when I worked at *Muscle & Fitness*, I've always been aware that when I'm writing something that there's some kid next Tuesday who is going to go in for a chest workout and he's going to be reading what I wrote. I have to try to tell him exactly what he needs to do, not just the facts, but enough to tell him the complete information. Remember if I give you three numbers of a five-number combination lock, I'm giving you accurate information, but I've not told you enough. So you have to be careful when you're writing 'how to' stuff. You could tell somebody enough as well as just being accurate in what you do tell them. I'm very, very conscious about that. And Arnold was totally behind that. That was his attitude. He remembered when he was in the 1960s, when he would go into a gym and he would need to know how to do a certain exercise. He wanted to really know how to do it. So the *Encyclopedia* has really helped people in that way.

I've worked with Arnold on his columns for *Muscle & Fitness* and *FLEX* as well. It was the same thing: how do you tell people what they really, really need to know and something that would work for them? Not just do something that looks good but does really help. Anyway, Arnold is by all means to bodybuilding what Bruce Lee was to martial arts. And the interesting thing is that in both these cases, you had people who were really deserving of that – they weren't just hype, they weren't creatures of publicity where you see that. In some cases, you see a lot of people who are known for martial arts and they're not martial artists. Someone like Jean Claude Van Damme, who was never a fighter. But Arnold was Mr. Olympia and he did dominate bodybuilding. He was a person who deserved to be an icon.

**Q: Do you feel bodybuilding became the core base he used for his future success as a movie star and a successful businessman? In your own words, can you elaborate on this?**
Bill Dobbins: I don't have to use my own words. Arnold has been very clear about this since the beginning. Arnold, by nature, is a very disciplined and structured person. When bodybuilding came along it suited him perfectly. Because to be successful in bodybuilding, you have to be very disciplined and very consistent. You have to get up and do the same sort of thing every day for years, and you have to learn to do things correctly. You have to learn what works and apply that, and frequently that amount of discipline is difficult. So you have to really focus on it. Arnold has always said that bodybuilding

taught him how to focus and concentrate and how to develop personal discipline in order to achieve what he wanted. And he used exactly the same kind of discipline and concentration in each of the things he did throughout the rest of his life.

Again, by nature, he is this kind of an organized, disciplined person. I used to go over to Arnold's place and it always looked like the maid just left. You come over to my place, and you can see the last five things I've been working on because they're spread out all over. With Arnold, you would walk in and you'd think the housekeeper just walked out the door because the place is just perfect. He's very disciplined that way. Bodybuilding gave him the structure to really focus like this and learn how to put this in practice. He has always been adamant in interviews saying that the bodybuilding was the basis of the discipline he learned to apply to everything else he did.

When Bruce Lee first went to Hollywood, nobody wanted to talk to him. Nobody would believe this guy, martial artist, who was amazing. How could he possibly be of any interest to the mainstream public? And look what happened. You know his story. He had a very hard time being recognized. He had to be in the *Green Hornet*. You remember he was in a James Garner detective movie, *Marlowe*, in which he played a part. Can you imagine Bruce Lee losing control of himself and jumping off the balcony by accident (in the scene), that's pretty silly. When Arnold was first being taken around by the *Pumping Iron* people, nobody in Hollywood wanted to pay attention to him. He had a funny name. He was this big guy with an accent. He was in a detective movie about Philip Marlowe, in which he played a muscle guy. He played the guy who backed the gangster. His big scene was him taking off his shirt, showing his muscles and how big he was. He was in exactly the same situation like Bruce Lee, people like producers had no idea what his potential was. So Arnold and Bruce Lee have a lot in common that way.

## JON JON PARK

Reg Park's son, Jon Jon Park, had the opportunity to develop a close friendship with Arnold which can be traced as far back as when the Austrian stayed at their home in South Africa. As a former member of the British National Swim Team, Jon Jon participated in the 1976 Summer Olympic Games in Montreal. He later won a series of bodybuilding titles such as Mr. South Africa Maccabiah and Mr. Golden City. Today, Park is a gym owner in Los Angeles.

**Q: Before Arnold actually met your father, he wrote to him as a fan because he fervently idolized him. Can you tell me how they met, which lead to a friendship ensuing?**

Jon Jon Park: Yes. I believe the story goes, according to Arnold, that he walked into a magazine store in Austria in his hometown of Graz and there was a bodybuilding magazine – a Joe Weider bodybuilding magazine – and there was a picture of my dad on the cover. He was very intrigued. And he saw all my dad's *Hercules* movies. My dad had made five at the time, in the early to mid-'60s. He decided to train and mold his physique on my dad. When I first met Arnold, I was ten – I'm fifty-three now so it was forty-three years ago, when he first came to South Africa when he was nineteen. Actually, I was nine, so he's exactly ten years older than me. So, we're going back to 1967. What happened was, in 1966, it was the year after my dad won his third Mr. Universe. He was doing an exhibition in London. And the promoter of the show said to him, "There's a young kid here who's just won the Junior Mr. Europe, you're his idol and he wanted to meet you."

Of course, he introduced my dad to Arnold. And at that stage, my dad would bring the top star every year to South Africa to do a series of exhibitions. In South Africa, they would tour the country during the Christmas holidays, which was summer in South Africa. They would go to all the little towns and all the beaches, and they would have local contests in each venue. They would come there, and there would be Mr. South Africa in Johannesburg, where the star would do an exhibition at the end of the show. So, Arnold knew that my dad would bring these guys to South Africa every year, and he said to him, "When will you bring me to South Africa?" And my dad said, "Well, if you win the Mr. Universe I'll bring you." The following year he won the Mr. Universe in 1967. He came down during the Christmas time of that year and spent at least six weeks with our family in South Africa. That's pretty much how the relationship started.

**Q: Can you talk about the people Arnold was staying with in England – Dianne and Wag Bennett – back in the 1960s before he ventured out to America?**
Jon Jon Park: Wag Bennett was actually the promoter of that show where he introduced my dad and Arnold. I know that he was actually staying with them in their home at that time. There is a very famous picture in Arnold's book *The Education of a Bodybuilder*, and the picture has been published in numerous magazines over the years, where he's wearing a tank top with a large letter W on it, which actually stood for Wag's gym. Because at the Bennetts' house in London they had a gym there as well. The picture of him with the tank-top and my dad talking to him, my dad's wearing a cardigan. I know that subsequent to that he went and stayed in the United Kingdom several times with Wag and Dianne Bennett, and he kept up his relationship even when he went to the States. So, I think Wag also helped him and saw that he had a lot of potential. So, when he came to South Africa he had a lot of potential. He was big and had a lot of muscle mass. But he didn't have much definition, but did get it in later years. He was a little weak in his calf area. My dad was actually known for having phenomenal calves, and he said to Arnold, "If you get your calves up, you'll be the greatest bodybuilder in the world."

My dad always used to train first thing in the morning because he was running four gyms at the time. So he would begin his workout before the day started. At five o' clock in the morning, he would go to wake Arnold up – every morning. Of course, Arnold wasn't accustomed to it at that stage. The first time he woke him up, Arnold said, "Where are we going?" My dad said, "We're going to work out." They used to train every morning at five o' clock. They would do calf raises up to 1,000 pounds, squatting early in the morning 450 to 500 pounds, which he wasn't used to. I think he learned a lot. I think the intensity of his workouts certainly increased, and he applied pretty much what he learned from my dad to his training principles. He said he wanted to be Mr. Universe. My dad said to him, "Well, don't go for just one Mr. Universe, but win as many as you can." And the rest is history, as they say.

**Q: When your dad was in England in around 1966, your dad and Arnold went around England guest posing and competing. Can you shed light on this, please?**

Jon Jon Park: They weren't competing because my dad was a professional and Arnold was still an amateur at that time. And when he came to South Africa, he had just won the Amateur Mr. Universe. Then he turned professional. I believe they may have done several exhibitions throughout the United Kingdom.

**Q: How did Arnold fit into the environment the first time he went over to South Africa?**

Jon Jon Park: My dad brought Arnold out to South Africa several times to do exhibitions, and they kept up their friendship. And he would later be a guest at his show, Arnold Classic, in Columbus in Ohio. Numerous times, he was actually a master of ceremonies. The first time he came to South Africa, he could hardly speak a word of English. He was absorbing everything he could from my dad. I was a youngster at the time. We treated him like family. Everywhere we went, we took him with us. I remember when he first arrived in South Africa. He arrived in the coastal town of Durban. My dad brought him back to the beach. He was really white because he hadn't been exposed to the sunshine. Somebody asked him if he could take a picture of him, so he started posing at the beach. And the next thing, there was a crowd around like you can't believe.

They had local restaurants just next to the beach. The vendors walk up and down the beach selling soft drinks, sandwiches and hamburgers. That's how they make their money in the summertime. The beaches were crowded and there was a guy walking and shouting, "Cold drinks! Cold drinks!" Arnold could barely understand English, he said to my dad, "What is this 'old drinkz'?" My dad said, "No, he's saying 'cold drinks.'" Because here in America they call it 'soft drink'. He had the opportunity to come to South Africa in 1974 to do an exhibition. Then he came again in 1975 when he competed in Mr. Olympia, which my dad was the master of ceremonies. On both occasions he stayed in our home. He would go with the family to where we went – restaurants and the movies – it was great.

There was a time in South Africa in 1975, after he won the Mr. Olympia, there was my dad, there was Arnold, my mom's brother John Isaacs – who took my mom to meet my dad when they first met, he ended up becoming two-time Mr. Universe – there was Franco Columbu – Arnold's oldest and best friend – and Bill Grant from America, who was Mr. America and Mr. World. And they had been there to compete in the Mr. Olympia. There was a photographer, a long-time friend of Arnold's, one of his oldest friends called Albert Busek, they were all staying at our house at one time. My mom was cooking for these guys who had a huge appetite. Arnold loved her cooking. He actually said jokingly, "Come back to America and you can look after me and cook for me. I need to find a woman like you." He really became a part of the family. Then a number of years later, my sister came to the States for a while. And her and Arnold saw each other and dated each other for a while. So there's been a long-time family relationship. I don't see him much these days, but once in a while we bump into each other. But being the governor, he certainly had a lot on his plate.

**Q: Early stage of Arnold's career, in the late 1960s leading to his peak in the sport, did he effervescently have any conversations with your dad reflecting his desire to become a worldwide phenomenon?**

Jon Jon Park: He set his goals. He said to my dad that after bodybuilding he really wanted to follow in his footsteps. He said he wanted to get into the movies. And, of course, when he came back to South Africa, a number of years later after having stayed in America, he was completely different. He was polished. He was articulate and, you know, he had a full command of English. He was just more sophisticated and polished. He actually shared with my dad that he had a list of things he wished to accomplish, which he crossed off one by one. He wanted to get into the property business among other things.

My dad said many, many years ago that he felt Arnold would get into politics, long before Arnold even made it public. Arnold never even really discussed it with my dad, but my dad felt that it was going to be natural for him because he was just so driven. In fact, my dad said he was the most driven person that he knew. He felt that his articulation and his drive would be natural for him to get into politics. In fact, when he was elected governor he called my dad in Johannesburg, and he said to him, "The first person to call me was Nelson Mandela." So, my dad said to him, "And who are you calling now?" He said, "Well, I'm calling you because that's where it all started." My dad was kidding around, they had a very good relationship. They respected each other. I think Arnold regarded him very much as a father figure. When he passed away, he made a speech, because he was his mentor and a father figure.

In 1970, he issued my dad a challenge to compete in the Mr. Universe in London. My dad actually had retired from bodybuilding competition, but he accepted Arnold's challenge. Arnold, at that stage, was living in California, sponsored by Joe Weider as a fulltime bodybuilder. My dad was running businesses. There was almost a twenty-year age gap between them two. But my dad accepted his challenge, and he beat my dad by half a point, which was quite an accomplishment. He said he wanted to give him the opportunity to compete against him and issued him the challenge. He was asked many times if it was great to compete with my dad when Arnold entered. He said, quite frankly, it wasn't really about ego. If it wasn't for him Arnold wouldn't have been an

Arnold. Arnold made it clear on many occasions that he got into bodybuilding and was inspired by my dad.

**Q: When the 1975 Mr. Olympia in South Africa took place, a country where certain people were subjected to the vilest racial epithet possible, how big was bodybuilding in that country in those days?**
Jon Jon Park: Well, at that stage bodybuilding was pretty big. I mean, my dad really put bodybuilding on the map in South Africa. By bringing the top stars over, which he did, people were able to keep up with the sport. The whole bodybuilding scene, and, of course, the magazines we had. So, Arnold established it in South Africa by being there, bodybuilding had certainly grown. So, when Arnold came out there in 1974, he said he would like to hold the Mr. Olympia in South Africa. Arnold was very much liked by my dad and asked my dad to get involved in the master of ceremonies. And the Weiders asked Arnold to have a conversation with my dad. My dad wasn't really a Weider bodybuilder when he started off. After he won the Mr. Universe, there was a knock on his door. And the late Ben Weider was there, who ran the political side of the International Federation of Bodybuilders.

Ben came to my dad and said we'd like to sponsor you. It was to their advantage, and, obviously, they were very, very successful and it became the number-one federation in bodybuilding in the world today. They said they wanted to sponsor him. And he appeared in a lot of the magazines and different covers. He went to the States in early the 1950s, maybe '55 or '56, and worked for the Weiders for a while. But then they had a falling out through his late father. My father's late father felt he didn't need them (Weiders), and so my dad never really had any more association with the IFBB. But fortunately he did keep a friendship with the late Ben Weider, and I think it would've been a more positive effect on his career. But, you know, he was young, his father interfered – and Weider actually said that. But, anyway, my dad agreed to be the MC of the show in South Africa. At that stage, they had a 200-pound class weight and over 200-pound class weight. But also going as far as the movie *Pumping Iron*, they decided to make the movie.

Obviously, Arnold was the star of the show, but they (producers) wanted to set up a competitor thing between him and the up-and-coming Lou Ferrigno. Well, Lou was still very young. He also had a lot of potential like Arnold in his younger days. But he didn't have the polish and certainly wasn't as muscular. Arnold completely psyched him out onstage. He just wasn't polished to compete against Arnold so he came second. Franco Columbu beat Serge Nuberet in the under 200-pound class. Then they had the overall category afterward, which Arnold won and Franco came second. After that they just did the open-class weight, which is how it should be on the professional level. He won the Mr. Olympia for the sixth time and decided to retire. They made some movies with him later. One was *Conan the Barbarian*, which was his first proper movie. He had made one earlier in New York, which the Weiders pretty much set up, which was a bomb. It was called *Hercules in New York*. At the time, he couldn't speak English properly and the movie didn't do well.

Then he decided to make a comeback in 1980 for the Mr. Olympia. He was training very hard for the *Conan* movie, and he felt he was getting in good enough shape to compete against whoever competed at the 1980 Mr. Olympia in Sydney, Australia. Many felt he didn't deserve to win it because of his condition, the judging was advanced, he was releasing more and more water from his physique. There was a guy called Chris Dickerson who came second. Some said he should've won. And finally he retired after that. He won seven Mr. Olympias.

**Q: At the 1975 Mr. Olympia, what was the atmosphere like at the show? Any backstage stories after or before the show, which you would like to expand on?**
Jon Jon Park: They also held it in combination with the Mr. Universe, which was held a day before. So a number of guys who had entered the Mr. Universe and who'd won competed in the

Mr. Olympia as well. The whole city, which was Pretoria, was just taken over by these bodybuilders from all over the world. Unlike the Olympia today – it's just Mr. Olympia. Those days, it was Mr. Olympia and Mr. Universe in one venue within two days of each other. And they did that on several occasions, I think. But that may have been the last one at the same venue. So, it was a wonderful atmosphere. Because those days, in the 1970s, there was a lot more camaraderie with the bodybuilding than there is today. They don't have the same camaraderie today. All of the guys used to train at the same gym at the same time and all supported one another. So the intensity in the gym was fantastic. There was just this atmosphere with all the top guys working out in the gym at the same time. But nowadays it's not like that at all. It's almost like a bodybuilding expo so to speak. Then after the Mr. Olympia, Arnold stayed on in South Africa. And with my dad, certain venues that my dad had organized, they did certain shows around the country, Cape Town, Durban and back in Johannesburg in the end.

**Q: When Arnold's movie career started to prosper with the release of *The Terminator* and *Commando* in the mid-1980s, can you relate any stories pertaining to your father visiting him in California and seeing him advance in a new career?**
Jon Jon Park: Yes. My dad visited California on several occasions because my mom's brother lived there. Then I immigrated to the States in 1985. As a result of me being here, my dad would come over quite regularly. Every time he came over, he and Arnold would meet up together. They would meet each other at the gym and eat meals together. They always kept in touch. I went to several of Arnold's premieres. The after-parties were where the atmosphere was. I mean, here in America when they have a premiere they go all out. You get a choice of wonderful food. You see all the who's who walking around. And they give everybody, when they leave, a bag, which always has some goodies like a t-shirt and a cap, maybe some perfume for the ladies and cosmetic products. So, you know, they go all out. It's pretty exciting to go to these events and rub

shoulders with all the top stars. I mean, anyone who is anyone in Hollywood, you see them there. Of course, Arnold was a very, very big box office, a huge box office, which I think was the platform for him to become the governor.

I wasn't sure what he would do after he left the governor's office. I thought perhaps he'd continue the movies, production side of it. I think he'll carry on running the Arnold Classic every year because it's such a huge, huge thing. It's the biggest sporting festival in the world, a three-day event, barring, of course, the World Cup and the Olympics. But it certainly is up there, one of the big sports events because it's not just bodybuilding that they have, but other fields you're involved in. They have mixed martial arts, they have wrist wrestling, powerlifting, weightlifting, you name it – it goes on and on. So, the whole city of Columbus is taken over for approximately three days. My dad did go on set when Arnold was doing *Terminator II*. He spent a day with him on the set. Once I immigrated to the States, my dad and my mom would come over quite regularly. They were always the guests at the annual Arnold Classic. In 2001, he gave my dad the Lifetime Achievement Award at the Arnold Classic.

**Q: What's the most significant advice your dad gave Arnold?**
Jon Jon Park: I think what Arnold learnt from my dad was the importance of his family. Because from my understanding, Arnold didn't grow up with a close family. Certainly not to the extent what my dad had with my mom, myself and my sister. I think he was very impressed that at the end of the day, there's a time where we all sit down as a family and we talk. My dad would ask my sister, how was your day at school? He'd ask me, how did you perform at the athletics? I was a competitor, so I used to work out every day. I think that left a mark and the importance of the family to Arnold.

Secondly, my dad emphasized to him, he said, "OK. Go and win the Mr. Universe. But instead of one, go win as many as you can. Do not just be satisfied with achieving a goal and stopping, but just keep going as long as you can." I think the third thing was, you have the sky as the limit. He said to him, "You can do anything you want to as long as you set your mind to it." Just with determination and hard work it all pays off. It certainly has. Getting back to the Arnold Classic, in this little town, Columbus, I think they get over three hundred to four hundred thousand people in two, three days – unbelievable. The whole city is taken over by bodybuilding, weight training, martial arts, fantastic effort – it's unbelievable. They have a huge expo. And the booths, there are over a thousand booths there.

**Q: Your father ran a number of gyms in those days as businesses. Do you feel Arnold's business acumen kicked in as soon as he moved to America?**

Jon Jon Park: Most definitely. I think Arnold is a very, very shrewd businessman. One thing, the secret of success for people, and Arnold took advantage of this, is that they surround themselves with successful people – with the best. I mean, Joe Weider has a huge, huge art collection, which he's had for many, many years. He taught Arnold an awful lot about the art business, which Arnold invested in. He got into the property business. He only chose the right people to be involved with. And he's worked with people. He's a very astute businessman, very calculated and he doesn't do anything without thinking. He just doesn't rush into it. With his head first, he makes calculated decisions, wise decisions with the right people, the right money people, the right property people, the right legal advice – all the best in these fields. That's how he became successful.

To be successful in anything, you've got to learn from the best in their fields, and he certainly has. I think his drive is really the thing. There are not many people with that drive. Being a politician is not an easy position because not everyone is going to like you. But he seems to thrive on that power. Certain things that are challenging and certain goals he has, he's never left. He seemed to be very resilient, even if it doesn't go his way.

**Q: When Arnold became the number-one movie star in the world, did your dad and Arnold get together and exchange thoughts and stories about the movie industry?**

Jon Jon Park: Mostly on an annual basis, once a year, and it was normally at the time of the Arnold Classic. My dad would come to Los Angeles, either before the event or after the event, and spend time with me and my family. He would see him in Los Angeles and in Columbus. Often times he'd invite us out to meals, when my parents were here, or to his home for meals. So, he always made a point of seeing him and spending time with him. When my dad passed away I was in South Africa. Arnold called our home. I told him that when I get back to America I want to hold a memorial. And he said to me, "Look, if there's anything your mom needs I want you to let me know. And I want you to see me as his second son." I told him I want to have a memorial service when I come back to the States because my dad certainly knew a lot of people. He said, "I would like to host it." It was done at a hotel here in Santa Monica, and there were over five hundred people at the service.

Arnold got up and talked. People were really pleasantly surprised because when he spoke, there was no ego whatsoever; he was talking like he was the young kid meeting his idol for the first time. He was extremely humble. He basically spoke about his early experience with my dad, and how my dad had given him so much encouragement. He said he had called my dad in South Africa, and my dad had said, "How are you?" He said he was deflecting it off himself. He said he didn't only teach how to love, but he taught people how to die and that he died with dignity. He said if it wasn't for my dad, if it wasn't for Reg, he wouldn't be here today. That's a pretty much powerful statement coming from a guy in his position as the governor of California in a room of five hundred people. He left a big impression on everybody. To call my home and say to me, "I want your mom to think of me as a second son," I think that sums up his relationship he had with my dad and how he felt about my dad's family.

Arnold made a speech at Reg Park's Memorial in December 2007 at the Fairmont Hotel in Santa Monica, reflecting with reverence on the influence his idol had on him. "He has had an effect on millions and millions of people. I mean, we don't really know exactly how many people he has affected. But I'm just one of them, you know. When I think back, when I was walking down in Graz in Austria on the street and I saw this store that sold jeans and different clothing – American clothing, all American stuff. And there was a muscle magazine – there was a few muscle magazines in there – and Reg Park was on the cover. And I was looking. And I looked at the slides if the photograph maybe appeared, but it didn't. It was a shot of him standing there with his hands on his waist, as Hercules! And it was (written) on there 'Reg Park: Mr. Universe'." In the article Park explained how he got involved with the movies, which invoked the young man's interest and he purchased the magazine and read it from front to back. "It inspired me so much to finally realize what I wanted to do in life. So it was because of that I started to do bodybuilding. I was fascinated by the stories inside, how Reg trained and all this."

# TWO

## FRIENDS & COLLEAGUES

### CHARLES GAINES

Charles Latham Gaines Jr, an author and journalist, was one of Arnold's closest friends. During his coverage of the golden age of bodybuilding, Gaines wrote the classic *Pumping Iron* book and went on to narrate the film of the same name. He also wrote the novel *Stay Hungry*, first published in 1972, which went on to be adapted into a film that gave Arnold one of his first roles. He's currently active in the conservation movement and lives in Jacksonville, Florida.

**Q: How did the concept for the *Pumping Iron* book come about?**
Charles Gaines: I had written my first book, which was a novel called *Stay Hungry*. And after the book came out, it was bought for a movie by a director named Bob Rafelson, a well-known American director. He directed *Five Easy Pieces* and lots of other fine films. Anyway, he bought the rights to *Stay Hungry*. *Stay Hungry* is a novel about bodybuilding, and in the novel there's a character – a main character – named Joe Santo. Bob and I started looking around for an actor who could play Joe Santo, but we just couldn't find any actors who were as big as they ought to be. In the meantime, I had

been reading muscle magazines because it was part of the research I was doing for *Stay Hungry*. And I kept seeing stories about this new Austrian who had just come over to America, who was Arnold Schwarzenegger, and how he sort of set the new gold standard for bodybuilding and so forth. So I got curious about him in terms of whether or not he'd make a good possibility for Joe Santo.

So I got an article assignment from *Sports Illustrated* magazine to go down and write a story about a bodybuilding competition in Massachusetts. And they asked me to find a photographer to go down and photograph it. I had not met George Butler yet, but I talked to him on the phone. I called him up and asked him if he wanted to take pictures at this bodybuilding competition for this article I was writing. And he said yes. He came and we went. At this competition, which was called Mr. East Coast, we kept hearing about Arnold Schwarzenegger. One of the guys there who was in the competition knew him. We found it interesting, both George and me, so we got another magazine assignment for *OUI* magazine, which is now defunct in America, and went down to the Brooklyn Academy of Music for Schwarzenegger's second or third Mr. Universe competition.

At that competition, we met him and talked to him and we were impressed by him. I told him about the movie and my novel. I asked him if he was interested in being interviewed by Bob Rafelson. He said, "Yes, of course," and so forth. So, at that contest – Mr. Universe contest – I think it was 1970, '71, George and I both were really impressed with Arnold and thought he could be a big star if he was handled right. Anyway, we went back home and I went out to California to write the script for *Stay Hungry* with Rafelson. Arnold was living there. Bob had him came over to his house and interviewed him. Bob told me afterward, "No, I don't think so. He's too unpolished. I just don't think, unless he can learn to act." I kept on telling Bob he's perfect and that we should use him.

Anyway, to make a long story short, after about a month looking at and interviewing all kinds of Hollywood guys, minor actors who happened to be bodybuilders, we couldn't find anybody who was right. Bob decided to take a chance on Arnold and hired him. That movie was shot in 1973 or '74, in Alabama, and it starred Arnold. That was the first movie Arnold ever made, other than a movie called *Hercules in New York*, which was a little film which was not really good. *Stay Hungry* was the first legitimate movie that Arnold made. It starred Arnold, Jeff Bridges and Sally Field, and it won a bunch of Golden Globe Awards. It's still sort of a cult classic. Arnold did very well in it. It was directed by one of the truly great directors of the 20th century – great American director. He did very well, he did well enough to win a Golden Globe for Best First Time Actor. And working with Sally Field and Jeff Bridges, who were both pros, I think was a big help to him, too.

Anyway, Bob came down to visit me when they were filming in Alabama. There was another guy down here, who's still a very good friend of mine, who lives in California. He was, at that time, a young entrepreneur who started a waterbed company, different things in California. He had some money and he was a little bit of a playboy. George had met him at Cannes. And this guy had expressed interest in producing a documentary movie about bodybuilding, which was a concept George and I had been talking about for some time. In the meantime, George and I went to an editor in New York named Dan Green, while we were actually filming *Pumping Iron*. We had been to my editor, the guy who had published *Stay Hungry*, a man named Sam Richardson, at Doubleday. We had gone to Sam Richardson and said we'd like to do a book on bodybuilding – a non-fiction book on bodybuilding.

He said my book had been quite successful and he wanted to have me stay with Doubleday. But he said, "I think it's a lousy idea. I don't think anybody will buy a book about bodybuilders." He said a lot of bodybuilders are homosexuals, you know. Bodybuilding at that point was not what it is now. It was considered as a sort of a sleazy occupation, and it was kind of under the overcoat of the society at that point. So not many people wanted to touch it. Anyway, we saw four or five publishers, but nobody would buy it. But we ran into another guy. My agent had given up. He had really given up trying to sell this book about bodybuilding because nobody would do it. So, this guy that I met was an agent, and he said, "I like this idea. I'll take it on and I'll guarantee you I'll sell it for you." So George and I went to his office, and he got an appointment for us with Dan Green, who was at the time one of the top editors at Simon & Schuster.

Dan just saw it. He was one editor out of six, seven or eight that we had seen. He saw the book and said, "I think you might have something. I'll take a chance on it. I'll give you the money you need to fly around and do the research." So, that next summer, I guess it was the fall, right after the film *Stay Hungry* finished shooting, George and I took off and spent about five or six months on the road all over the place tracking bodybuilders. A lot of it was down in Santa Monica, California, Gold's Gym, and a lot of it was in European countries, too. And we produced this book *Pumping Iron*, which was an immediate hit. George was a great photographer, and the photographs were wonderful.

A number of celebrities got behind it. And George had the foresight to hire a terrific public relations guy in New York, and this guy really made a meal out of *Pumping Iron*. I mean, really took it to the next dimension and got all kinds of celebrities involved. So the book became a bestseller. In the meantime, we had been – George and I and this guy Jerome Gary – talking about making a film out of the book, loosely based on the book. So, when the book came out and was a success, it made it easier to raise the money that we needed to make the movie. George and Jerome were the two producers of the film, and it was their responsibility to raise the money. Between the two of them, they raised whatever the budget of the film was. And the film went on from there.

**Q: Arnold and Lou Ferrigno, who were the two major stars of *Pumping Iron*, had competed together at the 1974 Mr. Olympia. Did you cover this competition when Arnold beat Lou?**
Charles Gaines: I covered a lot of them because I was a judge – an IFBB judge. I was a judge for many of those competitions, and I judged at least four Mr. Olympias. I was in New York when Arnold

beat Louie. What Louie had going for him was fine. I think I'm right about this, at that point he was the largest competitor ever in the Mr. Olympia contest in terms of both height and weight. I think Louie in his prime weighed something like 265, 270 pounds, which was 30 or 40 pounds more than Arnold weighed at his top weight. Louie was much bigger than Arnold. He had more muscle mass than Arnold did. But he had a lot of glaring deficiencies that Arnold more than made up for. He didn't have the symmetry and the proportion that Arnold had. His legs were a little bit weak. He was not a good poser; Arnold was a great poser.

I think more importantly than any of those things is that Arnold was so intelligent. And by that I mean Arnold had a huge advantage over all of his competitors in all of his competitive life because of his mind. And what that mind allowed him to do was not only to train harder than most of his competitors, but to psyche people out, to figure out what their weak points were and how to exploit those weak points on the posing platform. And this is dramatized in the film *Pumping Iron*. I saw it happen at more than one Mr. Olympia contest, when Arnold was pitted against Louie or Serge Nubret or Sergio Oliva or Franco Columbu, Frank Zane or Ken Waller, or any other people who had set for beating Arnold. He could always find in those people a psychological flaw, something they were afraid of or ashamed of, knew they were deficient in, and then he would work that. As I said, it is dramatized in *Pumping Iron*.

You know where he has breakfast with Louie and Louie's father, and he begins to work on Louie. He says, "Maybe next year you'll be right for the competition. You're just a little bit too smooth." Louie was smooth. He had not been as cut up as he wanted to be. And both Louie and his father knew that. By bringing that up a few days before the competition over breakfast, he was trying to get into Louie's mind that Louie's not quite in the shape he would like to be in, not as cut as he would like to be – that the guy's already been beaten almost. Arnold had a phenomenal capacity to psyche people out like that. A phenomenal capacity to outpoint them when he was on the posing platform in the pose-offs – the judges give a lot of credit. When you've got five guys doing the pose-offs, then you have two guys to pose off, Arnold always won those pose-offs even if he wasn't the best body out there. He usually was, by the way. But even if he wasn't, like in some of the later competitions, like the one in Australia with Mike Mentzer. I didn't go to that competition, but I read a lot about it, heard a lot about it. George was there.

But Arnold was probably not the best body in that competition. I mean, there were probably guys in that competition who were more cut and in better shape. A lot of people felt that he didn't deserve to win it, but he won it because he's smarter than everybody else. And being smarter than everybody else certainly has advantages if you're not the top body in the competition. If you are the top body in the competition, then you don't really need it, but it's a good edge to have on everybody. Louie was gone, he was gone. At the time, not a lot of people know this but he had a little bit of a speech defect. He's a big guy, but he's shy and he didn't like to talk to strangers. His father did most of his talking for him. When he did talk he sounded a little funny because of his speech defect. Louie was never dumb! He was quite a bright guy, in fact. And, you know, later his movie career proved that he could be quite confident. But he just wasn't as smart as Arnold, but that's no insult. There are very few people in any line that are as smart as Arnold.

So, when I think back on the series of competitions that they had and their relationship in the film, what I think of is a pro Arnold who's been through at that point and seen it all, done it all, knows how to win on fifteen different levels. And a young very talented guy, who didn't know how to train that well and took a lot of bad training advice from his father, with a hero-worship thing going on for Arnold, but also made it acceptable to be conned by and psyched out by Arnold. Arnold, more in good nature than anything else, didn't mean to insult or hurt Louie. But it was just his nature, just, you know, con him all the way to the bank.

**Q: Let's talk about the 1970 Mr. Olympia, when Arnold was crowned Mr. Olympia for the first time. Famously, Arnold was**

**able to utilize a trait – sly manipulative behavior – to get the edge over his competitors. What are your recollections of this monumental achievement, which laid the groundwork for his bodybuilding achievements?**

Charles Gaines: I covered that. That was the turning point for Arnold in bodybuilding. I think he was surprised that he got beat by Sergio Oliva in 1969. And I think he made up his mind then that he's never going to be beaten again. He realized that he hadn't done the work he had to do. Sergio was huge! He was as big as Arnold and had a great body, great proportion, great symmetry, and great muscle mass – everything was terrific. He just outworked Arnold. He just looked better. He said he was never going to get beaten again by Sergio or anyone else. He went back out and he had Sergio onstage where he paused against him during the competition, and then out-posed him. He knew he had to put some muscle on his legs because Sergio had fantastic legs. Arnold's legs at that point were still a little bit weak. He went back and worked his legs. His back got harder in the next competition. He got more cut-up and he worked on his posing.

In 1970, he looked every bit as good as Sergio did, but he also worked on his posing, so he knew he could blow Sergio away in posing. He also did the same psychological thing that I was talking to you about earlier in reference to Lou. In the pose-off, when Sergio would go into his most muscular pose, Arnold would go to a double bicep, which was his best pose. And he psyched Sergio out during that competition as well. Arnold was smarter than everybody else, and he used his mind to help him compete. When he was in the pose-offs, he hit a bunch of poses. Then Arnold says to Sergio that's enough, we've done all they need to see, let's go. Sergio walked off and Arnold starts to walk off. Then Arnold, with his great big grin, starts posing again. Sergio had already left the stage. So he got five to six extra poses that the judges kept seeing after Sergio had already gone. There's no rule against that, there's no law against it. He wasn't breaking any rules, he was psyching the other guy out. That's what he does.

**Q: Obviously, Arnold won the Mr. Olympia again in 1971 and 1972. Joe Weider offered Sergio $1,800 to compete in the 1973 Mr. Olympia, but he dismayingly declined. Why do you think Sergio stopped competing in the prestigious Mr. Olympia competitions, what's your opinion?**

Charles Gaines: Sergio was a great bodybuilder. He was older than Arnold. When Arnold came on the scene, I think Sergio just thought, *I'm never going to beat this guy, so I might as well retire.* That would be my guess. I didn't really know Sergio. I just met him a couple of times, never had any conversations with him. So I don't really know what he was thinking, but that would be my guess. It was held in New York at the Brooklyn Academy of Music. Serge Nubret was expected to win, possibly to beat Arnold. But Arnold, again, psyched him out. Arnold joked around and he never got nerves before his competitions. Even after South Africa, when I was a judge for three or four years, seeing him backstage he never got nervous. Most of his competitors got real nervous before the show, but Arnold never let anything bother him.

**Q: You and Arnold became close friends. What is one of the most stimulating conversations you had with him?**

Charles Gaines: We've been friends, and we still are friends, since 1968. We had a lot of conversations. One that stands out in my mind is when we were doing research for the book *Pumping Iron*. George Butler and I were practically living in Santa Monica, California, and we were spending huge amount of time with Arnold. I remember one day we were driving back from Woodland Hills, which is where the Weider magazines were based. George and I had rented a car. Arnold was in the backseat. George was in the front and I was driving. I asked Arnold, and it had been in my notebook to ask Arnold this question, which I had never asked before, I said, "Let me ask you something. I know it's going to sound strange, but have you ever thought of your body as a work of art and yourself as an artist? In other words, Michelangelo had his clay. Do you ever see yourself as a sculptor? And your body has been the material that you're trying to work with?" He had a long, long pause in the backseat – silence. He said, "No, I've never thought of that. But now that you mention it, it's a really good analogy."

Then he just started spinning off this whole thing as we are driving, and he said, "It's interesting because I can look at my forearm and I can say by two weeks by the time competition happens that forearm needs to be half an inch bigger." He said, "Just by eating and exercising, I can cause that half inch to happen." He said, "I don't even have to think about it consciously. I look at the forearm and say in two weeks you're going to be a half inch bigger. Then I eat and I exercise and two weeks later that forearm is a half inch bigger." He said that's a good similarity to how an artist works. And another similarity is that an artist has to be incredibly honest about his work. He has to be able to look at the painting, sculpture or whatever, and say, "That's really not the way I want it to be; I've got to make it better." He said, "I think that one of my strengths as a bodybuilder is my honesty, that I can look at myself and say my calves . . ."

He had a big problem with his calves for a long time, before he got them up to where he wanted them. He said, "I could look in the mirror and say my calves are not what they need to be. I can be ruthlessly honest about it. Then I can put in the work that I need to put in. Most bodybuilders won't or can't. I can put in the work that I have to in order to get them there." So, he said, "Yeah, yeah." The more he thought about this, the more he kept finding analogies. He finally said, "You know, it's brilliant! That's exactly what a bodybuilder is like. I'm exactly like a sculpture, and my body is like a material of a sculpture in that I bring it up to the vision that I have for it and put my heart and soul into it." From that conversation on, Arnold used that analogy over and over again. I mean, you'll see it in half of the interviews he has given about bodybuilding – not about movie acting – he talks about how a bodybuilder is a sculpture and an artist of his own body. I think that was one of the most interesting conversations we had because it kind of lit a light bulb in Arnold's head that went on to be a gigantic spotlight.

**Q: Do you feel there was an evolutionary process that took place as far his personality is concerned? Do you feel a personality transition took place, and what was the contrast between the era when he was a bodybuilding star to when he became the biggest action movie star?**

Charles Gaines: I would say yes and no. I think Arnold came to the United States with all of the essential psychological armor he had, which is to say that he was ambitious from the beginning. He knew more or less what he wanted to accomplish. In fact, he told George Butler this. I think he came over to this country knowing the good strokes of what he wanted to accomplish. He wanted to be the best bodybuilder that there ever was. He wanted to make a lot of money. He wanted to become famous as a movie star. He wanted to marry a beautiful and rich and famous woman. The only part of what he has done with his life that I don't remember him having said he wanted to do when he first came to this country is the political part. That might have been a part of his plan, too. So, in a sense very little psychologically changed about Arnold the time he got here until now.

But on the other hand, quite a lot has changed because there were a lot of subtleties, a lot of things that allowed Arnold to make use of. He came over here with this fierce intelligence and fierce independence, and one of the greatest bodies ever given to a human being in the history of the world, a fierce willingness to work and a fierce discipline – all of those things going for him. What he didn't have is a sense of how to put all that together. And another thing he didn't really have was taste. I think what Arnold has done is to acquire that good taste. I don't mean being wise and charm and things like that because he's always had good taste in that regard. But I mean in things like art, clothes and how to dress, how to speak, how to carry yourself. All those things, he pretty much had to learn from scratch. And he was the quickest learner that I have ever seen.

He learned things unbelievably quickly. If he saw something you did that he liked, the way you carried yourself, the way you spoke, the way you dressed, drank wine, or how you smoke cigars, or any of this, the next day he 'owned' it. He would study you, and the next day he would be doing it. He'd be going to your tailor, and he would be buying the wine from the guy you bought your wine from, and smoking the cigar that he saw you smoking. So, he developed an incredible curiosity and ability to learn and develop that into yet another weapon that he had over you.

To answer your question, I don't think he changed psychologically much. I think he came over with all the essential tools that he needed to do what he needed to do. Which are, in my mind, very, very high intelligence, a very high curiosity, an incredible discipline and a willingness to work hard to aid him in what he wanted to become and what he wanted to accomplish. He's often quoted the title of my book, when people ask him his secrets to success. He says 'stay hungry'. That was the title of my first novel, the first movie that Arnold ever had been in. That's what he's done: he's stayed hungry. He stayed competitive. He's kept eating one thing after another, all the way down the line and all the way to where he is now.

**Q: When *Pumping Iron* was being made, Frank Zane, who was one of the most intelligent bodybuilders, made a rather sarcastic remark, "Why don't you call it *Pumping Arnold*?!" It seems like there was a competitive element going on between Arnold and Frank.**

Charles Gaines: Frank Zane is a great guy and happens to be a good friend of mine and was quite bright. As you say, as a bodybuilder he was quite intellectual. He was well-read. He and his wife Christine, at that point, had a fascination with Buddhism, writings and philosophies and so forth. Very interesting people. Frank also was one of the early experts on nutrition. I think at the time. when he started to hang around bodybuilders, they didn't know as much about nutrition. Frank was in the vanguard of a group of bodybuilders who took nutrition very seriously. He really understood it better than most. He understood supplements better than most and so forth. He was older than Arnold. He had been a star before Arnold got to this country. He was a small man, small boned and not very tall, with a beautiful physique. I mean, he really was one of those bodybuilders who had more symmetry and proportion in his body than 98 percent of all the bodybuilders.

But because he was small, he was not able to put on the kind of muscle that these small guys have now. Nor do I think Frank wanted to because he was more of an artist. He had a lot of proportion and symmetry. So, he never was in a position to beat Arnold and I think that probably caused Frank, if not jealousy, a little bit of mild annoyance because he had been a star before Arnold had got here. And he knew he will never win a Mr. Olympia, or a Mr. Universe contest against Arnold after Arnold did get here because Arnold was so much bigger, so much heavier. Arnold also had a lot of symmetry and proportion. So I think Frank, as I say, might have from time to time been annoyed about Arnold of how really big he became and how everybody paid so much attention to him, and, therefore, conversely a little bit less attention to him. But on the whole, they got on very well.

And because they were two of the brighter of the then bodybuilders, they had more in common than Arnold had in common with most of the rest of the guys at Gold's Gym. Frank was a regular at Gold's Gym. They were quite good friends. I wouldn't say they were real, real close the way Arnold was with Franco, but they were good friends and they respected each other and they admired each other. Arnold admired Frank's posing. Frank not only had a beautiful body, but he was a beautiful poser – next to Ed Corney, who may have been the finest poser in bodybuilding. Arnold admired that. He admired his mind and he admired his body. Frank certainly admired Arnold. They were good friends, but they were never, never, at least in my memory, great best buddy types.

**Q: When filming *Pumping Iron*, what was Arnold like to collaborate with?**
Charles Gaines: He was great to collaborate with. He had great suggestions. Of course, he knew the bodybuilding world way better than we did. He was very helpful. In terms of making the film from

day to day, he was tremendously helpful and always fun to be with, fun to work with.

**Q: Can you reminisce on some of the more social moments you shared with Arnold?**

Charles Gaines: I went to lots of parties with Arnold. The thing about Arnold is he's always himself; he's not a different person at a party full of movie stars than he is at Gold's Gym. He's always himself. He's always in tease. He always loves to tease people. He's always got a great sense of humor. He's always kind of the life of the party. He never pretends or tries to pretend to be anybody he's not. He's always himself. I think the most remarkable things about – one of the most remarkable things – Arnold is that he has an absolute rock-hard confidence in himself.

Most of us, if you and I went to a party full of A-list movie stars, or went to a party before the Academy Awards or whatever, we might be a little bit shy or a little bit different than we are in everyday life, a little bit quieter, or maybe a little bit louder, who knows. Arnold is always the same, no matter who he is with. He's always the same. He's never impressed by anybody, whether they're politicians or movie actors or whatever. He feels he's as good, as big, as smart as everybody else in the world and there's no need to be self-conscious. I would characterize him at parties, the main characteristic I would say is that he is always the same in person. And secondly, that he's always the life of the party because he loves to have a good time. He loves to kid people and joke around, so he's great at parties.

**Q: Were you invited to Arnold's wedding and did you go?**

Charles Gaines: Yes, I did. I went to the wedding. It was a great wedding, you know, it was held at the St Francis Xavier Church in Hyannis, Massachusetts. We were there for three days, I think. We went to the bachelor party and all the different parties before the wedding. And then the wedding itself was in a small church and the reception was back at the Kennedy compound, there were all kinds of people there. There were also some people who were not that famous, but were going to be famous, like Oprah Winfrey. That was the first time that we'd ever met Oprah Winfrey. She, at the time, had a TV show in Baltimore or Washington someplace. Nobody had heard of her. It was kind of an odd wedding because Maria has such a huge powerful family, and I'm not sure that they were all that sure that Arnold was the right person for Maria.

At that point, 1987, he was already becoming a movie star, but he was a bodybuilder. He was a Republican, they were all Democrats. I think there was a certain amount of doubt on the part of some of the Kennedys as to whether or not this was the best choice for Maria. And you could sense that quite a bit if you paid attention to it. Otherwise it was a beautiful day. I remember the food was unbelievably good. The bands were great. Arnold had one of those Austrian suits with kind of a long skirt, green jacket with a kind of button kind of thing. He had a bunch of Austrian friends there, so it was a combination of Austrian and Kennedy, Republican and Democrat, movie stars and politicians. It was an interesting combination. It was a tremendous amount of fun.

**Q: Can you tell me about visiting Arnold at his home, when he was in the peak of his movie career, and was he more inclined toward being a family and homely guy?**
Charles Gaines: His family life has always been wonderful, and I think that was partially a function of Maria. She has such a big close family, and that's what she wanted for her family. She also was born into a famous family, but the family managed to keep their privacy. They insisted on privacy and people not violating it. So, the very few times that I visited Arnold at his home, and there were not many, during the time he was a movie star, I would say that it was just like being in a normal family. His kids were not spoiled. They're all wonderful kids; they're not like brats like some movie star kids tend to be. They're really brought up well and well-disciplined by Arnold and Maria. They were just little gentlemen and gentlewomen. They couldn't be nicer. They had a great relationship with Arnold. There were always dogs around. I would

characterize his family life as being informal. I've had dinner at his house, and we would just sit around and bring out the food and the kids are there. Just have conversations like old friends, smoke cigars and drink some wine. To answer the question, his family life, to the extent I've experienced it and knew something about it, was quite informal, quite happy and completely family-centered.

**Q: Arnold has lived a life that is far from being mundane; he's inordinately been an active individual. Did you and Arnold share any interests and hobbies away from bodybuilding and movies?**

Charles Gaines: We have different enthusiasms. My enthusiasm had to do with the outdoors. I'm a fisherman, bird hunter, hiker and I like to canoe. I could never get Arnold interested in any of those things. We did do a television program for ABC, I forget what year it was, that I directed and produced and George Butler co-directed with me. We got Arnold to come out. One of my great interests in life has been grizzly bears. We got Arnold to come out and do this TV show. We went into Ellison Park to track grizzly bears. That was about the only time I've been with Arnold in terms of being interested in the kind of things that I like (other than bodybuilding and movies). I don't care a thing about cars and motorcycles, the things that he tends to be into. So, I don't recall any conversations about those kinds of things.

**Q: What was Arnold like as a traveling companion?**

Charles Gaines: We traveled together a lot in South Africa and in Europe. We traveled together in London. I remember London in particularly and Paris on the way to South Africa. Then we traveled together for the documentary I was talking about. We traveled over Wyoming, making that documentary about grizzly bears. It was great fun traveling with him. This was mostly before he got famous. Also, I flew around with him when he was the head of first George Bush's fitness program – whatever it's called. He had a plane at that point. He had a jet. He picked me up and we flew around for a number of days. I went with him to talk to these governors about the program.

I remember we flew down to see Bill Clinton when he was the governor of Arkansas, but he was late and he had his secretary to tell Arnold that he'll be half an hour. We sat there for half an hour. Then he called back and said tell him I'll be there in another half hour. Arnold got tired and we left. So we never met Clinton. But we saw lots of governors and flew around to try to get the governors to embrace the fitness programs in their states. It was a lot of fun. We had been on the road flying in his plane. I've traveled with him lots. Being with Arnold is always the same. It doesn't matter whether you're traveling or at his house, or in a restaurant or at a party, he just pretty much sucks up all the oxygen in the world. And you are on his conversational schedule, and you're doing whatever it is he wants to do. It's always great fun, always amusing and always rewarding when you're with him on any of these occasions.

## Q: What was the core concept of President Bush's physical fitness program, for which Arnold became the head?

Charles Gaines: The aim was: American kids are in terrible shape, they were back then and they still are now. That was something that bothered Arnold, it bothered me. It was big back in the 1980s and '90s. I also had a lot to do with that, to try to help kids and adolescent fitness levels improve in the USA. And this was one of the things that Arnold wanted to do as the head of the program. It was called The President's Council of Physical Fitness, and he (Arnold) was the head of it. He had been made head of it by George Bush. One of the things Arnold wanted to accomplish was to improve fitness levels around the country for young people. He figured the best ways to do that was to go see all the governors in the states – every governor in every state, fifty-two states – and talk to the governors into starting state physical fitness councils, that would go down the grassroots level in the states and get kids on fitness programs in the schools, which would be funded by the states. So, that was what I was doing with him.

I didn't go to all fifty-two governors, but about five or six with him. But he went to all fifty-two. Arnold would say, "Governor, your state has got terrible fitness levels for kids. I want you to get them improved. I want to give you an incentive to get going a State Physical Fitness Council and the National Physical Fitness Council. I'm going to help you out with it." And the governors, almost all of them, said yes. So, I went back to Hampshire – I lived in New Hampshire at that time – and started the New Hampshire State Physical Fitness Council. We were quite successful, as I think most of them were. So, that was the point of the thing that Arnold was doing.

**Q: Were you in the presence of Arnold when he was with the first President Bush?**
Charles Gaines: Yes, I was. The first physical fitness day that they had in Washington, right after Arnold had been named the head of The President's Council of Physical Fitness, George Bush put on a big physical fitness day on the lawn of the White House. I was there. I remember Randy Travis was there, the singer. I got to meet President Bush.

**Q: Having known Arnold and been a close friend of his, what it the most vivid memory that stays with you?**
Charles Gaines: I don't know. It's kind of a blank. The most distinctive thing about Arnold, and I saw this over and over with him in all kinds of different circumstances, is his ability to create a dream for himself and then make it happen. I'll tell you one conversation. I did an article for *Men's Journal*, a cover article, when he was running for governor of California. I called him up and we had a long conversation on the phone. This is the result of that conversation. The trick in bodybuilding is to be able to turn a normal body into a competitive piece of art that is going to beat other pieces of art. That's the trick. That's what bodybuilding is all about. It is to take a normal body and turn it into an abnormal body according to a set of esthetic criteria, and allowing it to compete with and win over people who try to do the same thing. So there's

an element of brawn in there, there's elements of imagination in there and there's a tremendous element of will in there.

Another thing about Arnold, when I was talking to him about this article, you look in the mirror and be ruthlessly honest with yourself about what you see there and then decide by one to twenty seconds: I have to weigh 6 pounds more, my biceps have to be two inches bigger, or whatever, whatever esthetic demands you want to put on yourself. Then you go out and accomplish it. Well, most people in their lives, they might come over to America from Germany and say to themselves, I want to be the best bodybuilder there ever lived. I want to be rich. I want to be famous. *I want to be a movie star. I want to marry a rich and famous wife. I want to go on to be the governor of the biggest state in the country.* Most people could say that sort of thing to themselves, but they could never make it happen because they don't have the discipline. They don't have the vision and they don't have the talent. You've got to have so many things in order to do that.

So, the point I'm making is, what Arnold did was to take the sort of the magical transformation that a bodybuilder goes through in changing his body with will and discipline, changing his body into a thing he has only in his mind. Arnold did the same thing with his life! He looked in the mirror when he got to America, and instead of saying his bicep has to be two inches bigger, he said to himself, *I've got to learn these things in order to become a movie star. I've got to meet these people. I've got to be in these things. I've got to take these classes.* And then through his phenomenal willpower, he just went on and did it. He did the same thing for everything else in his life. So, in a way Arnold's life has been all of these pieces. Because the same things that allowed him to become a great bodybuilder have allowed him to do and use his mind, his will, his imagination and his vision of himself to become anything he wanted to become. I think he's really unique among 20th century people. He's kind of a completely self-created human being. He took raw material and made it into what he wanted to be.

# GEORGE BUTLER

Many acknowledge George Butler, born in the United Kingdom, to be responsible for starting Arnold's film career when he produced the classic *Pumping Iron*. A photographer and filmmaker, Butler became a close friend of Arnold's and got to know him personally, producing a series of life-sized portraits of the Mr. Olympia winner. A lifelong conservationist, he has worked on many of the most critically acclaimed documentaries ever made.

**Q: George, you were the mastermind behind *Pumping Iron*, how did this all start?**

George Butler: I had an assignment from *Sports Illustrated* magazine to do an article on a bodybuilding contest in Massachusetts. I went there with Charles Gaines, who went on to write the book *Pumping Iron*. I took the photos for the book. We noticed that the crowd was going crazy over the bodybuilders, and we decided to do a book. One thing led to another I guess. The last overseas assignment that magazine gave us was to go to Baghdad to cover the Mr. Universe contest. Once we finished the book and when we turned it in to the publisher, they rejected the book and said no one ever will be interested in Arnold Schwarzenegger. They were wrong.

**Q: What kind of personality did Arnold project when you were filming him in *Pumping Iron*?**

George Butler: He was very quick, very eager to learn and very good at what he did – very ambitious. He worked very closely with us at that time when we did the film. He was an ideal collaborator.

**Q: In your opinion, what was some of the more interesting footage you shot?**

George Butler: It was all interesting. He holds the screen very well. We shot about a hundred hours of film. Arnold was very cooperative. So we got a lot of good footage all over the world. We shot in California, Connecticut, Massachusetts and South Africa. Arnold was very helpful. There's a scene where Arnold went to the zoo in South Africa, where they were keeping some rhinos. I was very nervous because Arnold was very transfixed with this big rhino, but that scene did not make it into the movie. Let me give you another example. I filmed some footage with Arnold and Mike Katz. Mike Katz was part of the movie *Pumping Iron*, and they were doing Roman chair sit-ups. I remember Mike Katz saying, "This is the most boring exercise I've ever done," and Arnold laughed at him and said, "It's perfect for me, Mike. I sit on the Roman chair and do those sit-ups, and I take the extra time to think how I'm going to make my next movie."

**Q: Of course, Lou Ferrigno was the other prominent bodybuilder who appeared in the film. What influenced your decision to have him play one of the main roles?**

George Butler: Well, I was very insistent to have Lou be in the movie because at 6ft 4in, 270 lbs, he was a giant and he looked like he could beat Arnold. The rivalry between Lou and Arnold was visible. There was Serge Nubret, who was a French bodybuilder who lived in Paris. There was Mike Katz, who was a professional football player. There was Ed Corney, who was a professional surfer. There were a lot of interesting people in the movie, including Franco Columbu, who is a chiropractor. We all got along and had a good time and shot very good scenes for the movie.

**Q: Can we talk about how you got the film financed, what obstacles lay ahead?**

George Butler: Everyone thought it was a crazy idea for a movie. Everyone said, "George, you're wasting your life making a movie about Arnold Schwarzenegger." I stuck to my guns and we made a very good movie, and that's where I overcame most of the obstacles. It was very difficult to finance, but eventually we got it done. Most people thought that bodybuilding was a ridiculous sport – that was the enemy. So the more exposure the movie had the more cities we went to and the more interested the people became. Eventually, I think the movie caused a hundred thousand gyms to open up around the world and bodybuilding became a bigger sport than jogging, but it all took time.

The budget for *Pumping Iron* was $400,000. Jerome Gary, who was one of the producers, contributed $25,000, and a further $110,000 was invested by Butler's wife. This was a very modest budget for a film that took three or four months to film. Short on money, Butler asked for $15,000 in credit from a lab in New York after coming back from filming the initial parts of the docu/drama, which was then standard practice during production. After Butler divulged to the lab that the credit was for a bodybuilding film, the curious owner asked whether this unusual venture of Butler's had anything to do with Arnold Schwarzenegger. Butler, of course, said yes, and was promptly denied the credit – only to learn that years earlier, the lab had done work for *Hercules in New York*, but the company never got paid, losing out on $30,000. When *Pumping Iron* was released, it was embraced beyond the confines of the bodybuilding fraternity. One reviewer in a prominent newspaper wrote, "Mr. Schwarzenegger is the central figure in *Pumping Iron*, an interesting, rather slick and excessively long documentary about the small but intensely competitive world of bodybuilding. The first thing the outsider realizes watching the film, is that the object of all that weightlifting is neither strength nor prowess, but appearance. Mr. Schwarzenegger calls himself a sculptor of his own body."

**Q: It's generally considered that Arnold's exposure to a much wider audience through *Pumping Iron*, which was no doubt a seminal film, led to open doors in Hollywood. Would you say you were responsible, to a degree, for this?**

George Butler: You must remember Arnold made three movies before he made *Pumping Iron*. One was called *Hercules in New York*, which failed in the United States. It was a total flop. It was a ridiculous movie that got no distribution. Arnold should not have done it.

Then there was a second movie called *Stay Hungry* for United Artists. Bob Rafelson was the director. Jeff Bridges and Sally Field were in the movie. And it, too, was a failure at the box office. And it took *Pumping Iron* to come along and elevate Arnold to a much higher plane and the national interest in Arnold. He went on a wonderful publicity campaign in New York, and it all worked out very well.

More than fifteen years later, at the height of his fame, Arnold was on *Late Night With David Letterman* promoting *Terminator II* when Letterman showed a clip of Arnold's first movie, *Hercules in New York*. "I cannot believe it!" Arnold laughed as the audience joined in. "I have to tell you, every single time I come to this show there's some kind of a surprise. I said to myself, *What could it be today?* There you have it, a movie I tried to hide for centuries," laughed Arnold. At the time, the young Austrian had literally just got off the boat basically in his quest to conquer America. He could hardly speak English fluently. The production company dubbed his voice. "I didn't even know what I was saying, it was dubbed," Arnold continued. "And it was one of those dream stories, in a way, you say to yourself, *This is true, there's such a thing when you come to America someone comes up to you and says, 'Do you want to star in a movie?'* That's what this was." He said he was ecstatic and had made $3,000 doing the film. Arnold had come a long way from his initial exposure into the film industry, and was now polished and the highest-paid star in Hollywood.

**Q: You were a photographer and shot Arnold. Can you tell me about some of the photo sessions you did with Arnold?**
George Butler: Arnold was always willing to be photographed and he loved the cameras. I took my camera and my lights everywhere I went. I took about five thousand photos of Arnold. The photos worked out cool.

**Q: Your relationship with Arnold went beyond the confines of business. You and Charles Gaines developed a close-knit friendship with Arnold and became very close friends with him.**
George Butler: Arnold and Charles Gaines and I were very good friends. We always had a good time together when we joined forces. We traveled a lot together. We did the book and the movie, and Arnold helped a lot because he was always willing to talk to someone we introduced him to. He enjoyed the whole process. When the movie came out, he did hundreds of interviews and he wanted more. The premiere of the movie was on January 7, 1977, in a hotel in New York. There were a lot of celebrities at the theater, which was near Fifth Avenue. There were lots of news people and lots of television cameras. It was a very successful premiere because we got a lot of attention. A lot of people turned up to come and see the movie. The book that we did and the movie that we did spoke to the audience outside of bodybuilding. The project was successful because we succeeded in making Arnold famous, when people had no interest in bodybuilding, and he handled it very well.

**Q: Would I be right in saying some of the scenes in *Pumping Iron* were dramatized? Arnold has said some scenes were made up and dramatized to make it more interesting, can you elucidate further?**
George Butler: All of the scenes in *Pumping Iron* were true to the sport – truth in the scenes from the movie. He wanted to move bodybuilding into an acceptable arena. And everything in the movie is true to the individual. Nothing in the movie was pure fiction.

When promoting the 25th anniversary of *Pumping Iron*, Arnold said, "Every time anyone sees *Pumping Iron*, they will come away, you know, loving the movie, being inspired by the movie." Over the years, many of these questions have persisted. Arnold himself has said it's important to clarify there are certain elements in the film –

such as the results, competition and intensity of the training – that are presented absolutely, even if others are fabricated. These days, *Pumping Iron* might be more appropriately labeled as 'docu-drama' – certain things were created in order to make it more compelling because it was very clear that the only way the finances could be raised, for what was perceived as a risk project by certain backers, was to make it more dramatic. "All the investors always said, 'Look, the training is terrific and what they are doing is terrific, and all this,'" Arnold explained later. "But how much can we look at this footage of them doing squats and chin-ups and sit-ups and all this? It's boring. Even though it's exciting to them, it's boring for us to watch." It was therefore decided to add some drama and some conflict, which would raise the audiences' temperature. To this end, certain things and a storyline were created as the filmmakers went along and a villain and a hero were created.

**Q: There were certain controversial elements attached to the movie, like Arnold smoking marijuana cigarettes. He seemed to be quite open in those days, conversed frankly about various controversial issues. Can you expound on this, please?**
George Butler: Arnold behaved the way he always behaved. There's nothing in the movie that cause the police to arrive and arrest him for smoking a joint. That's just part of life. I can't think of any other controversial elements. In various newspapers, there's been a score of articles about things that were in the movie, but they never were. So they (writers) were just wasting their time.

**Q: Did you have any new projects you wanted to work with Arnold on after *Pumping Iron*, and what did the general public learn about the sport and Arnold after being exposed to *Pumping Iron*?**
George Butler: The truth of the matter is, after I finished *Pumping Iron* and went on to make other movies, Arnold was, obviously, making his own movies. I was working on a movie somewhere for

some time, and Arnold was working on a movie in Indiana. I hadn't seen Arnold for a while. The last time I saw him was here in New York. He seemed very well. I went to a lot of dinners with Arnold and birthday parties to his house. I went to his wedding. You have to remember we were close friends.

Everyone changes when they become a big star. And Arnold's life has taken about his work. Whenever I see him we talk the same as we used to talk in the good old days. It's (*Pumping Iron*) a father and son story, about Lou Ferrigno and his father, about Arnold and his father, who, as you know, by then had died. It's a story about fathers and sons. Arnold is absolutely the epitome of the American Dream. He came to the United States with nothing more than a gym bag and no money in it, and he's become one of the wealthiest people in California, if not the United States. He's been a bodybuilding champion. He's been the governor of California. He's been a movie star. He's quite extraordinary. We did some television work together and made a show for ABC TV. There were several things I'd like to have done with Arnold over the years. Essentially, I make my own movies now.

## BARBARA OUTLAND BAKER

Barbara Outland Baker was Arnold's first girlfriend when he moved to America, after he asked her on a date when she was working at a San Diego delicatessen. She went on to date him for six years.

**Q: You and Arnold met in 1969 at your workplace in Los Angeles. Can you talk about your first meeting?**
Barbara Outland Baker: Right. What happened with meeting him was, it was the year between my junior year of college and my senior year, and I worked in a delicatessen – a Jewish delicatessen – that he came into at least once a day, if not twice a day. So, one day, all of a sudden I'm sitting at the counter eating lunch, eating French fries, he just came over and said, "You are so sexy. I must ask you out on a date." I was a college girl, little sorority girl. I had never been spoken to like that in my life. But he was interesting and I gave him my number. It took a week or so for us to go out, but we did and really had fun on the first date.

**Q: How was Arnold adjusting to life in America when you met him?**
Barbara Outland Baker: His English language was at a really low level. So his communication had to happen with a lot of body language and asking questions. So, with that element, and from my end, I kind of felt I could be the English teacher and have fun with it. And then on his end, he loved everything. He loved American politics. He loved the American movies. He loved the American beaches. People were so nice to him that he had instant friends, of course, surrounding the bodybuilding world. He struggled financially, for sure. Joe Weider was a very hard person to negotiate with. But you never really had the sense that Arnold ever worried that he never had enough money. He really didn't have very much money at all, but he was still able to have the life he wanted to have.

**Q: Bodybuilding never really invoked your interest. Did Arnold relate his dreams and ambitions to you in those early years?**

Barbara Outland Baker: No, I was not part of the bodybuilding world at all. You know, what's funny is he really is somebody who was so much into the moment that he didn't really talk on a daily basis about long-term goals. It was always about building his body for that day, for the upcoming contest which was next. So it was probably a two- or three-month plan to get the goal of building up his body, and the overall goal wasn't so much in view. I think he just wanted to keep developing contacts, networking, writing letters, and getting to know as many people as he could. He had realized the value of networking very early.

In his mind, he may have known more about what he wanted to do with that than he said, but really none of us from those days can remember him talk about any big dreams of being a businessman. Not even owning a gym like, say, the Jack LaLanne chain we had. He just felt it would just unfold. Even his movie career was something I never really heard him talk about except through his fascination with Steve Reeves. There was kind of an understanding that he would love to be the next Steve Reeves, but that was never going to happen. So it didn't really need to be discussed because they weren't making Tarzan kind of movies anymore. Again, he just kept doing his best in the moment. I'm certain he had a strong belief that it would pay off some way, somehow, but I didn't quite see how it was going to.

**Q: Did Arnold talk to you about his childhood, growing up in Austria?**

Barbara Outland Baker: He did a lot. He was very much Austrian. Even though he had a difficult childhood, he was a highly individualistic child that his father, in particular, didn't understand. Our childhoods are so pivotal to our lives, so he couldn't help but tell stories about his brother Meinhardt and various stories about his father being demanding and his mother indulging him a little bit more. And his other friends, their fathers would be surrogate fathers to him. They gave him more attention. They gave him more acknowledgment than his own father did. So there was a huge struggle that went on with his father, really, to the point that when I met him there was no desire to see his parents frequently. He felt he had to do it out of duty, but there was no real loving desire to see his parents. So, when he would go over for contests, he would attempt to see them. And then suddenly it was too late because his father died of a heart attack quite young. His brother died first. It was like all that was left was his mother from his childhood. When he was aged, I would say about twenty-four, those deaths had occurred, that's pretty young to only have a mother left.

Arnold had first expressed a strong desire to become an athlete when his father took him to Graz to see Johnny Weissmuller, the Olympic swimming champion and actor who became best known for playing Tarzan. Arnold's father was a curling champion and had a penchant for sports, and encouraged his young sons to compete in soccer, which was the most popular sport in Europe, as well as boxing and skiing. But weightlifting, which Arnold initially took up to strengthen his legs for soccer, was something else entirely. "I still remember that first visit to the bodybuilding gym," Arnold later wrote in his semi-autobiography *The Education of a Bodybuilder*. "I had never seen anyone lifting weights before. Those guys were huge and brutal." The bodybuilders started paying closer attention to just how hard the young man, who at the time was fifteen and weighed 150 pounds, was working out, squatting with fairly heavy weights despite his age. According to Arnold, the bodybuilders at the gym encouraged him to pursue the sport of bodybuilding.

**Q: Do you feel that Arnold had to prove himself to his family, especially his father, because they weren't really keen on bodybuilding and they wanted him to get a proper job?**
Barbara Outland Baker: They sure did. I think he was in such a

habit of trying to get attention from his father that it has worked itself into his personality. I really think his drive was so dramatic in getting attention from his father, getting him to acknowledge he was at least as good as his brother Meinhardt, if not someone really special. So, yes. I think his whole life was about that drive to get attention from his father – and now it's patterned into his later life.

**Q: Arnold's brother died young, but his father favored his brother. How would you define Arnold's relationship with his brother?**

Barbara Outland Baker: Yes, the father definitely favored the brother – he was firstborn. He was naturally a good student. He was probably more naturally an all-around good athlete. They did things together like ice curling, which was, I guess, a special sport in Austria, you know, when you're living in a snowy climate. The father believed in competition. So he always set it up that Meinhardt or Arnold had to be the better one in whatever activity they did. So it was never really about having fun; it was who could get the biggest handful of flowers for their mother on Mother's Day, or who could run the fastest. So, you know, Arnold always felt, being the youngest, he never could be better than Meinhardt. His brother was a year ahead of him and did everything bigger, better, wiser, smarter. So that doesn't give a lot of room for having a loving relationship. When his father and brother were alive, there was more conflict than there was resolution.

**Q: His father inculcated his sons with a sense of duty. When Arnold's father passed away, you say Arnold showed little empathy. Was there any vestige of sympathy, why did he miss the funeral?**

Barbara Outland Baker: He really did make a very conscious choice that it wasn't good timing for him. He had shattered his knee in Australia in a competition. So, he had come home from that. Once he got home from Australia, maybe even at the airport in Australia, it was really bad timing – his knee had gone out on him. He got a phone call that his father had died. This was in early December. It's not, like, he had the surgery right away, because he was trying to postpone having the surgery. He had a miserable journey coming home because he was on crutches. But there's a secondary plot to that, too. He really did not feel the obligation and the love of needing to be there. He figured his mother had the rest of the family there. And there was no warmth Arnold had felt for his father, so he already had missed his father – the missing had already occurred. So, to go home to show that he was going to miss his father, he really felt that his father had sort of abandoned him and the relationship, I would say, had already been severed.

**Q: Did Arnold have a tender side to him? Of course, being an athlete, he was a macho guy. Did you see any side that wasn't obvious to outsiders?**

Barbara Outland Baker: I'm sure people have heard some of the sweet and tender stories of things that he would do for people. Certainly the bravado and the macho side, the gym, the teasing among buddies, that dominated 95 percent of the time. But definitely there was a soft side to him, where people he really loved and cared about, whether it was my mother or me, even a little old lady who he saw fall off a bench in the park, he would run to the rescue and see if he could help. He loved to tease people lovingly. He would love to brush my hair. There was a side to him which was very kind and soft, and I really appreciated that side to him. Throughout his adult life, he continued to show that for certain people. He had a lot of surrogate fathers. One of them was Mits Kawashima, Arnold was so wonderful to Mits – even as governor, he would call him to make sure he was OK. Before his wife died, Arnold made sure he had all the care in the world – the best care. I don't want to say hospitalization – I'm sure he didn't pay for that, including medical bills – but he made sure that she was healthy and happy as he could be as she was dying. He did that for quite a few people. Artie Zeller, the postal worker and the photographer that took his pictures. Again, when Artie was dying, he made sure that he had absolutely everything he needed. So he's really been there for his lifetime friends as they come to their deaths. He still supported them. He's been good to their needs. So, yes, there's a very tender side to Arnold.

**Q: Arnold was obsessed with his sport; you wanted to settle down and get married. Can you relate any conversations you both had reflecting this issue?**

Barbara Outland Baker: Well, they were fairly constant. Probably for the first year, you're typically dating, and my world was such that if you dated for a year you got married, because that's what all of my college friends were doing. But for him, I guess, culturally his upbringing – and maybe in different parts of Europe – is that you didn't really need to get married. If you loved one another, you could live together and maybe someday you would get married when you wanted children. But for him, that wasn't now. So, once we started moving in the second and the third year, I was starting to get extremely impatient and worried and thinking I wanted to have children. I'd say that at least once a year, there was a serious conversation. I would say to him, "Where's this going? Where do you want to go? I desperately want to have children and we have such a great relationship." It just went nowhere. As people today get into those kinds of relationships, when the man isn't ready – or woman – or one of you, it can't happen. He couldn't really explain himself well enough to me that I understood it. So I was really frustrated that we weren't getting married, but I wasn't strong enough to leave him.

**Q: You were together for six years. Over that time, what is the strangest conversation you had with Arnold?**

Barbara Outland Baker: Actually, one that occurs to me is where I was absolutely shocked after we had broken up. We really did maintain a beautiful friendship and we would still meet for lunch. So, I went to Santa Monica and by now he owned an office building along with his apartment building. I don't think he owned the restaurant yet, but there was a restaurant he liked to go to frequently. And he's sitting there talking – this would be 1977 or '78. He said to me, "You just wait, I will be the governor of California." And it came so out of nowhere. It was such an impossible thing to say, that you'd out of most people just laugh at him. I felt, because he was with Maria Shriver then, maybe he's going to learn something about how to get into the political arena. It did take him more than twenty years or so to achieve this dream after he said that. But to think he predicted that he would be the governor of California, it was a shock. I drove home that day thinking to myself, I don't believe what I just heard. *What if my ex-boyfriend becomes the governor of my home state?*

**Q: Barbara, please can you reminisce on spending time together? Did Arnold go out often or was he the type of a guy to stay in and watch a movie?**

Barbara Outland Baker: I would say he was very much a doer. It wasn't drinking – he might have a beer here and there – and it wasn't like a party scene, like today's youth would do; it was more dropping in on his bodybuilding friends, talking and laughing. He would rather have a cup of coffee in the evening as opposed to a drink – a cup of coffee and a little tiny dessert. But we would do that with Italian friends, or Jewish friends, and there usually would be couples, long-term married couples. And they would have this hospitable open-house policy. So, there was a lot of that going on spending time with friends. Or he and his friend Franco Columbu, the three of us, again, would go out to a restaurant and go to every movie. There was hardly any movie that was made which we didn't go to see.

We spent a lot of time with my family, who lived about half an hour away. Usually, we'd go over every Sunday and have dinner with my family. And just laugh and maybe play a little poker, just wear silly hats, and he would laugh and tease. He loved getaways, whether it was going up to Santa Barbara, Palm Springs, just day drives. You could be gone for one night. He loved getting out of town. But he wouldn't let it disrupt that much because he was so driven to be back at the gym and back to his schedule. But he was a goer and doer and loved meeting new people. He really liked it if they could advance him. Again, that takes us back to the networking.

**Q: Would I be right in saying that Arnold's mother visited America for the first time in the early 1970s? How did she settle down with Arnold in her new environment?**

Barbara Outland Baker: After his father died, I would say he already bought his apartment building, so she stayed with us in a rented apartment. So I would say that was probably 1972 or '73 at Christmas time. She stayed for quite a long time, maybe for six weeks. You know, he didn't spend much time with her. He visited her in Austria, certainly. I had met her there by then, when I went to Europe with Arnold once. She was a very simple village woman and didn't have any kind of disposable income. She came over here with a very simple heart and a closed pocketbook. And I know that it was a little bit hard for him because she was so Austrian and he was so American. So it was almost like he had a cultural conflict with his mother.

Eventually, she really learned to have a better life. She had a boyfriend called Franz for fifteen years after Arnold's father died, and they had a wonderful relationship. She, and even Franz, would eventually come over. This is after Arnold and I broke up, but our friendship allowed me to know that she and this man had a great relationship. She developed her personality. She was a lot more fun. She was looser. Arnold could help support her financially, so she wasn't as worried and nervous about her finances and she really started blossoming more in her personality.

**Q: When you visited Austria with Arnold, how did you find the experience?**

Barbara Outland Baker: I would say it was in the summer of '73. I don't think it would've been '74. We went over for a couple of weeks. It was for an exhibition in Belgium and Germany. So it was more that he had these business deals where he would get paid for his exhibits. In Germany we were close to Austria so, of course, it was an opportunity to go and see his mother. And what had happened by then, of course, you can't call her a sister-in-law because she and Mienhardt never got married, but Erika was really like his sister-in-law. She had a son named Patrick. We went to see all three of them and just had the most loving, wonderful, sweetest and kindest time. It was really a joy to be there, being in his mother's home and the home he had grown up and meet his little nephew, who later, of course, worked for Arnold as a lawyer. So, it's really ironic to see that child, who had been fatherless, taken on by Arnold all those years later and now living in Santa Monica and working for his uncle.

**Q: Like any relationship, there must have been tumultuous times. Can you tell me what these were and how you overcame them?**

Barbara Outland Baker: Well, I think I would go back to the conflict of how we each perceived marriage. So, other than that we really were compatible, we had a good time together. I do recall being dismayed by a little bit of a sarcastic side to him that was hurtful to other people. So, sometimes his nature, I felt, it really hurt my soul. It's like, you have got to learn to be kind to people! You can't go hurting people's feelings for your own pleasure. So that definitely was a source of conflict. But mostly it was my selfishness – I just wanted to get married. So, any of the ups and downs would affect my emotional nature. I was so depressed I couldn't make myself leave him. It was more my issue. I was caught in the relationship. I couldn't stay and I couldn't leave. It was really, really tough.

**Q: Did Arnold have a penchant for anything else other than his sport?**

Barbara Outland Baker: We're talking in the early years. As he would say today, "I collect everything." There's not one thing that man doesn't collect. But back then, no. He wasn't into clothes; he pretty much looked like a slob, like a gym slob. He was a monomaniac. Bodybuilding was pretty exclusively it. It doesn't mean he wouldn't like to go skiing or horseback riding or driving his cars fast or hang out at the beach. I mean, all of that aliveness was in him. It was business, business, business, learning how to develop his business; his bodybuilding courses; develop his body; win contests – apply that to better business. And it was about how he could make more money through exhibitions, through selling more courses to negotiating his contract with Joe Weider. So, the years I knew him, it revolved around bodybuilding as a vehicle to become a businessman.

**Q: What food did he favor?**
Barbara Outland Baker: He certainly was a protein person, as they all were in those days. It was all protein powder, with raw eggs and meat in on top. In the morning, little steaks, all kinds of eggs – scrambled or boiled – cottage cheese, protein any way he could get it in there. Vegetables, salads, he and the other guys, they wouldn't want too much carbohydrates so they would have almost nothing on their salads, maybe vinegar and oil. But he had a little weakness for sweets, especially when it wasn't training time. He would have his apple strudel, which was his favorite. And he loved my carrot cake – that was his favorite thing. I had a special recipe where I would mince the carrots with my hands. And I would take the cake to New York when he was competing at the Mr. Olympia. So, I even made a cake in California and physically hand-carried it to New York, so we could have it to celebrate his win in New York City. It was pretty repetitious. He was very protein driven.

**Q: What kind of restaurants did you frequent with Arnold?**
Barbara Outland Baker: We went to Zucke's Delicatessen so many times. That's where we met. We lived very close to it, so we would either walk over or drive over. That was totally a second home for us. They kind of knew what he ordered. So they would bring it to

him without him even requesting it. We would go out for Chinese food a lot of times with Joe Weider. That was an unusual taste for him to venture into. It wouldn't take him so long to get a little tipsy, so it was funny sometimes seeing him have one beer. And, you know, I guess even though you're that big, if you're not used to alcohol it could get to you, and he could be really, really funny.

**Q: Arnold eventually admitted to steroid use. What do you think about this?**
Barbara Outland Baker: Well, many of the guys took them. Sure, the guys in the Jack Lallane era didn't, but for all those guys it was pretty normal and they were quite easily able to get them. They had doctors to figure it out. Personally I didn't like it, it just seemed really wrong to put such substances into your body, but there was no way I was going to stop Arnold. So, he definitely admitted he took steroids, and he did.

**Q: How would Arnold relax at home and kill time?**
Barbara Outland Baker: I don't think he'd know the phrase 'killing time'. He would watch a little bit of television, like the news, at the end of the day. And our last year together, we had a terrible gasoline crisis in the country. He was really focused on that and the politics at the time. So, he certainly had an avid interest in keeping up with the news, international news, state of California news, American news. But it wasn't really killing time; he really wanted to know what was going on in the world.

**Q: Did Arnold have a penchant for any particular TV programs?**
Barbara Outland Baker: You know, isn't it funny that he loved movies so much? But unless there were reruns of cowboy movies, he really liked the Western genre. I can't think of anything that was valuable enough for him to look forward to see on television. Remember television wasn't as advanced in those days as the productions they have today.

**Q: Would I be right in saying that Arnold wasn't very polite like he is today and he had bad table manners, is this true?**

Barbara Outland Baker: Oh, gosh, that stems from his childhood. His father was of a military background. And you are brought up like military style, which is spoon and fork up, and right range in your mouth. Arnold was raised in that manner and he eventually completely rebelled. He made a choice that eating like this, like sort of a beast and an animal, he didn't really care and it wasn't important to him. Then he started realizing that having refined manners was going to get him more socially accepted by the higher classes of people that he was surrounding himself with. All of that improvement – the refinement. Early on he had a taste in classical music that was an Austrian inheritance. So, he did have some refined aspects to him. Mostly he was a gym animal and he acted accordingly until he decided that it served him to become more refined.

**Q: You were a teacher. We know Arnold enrolled in college, but what was he exactly studying and how did this help him?**

Barbara Outland Baker: He really wanted to work on his English, so he started at the Santa Monica Community College. He struggled and he was not a natural student. So, getting the writing down and everything else, it was very helpful that I was there, being an English major. So I could tutor him more or less. So, from Santa Monica College, he then started taking classes at UCLA. But in there there's adults, or people who are continuing education programs, because he wouldn't have had the units or the grades to have gotten in as a regular student in UCLA. But he did do a lot of work in there, whether it was philosophy classes or history classes.

Then somehow he had enough of an academic resume that the University of Wisconsin gave him a degree. They're very creative in how they give you credit for your life experience for your education that you have had. They arranged to deal with him where he could go back to Wisconsin. I think it was for some classes he could do by correspondence. It's not a world that I really know very well because I have a more traditional history with how education works, or you take classes on the campus and you go to them and they are credited. But in his case, he pulled it off and got his degree in business. I'm not really sure what the title would be, but I think it would have to be a B. Then after that, he got countless PhDs, honorary PhDs, from various colleges. So, for somebody who was not academically oriented, he does have a resume to show – it's very interesting.

**Q: Did it ever surprise you that Arnold went on to become so famous around the globe?**
Barbara Outland Baker: Well, I don't know, if you've personally known somebody before their fame, it is really odd because they're just the person they are. And you like them, you laugh with them and you know them personally. They're really like this person you're hanging out with. And it's like, OK, fine, the reason you like being with this person is because they're so exciting. So, that's how I perceived Arnold. That he was the most unusual person that I ever met. He was just incredible fun to be with. He was the life of the party. Yes, of course, with that came narcissism. And often life was all about Arnold 100 percent. And most of the time, that was OK with me because I was included in everything and it was really great fun.

So, I never would have pictured how far it would have gone because I had a small enough mind that I thought, Hey, this guy really could have a successful chain of gyms. And that's kind of where I was going with what I could see him doing if I kept it in the same domain that he'd been training in. So, to see him venture out in real estate, I got to witness that even being with him when he bought his first apartment building. I'm thinking, *That is absolutely amazing. He didn't buy a home, but he bought an apartment building where six other people are going to have their homes within his home. And he's going to own their homes, too.* I definitely thought this guy was really unusual. So I imagined him to be wealthy. I figured he would be a real estate mogul.

Then after we broke off, he ended up buying this office building in Santa Monica and really restoring it. Actually, it was Venice. Well, they're kind of one and the same, but Venice was really rundown.

And by Arnold buying this office building, he upgraded it. All of a sudden, I felt he was very much at the core of restoring the bad part of Santa Monica. I thought, *Well, that's powerful!* That's really huge – that you'd take a city that's so famous and rundown and become part of the restoration process. I kept seeing him buy more expensive homes. Of course, at the end of our relationship he had already been working on two movies – *Stay Hungry* and *Pumping Iron* – and that was why we broke off because I felt: OK. This isn't going to change. Arnold's not going to marry me now, just because he's going to quit his bodybuilding career. He's going to be now married to an acting career or whatever else is going to come in the way. I did see him in the *Stay Hungry* movie, which came out after we had broken up. We were together for the filming of it, but we split up during it.

The *Hercules* movie before that was such a joke that I never expected that he could succeed in that industry. The *Stay Hungry* part was a little weird. I know he won awards for it but, I mean, I just didn't see that was going to result in a big acting career. In *Pumping Iron* he kind of looked like a goofball. When he hit the big time with *Conan*, I couldn't believe that he was becoming a household name. I started hearing it on the street, strangers talking about Arnold Schwarzenegger. And in my classroom, where I taught students, they would say, "I like Arnold." And it just seemed everywhere I turned around, I started hearing his name. But they didn't know that I was in any way related to this man's life. So, that continued forever and you get used to it. It still continues and you get used to it. But there's something very surreal about knowing a human being who once was a normal person and now they're completely iconic, you know. They're known worldwide, not even in a small little arena. It's just pretty phenomenal.

**Q: Did you see Arnold in the 1980s and 1990s, when his movie career peaked, as he basked in his newfound fame?**
Barbara Outland Baker: Yeah. We really did maintain a friendship. Most of the times I'd say it was on the telephone. I think he would

just get lonely in the hotel rooms, making movies and stuff, and he would probably have a list of twenty or thirty people he felt like calling. Because Arnold is really not a person who likes being alone. He would call frequently enough when he was on the road. I can't tell you whether it was once every month, two months, or six months – it changed over the years. But certainly we kept up. And occasionally I would go down to visit him on a movie set. I went down when he was making, I think the Belushi movie, *Red Heat*. So, things like that would happen. Then in 1992 or '93, he invited my mother and me to a really big art exhibition that he had thrown at a museum in Los Angeles. That was really sweet. As late as 1992, he extended this formal invitation to my mother and me. It was a great night where we had a wonderful reunion to see old friends. Then I got married in 1993 and it was interesting that the phone calls did start dropping off a little bit more after that. It was rare that I would hear from him. But we still would keep in contact. It was less when he became the Californian governor. I think that his world is so ascended into this . . . at this point I just don't see a real need for us to speak with one another. But the feelings are fine, you know, we're good with each other. It's just that after a while you do grow apart. I think we might have hit that place.

**Q: Do you feel Arnold, from when you knew him when you were together in the early period and Arnold at the height of his fame, went through an evolutionary process as far his character or personality, and did you perceive any elements of pompousness?**

Barbara Outland Baker: When I interviewed him once I really left the office sad that day. Remember it's all subjective – it's just me and how I perceive it. But I feel when you get that famous, most people are so locked off by your protection. Your security guards, your office staff, everybody is there to protect you so that you won't get killed, so you won't get burdened by the use of your time. And I could see that his life was so large and so small at the same time. It seemed to me it would be a real burden living like

143

that. So, as a process maybe he has developed more of a harder shell in protection. He's lost the spontaneity that a freer life would allow you to have. I think anybody might have fallen into this kind of situation, although, I don't know any other famous people, so I can't compare. But I just have to believe that that's going to be a certain direction for anybody who becomes so famous that you are no longer openly accessible to the public – you're more of a robot.

**Q: A lot of controversial stuff surfaces when someone becomes famous. Arnold had his fair share of negative media, especially when he was going to pursue politics. What are your views and was it something you were surprised about when you heard about his treatment of women?**

Barbara Outland Baker: Well, as I explained going on Fox News network when all this came out, Arnold is certainly no saint. He has loved women his whole life. Certainly in my time, he had a more open morality about what constituted fidelity, the need to have it. So I knew that Arnold really had reached out to plenty of women in his life, and I watched his flirtation even when I was with him thinking, *That was really inappropriate, why did you do that?* But on the other hand, these women would reach out to him. They would expose their breasts to him. They would go offer their bodies to him. It's incredible, even way back in the 1970s, what women were capable of doing. So, I think he got so used to women being like that. He's got two perspectives: on the one hand, he completely respects a woman who is worthy of his respect. But on the other hand, if you're going to put yourself in to being just raw meat for him, he's going to treat you like raw meat. And sometimes he's going to miscalculate, and he's going to treat somebody poorly who should've been respected.

There was just a big mismatch that he said the wrong thing to the wrong women at the wrong time, and he went too far. But I don't think he's 100 percent to blame for it because the women had fed him this all his life and also exploited him. So, I don't know, he got himself into a really big mess. But nothing stuck; he sort of was tough throughout the whole deal and escaped. I think there were a few little lawsuits, but I think they went away, really, nothing stuck while he was the governor of California that really mattered to his reputation. Since that time, when I even asked him during the interview, he replied, "We've learned! We've learned!" I thought to myself, *We've learned?* How interesting to phrase it in that way. He and his committee decided that Arnold better keep his mouth shut and not be flirtatious around other women.

**Q: Of course eventually his marriage broke down. He had everything a man could want, but made a big mistake that cost him.**

Barbara Outland Baker: I think we always have a flaw that we need to work on. You can call it a male flaw. Arnold's flaw was his sex drive. He made a horrendous mistake. You don't go to the maid, who is living in your home, who Maria knows dearly just because of convenience. So it was just too big of a mistake. How can a wife forgive something like that? I mean, she knows this housekeeper. You just have to wonder how he could've rationally made that decision. I think when you're that wealthy, famous and powerful, you lift yourself out of the normal human beings and you really think you're never going to get caught. But finally he really got caught in a really big way! Yet, I don't think he fell far; he picked up the pieces. And as I understand, he loves his child from the housekeeper and I think he cared for the housekeeper.

**Q: Do you feel he had the chance of him becoming the president had the lovechild story not hit the headlines?**

Barbara Outland Baker: See, I stopped when he said to me that he would become the governor. I said, "Nope, there's no way." I think running for president would have been a much harder platform. He would really have been exposed. I mean, the American process of being the president is long and look how nasty it is. I don't even know if it's a function of money, who knows. Politics is a strange game and a lot of people grew to not appreciate Arnold as the governor of California. So, I'm not really so sure he would have got Californian votes, either, let alone the whole of the country. They were more conservative in the Midwest. And snobs on the East Coast, would they ever have embraced a bodybuilder and actor?

I really don't think he would have become the president. He was so fortunate to become the governor. If he did, if by any rare chance that he did become the president, then that would have been surreal to me. I would've thought to myself, *My past boyfriend of six years is now the president of the United States.* How do I comprehend that? What am I supposed to do with that? Because already he's such a legacy in my life to live with and sometimes I tell people about our history together. And with great surprise people say, "Really, are you serious?" and I say, "Somebody had to be his first meaningful girlfriend. I just happened to be that person."

**Q: Finally, what would be your most enduring memories of Arnold during the time you spent with him?**
Barbara Outland Baker: Instantly, I had the picture of us meeting his nephew for the first time, just a poignant bond that developed. That was like the birth of his fraternal feelings when he met Patrick, who was probably two years old. So, just seeing his tenderness, that was a surprise because I didn't know that he had that side. I don't know him as a father. I've not met his children, but I have to believe, even though he's known to be strict, he's probably incredibly tender, funny and really, really a good father.

# JAMES LORIMER

James Lorimer is one of Arnold's closest friends – a friendship that can be traced back for more than four decades – and one of his key business partners. Lorimer, who early on in his career served as an FBI agent, is still the promoter of the annual Arnold Classic.

**Q: You and Arnold joined forces back in the 1970s. Can you tell me how you got involved and how the friendship ensued?**
James Lorimer: In 1970, I was promoting the World Weightlifting Championships here in Columbus, Ohio. And in connection with the World Weightlifting Championships, I obtained television coverage from Wide World of Sports programing here in the United States. I knew I wanted to have an addition to the World Weightlifting Championships – a Mr. World contest. So, I promoted the Mr. World contest that year because it was going to be the first time bodybuilding and weightlifting were on international TV, right here in Columbus in 1970. So, as I put the contest together, I identified the top six bodybuilders in the world. Among them were, of course, Sergio Oliva, Franco Columbu, one was a new young Austrian who had just come over to the United States.

And I called Arnold and told him that this was going to be on a national TV program. He said he understood the importance of that and he very much wanted to be there. The event was in September of 1970. He said that the day before your event – Mr. World contest – is going to be the day before on Saturday, and I'm scheduled and I've made a commitment to participate in the Mr. Universe event in London, England. He said I don't know how I can make your event on Sunday. I said, "Well, if you compete in the Mr. Universe contest on Saturday evening, and go directly to Heathrow airport right after the competition and get the last flight out of London for the United States, we will meet you by private plane in New York City and bring you to Columbus and you can compete here." He said, "Well, if you will do that, I'll do that."

So, in September 1970 he won the Mr. Universe competition in London on Saturday evening. Then he got the plane and we picked him up in New York and he came here and competed in front of four thousand people, in connection with the World Weightlifting Championship and the Mr. World contest. He beat Sergio Oliva that evening on our stage for the first time. After the contest, he came up to me and said, "This is the best competition I have ever been in. When I compete and I'm done competing in the sport of bodybuilding, I want to go into the promotion side of the sport, and raise the energy of the sport up and professionalize the sport making it a great sport worldwide." He said, "I'm going to come back to Columbus, Ohio, and ask you to be my partner." I said, sure. I didn't know who he was, really. So, the next five years he won everything. He won the Olympia every year.

And in 1975, he won his last Olympia, as you may know, and he stopped by on his way back from South Africa in '75. And he said, "As I told you five years ago, I'm done competing now and I want to go in the promotion of the sport. The next year we'll hold the Mr. Olympia here in Columbus, Ohio, in 1976. And if you will help run the competition, I will help get the athletes and help get the sponsors. And we're going to raise the cash prizes." He was still only making $1,000 in cash prize when he won in South Africa. He said, "The first year, we'll raise our cash prizes up to $10,000," ten times whatever was being made. And he said, "In three years, we're going to have it up to $100,000 in cash prizes for the athletes." We shook hands and thirty-five years later now, on a handshake, we're still partners. We did everything we said we'd do. The first year we had ten thousand, and three years later we had a hundred thousand in cash prizes. We've expanded over the years, as you know, we're giving $500,000 in cash prizes, still promoting together all of these thirty-five years later.

**Q: Can you tell me what the core concept of the Arnold Classic is?**
James Lorimer: Absolutely. We ran the Mr. Olympia contest for several years very successfully, and then the Weiders suggested that

they wanted to run the Mr. Olympia contest in Europe. So we then began running the Mr. Universe contest. And during the 1980s, we ran several international contests in Europe, but then in 1988 Arnold said, "Really, we've been running the Olympia contest and some years we've been running the Mr. Universe. I think we should have a contest which carries my name – the Arnold Classic." So in 1989, we ran the first Arnold Classic. The reason for that was, again, a title that was his, nobody could take it away. And every year since 1989. This will be our twenty-third year that we have ran the Arnold Classic, raising the cash prizes up every year.

In the early 1990s, while Arnold was the chairman of the United States President's Council of Physical Fitness of Sports, and I was on that council with him, and at the time we began to get more opportunities to work with a number of other sports like martial arts, gymnastics and the like. So in the early 1990s, we began to expand the Arnold Classic weekend to include other sports in the weekend. Each year we've added some different sports. So, now twenty years later we have the largest multisport event that we know of anywhere, which involves athletes from seventy-one nations competing, eighteen thousand athletes competing in forty-four different sports and events. Olympic Games in Vancouver usually had six thousand athletes competing in about eighteen events. We had a hundred and seventy-five thousand people who attend the weekend, plus booths involving seven hundred booths with exhibitors around the world. So it's a huge, huge event. But it's become a huge event because each year we've added new events in a twenty-year period.

Driven by an immense desire to succeed and an unparalleled determination, Arnold cultivated a no-lose attitude. He put his entire mind and focus into fulfilling his ambitions. Arnold once said, "When I used to do seminars on how to become a champion, I would always ask people, 'Why do you want to be a champion? Or, 'What do you want to accomplish? Or, 'Why are you training?'"

Arnold has always had a blueprint for success in life regardless of what endeavor. He added, "And if a guy would get up and he said, 'Well, I want to train because I think that if I get muscular and I feel like I'm getting the definition, then maybe I can enter a bodybuilding competition,' I said, 'Sit down. If you think this way, you're going to be a loser. You're never going to make it because there's no 'maybe'." A person should say to himself with great conviction that he wants to be a champion, Arnold believes, and do whatever it takes to reach that goal. The amount of hours it takes, the visualization and research looking at training footage and immersing oneself fully. "'I'm looking at motivational books, reading this and reading that. Whatever it takes, I would do it.' That's the answer I want to hear from you.'"

**Q: What was Arnold's vision, ultimate vision of achieving goals promoting bodybuilding and fitness?**
James Lorimer: Well, the original vision, of course, was to do everything we could to enhance and professionalize the sport of bodybuilding, which is his first love. And, of course, as he moved through his career, he's become very much involved, always involved and committed to bodybuilding. At the same time, acknowledging the fact the whole physical culture movement involving many sports is very important in our society. We have great problems with child obesity and the like. So his vision has gone from the focus on bodybuilding to a focus on the entire sports community. How do we bring more opportunity and more fun for youngsters to compete in a wide range of sports? Because there's a sport there for everyone. One of the Olympic sports we have in our program is archery. We have thirteen hundred archers come into the Arnold Classic. Archery is, you know, an Olympic sport and so is fencing, gymnastics, weightlifting. And all the Olympic sports that we have in the program. We focus very much on the Olympic sports now, but also other sports like cheerleading and the like, which add to the opportunity to participate and

compete. It's a combination of all the sports, adding a sports festival feeling to the weekend.

In 2011, at the Arnold Classic, Arnold expressed his admiration for mixed martial arts (MMA), a sport that has now enjoyed immense success and has become part of the annual expo with many stars and companies promoting themselves in Columbus. "I just love to watch the fights," the bodybuilding legend told a reporter. "I think they're very entertaining, and you get a kind of a combination of things. You get inspiration because they're in extraordinary shape. It's entertaining because it's fighting. It's just like basic stuff, just like the gladiator days. They don't have as many restricted rules, which I think people enjoy." These modern-day gladiators have great personalities and are intelligent athletes, Arnold added. "They can explain what they've done, why they won, why they lost. It's also very important." Arnold believes the UFC is very organized. Moreover, it's sport and show business. Impressed by the new brutal bone-crushing sport, Arnold believes the relatively new combat sport has caught the imagination of the new generation. He told the reporter that he watched every one of the fights. In 2000 Arnold had approached Relson Gracie to start the Arnold-Gracie World Submission Championships at the expo. Many years later, he presented the greatest icon the sport of MMA has ever produced, Royce Gracie, with a Lifetime Achievement Award.

**Q: What is Arnold's role in attending the event?**
James Lorimer: For the past thirty-five years, Arnold has been here every year without fail. He makes a tremendous contribution to the weekend and advice throughout the year, especially on that weekend. Because I told you about all the different competitors we have and the booths we have at the expo, and he has a full weekend of moving around. He goes to every competitor site. He goes to all of our major sponsors' booths at the expo. He participates in the

award ceremonies and recognitions throughout the weekend. We give twelve college scholarships on the weekend. He participates in the awarding of the college scholarships in various sports. So he's very much involved, has very much output and is very much committed to the sports festival.

**Q: As a business partner and a close friend, what is the most intriguing conversation you've ever had with Arnold?**
James Lorimer: I think one of the most interesting things about Arnold and myself, an interview I had with a *Time* magazine writer a few years ago. She called, like you did, and interviewed me for quite a while. The last question she asked was, "What is the one thing that distinguishes Arnold Schwarzenegger from anybody you've ever known?" And I said, "I feel it's his capacity for enjoyment." I said, "Everything he does, he seems to enjoy. And that's not just from a humanistic standpoint necessarily, but it's just from a pure joy sense. And if he doesn't enjoy something, he isn't likely to do it very long, that's for sure." So, after that conversation with that writer, I called Arnold and told him what she had asked me, and he said, "Well, that's interesting." He said, "Because if she asked me one word that I would use to describe myself, it would be 'joy'." Here is a guy who defines himself in terms of joy. And that's part of his charisma, that's part of what comes through to people. Here is a man who is enjoying life to the fullest. And it speaks to us! We all can relate to a person who is feeling that way about life.

Just recently I called him, and I said, "Arnold, I Google you every day, and in the political environment it's so nasty. They are always coming after you." I said, "How are you feeling about that?" He said, "I'm loving every minute of it. I'm enjoying every minute of it. The challenges are so great, so fantastic. I feel I have an opportunity to give expression to everything I've learned. And I'm doing the best possible job I can. But the opportunity to give everything I have to a mission is very, very rewarding, very, very enjoyable to me." Again, if I was standing in what would normally be a very, very troublesome environment for a person . . . I think it's an attitude toward life, an attitude of mind and the attitude of joy that distinguishes Arnold to anybody else. That's also, to respond to your question, a very interesting conversation with me about Arnold how he sees himself.

"To me. it's fun to have a movie come out and make $500 million worldwide," says Arnold. "It's not fun to get beat up by some creature, or be in *Predator* and freeze my butt off. I think in general, what I do with my life, everything that I do I have fun, or otherwise I don't do it." Arnold said that every movie that he made he had some fun, which doesn't mean that he avoids danger. In early 2011, Arnold told a prominent magazine, "I can only operate to the utmost and to 100 percent of my potential if I have no safety net. Because it's only then that I'm at my peak. That's one reason I never did a TV show. I didn't want to have that security." Arnold translated this approach to his political ambitions. "What I liked about being governor was never knowing how a meeting would end," he said. "The legislative leaders could leave and destroy you to the press. Or they go out and compliment you. So you don't know." He understood part of the unpredictability of people. One year something may be embraced, the next year it's number seven on their priority list. "That brings excitement and spice to life," Arnold said. "And that, to me, is the difference between living and existing."

**Q: Arnold is also known for being a facetious person.**
James Lorimer: He's a part of a joyful atmosphere and joyful attitude that he has. He's always good with a line to come up with in respects to any situation. He's always fairly critical of himself. He can make fun of himself. And a lot of his humor really has a political pitch to it. But I can think of so many humorous things that would be really significant in the political environment in the United States. When Arnold was the chairman of the President's Council for Physical Fitness and Sports, I traveled with him quite

a bit. He went to every state in the United States and met with the governors and educational leaders, telling them his message about fitness. I remember one time, when I was in his own jet when we went to Washington DC. He was going back to California, and I asked him, "Would you mind dropping me off in Columbus because you're flying over Columbus?" He said, "From how high?" I was at Arnold's and Maria's wedding and I gave the reading on behalf of Arnold's side of the family. Ted Kennedy gave the reading from Maria's side. Arnold said he selected me to be the reader because I was the only one of his friends who could read.

**Q: How would you describe him as a family man, irrespective of the mistakes he's made, away from the public eye?**
James Lorimer: He's a tremendous father, caring dad, very much involved in his youngsters' life. Of course, he and Maria have been very protective of their family, which is important in the political environment. But he is absolutely a great father. And the family did things together, went skiing together and sailing and did just about everything. It was a great family. There's two girls and two boys (born to Maria), and that's a good size family with a lot of caring and a lot of sharing.

**Q: His movie star status propelled the sport of bodybuilding into a much more mainstream arena. What are your thoughts on this?**
James Lorimer: There's no question about it, he's the most iconic figure that ever competed in the sport of bodybuilding. He's always identified in the public mind as a man who came out of the bodybuilding culture, so that has been a tremendous help to our sport, giving it legitimacy. A man who could go on to be one of the top movie stars in the world, and still go on further from his bodybuilding background to become governor of the largest state in the United States. That shows quite a bit about the fact, the discipline and training and the experience in his early career of bodybuilding certainly did nothing but help him. And he got into one of the great fields in which he attained a high level of achievement.

**Q: When he initially became famous, winning all the coveted titles in bodybuilding, did he talk to you about pursuing even bigger things which went beyond the confines of his beloved sport, which may have been imperceptible for some?**

James Lorimer: You have to understand that Arnold was a goal setter, and he consciously sets goals five years out. That's, of course, one thing that distinguishes him from other people, too, because a lot of us just go along. But he says setting a goal gives him a track to run on. He knows where he wants to go. He knew that he wanted to go in the movie field. He bridged over from the bodybuilding, starting off with bodybuilding-related movies then going more over to the straight action films. But I also knew very early on he found a great and abiding interest in politics. And in the long run, he was going to go into the political field. So, he also makes his plans and he's moved from one pathway to the other with a goal in mind, always.

**Q: Arnold has also been involved in charitable ventures, would you care to elucidate on these?**

James Lorimer: He's involved in a number of charities. Of course, he established his own charity called The After-School All-Star Charity, which is in thirteen major cities in the United States. It's aimed at children in the inner cities. They have periods from 3 p.m. to 6 p.m. every day after school, giving them places to go and activities to participate in. This is a major, major charity of his. Of course, the Special Olympics, which the Shriver family has been involved in for many years, is another major attraction for him which is aimed at disadvantaged young people throughout the world. He's traveled worldwide in support of the Special Olympic program.

**Q: Can you explicate, from the perspective of a close friend and a business partner, how you perceive Arnold as an entrepreneur?**

James Lorimer: He proved very early on, because of his discipline and training, that he is an extremely successful businessman. He owns a great deal of real estate. He's had heavy, heavy investments.

Because of his success in the film industry, he was able to invest in real estate. And he is positioned financially so that he wouldn't have to work again. He's got the income. The fact of the matter is: he's been like that for some time. All the time he was the governor, there was a salary that went with that job – about two hundred thousand a year – but he never accepted any salary in the seven years he was the governor. So, he's economically independent because of the great business judgment he used earlier in his career building on his film advantage. So, it's a beautiful business partner to have.

He's trying to do a lot of good now. He's not necessarily motivated by money. Arnold is the best possible friend you could have. His attitude shows you what kind of a man he is. On a handshake over thirty-five years ago, we still have that partnership over thirty-five years later. We've been part of each other's lives for all those years. I've been there for every major thing that has happened to him. And he comes into Columbus, Ohio, for all our events, several of our birthdays and activities like that. So, from a close personal friend you could not have a better friend over a lifetime than Arnold, and I've been very blessed and very fortunate to have that friendship to enjoy. I'm encouraging him to continue to be involved in the world of physical culture and sports promotion, opportunities for that to move forward worldwide.

# JOE LEWIS

Joe Lewis, a training partner of the late Bruce Lee, reigned as the U.S. Nationals karate grand champion from 1966–1969, and is commonly regarded as one of the greatest karate fighters in history. The former actor and fitness aficionado met Arnold in the late 1960s. Later, both men were in the same acting class in Los Angeles. Lewis died in 2012.

**Q: Joe, did you come into contact with Arnold for the first time back in the late 1960s or early 1970s?**
Joe Lewis: I met him in the first year he came to this country. He came here in 1968. I met him right in the end of 1968. He was living with a buddy of his, Franco Columbu. Joe Weider had brought him over to this country to pose for the magazine. And he was paying him to live here. They told me that all he had to do was work one day a month for Joe Weider. They were to take pictures and it was kind of nice. Arnold was going to college. They lived in a little apartment. Arnold slept on the top bunk and Franco slept on the bottom bunk. They just had two really nice bodies. I walked with them to their place one day after they finished the workout. The first thing they did is that they ordered a pizza to eat. Junk food! You know, when you're training so hard you can eat anything you want.

Years later, in the mid-1970s, he actually joined my acting class in Hollywood. Eric Morris was the acting coach. He was more of a loner; he didn't really hang out with the guys so to speak. He was kind of like me – I didn't like hanging out with guys, either. People didn't think he was real friendly. It could've been the fact he needed to learn the language. He probably went through the same nonsense that I did in the film industry: if you want to do a movie, you better get rid of those big muscles. You've got to get rid of the accent – because that's what they did to me. Then the kid named Jean Claude Van Damme and Arnold came along and said, "Well, you can have the muscles and you can have an accent and it doesn't matter. You can still do the movies." But that wasn't how it was when I went through Hollywood. Bruce Lee had the same problem. They said, "No Chinese guy is going to be taken on by any major studio to become a big film star." So he had to go to Hong Kong to get started. Arnold was lucky.

**Q: What was Arnold like in the acting class and did he possess an austere style?**
Joe Lewis: The classes that he and I were in met once a week. I was taking private lessons on the side because you get a lot of extra knowledge that you can pick up from the coach. He was studying what they call 'method acting'. It's the most difficult form of acting. It's more for, like, stage than it is for preparing you for the actual film. For some reason, I don't know how he got involved in the class. I don't know who recommended him to go there. But he had a persona, an image and reputation, which he can use rather than a lot of that acting preparation stuff and go right into doing films. He was like kind of Clint Eastwood, Charles Bronson and John Wayne. They weren't what we would call 'character actors' like Lawrence Olivier and Robert De Niro. While actors such as Arnold and Clint Eastwood are what we call 'personality actors', they play themselves on screen. If you watch their roles, they're the exact same character. And the only thing that changes is the plot, the wardrobe and the storyline. So, Arnold became what we call a 'personality actor'. And what's interesting is, personality actors actually make more money than the real authentic character actors.

**Q: Did he relate his ambition in class, as far as what he wanted to pursue and achieve in the movie industry?**
Joe Lewis: No. You're not allowed to do that in class. No one cares that much about what you're doing professionally, whether you're doing commercials or you're on stage or you're doing films or television. There are some famous people in class, for example, but nobody really cares. So, you don't talk about those things. In class it's a hundred percent you're there to train, and it's all about training. An acting class has nothing to do with getting you jobs,

or send you up to be hired to do a movie, or anything like that. So nobody talks about that stuff. You'll have famous people in class. Sometimes you'll have a famous writer or producer or a director come by and visit the class because, especially people who are casting, they're always looking for new talent. I don't know how Arnold got discovered outside of that. He did that *Pumping Iron* film and he did that real low-budget film *Hercules in New York*. That just kind of catapulted him into the big time. But, you know, a lot of actors are poor. Back then in the early 1970s, Arnold was doing really well with his mail order. He was doing mail order bodybuilding stuff. I heard he was making at least $300,000 a year, even way back then. Of course, now he's worth millions of dollars.

**Q: You had an interest in weight training and bodybuilding, was there ever any inclination to talk about this subject?**
Joe Lewis: I would talk to the guys who competed in the Mr. Olympia contest, or the Arnold Classic. They would tell me, if you don't do steroids you're never going to be a world-class bodybuilder – they all do steroids. That's kind of interesting, because they keep that hush, hush. Then if you talk to the experts, they say if you train hard and you're dedicated then anybody can become a champion. That's not true. World-class bodybuilding, world-class powerlifting, in my opinion, is 97 percent genetics. For example, if you're not born with long muscles, you're never going to be a world-class bodybuilder – you've got to have long muscles. Number two, if you're going to be a world-class arm wrestler, then you've got to have the long tendons, the large thick tendons, what they call 'the bicep tendons'. For example, my bicep tendons are an inch thick. That's incredible. When I had my muscles measured by some physicist at the University of California, they told me that my muscles were two-and-a-half times as dense as the current Mr. America. That's kind of important.

It's no secret that Arnold has publicly admitted to using performance-enhancing anabolic steroids, when it was legal to do so. Sergio Oliva told Brian Johnston in an interview: "I don't care who wants to take steroids because that's a personal choice. That's his life. Now, today, everyone has them. I even saw in one of the big magazines that Arnold denies having used them, but Arnold was one of the first to bring steroids over to America." Oliva conceded he himself resorted to steroids and that everybody in the past used them: Zane; Columbu; Arnold; Larry Scott; Harold Poole; Dave Draper and even Steve Reeves. "There's no way to deny it," he added.

Arnold conceded that he used them for muscle maintenance when cutting up; not for muscle growth. They aided him in maintaining size, he explains, while he was on a strict diet when preparing for a bodybuilding competition. Once the talk show host David Letterman asked Arnold on air, "If you had to do it again, would you use steroids, do you think?" To which he replied, "No. I think that drugs, the name already says 'bodybuilding', you know. This means you build your body and that you build your health and you want to stay away from any kind of drugs. And I always tell people on seminars, you must create the body without the steroids, without the drugs. No matter what it is, if it is acting or anything else, drugs are temporary." When asked whether he could have achieved the same results without steroids, Arnold replied, "Absolutely, oh, yeah. It would take maybe an extra half year or a year. But it's such a small percentage you get." And then when you stop taking steroids, your body soon goes back to normal. It really is just a temporary thing and it doesn't pay off in the end, Arnold said. In those days, you could go to a physician and merely say you wanted to gain some weight and take something. And the physician would advise the athlete to take the steroids for six weeks before the competition, and this would be safe. The dosage taken by bodybuilders back in those days in comparison to what is taken now was less than 10 percent some have claimed.

**Q: Did you spend time socializing with Arnold in the early days, when he was settling in and competing in the sport?**

Joe Lewis: We had a mutual friend who brought us together. I don't know if anyone really socialized with him. I got along much better with Franco Columbu. Dave Draper and I were pretty good buddies. He did that *Don't Make Waves* movie. I think he beat Arnold in a physique contest early, just like Frank Zane beat Arnold when Arnold first came over here because Arnold had that big bulky body that was very popular in Europe, but that wasn't very popular in this country back in '68, '69, '70. Arnold was kind of a unique figure. He was a man's man. But he wasn't necessarily somebody you could befriend easily because he was kind of a loner. He was always working. I remember he talked about how he only slept for four hours at night, and that that was the only sleep he needed to get. And that means you're up twenty hours every day. You could get a lot done if you're up twenty hours working every day. There's not that many people that have that kind of pace. So he was kind of like a unique person that's just very different than all other men.

**Q: Were you surprised when he became a big movie star? He wasn't exactly the best actor in the pure sense of the word, but he became the biggest box office draw?**

Joe Lewis: No, but John Wayne wasn't, either. Bruce Lee wasn't, either. But that's not what makes money on the big screen; it's your persona. It's that ability on the screen and the presence and the energy that you project which affects people emotionally. And they've not been affected by how good an actor you are. So, there was something that they could identify with him when they watched him on the screen, and that was the special energy which made him a big star. I was shocked!! Because first of all, his accent was very strong. I'm thinking, *What kind of role could you get?* You can only get the roles where you need that accent. And then it's kind of hard to put him on the screen because when you're in front of the camera, you always look 20–25 pounds bigger than in real life. I'm thinking, *How are you going to get any roles unless you play a role of some kind of a bodybuilder?* So, he kind of changed Hollywood in a way. He made Hollywood his world.


One may ask if it ever was suggested to Arnold to change the name Schwarzenegger when he pursued a serious career in Hollywood. According to Arnold, a lot of things were suggested to him to polish him up – from changing his name, to changing his body and changing his accent. He told an interviewer this when promoting his 1985 high-octane movie *Commando*. When he made the transition from bodybuilding to the motion picture industry, the industry fraternity felt that those obstacles were going to be an impediment. The experts felt that it would hold him back from ever becoming a major player in the movie business, and achieve the status he had achieved in bodybuilding. "But I felt that, you know, if anybody could pronounce Gina Lollobrigida and all those kinds of names, I felt they can also pronounce Schwarzenegger," remarked Arnold. The ambitious actor said he had no special interest in getting rid of his accent, remarking that if you were born somewhere outside of America then it was almost inevitable to have somewhat of an accent. As for the physique, Arnold affirmed that eventually people would comprehend that his body would be fashionable enough and appealing enough that it would be considered an asset rather than being an impediment. It, of course, became the norm and almost a necessity to have a well-developed physique in order to play a heroic role in the action genre – first in the 1980s and then again more recently. Indeed, Arnold was aware there was a natural pressure to conform even in Hollywood, to do things the way they had been done before. However, he always felt the only way you make an impact is by being unique and break that barrier by doing things in your own unique way. If people had followed the flock by changing their name, maybe he should be different. If everybody had gotten to the top with a perfect American accent, maybe he should be the exception and be the first one who didn't. His determination and drive to succeed at all costs was apparent right from the start.

**Q: How much of a motivated individual was Arnold? A lot of people say he had an immense level of motivation, and he just wanted to be a big movie star rather than the best actor?**

Joe Lewis: It's true, it's true. He wanted to go beyond bodybuilding. When I met him, he was going to college every night to study economics and business, because he knew that's where the money was. That was his real passion. Then when he became the governor of California, they had bankruptcy problems in that state. But he was real good with finances and money and marketing, and that's an asset a lot of politicians don't have. Most politicians come from law school. They don't teach you how to motivate people. They don't teach you how to run a business in law school. So, he was unique and different in that respect. I don't know what his real passion is now. I'm kind of curious.

I was talking to his wife on an airplane – we sat together – about four years ago. What was interesting is we talked about him about the acting class with Eric Morris. But I was kind of curious as to what next Arnold would do when he left the office. Will he really go back to acting? Does he really want to go back there, or is he just going to retire? He's a businessman, he owns a lot of property in the Santa Monica area, California – that's part of Los Angeles right on the beach. I heard rumors that he's worth close to $600 million. I don't know if that's true or not. I think his real accomplishment in life is, that all the young people he motivated around the world, not so much with the movie acting, but with his bodybuilding accomplishments. For example, I get guys saying, "You were my idol when I was a kid thirty years ago." I get that all the time. So I know he's getting at least ten times more than I am.

**Q: Did you bump into him at the height of his movie career, and did you see any change in the man you first knew?**

Joe Lewis: Yeah. I'd see him and say, "Hey, how you doing, Arnold." One time, I met him at the Arnold Classic bodybuilding contest. He was sitting with Joe Weider, and his wife and Weider's wife. I just walked up to him and I just said, because his two daughters were taking karate lessons with an instructor I knew, "How are your kids?" You talk about the little stuff. You don't talk about making movies. You don't talk about bodybuilding. None of that stuff is important. You know, when you've done it all it's no longer of any importance. You just talk about personal things. He became, in my opinion, humbler than he was back in the late 1960s when I first bumped into him.

**Q: You, of course, knew and trained with one of the greatest icons of the century, Bruce Lee. Did you ever talk to Arnold about Bruce and share your experiences?**
Joe Lewis: When I met Bruce Lee, he wasn't that much into the bodybuilders and Arnold wasn't that famous. I was with Bruce Lee from 1967. Arnold didn't get really known till he beat Sergio Oliva in the Mr. Olympia contest in 1970. So my thing with Bruce Lee did not come up. I mean, Bruce Lee has a lot of fans who are famous people. Today, for example, Mike Tyson thought a lot of Bruce Lee. Klitschko brothers, the famous world champion boxers, think a lot of Bruce Lee. Famous basketball player in this country – probably the best basketball player in the world – Kobe Bryant was a Bruce Lee fan. So it's kind of odd talking to Bruce Lee about other famous people when he was going to become probably more famous than they were.

**Q: What kind of an acting student was Arnold, was he a fast learner and did he blend into the class quite well?**
Joe Lewis: No, because in bodybuilding you're taught to insulate your emotions. In an acting class, he was going to . . . One of the key things to work on is to get you to open up emotionally – they want to see you cry. They want to see you look embarrassed. They want you to be humiliated. And they want you to show that – don't insulate that from the outside world because to be an actor you must be able to show all those colors of the rainbow. And that's very difficult for a fighter, and it's very difficult for a bodybuilder. Because

in my opinion, a lot of the bodybuilders, all that muscle around the body, to me it's insulation. It insulates emotionally mostly from the outside world. So one of the reasons he was in the class was to break that barrier. The more appealing you are emotionally the more interesting you're going to appear on the screen. You don't want to see a person on the screen who's one-dimensional from the beginning of the movie to the end. His voice never changes. There's no fluctuation in his emotion. There's no fluctuation in his voice. There's no fluctuation in his attitude. People who are uptight and afraid to show their emotions, they're not going to make it on the screen. So, I thought Arnold was smart that he went to a class, which was designed to teach you to open up that way and to show those emotions. That's what method acting is all about.

**Q: Did you two talk and see each other often?**
Joe Lewis: I had my friends when we met, and he had his friends. So it's not like I was looking for a new friend, and he wasn't looking for a new friend. Little things. I remember once when we walked into a magazine office. It was called *Inside Kung Fu*. And he saw me on the cover of the magazine. And he told the publishers, "Hey, that guy's got a good body." Little things like that. There wasn't a lasting relationship; we were more acquaintances and not really what I would call 'friends'. So, if I bumped into him today, I'll say, "Hey, Arnold, how's it going? You were supposed to give me a Lifetime Achievement Award a couple of years ago." They forgot to call me up onstage when he was up there presenting awards, and that kind of peed me off a little bit. But I would never bring that up to him and say, "Hey, Arnold, remember you were supposed to give me an award?" He doesn't know what awards he's supposed to pass out. The promoter doesn't tell him.

And wherever he goes around now, it was kind of hard to be around him because he was married to Maria Shriver, who is part of the Kennedy family. Everywhere she went, she had two Secret Service agents with her. Now I think she's free of the Secret Service. But when Arnold became the governor, you've got a Kennedy with two Secret Service and you've got a governor of a state with Secret Service. So wherever he went, there was an entourage of six or more people around him at all times. So it's kind of, you can't just walk up and say, "Hey, Arnold, how's it going, old buddy?" You have to realize that. Then you've got all the hangers-on, photographers and the news reporters, and they get first contact because the promoter wants to use Arnold to make money. And to make money, he's got to do a quick interview here and a quick interview there and then move on. Times have changed.

I remember seeing Sylvester Stallone at the Arnold Classic a couple of years ago. He's pumped himself up with weights, and everybody thinks he's done steroids, but that's no one's business. Arnold had a crowd of people. Wherever he went there was twenty people around him, like bees around a flower or something. And I'm thinking, *Would you really want to live like that?* Because if you've got to go to the bathroom to take a leak, you'd say, "Hey, you guys mind waiting here? I'm going to go in by myself." When you're sitting out eating, you want to eat in peace at an event. You don't want twenty fans walking up to you trying to shake your hand. How many germs are you going to pick up putting your hand in this guy and putting your hand back on the food? So, there's a certain kind of space that you want to grant celebrities.

When I see Arnold or somebody – I know Jack Nicholson – I'm not going to approach him. I'll make eye contact and he'll make eye contact with me. I know Lou Ferrigno, who worked with Chuck Norris at one time, and I'd say, "Hey, how's it going?" If Lou saw me walking in the hallway, he'll say, "Hey, how's it going, Joe?" If I see him at a contest and he's sitting behind a booth and he's signing autographs – twenty bucks an autograph – I'm not going to walk up to him and say, "Hey, how's it going, Lou?" Because he's got two or three guards who'd say, "Hey, get in line." So I'll look at Lou and he'll look at me. I'll wink at him, he'll wink at me. And it will be, "Hey, I'll see you next year." That's just the way it is. Probably the same thing with Arnold. To me, it's like: hey, I just want to go out in public, do my job, come home and turn the TV on. Not have an over-long conversation just because they are a celebrity.

**Q: Did you train Arnold in martial arts, and can you relate any conversations you both had pertaining to the martial arts?**
Joe Lewis: No. He did an article in *Black Belt* magazine about six or seven years ago. In the very first paragraph, he said that he trained with me and Chuck Norris. Now, I don't know if he said that for real or the magazine just says he said that. But I gave Jim Lorimer, who was his partner, the magazine and said to him, "How about having Arnold sign this for me?" Jim threw the magazine away. So, when I saw Arnold that night, the night before, I'm backstage at the Arnold Classic and Arnold's entourage come walking in backstage. As soon as Arnold sees me, there's about a hundred and fifty people and I'm back there with Bill Wallace. Arnold yells out to everybody, "Joe Lewis!! Joe Lewis!! Champion of champions!!" He makes a scene straight away. I know why he's doing that: to make everybody jealous. But that's three decades of friendship. It goes way back.

So the next day, I asked his partner to have that magazine signed. I don't get autographs, but I thought it's kind of neat he's used my name in there. If he wants to tell people he trained with me, let him say that, you know. I don't know if he's got any martial arts training outside of films, besides who taught him to work that sword for the *Conan* movie. Now, he must have some interest in martial arts because he and Maria had their two kids taking karate lessons. And he felt that was kind of neat because that's something I've talked to him about. You have to keep in mind that, how much time does he have to take lessons and learn how to move a sword, or take lessons on how to throw a kick? I mean, if you look at pictures of him, he probably doesn't have time to work out anymore.

## ERIC MORRIS

One of the most prominent acting coaches in Hollywood, Eric Morris' clients have included Jack Nicholson, Johnny Depp and Arnold Schwarzenegger, who he first worked with on the latter's role in *Stay Hungry*. He lives in California.

**Q: Can you tell me how and when Arnold came to you for acting lessons?**
Eric Morris: Jack Nicholson recommended me to Bob Rafelson, who was directing a movie called *Stay Hungry* with Sally Field and Jeff Bridges. Bob Rafelson called me. He was going to cast Arnold. You know, it was about Mr. Olympia. It took place in the South. He told me that Arnold had not done any movies except that documentary *Pumping Iron* and would I work with him. I said, "Well, how long do I have?" He said, "About twelve weeks." I said, "That's a very short time to work with somebody and teach them my system, my work." He said, "Well, you come very highly recommended to me, so would you at least meet with him?" I said, "Of course!"

So I met with Arnold and we hit it off. We got along very well from the beginning, and we worked for about nine weeks together. I found out all about his life, about certain things that he could use as choices, etc, etc. Then he went to Alabama to shoot the film. He did very well and he won the Golden Globe Award for the Promising Newcomer. Bob Rafelson called me from Birmingham very early morning once. It was five o' clock here, but eight o' clock there. He apologized because he'd forgotten what time it was here. He said, "I thought I'd call you and tell you Arnold's doing really well. And I'm very grateful to you, Eric, for the work you've done with him. He's incredible." So, that's how it started.

After he finished this film, he began to work with me in my classes for about a year or nine months. After that he kind of went out. I guess the rest is kind of history. But he was with me for eight or nine months in class. And I worked with him privately. Recently, a couple of years ago, he called me and asked me if I'd work with his daughter, who wants to be an actress. She wanted to work on weekends, but I don't teach on weekends. So that never worked out. But I told him I finished my book *The Diary of a Special Experiencer*. And he said, "I want to write the foreword." I said, "Arnold, you're the governor of California, do you have time to do that?" He said, "Send me some information and I'll write something. I want to do it!" So he did. The last book that's in publication, he wrote the foreword to.

**Q: What was he like in the acting classes? Did he earnestly pursue coaching and what was your impression of him?**
Eric Morris: Well, you know, he was very committed. He was very good and we did a lot of stuff. He was very vulnerable in some of the exercises, and he did a scene or two in class. I really always believed Arnold was very talented. He chose to do action and adventure films. If he wanted to do serious dramatic films, he could. First of all, I think he's the smartest human being that I have ever met in terms of intellect. He has a mind like a steel trap. He took to the work very well. And then he visited my class after he had been out of it for a while. He said, "I love the work you do, Eric. But the kind of work I want to do, I really want to do action and adventure. I'm an athlete and I want to do those kinds of films." So, I wished him well and he went ahead and created a career in that area. I don't see him very often, certainly, after he became the governor. But I am in touch with him in terms of I know how to reach him if I need to talk to him or something like that.

**Q: Arnold seemingly was looking for adoration through fame. Can you recall some of the dreams and goals he related to you pertinent to making it in the movie industry?**
Eric Morris: He wanted to do action and adventure films. He came to me one night and watched a class. He said he liked the work I did, but the kind of work he wanted to do was physical. I wrote him a letter once. I guess it was a documentary; somebody

introduced me to a documentary. I said, you know, if Arnold wanted to play Hamlet, he could do it. I mean, with an accent or no accent. He certainly could fulfill emotion. He wrote me a letter saying, "Well, Eric, I'm a little too old for Hamlet, but if I ever do Macbeth then you can come and coach me on that. "I think that was very humorous. He's got a great sense of humor. His career was mostly about action and adventure (films). I had the feeling that after he is released from the governor's office, he might return to acting. I thought he won't return as an action and adventure hero. I thought he would probably want to do serious work. He told me once, when we were having coffee in Cafe Roma in Beverly Hills, he said the kind of acting he wants to do is character acting, like the actor Armin Mueller-Stahl. He's a German actor. He said I'd like to do scenes like that. And I thought if he goes back to acting, he'd probably do much more serious and meaningful and dramatic types of work. He's capable of it.

**Q: Did Arnold ever give you the impression that he admired any particular actors? He expressed that he admired Clint Eastwood and Sean Connery.**

Eric Morris: The only thing I could tell you about that is that he never mentioned any of those people to me. He did say that, as he got older and matriculated out of the action and adventure, he'd like to do characters like Armin Mueller-Stahl, the German actor. He did the movie *Music Box* with Jessica Lange. He's a very good actor, a character actor. He's much older than Arnold, but I think Arnold kind of admired his work. But he never mentioned Clint Eastwood, or any of those people to me.

Even though Arnold didn't let on to his acting coach, he had long admired Clint Eastwood well before he moved to America, and he hoped one day that he would have a career just like his hero. "First of all, you have to understand that Clint Eastwood was, like, my inspiration," Arnold later told interviewers. "I remember when I first came to this country, there was, like, John Wayne, Clint Eastwood and Kirk Douglas. There were two, three guys like that that I really admired and I wanted to have a career like them. And Clint was one of those guys that I always thought – even from the Westerns he had done before *Dirty Harry* – I want to be like him." Arnold wanted to model his career on Eastwood and do his kind of movies. His hero had already left an indelible impact on Arnold and was the motivating force for the Austrian to come to America with a long-term goal being Hollywood after triumphing in bodybuilding.

**Q: What advice did you impart on him in your role as the acting coach?**

Eric Morris: After working with him, I told him he was capable of doing really serious, meaningful work. When he came and watched a class and said that he had decided to do action and adventure work, and that he was very physical, I encouraged him to do that. That's the direction he went into. When I had coffee with him in Beverly Hills at Cafe Roma, he did say that he would like to do more serious and dramatic work later in his career. That was before he became governor. I thought when he leaves the governor's office I don't know what he's going to do – whether he's going to continue with politics or not. If he returned to acting, I thought he would return as a serious actor, serious dramatic character actor. That's what I thought. And I hope if he did that I can work with him. He was very effective in class.

**Q: Do you think he is the epitome of the American Dream?**

Eric Morris: Are you kidding! He came to this country without any money in his pocket, and he's become a multi-millionaire and a super movie star. Are you kidding, the epitome of the American Dream? I would like to have a dream like that. I'm pretty successful, you know, but that's some American Dream.

Arnold received the 1,847th star on Hollywood's Walk of Fame on 2 June 1987. "Well, I think this is the first time a Schwarzenegger has been on the Hollywood Boulevard represented on a star," Arnold told a reporter. "It was like a dream of mine. When I first came to Hollywood, I walked up and down Hollywood Boulevard and I saw all those stars. And I said, 'God, this must be incredible, to be forever on Hollywood Boulevard.' Well, for those young girls and guys that have dreams, it just shows to you that dreams can become a reality. Set a goal, believe in it and go for it."

Many celebrities go through a phase of wanting to be left alone when they are hounded by fans and the media. They lose their privacy and start to complain. "That is movie star bullshit, loss of privacy," Arnold told James Cameron's biographer Christopher Heard, several years before moving into politics. Arnold says that all actors want the public to see their movies, and it's the public that allows the stars to make a good living. "Every actor dreams of being successful, dreams of being famous," he added. "One goes with the other in this business. So to say, once you get what you dreamed of, that you wish people would leave you alone is fucking bullshit. If no one wanted to see you, or nobody was suddenly curious about you, then you would no longer have a fucking career and you would be back to saying, 'I wish people would ask for me again.' Any actor that wants his privacy back should stop making movies and move to a cabin in the fucking mountains."

**Q: Can you tell me about the more social side to your relationship with Arnold?**
Eric Morris: Actually, he sent me a couple of people to work with. I had dinner at one time and we talked. And I talked on the telephone a couple of times. And he volunteered to do the foreword to my book, and he did. I talked to him and his secretary when he asked me to participate in a couple of documentaries. I can't remember if he asked me or they (producers) asked me, but I did participate in two or three documentaries on Arnold. Then there were a couple

of other ones, one from England. So, I appeared in three or four documentaries on Arnold and talked about him in those.

**Q: Once in class, Arnold complained that no one liked his accent. Can you elucidate on this and tell me exactly why he was disconcerted on that particular day?**

Eric Morris: He came in one night very angry. I saw him sitting there and I could tell he was angry. So I got him up onstage, and I said, "What's going on, Arnold?" He said – in his accent – he had just had a very disappointing interview with an agent. This was before he did one of his action and adventure movies. He said, "I'm pissed off! They don't like my accent. They don't like my body. They don't like . . ." I forget what else he said. He said, "To hell with them! I'm going to be a superstar." And everybody laughed and applauded him. Then he did an exercise in class where he recreated a Christmas morning in Austria. He was playing with some of his toys and he became very vulnerable, it brought tears to the eyes of everybody in the class. He was recreating a Christmas morning when he was a child in Graz, Austria. It was so effective that it brought tears to everybody's eyes in the class. Arnold is a great man, he's a good guy. If he loves you or he likes you, he'll do anything for you.

**Q: What would you say were Arnold's attributes and vulnerabilities, plus points and minus points, when you were teaching him the craft of acting?**

Eric Morris: He was very receptive. He was very bright and he understood the work immediately. He's a very sensitive man, you know. He plays all these action picture heroes where he kills people and all of that, but, you know, Arnold is a very, very sensitive man. He's a very loving man. I don't know that a lot of people know that. He's a very, very deep, sensitive, caring human being and I love him. I would still say that if he wasn't a movie star and he wasn't the governor. As a man and as a person, I love him.

## SVEN-OLE THORSEN

Originally from Denmark, Thorsen won Denmark's Strongest Man in 1983 before moving to LA. He played the hammer-wielding Thorgrim in *Conan the Barbarian*, and went on to be credited in fifteen Arnold Schwarzenegger movies – twelve as actor, three as stuntman or trainer – making him Schwarzenegger's most frequent collaborator. He's one of Schwarzenegger's closest friends.

**Q: Before you immigrated to America, how did you meet Arnold and become close friends with him?**
Sven-Ole Thorsen: In 1978, a cinema owner in Denmark who owned a theater told me that she had invited Arnold Schwarzenegger for the premier of *Pumping Iron*, and asked if I would go into business with her and pay half of the cost. And I said, "Of course." In those days, I had started a gym, which still exists in Copenhagen. And later, she came back to me and said that it was too expensive to invite him. I said, "Let me pay the expenses." Then when he came to Copenhagen, we picked him up in a 1926 Rolls-Royce. We gave him a tour of Denmark. Then he disappeared – last ten minutes of the movie. Outside they had two double-decker London busses to bring all our guests to downtown Copenhagen. We had ladies onboard the busses dressed in t-shirts, which read 'Arnold is Numero Uno', which were the t-shirts from *Pumping Iron*. And we served champagne. In my gym, we had set up three hundred chairs for the press. He came and he gave a great speech and a great seminar.

Back then the sport of bodybuilding only existed in Denmark in two or three gyms, but then it exploded. I started off the Danish Bodybuilding Federation in 1979, and when I stopped in 1981 we had many gyms in the federation. So by his visit, he actually created the foundation for the sport of bodybuilding, and we became friends. The same year, I went with Arnold skiing in Austria. And then I went to Los Angeles for some martial arts championships I was involved with. And Arnold and I went to a meeting with John Peters, who was writing *Conan the Barbarian*. In those days,

I was kind of a big guy. I was 330 pounds. So when John saw me, he asked for me to give him a famous Viking name for his picture, *Conan the Barbarian*. I said Thorgrim. So, the next year I got a phone call from John. He wanted to hire me and take me to Spain to play Thorgrim in *Conan the Barbarian*. He also asked me to bring nine other Danes.

So in 1980, I went to Spain for seven months with my friends from Denmark, all champions in track and field, weightlifting, powerlifting, boxing and martial arts, and we worked seven months in Spain. That created a relationship, which led to the second *Conan* picture, which we did in Mexico for six months. Then for the third *Conan* picture, *Red Sonja*, we spent four months in Rome. So, when I immigrated and came here five years later in 1985, I'd done three American pictures whilst still living in Denmark. The only person I knew in Hollywood was Arnold. So I called him and he invited me to come and play a part when he was shooting *Commando*. I arrived in 1985 as the Strongest Man in the World. I was quite huge. I was 340 pounds.

So Joel Silver, the producer of *Commando*, invited me to work on *Commando* for three months for $22,000. But I had to be a member of the Screen Actors Guild. From then on I was in the business. Actually, I came here for the sunshine; not really for the movie business. But when I wrote my memoir, *Viking in Hollywood*, I realized that in twenty-six years I have done over a hundred movies and TV shows. When we did *Conan the Barbarian* in Spain in 1980, which lasted seven months, the last days of the show Arnold said to us that his dream one day was to become the president of the United States. That's what he said in 1980.

*Conan the Barbarian* producer Dino De Laurentiis left his native Italy to pursue a Hollywood career in the mid-1970s. Several years after settling into the Mecca of movie-making the producer along with Edward R. Pressman – also a producer of *Conan* – signed Arnold to a three-picture deal. For the first film, Arnold would be paid $250,000, and the same for the sequel. The action-adventure movie turned into a big hit and the producers sold the sequel rights. Subsequently Arnold was able to negotiate an attractive salary for the sequels. *Conan the Barbarian* set the stage for the bodybuilder-turned-actor to eventually become one of the biggest and highest paid movie stars in cinema and an international icon. Arnold's path to his role in *Conan* was anything but smooth. His agent had first arranged a meeting with the Italian producer hoping his client would be cast in *Flash Gordon*, a part which would later go to Sam Jones. Both men arrived at De Laurentiis' office in Beverly Hills to discuss the project with great anticipation where, to his surprise, Arnold saw a diminutive man sitting behind a large desk. Somewhat naively, Arnold blurted out, "Why does such a tiny guy like you need such a big desk?" The producer, incensed by the remark, shouted in his thick Italian accent, "You have-a dah accent! You cannot-ah be in-ah *Flash Gordon*!" and had him thrown out of the office. Arnold's agent was furious with his client. He had spent several months setting up this meeting, which was an opportunity for Arnold to crack Hollywood, but it took under two minutes for Arnold to blow this. Outside the agent furiously told his client, "Schwarzenegger, you idiot! Mark my words, Arnold, you will never amount to anything!"

After this initial mishap and disastrous first meeting, Arnold eventually did get signed up by the Italian who flew to London to meet and sign up the director Ridley Scott. However, the British director told the Italian producer that he was interested in collaborating with the producer, but he was adamant that the producer find someone else to play Conan. Scott wanted to work with an 'actor', not merely a huge muscleman with limited experience. As we know, John Milius ended up directing – and finally, Arnold had the part.

The studio invested in the film quite heavily. *Conan the Barbarian* cost $17 million to produce at the time, which was big-budget for an action adventure fantasy film. It grossed around $70 million worldwide. Once the movie was released John Milius didn't hesitate to praise his actor, "If I had movie stars, veteran actors with inflated egos, they never would have done what my people did. Arnold's a great man. He's very disciplined – the closest thing to Conan in real life. He has built his own character and career just like Conan did." According to the director Arnold was willing to work endlessly, training with a sword master, the physical conditioning to keep his body in great shape, the horseback riding, and, of course, practicing his dialog. Apart from the work that was needed to polish his acting skills, Arnold often found romantic scenes onerous to film. "The love-making scenes, they were very, very difficult," he explains. "It's so strange when you're used to doing these things within the privacy of your own four walls, and then all of a sudden here we are naked with a hundred and twenty horny Spanish guys breathing down our necks. And we're not even sure who they want to get a look at – Sandahl or me."

The movie received ambivalent reviews from critics. Vincent Canby wrote, "*Conan the Barbarian* is an extremely long, frequently incoherent, ineptly staged adventure fantasy set in a prehistoric past. One has the impression that it cost a lot of money, though not all of it is on the screen. One is never unaware that one is watching a lot of extras trot around Spain wearing goat hair, jogging shorts and horns on their hats. *Conan the Barbarian* contains plenty of ambitious scenes – episodes of magical transformations, battles in which skulls are split if not lopped off – but it's not engaging even on a primitive level."

The weekly entertainment-trade magazine *Variety* described the movie in its December 1981 issue, "Director John Milius does a nice job of setting up the initial story. There is a real anticipation as Schwarzenegger is unveiled as the Barbarian and sets off on the road to independence. But for whatever reasons, the actor has a minimum of dialog and fails to convey much about the character through his actions." Either because or in spite of Arnold's acting performance, the sword-and-sandal action flick triumphed at the box office. What was apparent was that he had improved hugely from his first film, *Hercules in New York* – and he now had success to build on. Arnold has stated that he knew the movie was going to do really well when it was screened. But it was beyond anything he expected. "I've never been wrong yet with my instincts," he explained. "And they tell me this is going to be a really big film, a whole new phenomenon." Equipped with determination and an unparalleled thirst for being embraced by millions beyond the confines of the bodybuilding arena, he was willing to do what it took to achieve his goal. And if he had to dedicate a whole year out of his life focusing solely on this new project, he would dedicate himself completely to the cause.

**Q: After Arnold immigrated to America, his subsequent investments, mainly real estate, enhanced his reputation for shrewdness. Did Arnold already have properties and restaurants when you moved to America?**

Sven-Ole Thorsen: During the 1980s, Arnold started to buy the whole building there. We created together a Cigar Night, which took place the first Monday of the month. We had people who came over for dinner and we traded cigars, which became extremely popular. Some movie stars, movie directors and producers were standing in line to get into this intimate kind of cigar event. He worked with a gentleman in town and they owned a lot of real estate on Main Street in Santa Monica. They had several properties there. Also, he built his own office in his own building on Main Street where he also had a restaurant called Schatzi on Main. He recently sold that building for, I think, $40 million or something.

**Q: Can we talk about *Red Heat*, Sven? You have a fight scene in the snow with Arnold. Can you tell me more about working on the film with Arnold?**

Sven-Ole Thorsen: Absolutely. *Red Heat* was a movie where all the interior stuff was shot in Hungary. And most of the exterior shots, for the snow and stuff, were shot in Moscow and Austria. So, in the opening sequence we are in Hungary, the interior shots in the sauna with all the naked women, we have a fight and fly out of the window. But then all the snow scenes, after jumping through the window, were shot in Austria because there was no snow in Hungary. So it was shot in two sequences. The interior in Hungary and the rolling down and fighting in the snow was all done in Austria. And the sad part was that it was so cold there, so our stunt coordinator, Bennie Dobbins, who was a close friend of Arnold and me, unfortunately died because it was so cold. In the movie you see there's a special credit for Bennie Dobbins. That particular day, we stopped filming and Arnold and I took a walk smoking a cigar. And actually, Arnold and I cried with tears because of Bennie Dobbins' death because he had been trying to protect us from freezing in the snow. By doing that he had a heart attack.

**Q: Can you tell me about choreographing the fight scenes with Arnold? And what was the cast and crew like on this movie, were their elements of melancholy or was there always high spirits pervading?**
Sven-Ole Thorsen: First of all, Arnold liked to work with me because I never hurt him. We had sword fights in the Conan pictures, and later on different fights in different movies, so we coordinated our stunts and fights pretty well. I didn't have a stunt double because I'm playing myself. It worked out pretty well. When there's a big crew that goes to another country, three or four hundred people, it's like a military operation. So, when you come to Budapest with all those people, later in Austria, it's like an army coming. The whole army. At the same time, it's like a traveling circus. So three, four hundred people are like one big family. Very often in situations like big movies, it's not so much based on people's talent – which is good to have, a hairdresser or a makeup person or an actor or stuntman – but it's all about how you are to be with socially.

Because very often when you work together with people for seven, eight months you need to have good chemistry. So talent is very often secondary, whilst social behavior is more important because you have to work with people, very intimate, different countries, living in hotels. So, if there's too much bad chemistry it influences the production of the movie. When you're hired to do a job, you do it! When we did *Red Heat*, every morning at four o' clock it was wakeup time. It was winter time. We went to a gym which was in a basement. We had gloves to work out with. Then we start work at six o' clock in the morning. So the discipline you have from being an athlete is going to make you a good team player on the movie. Because they can count on you, you're there on time, you're prepared, you are willing to go all the way and you don't mind doing it again and again and again. So discipline is a big factor.

**Q: You played a security man in Arnold's *The Running Man*, how did you get this part? What was it like to work onset with Arnold on this movie?**

Sven-Ole Thorsen: One day I was called in to meet the director. And there was another man who was a bad guy. He had had a fight with Muhammad Ali. He's a tough guy, very tough guy. I'm sure if you investigate his name, you'll see his resume. Anyhow, now the director says to me, "OK, you guys go ahead and start threatening each other." The other guy was more experienced than I was. He really put his face in my face and was spitting on his lips. He chewed my ass! I was so shocked I was almost speechless. So, finally after threatening me with all kind of verbal attacks, my reaction was, "If you touch me you're dead." And based on that, I was hired to play the part in *The Running Man*. That was my casting. It was a little unusual way of getting a job. He put two guys up against each other and wanted to see who is the toughest, and according to him I was the toughest because I stayed calm. He didn't know I was shocked and he liked my reaction. Strange way of casting people, but that was the director's choice.

First of all, everybody in town likes to work with Arnold because he pays attention to every employer who is working on the movie. Meaning, if one of the grips has a birthday there's a birthday cake, there's a birthday gift, there's a speech from Arnold and there's a song. So the crew and the cast, they really love Arnold because he's a team player. He's very considerate, has a great sense of humor and makes it fun to make movies. It's always fun because of his personality. He's a very charming gentleman and very easy to work with. He never complains about eighteen-hour days, or never complains about being cold, never complains about being uncomfortable.

He actually told me once that what he loves the most in life is to work on a movie because there is a call sheet every day that showed you what to do that particular day. He likes that. He likes to be told what to do without thinking. So, every day you get a call sheet telling you what to do. He's very easy to work with. He's probably the best guy to work with because I've worked with Sean Connery, Mel Gibson, Steven Seagal. I mean, all the big stars I've worked with, Clint Eastwood, Chuck Norris, Jean Claude Van Damme as well.

*The Running Man* was directed by Paul Michael Glazer (*Starsky and Hutch*), and produced by Keith Barish, who would later team up with Arnold on the Planet Hollywood chain. Arnold had read the novel by Steven King and liked the concept. Arnold said, "I think it's a great, great concept." And he was very happy with the fact someone picked up on it and had written a script to make it into a motion picture. When Arnold read the novel, he said to himself, *I hope someone is going to make a film because I would like to play Ben Richards.* And two years later, it was brought to his attention that it was going to be made into a film. Arnold was very delighted that he would be playing the role. Sven was one of the few friends Arnold looked after by having him in most of his movies playing bit parts. However, another former bodybuilding friend and training partner says, "As he grew in the film business, he gained new friends and some of the old ones were set on the sidelines. He gave his roommate Franco a small part in *The Terminator*, but that was it. As far as using any of us as actors, it never happened for some reason."

**Q: You worked with Jean Claude Van Damme on *Hard Target*. Did Arnold and Van Damme ever have plans to work together on film projects?**

Sven-Ole Thorsen: When we did *Predator* in Mexico, Joe Silver, the producer, had hired Jean Claude Van Damme to play in a blue outfit playing the monster. They photographed it in the blue suit, and upside down and stuff, so later on the CGI can put the monster, the alien, in *Predator*. But Jean Claude Van Damme had claustrophobia. So after a week of work, he was whining and complaining. So Joel Silver fired him and promised him he would never work in town. Then a year later, he became a star himself. Very skilled martial arts guy with a lot of talent. But there was never any thought of him and Arnold working together. Then later on, Jean Claude Van Damme had his own career.

**Q: Being involved in the Hollywood motion picture industry and being a close friend of Arnold's, what's the first premier you went to with Arnold?**

Sven-Ole Thorsen: Actually, it was in Copenhagen for *Conan the Barbarian* in 1982. And as you know, he was charming and the press liked him. I can't remember in detail. I think that was the only movie I went with him for the premiere, actually. There is a very interesting story I would like to share with you. I worked for a couple of weeks on the movie called *Twins*. I'm on the screen for maybe only thirty seconds. But as an actor, member of the Screen Actors Guild, you get residuals. So, next year I got a residual check from *Twins*. I got $15,000 and I was so proud of that. So, when Arnold was visiting me for a cup of coffee a couple of days later, in my little apartment, I said, "Hey, can you believe it? Thank you very much for having me in *Twins* because, look, I got a check for $15,000." He said, "Great." Then he said, "I never see my residual checks, but I think I remember one. I think it was from *Twins* and I think it was either $14 million or $15 million." For *Twins* Arnold made about $17 million based on residual. The movie made five hundred million worldwide. I have made, since that movie, I probably made $400,000 in residuals.

**Q: *Twins* was the first movie where Arnold was paired with his co-star Danny DeVito. Both men pulled it off and Arnold really was able to show the humorous side to his character, which wasn't intrinsic to this movie alone because he continued to make comedies. Can you expound on this side to Arnold which he portrayed in this movie?**

Sven-Ole Thorsen: Arnold has a great sense of humor and he loves to pull practical jokes on people. And all those years I worked with him, I always pulled practical jokes on Arnold. And for him now to actually be himself, in *Twins* he was more like himself, more than any other movie. He was very relaxed and very much himself. Because when he is himself, he's an extremely funny guy who loves practical jokes. That's probably one of the reasons why he likes me because if people are too serious, they take themselves too seriously. I'm there to put a practical joke on them in a second. They had a great relationship, they laughed a lot. Danny DeVito is probably one of the most skilled actors in town. Everybody likes to work with Danny DeVito because he's very professional and he's also very sweet and very funny. But I can't recall any particular situation for the moment.

**Q: Arnold cultivated a penchant for Hummer jeeps, can you expound on the story where you went car shopping with him once?**

Sven-Ole Thorsen: When we did *The Running Man*, we filmed a lot of the times at night in Fontana steel mill. Most of the shooting for *The Running Man* was at night, so during the day him and I went to different car dealers who were selling Porsches because he wanted to get a Porsche for the right deal. After visiting for three months maybe fifteen, twenty different Porsche dealers, I said to Arnold, "This is ridiculous, why don't you call Porsche in Germany and have them make an 'Arnold Porsche' for you?" He said, "Sven, you don't understand. I want to deserve it when I buy something. I can buy an airplane. I can buy a yacht. I can buy an island. But I want to feel when I buy something that I deserve it."

Now, he was doing *The Running Man* for four months and hustling and visiting car dealers. When he finally found a deal, which was to his liking, he probably saved $5,000. He felt he deserved to give himself a car. So he's not a guy who just buys stuff, you know. Once he said to me some years ago, "Sven, there are so many millionaires in town, but there's not too many billionaires. And I'm actually a billionaire." I said, "Good for you." Also he uses phrases from his past like he wants to stay hungry. Meaning, even though he could buy anything he likes, he feels he has to do some work before he gives himself a gift, like a car or whatever – a very healthy way of thinking.

**Q: Arnold also enjoys motorcycles. You often, along with Arnold's other close friend, Franco Columbu, enjoyed riding with Arnold.**

Sven-Ole Thorsen: When we did *Raw Deal*, in the movie there's four motorcycles. And Arnold's riding a Harley-Davidson in *Raw Deal*, which was shot in North Carolina. After the movie was done, one day he called me and Franco to his home and he gave us one motorcycle each – Harley-Davidson, which both were used in *Raw Deal*. After that he had several hours of enjoyment on Sundays riding the bikes off to a place in Santa Monica Mountains called Rock Cafe, where thousands of people are on Harley-Davidsons who are meeting on a Sunday to hang for a cup of coffee and gossip and stuff. So we had a lot of pleasure riding the motorcycles.

**Q: Arnold had a motorcycle accident in 2001. Do you feel because of his bodybuilding it helped him to recover more rapidly?**

Sven-Ole Thorsen: The thing is, if you're physical, if you're an athlete, if you have an accident you kind of roll yourself out of it. You know kind of how to fall and react. Him being an athlete, it probably saved his life a couple of times when he had accidents, yes.

**Q: Arnold put on parties, what celebrities and people attended these house parties? And what would be one of the most significant anecdotes you remember?**

Sven-Ole Thorsen: July 30, 2010, it was his sixty-third birthday and I was invited. There was a big crowd. There were sixty people. And in his speech, he told the people there who were at the party. Most of the people who have been with him from the beginning, me and Franco, also his heroes Clint Eastwood and Sylvester Stallone, and, of course, people from his office in Sacramento, so the people at that particular party were people who have been around him since he came over here. I worked with Clint in a movie called *Pink Cadillac*. So, when you kind of hang with those kind of people, who are superstars, they actually act like normal people. They have the same needs of being complimented, of being loved, so there's no difference between a person who is a superstar and a normal person. They're just average people who have a kind of an unusual job. They're all very nice people, very highly educated and low-keyed. There's no star stuff there. You talk to them like you talk to normal people.

And that's one of my advantages of being a Dane – Danes are not easily impressed. I mean, if you see the Queen going somewhere in Copenhagen, it's no big deal. So for me, the only time I was impressed by meeting a so-called celebrity was many years ago – 1988 or '89. There was a fundraiser for a Californian politician. Ronald Reagan was supposed to be there, so I was invited there. Three months ahead, I had to give my passport to the Secret Service. Then before the fundraiser, there was a little get-together in the VIP room. There were about twenty-five security people and maybe twenty guests. Arnold and I were standing there side by side. Then Ronald Reagan came up with Nancy. He talked to Arnold about his wedding, and then Arnold introduced me. When I shook Ronald Reagan's hand, I said to him, "My name is Sven and I'm from Denmark. It's a great honor to meet you because I'm a big admirer of you and your country." Then Ronald Reagan said to me, "What do you want to do here?" I said, "I want to be an American."

He said, "Then you have no problem. I'm your friend and Arnold is our friend."

From then on when we went home in Arnold's limo, I was sitting there and got out my right hand. I said, "Arnold, you know what, thank you very much for allowing me to meet Ronald Reagan because I actually shook hands with a person who can decide if I can live here or not. I actually shook hands with the most powerful man in the world." So that was impressive. I said to Arnold, "I don't think I'm going to wash my hand for the next couple of days." It was really an experience for me to meet and shake hands with the most powerful man in the world, which is the president of the United States.

Arnold became a United States citizen on September 17, 1983, and has never stopped enthusing about the merits of his adopted country since. "I was born in Europe and I've traveled all over the world, and I can tell you there's no place, no country, more compassionate, more generous, more accepting, more welcoming than the United States of America," he proclaimed two decades later. "As long as I live, I will never forget the day, twenty-one years ago, when I raised my hand and I took the oath of citizenship. You know how proud I was? I walked around with the American flag around my shoulder all day long." At the Republican Convention in Madison Square Garden, Arnold explained, "In school when the teacher would talk about America, I would daydream about coming here. I would daydream about living here. I would sit there, watch for hours, watching American movies transfixed to my heroes like John Wayne. Everything about America seemed so big to me, so open, so possible. I finally arrived here in 1968. What a special day it was."

**Q: Did you often go shopping in Beverly Hills with Arnold?**
Sven-Ole Thorsen: There's a place in Beverly Hills called Cafe

Roma, which is owned by some Italians. And that's a place where I used to go to because it's very European, very relaxed and all kinds of people from the movie business come there. Then there's another place we go to smoke cigars called Havana Room. That's the only two places I go to in Beverly Hills. I'm not a guy who goes to Beverly Hills because it's kind of an unreal world with all the fashion shops, you know. It's not my kind of life. I'm kind of low-keyed. I don't go to so-called Hollywood parties or Beverly Hills arrangements – it's a different world. I never really participated in that. Even though people think if you live here, live in Hollywood, it's all rock and roll – which it's not. It's a lot of very hard work. And when you socialize in town, in Hollywood and Beverly Hills, it can take all your life. So you're more focused on being seen than actually working. So always try to avoid that kind of scene.

**Q: Can you tell me of the most thought-provoking conversation you and Arnold had?**
Sven-Ole Thorsen: I did *Dancing with the Stars*, and the week after I came out of my last surgery, which was for my right hip – in two years I've had six new joints put in my body, two new knees, two new hips and two new shoulders – I get a phone call. And Arnold says, "I'm in the neighborhood, may I come by for a cup of coffee?" I said, "Sure." So in my alley, there were two SUVs with eight security guards. Arnold came in and gave me a cigar and said, "Give me a call sheet, what's going on?" I told him, "I'm going to Denmark." He said, "Are you crazy? You've just had surgery." I said, "No, Arnold, this is a smart way of training. You have to train every day six, seven hours." He said, "You know, that's maybe a good idea."

So I said, "What is your call sheet now that the governor thing is over shortly?" I'll quote what he said, "Sven," still believing what he said in 1980, that he wanted to be the president of the United States, he said, "if I cannot be the president of the United States, or if I cannot be the secretary of state, I want to be 'Mr. Green' of the world because if I go up for a Nobel Prize, I want to have a Nobel Prize." I said, "Good for you." I thought that was the most intriguing thing I ever heard from Arnold. Even though it's impossible for him to be the president of the United States, based on the Constitution, he still believes he can be the president.

On his birthday party he's playing chess with Franco Columbu. And even though Arnold only has a king left, but Franco has a king, queen and a bishop and a couple of others, Arnold's still moving his king believing he could win. Stallone wants to say goodnight. He's standing there waiting to say goodnight, but Arnold's so focused and so occupied, still being able to beat Franco even though the odds were one-to-hundred. It just shows his strength that he never gives up and always believes in himself.

Another situation, actually, when we were in Mexico working on *Total Recall* – I also worked on *The Hunt for Red October* – I'm flying back from Mexico to Los Angeles and on one of the trips I'm flying with the producer of *Total Recall*, Andy Vajna, and also Arnold. Andy Vajna is now talking to Arnold about how he wants to do Arnold's next big *Terminator* picture. "What can I do to make it happen?" he keeps saying to Arnold. Arnold looks at me and says, "What do you think, Sven?" I said, "To start you can take over the fucking airplane we are flying in." Arnold looks at him and says, "What do you say to that?" Then there was a handshake and it was Arnold's airplane. And Andy was producing his second *Terminator* picture. It was kind of fantastic that my little crazy idea became a reality. It was one of a kind.

**Q: Hard work and persistence reflect the depth of Arnold's character, and his unparalleled desire to achieve the ultimate and reach heights which mere mortals can only dream of. Can you exemplify how he is able to thrive on achieving what he sets out to?**

Sven-Ole Thorsen: I think when he did the first *Conan* picture that really showed a great character there. I think that he had the most pleasure working on that picture because there is a lot of camaraderie. It was a long shoot. So, I think it's actually my favorite movie that I have worked on. And I also think that's Arnold's favorite movie, even though he hasn't said anything directly about which movie he liked the best himself. It's always interesting to work on a movie, very often you're on locations all over the world. An Arnold movie is a special movie because, as I said to you, they all become kind of family members. It's one big family. I mean, for example, they love Arnold because he gets on with the average Joe. He doesn't pretend to be a superstar – he's just a guy.

I always used to say that people like Arnold come around every thousand years. There's a certain person who has a higher call than anyone else. Because if he can say in 1980 in Spain that he would be the president of the United States, that's kind of an unrealistic thought. Also, for example, when he said to me one day, "I think I've found my wife." I said, "So, yeah?" He said, "I haven't met her yet. But I'm going to go after Maria Shriver because she's a Kennedy." I said, "Good for you." A couple of years later, he married Maria Shriver. I was one of the best men. When he does the opening sequence in *Conan the Barbarian* with the sword, he'd been training with Yamasaki with the sword, who was a sword expert in town, for over a year. So when he does that with the sword, it looks like a top professional.

When we did *Red Heat*, he was supposed to speak in a Russian accent. He had an Austrian accent. For a year he started to learn how to have a Russian accent. When he did one of the *Terminator* movies, where he hangs out on a truck with a shotgun and he used a six shooter, he practiced that in his backyard for six months. So when he does stuff he goes all the way. And he is able to focus a hundred percent and have tunnel vision. There's another skill he has, which is kind of unusual. Every time he has to go from one set to another set by a car, he power naps, even for five minutes or two minutes. That's one of his biggest skills.

Another example, when he became the governor I was flying with him to Sacramento and back to Los Angeles. When we got back to Los Angeles, I said to him, "Hey, look how big Los Angeles is. In reality, Arnold, now you are the governor, is that kind of a dream? I mean, now you're the kind of a king of a country. You're actually the leader and governor of one of the most important economies in the world, six or seven in the world. I mean, how do you feel?" He said, "Sven, I believe I have one talent only. That is, when I believe, it happens. I believe I can fix California's problems, and for that matter, United States of America's problems." Can you imagine a person can say that? He's one of a kind. Every thousand years, I believe a person is born with a higher purpose and he's one of them. He's not done yet, there's much more to come. I was at one of his speeches at his birthday party, where Maria said, "I know everybody here likes to ask Arnold what will he do after now not being a governor at the end of the year. That's why I love him. I never know what Arnold's going to do next." She said, "By the way, two days ago he told me we should have a birthday party." I got the invitation two days earlier. I never know what Arnold's going to do.

**Q: Any last words on your friend?**
Sven-Ole Thorsen: I think what I said earlier. I cannot come up with a better explanation, that I believe every thousand years there's a person born with higher purpose than the average person. And Arnold is one of them. Jesus was another one. And I really mean that. Even though I'm always the guy that kind of tries to make him humble, even though he is humble, but he speaks big words. And, again, every thousand years there's a person born for a higher purpose and Arnold is one of them. He's the kind of a guy whose charisma can't be explained, when he comes into the room he kind of takes over the room. That's one of his biggest assets – his charisma. I think that's something you're born with. I think he's one of those guys with the charisma which goes beyond what you can't explain.

# THREE

---

## FILM FRATERNITY

### MARK LESTER

Mark Lester directed *Commando* in 1985, the film that became an Arnold classic. Lester's credits include *Showdown in Little Tokyo*, which starred Dolph Lundgren and the late Brandon Lee. He's worked on many action pictures as a director, writer and producer.

**Q: How did the concept of *Commando* come to materialize, and how did Arnold come on board for this project?**
Mark Lester: There were two original writers, Mathew Weisman and Jeph Loeb, they're on the credits as associate producers, and they gave the script to Joel Silver. I met him at a party at the Playboy mansion. He said he had this great script. I said, "OK, let me read it." He said, "If you read it, you'll never do the movie. Let me just tell you the idea." So he pitched the whole idea to me. I said that sounds great and Schwarzenegger and I said we're in. So, then we hired Steve de Souza to write the script. It was pretty much different because it didn't have comedy in the original script. It didn't have the one-liners. So he wrote the draft and it was really well done. That's how it all started, preliminary first draft of the

script. He was brought in right after that. We went to the producer, who pitched the concept of the movie and told him the whole story with the writer. And then Arnold signed on right away after hearing the story. So, he was involved right from the beginning, from the whole script writing to the draft. He was involved from the beginning.

**Q: What was Arnold's personality like back then?**
Mark Lester: That was a thing, in the meeting he was a very fun guy, always telling and cracking jokes, very charming personality. But he hadn't been seen in movies yet, other than the *Conan* movies – and then he did *The Terminator*. And that's when I said that this character should just be like who you are – you should be cracking jokes and having fun and still be the commando. So it's kind of a cross between *Terminator* and James Bond kind of thing. That's what developed the screen personality, where he had this charm and humor, which went with the action.

**Q: How was Arnold to direct?**
Mark Lester: He was unbelievable to work with. He was like using a model. He followed instructions perfectly and he was extremely cooperative. He wanted to do all of his stunts, so he did all of his own stunts. There was one scene where he dresses up as a commando on the beach before going for the final attack. He had a knife fight. Because he was confident, we had to do it in close up. He even wanted to do that himself, but I tried to convince him not to. And that was the only time he got hurt. He really wanted to do everything – fighting to glass stunts. He was very excited and jumping. He was very exciting and cooperative. He had a lot of different ideas. One of the things people don't know about is, he wanted to pick up one of the guy's arm after he cut it off and slap him with his own arm. I think that went a little too far. But that was the only time we had a discussion about what not to do.

**Q: Were there obstacles in shooting the scene at the shopping mall?**

Mark Lester: We had to shoot it quickly because we had used it all night long when the doors were closed. So we had all the stores opened up and all the extras throughout the mall. But the interesting thing there is, when Arnold swings across the galleria there is no net. He swings across the elevator. So we hired a circus trapeze artist but he was so tiny and small. I said this is never going to match. He said don't worry, I'm going to swing moving so fast that no one will know it's me. That was done by a stunt double trapeze guy. That was the most concerning thing. He got up there and swung across and landed on the elevator perfectly. That was pretty amazing because there was no net or anything.

**Q: Can you tell me about Arnold socializing on the set and any intriguing anecdotes?**

Mark Lester: Nothing like that happened. People always call me, when he was running for governor, and ask, "Who did Arnold seduce on the set?" I said, "No one." Someone said, "The service girl said . . ."

**Q: What I meant was, how did Arnold socialize on the set?**

Mark Lester: Oh. He hung out with a lot of the bodybuilders that came. There was a trailer filled with weight equipment, and they all hung out and lifted weights between the takes. They were all smoking cigars with Arnold. It was a lot of fun. That's basically what he did between the scenes.

**Q: Can you shed light on some of the more intricate action scenes? There were a lot of machine guns firing and explosions.**

Mark Lester: We blew up three buildings. They had to be built on the beach. The Californian Environmental Laws, three days before we were to shoot the scene, wouldn't let us because it was the beach water ocean. So we had to find another place. We used a beach that was owned by Will Randolph Hearst, the old newspaper mogul in the 1930s. He owned a beach. So, we had to quickly go there – there were huge barracks on the beach – and make that major explosion. There was no CGI and animation in those days; we had to do it for real. We have Arnold running from the explosion near the building, and the explosion goes flying toward him and he has to dive for cover. This kind of stuff, you don't need to do anymore because they have CGI. But in the 1980s, it didn't exist. So we and Arnold had to make actual major explosions.

**Q: Were there any particular scenes that were an impediment to shoot?**
Mark Lester: There was a scene in the shed that was really hard – even though it was a small little scene, where he had to kill six people very quickly with garden tools. That was a hard scene to choreograph, getting all the timing to work with and kill so quickly with different tools in the shed. That's the scene that he wanted to pick up the arm and slap one of the soldiers. And the other scene, which was with the plane, was really difficult because we had to shoot it at the actual airport. In those days, when they used the airport to shoot they'd shut down the runway. So we had a plane out there, and Arnold had to get attached to the wheel. And we had a very complicated sequence with the airplane. Again, there was no CGI so we actually had to have this huge wheel apparatus brought up to the airport, which was attached to a truck. And then we had to run it down the runway. It was all very complicated. It would be easy if you put it against a green screen and put the airport behind it. Back then we had to actually do everything practically.

**Q: Did Arnold get involved in other aspects of the film beyond his role of an actor?**
Mark Lester: At that time, no. He basically concentrated on the acting. His haircut and his character, that became famous in the United States. In the 1980s, people wanted to cut their hair like Arnold's in the movie. That was more about the cut than makeup

of the hair. And in shooting, he wanted to make sure his body was right, the muscles flex a certain way. He was very meticulous about all those things.

**Q: He wasn't an actor, let's say, of the caliber of Jack Nicholson and some of these other actors. He was an action man. Did you encounter any problems pertaining to filming dialog scenes with him?**

Mark Lester: It was written for him. So I had to do it many, many times. It was mostly written with one-liners. There weren't a lot of long lines. It was written very much for him, so there weren't any issues like that.

**Q: *Commando* is one of the best action movies Arnold made, which imprinted his image on a generation of Americans. Do you feel this movie was the perfect vehicle to catapult Arnold into global stardom?**

Mark Lester: Yes, this was the vehicle. This launched his entire career because in *The Terminator* he just played a robot. This was the picture that launched him into the action movie career that he had. People could see he was really a very good actor as well. Then he did things like *Kindergarten Cop*, where he just played in comedy films. But from this movie, it launched him into *Total Recall* and all these big action films. Without *Commando*, I don't think he ever would have had as big a career as he did. We never had a premiere. The movie was finished a day before it hit the theaters. At the studio, we had a rough cut of the film and we had a big screening for the studio executives. They said the good news is we love the movie, but the bad news is we're moving the release date to November right away. So we only had forty-five days to finish the whole thing, edit the movie and do everything. So, I mean, literally the prints were done two days before it opened up in the theaters. There never was a premiere in the United States.

*Commando* was released on the big screen in October 1985 in America. Five months earlier, *Rambo: First Blood Part II* had been released, which went on to gross a staggering $300 million worldwide. *Commando*, on the other hand, with a budget of a meager $10 million, grossed $57.5 million globally. The marked difference from the box-office receipts made evident who held the number-one action star spot that year. When asked about how his film *Commando* differed from his nemesis' film, Arnold stated, "It's a different movie. Mine is a battleground right in Los Angeles. Stallone's battleground is Vietnam. His is a very politically oriented movie, and mine is not at all. Mine is humor oriented." Arnold stated that he didn't take himself too seriously in the film – he believed in comic relief.

Franco Columbu had trained Sylvester Stallone for *Rocky II*. The producers approached Columbu to ask him if he was willing to train Stallone and get him in shape for *Rambo*. Sly called Arnold's best friend and said that they had only seven weeks to get in shape. Columbu's biggest concern was the fact he would not have complete control over Stallone because the star loved to be the boss, and had an inclination to do things his own way. Columbu's main stipulation was that if he was going to work with Stallone, then he had to have total control as the trainer. He even went as far as drawing up a contract in which it was stipulated the actor was not to take anything without Columbu's approval – including steroids, but also vitamins and minerals. The bemused *Rocky* star looked at the contract and asked what all these stipulations were, but Columbu stood firm. He explained to his client that if you take steroids, you get pumped up but you don't get defined, hence the producers won't be impressed. Columbu proceeded to get his client in brutal shape and defined in the time frame by putting him through a vigorous training regime.

**Q: What was Joel Silver's relationship like with Arnold, and what were his sentiments on the finished movie?**
Mark Lester: Oh, he loved it. He loved the movie. I mean, he did

*Predator* later with Arnold. Everyone got along with Arnold. He was a great person to deal with. You'll have to ask Joe.

**Q: What do you remember the most when you look back at when you initially teamed up with Arnold?**
Mark Lester: The funny thing was the night before shooting we had dinner at the hotel before we went on the set the next morning. Arnold says to me, "I'm scared to death." I asked him why. "The first day of shooting, I'm always scared to death." I said, "So am I. Everybody is until we get the first shot, then we're OK." But I was kind of surprised to hear that. There were just two of us there. He became a big star. And I think he got more involved, that's what I hear, with different pictures with the technical aspects and production. And he had a lot more control of the various pictures than at the time, which was one of his first movies.

**Q: How would you define Arnold's *Commando* from a historical perspective in the genre?**
Mark Lester: *Commando* is considered as the finest action movie of the 1980s. Myself, I was always thinking at the time like John Ford who made all those Westerns. He didn't know those Westerns were classics. It's only years later they became classics. Now *Commando* plays almost every week in Los Angeles and on American Movie Classics. So, it's considered what everybody likes about the action movies of the 1980s. *Commando* is considered to be the major action movie of the 1980s, and in every magazine and so forth, and there's websites devoted to it on the internet. They're even making a remake at 20th Century Fox. It's considered as a classic action movie of the 1980s, and I'm proud to have done it. At the time, I didn't know I was making a classic; we were making an action movie. It's now that people consider that to be a landmark film.

**Q: After working on the movie with Arnold, did you continue to see him and stay in touch, or did the friendship dissolve?**
Mark Lester: We stayed friends, even to this day. He's a very nice

guy. He was busy as the governor, but I'm sure I'll see him again. We usually used to meet in his restaurant in Venice. I saw him with his wife at the Cannes Film Festival five, six years ago. And Maria and him, they told me *Commando* was their favorite movie that he made.

# BILL DUKE

Bill Duke, born in New York, is known for his physically imposing frame. He appeared with Arnold in *Predator* and *Commando*. Duke has appeared in many Hollywood movies, including *Sister Act II* and *Hoodlum*. He continues to act and direct.

**Q: You worked with Arnold on *Predator*, but also had worked with him prior to that.**
Bill Duke: I did a movie before that called *Commando*. Joel Silver was the producer on that. And we got along very well. Joel Silver did *Predator* also. The most impressive thing was that he (Arnold) was a professional. In other words, very gracious with no ego. It was, like, *Let's move forward, let's get the work done.* And as a result, the crew and cast were like that. He had a sense of humor and was a very good person. At that time, I think he had retired from the bodybuilding world and he was getting into the movie business. I think he was really beginning to move in as an actor. He was a good person, and a good collaborator and a professional.

**Q: Anything you would like to share about filming *Commando*?**
Bill Duke: When we have our fight scene, where I die in the movie, I told Arnold, "In real life I'd kick your butt." He said, "Yeah, but it's a movie and you get killed, so die!"

**Q: Can you tell me about filming *Predator* in Mexico, I believe the shoot was done under harsh conditions?**
Bill Duke: We filmed in Mexico and we filmed in Pacific Palisades. We had a great team of people, but when we were in the jungle, that part was not easy. For the first two weeks that we were there, they had netting around the place where the catering was, but still bugs got in our food. So we told the caterer that we refused to eat the food because there were bugs in it. And he said there was nothing he could do because we were in the jungle. By the end of the second week, we were eating the bugs and we caught something.

**Q: Did you have time to socialize with Arnold and was the hotel far from the location set?**

Bill Duke: Well, Arnold didn't socialize very much because he's very disciplined. He had to get up early with the other guys and be on the set, let's say 7 a.m. He and some of the other guys would get up at three or four o' clock in the morning, and they would go for a run for at least, I would say, an hour and a half. Then meet back and work out in the gym for two hours. And then they would eat breakfast and then go to the set. I couldn't do all that all the time because they were much more disciplined than me. But it was a real challenge. But they did that seven days a week.

**Q: What were some of the obstacles and extremities the cast and the crew had to endure when filming the movie?**

Bill Duke: Heat, humidity, spiders, scorpions, snakes, we had diarrhea – anything possible, we got! Because we were in the jungle. When we would go back to the hotel at night, everything was pretty much OK there. One day, something had broken down and we all got sick. It was a very difficult shoot.

**Q: In the past, Arnold has said it was a survival story and it was physically demanding. Can you define Arnold's professionalism? He's someone who never complained, his professional ethics set an example for everyone when working on _Predator_?**

Bill Duke: Arnold is a professional. Arnold is the kind of person, no matter what the problem is, he doesn't complain. He deals with it. And with his leadership, everybody did the same thing. In other words, he was the star of the show, but he had no better condition than anyone else. And after we go, everybody followed his lead because they had great respect for him, also because of his leadership. So we were all in the same kind of cage together. He didn't ask for special treatment. He didn't ask for anything. He simply did his job as an actor, and it was a very good example for the rest of the cast and crew.

**Q: In your opinion, what were the most demanding or stressful scenes to shoot which required maximum physical exertion?**
Bill Duke: Oh, yeah. Well, you know, the jungle affected us. When we were trapped in the jungle and blew everything up, we had to do that scene repeatedly. There was a lot of running up and down the hill in the sweltering weather, we had uniforms on. I mean, that was all real, the weather was one hundred degrees with humidity.

**Q: Was there a lot of hanging around in the jungle?**
Bill Duke: Everybody had a good time despite the obstacles, that's number one. But the main thing is: the irony of the conditions. In other words, we were playing these soldiers that were in this jungle situation, but our conditions were no better than the guys we were playing. In other words, snakes, scorpions, spiders, you know, it was, like, real. The conditions were so real.

**Q: John McTiernan directed *Predator*, who also later went on to work with Arnold on another movie.**
Bill Duke: John McTiernan is a good director. He was a wonderful guy. He did a great job I think. One thing that you might not know is that the Predator creature that you saw was not the original creature in the picture. The original creature was more adept and smaller. He had a suit where they could put green screen special effects. It was very hot and the humidity, and several times the person playing the creature actually passed out. The producer said if you pass out again I'm going to have to fire you. The name of that person was Jean Claude Van Damme.

John McTiernan believed Arnold had the potential to be another John Wayne. Prior to filming, McTiernan had been warned that he'd have to do over a hundred takes for certain scenes for Arnold to get things right. But they didn't do more than nine, and four of those takes were for camera problems and two for Arnold and another actor for breaking out laughing in takes. Prior to filming,

Arnold had lost over 25 pounds, which made him lean and better fit into the role of a special operative. Aside from the extreme conditions, the cast had their light-hearted moments to get them through the filming.

**Q: Would I be right in saying co-star Sonny Landham was unstable on the set, and as a result a bodyguard was hired to protect the cast and crew?**
Bill Duke: Sonny Landham is a great human being. He had trouble sleeping, so when he didn't sleep he would go up to the clubs. So they hired a bodyguard to watch him to make sure he didn't get into trouble or anything.

**Q: As far as conversing with Arnold, what do you remember that made an impression on you?**
Bill Duke: I'm into education and I have helped kids in education. I asked Arnold one time, I said, "If you were giving advice to young people for them never to give up on their dreams, what would you say?" He said, "Bill, very simple. Tell them to stay hungry." Arnold is a professional and money is not important to him. What's important to him is he does the best at what he does. I think his standards are excellent and got him to superstardom. Whether it's acting, whether it's producing, whether it's being a politician, whether it's being an entrepreneur, he has values and he wants to be the best at what he does. I think it's not competition outside of himself; it's an internal competition. He always wants to be the best at what he does. It's not your standards, it's his standards.

**Q: Did he talk to you about bodybuilding or working out? There were some big guys in the movie, notably Carl Weathers, Sonny Landham and you!**
Bill Duke: I was working out but those guys have a different standard. I mean, they worked out three, four hours a day! In other words, the workout ethics was three or four hours a day. The

average person works out an hour and a half. These guys worked out! I mean, hardcore working out.

**Q: Did Joel Silver frequent the set and what was his vision for this movie?**
Bill Duke: Joel came on the set all the time. He flew from the United States and came down to Mexico all the time. In the original script concept, it was written from an animal rights point of view. The original writer wanted the script that showed how people kill, how they hunt animals. He wanted people to know how animals felt being hunted. So they wanted it to be an animal doing the hunting. Now the man is being hunted and killed, like we hunt animals all the time. But we don't think of them anything but animals because we don't consider them as important. They wanted to make people feel how animals felt, and that's how the whole idea came about.

**Q: The movie did well when it was released. Would I be right in saying Arnold went to get married during filming (February 25, 1986) and the production was halted?**
Bill Duke: I don't think the production was halted, but he did go to get married. But we kept shooting. The premiere was wonderful. The people really, really loved the movie. It was a big major action film in the jungle and with the special effects. Some people hadn't really seen something like that, you know. It was really well-directed. And people like performances, so there's nothing negative that people responded to. Arnold was the kind of a person to take on the leadership role, not what he said but what he did. He never complained. He always was prepared. He didn't put down other actors. He was famous by then. He also was a human being. A lot of people in that situation don't have the great class or professionalism that he has, and they have the tendency to feel that they're better than other people. He was never that way, ever. He's not one of those idiots that throws it in people's faces. He has the personal depth of a human being.

A problem Arnold encountered while filming was that he had to leave the location after three weeks of filming *Predator*. The schedule was really strange. He flew to Hyannis to get married. The producers wanted him to come right back to film in the jungle after tying the knot. How do you explain this to your wife that you have to go back to working in the jungle right after your wedding? "So I took Maria to honeymoon to Antigua and I explained to her this is a beautiful vacation site, and all that," Arnold recalled, when promoting the movie. "She was very excited to go down, and little did she know she'd end up in the jungle in Mexico where we were shooting the film. But it was a fun honeymoon."

**Q: After *Predator* did you keep in touch with Arnold or did you both part ways?**
Bill Duke: We still keep in touch. I had a premiere of a film in Sacramento. Arnold changed his schedule and attended my premiere. He came to the movie and I was really grateful for that because he is very, very busy. He had another appointment, but canceled that appointment and came to see my film, which I really appreciate. I really respect him and have a really high regard for him as a human being and he's a great guy and person.

## VIC ARMSTRONG

When it comes to stuntmen and stunt coordinators, Vic Armstrong is without a doubt one of the greatest ever. Armstrong worked on *Conan the Destroyer*, *Total Recall* and *Last Action Hero* with Arnold. Among his impressive credits includes the Bond and Indiana Jones movies.

**Q: You worked on *Conan the Destroyer* with Arnold among other movies. How did you link-up to work together?**
Vic Armstrong: I had just finished *Indiana Jones and the Temple of Doom*, and Raffaella had called me to go out to Mexico in June. I went out there and finished the job. Then she said, "We need you to do another film with Richard Fleischer, and we'd like you to do that one. It's called *Conan*." So I went straight from Mexico to do *Conan*. That's how I got it. I had a wonderful time there in Mexico. I love Mexico. I've done a lot of films there. We had a great time at the Churubusco Studios and all over the place – loved it. It was fabulous. We did a lot of films together after that because Raffaella used to like to keep the same crew together – the same special effects, the production and everyone. We went on and did *Red Sonja* with Arnie and it was very good.

Arnold has always been immensely passionate about making movies. When working on *Conan the Destroyer*, he said, "It's like being a little kid again in many ways, and doing the things that maybe you were not allowed to do as a kid, you know, stabbing people with a sword and killing them with an axe and stuff like that." Aside from the light-hearted side to making films, he was well aware of the challenges and hard work that was required. So it had these two opposites. Filming *Conan the Destroyer*, he says, was the best paid vacation he had in his life.

**Q: Can you tell me about meeting Arnold for the first time?**
Vic Armstrong: He was fabulous. I met him when he was in the wardrobe having his wig fitting. I went in and introduced myself. He was great fun. I used to box and train at the time, so we used to work out every day together and go to dinner together. He hasn't changed at all. Actually, he was a wonderful social character with charisma, but really tough. In Mexico City, which is 8,000 feet, after work we would go out running and training, he was just amazing. He's an amazing strength of character. He's a good guy and good socially as well.

**Q: What was it like working with Arnold on the scenes on *Conan the Destroyer*, he valiantly despatched assailants in the movie?**
Vic Armstrong: He was very collaborative because, obviously, he's a big man so very difficult to double. So he did a lot of stunts himself. I did a percentage of them. I had a stuntman there in case we needed him. But because, as I say, he was doing it bare chest, you can't double that figure, you know. I worked very close with him, training him to do the sword fights and the horse riding. We taught him to ride. And the sword fighting, we'd rehearse every day with swords. He was just fun. We would discuss it and work out all the fight scenes and treat him as a stuntman. He'd come with the boys and we would work it out together. And he knew he had to do most of the fights himself because of his physique.

The film wasn't without its mishaps onset. According to Grace Jones, for instance, "I hurt a lot of people with that stick, yes, seriously. I clobbered about five guys and sent them to hospital." Arnold himself found working with Jones arduous – she was as real as they come when it came to filming the fight scenes. Nevertheless, he praised his co-star's performance and enthusiasm, which allowed the team to film some very realistic scenes. "I have done a lot of fight scenes in the first movie with stuntmen, dangerous scenes, and falling off horses and jumping 40 feet and everything," he said.

A young Arnold – eleven years old in school in 1958. A little boy with big dreams. *Getty Images*

Winning the Mr. Olympia in 1974 at Felt Forum in Madison Square Garden, New York. *Getty Images*

Arnold at home with his collection of bodybuilding trophies in the 1970s. *Getty Images*

Training at Gold's Gym in Los Angeles, 1974. *Getty Images*

Arnold and best friend Franco Columbu doing a photo shoot in Los Angeles at the peak of their bodybuilding careers. *Getty Images*

Arnold in the high octane action movie *Commando* released in 1985. *Alamy*

Arnold onstage with Arnold Classic-winner IFBB star Shawn Ray in 1990. *Shawn Ray*

On set the director of *Total Recall*, Paul Verhoeven, directs Arnold and Sharon Stone in a scene in the 1990 box-office hit. *Alamy*

*Terminator II*, released in 1991, is one of Arnold's most iconic films. *Alamy*

Arnold with Larry Scott.
*Bailey Hall/Larry Scott Inc*

Schwarzenegger family, UCLA, Westwood, Los Angeles. Arnold with sons Chris and Patrick, wife Maria Shriver, daughters Katherine and Christina, August 2006. *Alamy*

Former President George W. Bush shares a moment with Arnold, Govenor of California, at an awards show in Beverly Hills in 2007. *Alamy*

Arnold attends a photo call with Mayor of London (and current British Prime Minister) Boris Johnson for Barclay's Cycle Hire Scheme in London in 2011. *Alamy*

Dolph Lundgren, Sylvester Stallone, Arnold Schwarzenegger and Jean-Claude Van Damme at the French premiere of *The Expendables II* in Paris on August 10, 2012. *Alamy*

Arnold with bodybuilding friend and writer Jerry Brainum. *Jerry Brainum*

"I would rather do all of those things together than do one fight scene with Grace Jones because she really takes it seriously! But she looks wonderful on the screen because she really gets into the character." Jones, meanwhile, said the match between Arnold and her was fantastic because there was so much physicality, and so much humor. The movie was released in June 1984. This sequel to the original *Conan* was moderately successful domestically and very successful outside of America – as was the case with many of Arnold's movies – grossing $31 million domestically and a further $69 million internationally.

Soon, Arnold was asked by Dino De Laurentiis to do him a favor by doing a cameo role for another sword and sorcery movie he was producing called *Red Sonja*. Shot in Italy in 1984, the B-movie flopped, taking in less than half its budget costs, and was critically panned because of its bad acting and bad characterization. Arnold has admitted that *Red Sonja* is the worst film he ever made. "Now, when my kids get out of line, they're sent to their room and forced to watch *Red Sonja* ten times," he once remarked. "I never have too much trouble with them."

**Q: Do you have any good stories away from the set?**
Vic Armstrong: One night we went out, and he used to eat very wisely, you know, vegetables and salads and steak and red wine. Then we'd finish with some tequila. Then during the evening, I had agreed to go play tennis with him in the morning. At seven o' clock the next morning, I woke up with a terrible headache. The phone was ringing and it was Arnold. He said, "Where are you? I'm on the tennis court waiting for you!" I was like, *Oh, my God*. He was on the tennis court so I had to go play tennis.

**Q: What were the most arduous stunts on that movie? It was an action-packed movie with a lot of fighting.**
Vic Armstrong: Most of the stunts are difficult because he couldn't wear any padding. We did one fight in a room where there were all

mirrors. The mirrors smash during the fight with the Wizard. So poor Arnold's running around and there's broken glass exploding everywhere. There are mirrors exploding and breaking. That was very dangerous and difficult to shoot. And we had to keep the camera out of the reflection of the mirrors, and we had to break all the mirrors. All the actors are standing there with no padding on because they can't wear padding because they had to show the flesh.

**Q: Were there any sophisticated stunts on *Total Recall*?**
Vic Armstrong: Yeah, there were. In the end, we built the set vertically. Imagine the set being horizontal. Take a horizontal set and stand it vertically. And you put the camera vertically beside it, when you look through the lens it looks horizontal. But for all the stuff where Arnie's heading for space, it was really hanging from the ceiling, but it looks like it's hanging from a wall. So the ceiling became the wall. It's very difficult to do that on a diagram. But it was very tricky and complicated and made the film much more realistic in the world we were dealing with.

**Q: Arnold had matured as an actor by this time, 1989, when filming *Total Recall*. What's your impression?**
Vic Armstrong: Oh, yeah. When you think about it, Arnold is a very, very smart guy. I can't stress how intelligent he is. He's a very intelligent man. And he knew to improve and carry on in the business he had to learn the business. Everything Arnold does, he does one hundred percent thoroughly. So he had acting coaches. He watched films and he thought about his performances. I think he improved one hundred percent from *Conan* to *Total Recall*.

**Q: Did he have any input that went beyond his role as the lead actor as far as directing or coming with ideas and putting them forward to the director or the stunt coordinator?**
Vic Armstrong: Oh, yeah. I was stunt coordinating and we did rehearsals with Arnold. We rehearsed together and we talked together. Anything that would make it better for the movie or

for him, we would incorporate that into the fight routines. Then we would present them to Richard Fleischer, the director, or Paul Verhoeven, the director of *Total Recall.* It's a team effort.

**Q: What was Sharon Stone's and Arnold's collaboration like?**
Vic Armstrong: They're great. The fight routines have all got to be rehearsed. You can't do them without rehearsing them. So I had good stuntwomen that could double her. My wife was doubling Rachel Ticotin. It's a team effort; you have to work hard at it and train together. Every film we do the same, they (actors) have to become stunt people for two or three weeks whilst they rehearse their actions and everything else.

**Q: Were there any stunts that didn't go to plan in *Total Recall*?**
Vic Armstrong: No, not really. Everything was good. Everything worked out. If something didn't work out we'd change the action before getting around to filming it. But the time we get on the film set, everything has been rehearsed and perfected. So nothing was a problem on that. It's time and money to rehearse it properly.

**Q: *Total Recall* was also filmed in Mexico.**
Vic Armstrong: Arnold threw a party for the whole crew one day. He came up with this idea of giving everybody water pistols. So we had all these squirt guns on the table. As the dinner progressed and people drank more, we squirted these pistols at each other. But, of course, at the end of the evening the pistols were filled with red wine and vodka. So everybody was just squirting these things and going crazy, it was a mad evening. It was wonderful. Arnie paid for everything. I missed the premiere because I was working. I actually saw *Total Recall* in a midnight screening in Marble Arch in London. I never forget seeing it there. Everybody was screaming and enjoying it in the middle of the night. It was wonderful.

**Q: Arnold, a physical specimen, was cognizant of the hard work that went into stunts and the abilities of the stuntmen. Did you**

**perceive him to be appreciative to the stunt fraternity?**
Vic Armstrong: Arnold is a great supporter of the stunt world. He's always friends with his team. We all work very, very closely together because he knows from his upbringing what work goes into it. He knows it's an integral part of his movies and action, so he's always very, very aware of what's going on. Even since he became a governor, he still came and presented the World Stunt Awards. He presented me with my Taurus World Stunt Award. He's a great supporter of the stunt team and great friends with everybody.

**Q: You worked with Arnold on *Last Action Hero*, you did stunt coordinating. There were lots of stunts on this movie. Can you reflect on working on this movie with him?**
Vic Armstrong: I only joined *Last Action Hero* at the end, when they were finishing. I was doing another movie and John McTiernan and Arnold wanted me to go and do some stuff. So I did lots of little pieces that joined the movie together. So I'm afraid I can't take credit for all the movie. I was on it for about four weeks. I remember we had one sequence where he had to fall away from the camera about 100 feet, and we had a big swing set up. We had a 120-foot crane and a cable on it, and Arnie's swinging underneath it. He was amazing. I've gotta' say he does anything you ask him to do, he's really brave.

**Q: Critics and fans alike didn't like the movie, what are your views on the finished film?**
Vic Armstrong: I think the script was the problem. Action was good. Arnie was good. The script just didn't capture people's imagination. It was too confusing, I think.

**Q: Did you ever run into Arnold or keep in touch with him?**
Vic Armstrong: We went to the opening of Planet Hollywood in London with Arnold – that was great. Everybody from the film industry was there, it was a massive opening.

## PETER KENT

Peter Kent worked with Arnold for fifteen years on most of his movies as a stunt double. This led to a friendship ensuing on and off set. Both men enjoyed a camaraderie, which went as far as visiting each other's homes for dinner.

**Q: How did you become Arnold's stunt double, when was the first time you actually worked with him?**
Peter Kent: I went to Los Angeles with literally no experience. I was living in a YMCA and I found some small magazines for casting. I went to one of the casting sessions, and they said we're looking for somebody for this little movie called *The Terminator* and we need someone to stand in for Arnold. So I went over to the offices and James Cameron saw me, and he said, "You're perfect, you have the job." He said, "By the way, do you know how to do stunts?" I thought if I didn't say yes to the second question, I wouldn't get the job. So I lied basically and got the job. Then basically, I kind of worked my way through it. The night that we went through the glass backwards in the nightclub, the stunt coordinator, Frank Orsatti, came to me and said, "Do you want wraps for those?" I had no idea what he was talking about. He looked at me and he said, "You don't have any idea what you're doing, do you?" I said, "No." He said, "I better help train you so you don't get killed."

There's no doubt that *The Terminator* cemented Arnold's spot in the action firmament, with the Austrian's accented English and imposing physique providing a perfect match for the android assassin. Ultimately, however, it was a happy accident that Arnold ended up portraying that part. "The people at Orion passed the script to Arnold with the suggestion that he plays the so-called 'hero', Reese," explains director James Cameron. "He and I met, and neither of us felt very comfortable about him in that part. It had never occurred to anyone that he consider playing the villain, but that was the role he wanted! Now, Arnold is a half-man/half-machine in a black leather jacket with wraparound sunglasses. It does break the mold of what people think about him."

Mike Medavoy, the studio head, had told Arnold that O.J. Simpson had been hired to play the Terminator and that he should play the hero. Arnold remembers, "Basically, they were looking for someone to play the heroic character in the film, in the first *Terminator*. And they asked me to play the character and they asked to send me the script." As it happens Arnold had a slot open for spring and he asked to see the script first before making any verbal commitment. After reading the script Arnold felt that he could relate much more to the character of the villain than the heroic character the producers were hoping him to play. Furthermore, Cameron recalls that initially he had reservations about working with Arnold. "I'll never forget walking out of my apartment and telling my roommate, 'I've got to go have lunch with Conan and pick a fight with him.'" That was the director's agenda because he was adamant on not doing the movie with Arnold. "So I had to get in an argument and come back and say he was an asshole." However, Cameron had lunch with Arnold and found the actor so fascinating, amusing and entertaining that Cameron had a newfound respect for Arnold.

**Q: When you first met Arnold on the set, what was your first impression and working with Arnold on *The Terminator*?**

Peter Kent: We were shooting in the Department of Water and Power in downtown Los Angeles. I went down there. They had a chair set up in the corner. The first thing he said, when I walked up to him where they had the dressing and wardrobe, he looked at me and shook his head and said, "Too tall." I thought I'd just lost my job. And I turned around and walked away. He was, like, "I'm kidding, get back here." We got along great. It was one of those things we were kind of like brothers right from the start. It was really a good relationship. In fact, my mother had said to me, when she found out that I had the job with Arnold, "Don't treat him any differently than anybody else." I didn't. And I think that was the success to it all. We got along well. I would tell him anything. If I didn't think it was right, or he was doing something stupid, or an acting thing which wasn't working for him, I'd say do this or that.

**Q: The darkly hued science-fiction movie *The Terminator* gave you your first taste of stunt work. Was there anything that you found to be much more intricate than you imagined it would be?**
Peter Kent: Well, on the first *Terminator* there was some of the motorcycle driving, which we actually had a guy who came in and did some of the driving on that. I didn't have a whole lot of experience. I was physically body doubling him. So, really the toughest one for me was going through a window for Arnold, having never done it before. The rest of the stuff was doubling, walking with the machine gun and that kind of thing.

**Q: Would I be right in saying Arnold sometimes did his own stunts on his movies?**
Peter Kent: Yes. He did. He did almost all of his own fights, which he was very good at. And he would do whatever he could get away with. Obviously, when he got more popular the insurance company, which was funding the movie, wouldn't allow him to do any more.

**Q: What was the next movie you worked with Arnold on?**
Peter Kent: I worked with him directly after that on *Commando*. We shot *Commando* in Santa Barbara, California. We filmed in San Luis Obispo and then a bunch of it in San Pedro, too. Not much of it in central Los Angeles. We did a little bit of onstage work there, but mostly it was outside of town. Arnold and Joel got along really well. I never saw them arguing. In fact, we did *Predator* with Joel again later on. Joel was always a really gracious producer. I remember I was getting really tired of eating the food in Mexico (when filming *Predator*), so Joel sent food from a deli from New York City. He had flown down about 50 pounds of stuff, including potato salad and all kinds of great American food that everyone was

missing so much. He had it flown in privately for the crew because he wanted everybody to be happy and be comfortable. It was a very nice gesture.

**Q: *Commando* had a lot of action and explosions. Can you tell me the precautions you have to take when filming such action?**
Peter Kent: Oh, yeah. You have to be very careful. I mean, one of the things about doing stunts, when I had the luxury of working with Arnold, was with the safety factor. A lot of guys get pushed into things where the director says, "Hurry up!" or the AD says, "Hurry up, we've got to get this done!" And you're in a rush and put in a position where something happens and you get hurt or killed even. In my case, I was always careful and I watched everything because I'd seen that stuff happen before. I was thinking, *It's not gonna happen to me*. So I would watch what was going on. And if I didn't feel comfortable and felt that I was being pushed, I'd just get on the radio and call Arnold in his trailer and say, "Arnold, look, they're rushing it. I don't think it's safe." And he would say hand the radio to the AD and Arnold would say to the assistant director, "Give him time, let him get what he needs." So that may have saved my life in some instances, I don't know.

  I just know a lot of guys never thought like that. And a lot of guys get injured because of being rushed. A lot of those explosions are every bit as dangerous as a car bomb in Baghdad. A lot of the times I would say, "There's going to be an explosion here." And they'd say, "OK, show me one." I worked with a guy named Tommy Fisher, who is a special effects guy, he was the only guy I've worked with that if he said you're safe standing there, I would believe him. Everybody else I'd say, "Please show me one. I want to see you blow that stuff up first." And they'd say, "Oh, no, we don't want to blow that up right now. We have to wait when they're rolling." I say, "No, I want to see it."

**Q: What was your experience working with Arnold on *Twins*, which had elements of humor thrown in, the movie that gave**

**Arnold another dimension to express his character?**
Peter Kent: It was a lot of fun obviously. I mean, working with
Danny DeVito was a real treat. Danny kept it quite lively all the
time and had a good rapport with everybody. Arnold and Danny
DeVito threw a big party at the end of the shooting when we were
in Santa Fe in New Mexico. I remember Danny and his wife, Rhea
Perlman, who was there. All he did the whole night was drink
tequila and dance. And on the very end of the night, Danny turned
to some of the stunt guys and said, "Guys, do you still want to carry
on?" But we had a 7 a.m. plane to catch that morning. I think it
was 4 a.m. at that time. Danny took all of us to another nightclub
and bought each of us a bottle of wine. And we walked around with
beers in our hands until 6 a.m., and then we left for the airport
totally drunk and climbed on the plane.

Arnold got on very well with Danny. I don't think anyone doesn't
get along with Danny DeVito. Danny's got a fabulous sense of
humor. Danny is a professional and he's been in the business for
almost all of his life. He's one of those kinds of guys who's always
in a good mood when he comes on the set. He's always happy and
he always makes people laugh. So he's very fun to be around with
and a lot of fun to be with. Because Arnold is a joker and Danny is
a joker, there were a lot of pranks, just goofing off on the set with
Danny and Arnold. We were shooting in New Mexico, so it was a
nice place to be away, beautiful location, nice artwork. Arnold and
I took a trip to the R.C. Gorman, the famous artist factory there.
And Arnold bought a bunch of very large faces and was also kind
enough to get R.C. to lithograph for me 'happy birthday' because
it was my birthday at the time.

Arnold's collaboration with DeVito on *Twins* led to further
collaborations and a friendship ensued. Arnold cheerfully recalled,
"He was always insisting on smoking bigger cigars than I did because
he was short. But, anyway, we had a wonderful time. He was a great
partner." Arnold said that DeVito is a very talented actor and a

very talented chef, too. DeVito would cook everyone lunch literally every day. He would make pasta and Italian dishes and add some wine in, which sometimes led to the actors forgetting their lines because they'd be so drunk. The concerned director Ivan Reitman would always get upset and he would say to the pair, "Guys, you're losing me money. You've got to remember the lines." Working on the comedies was a lot of fun for Arnold and DeVito.

**Q:** *Kindergarten Cop* **was another movie that allowed Arnold to express his lighter side. What are your recollections working with him on this movie?**

Peter Kent: We had fun on that, too. As they say: working with kids and dogs very much slows down the process. I think also the kids were, in fact, really great. They took direction very well. And, in fact, sometimes they weren't required to take any direction – the director Ivan Reitman just wanted mayhem from them. But the kids' mothers, who were Hollywood moms who had been failed actresses themselves, were just miserable. They would be bickering backstage saying their son was the better actor, or their daughter was better. They would go to the director whilst he was trying to shoot and say, "Why doesn't my son have lines whilst so and so has lines?" He'd be, like, "I don't know what you're talking about. Your kid wasn't hired to have dialog. He's here in the background. He has a line later on in the movie. Why am I discussing this now?" It was pretty crazy. The going-ons behind the scenes of the moms was quite something.

We shot in Astoria, Oregon, which is a real great little town. I'm from the Pacific Northwest, so it was a real great taste of home for me to be back up there so close to where I live in Vancouver. But I had been in Los Angeles for quite a while and I missed the home thing. It was really a nice small town. The whole town turned up with open arms, it really helped us with the shoot. It was a lot of fun. One thing working with Arnold, whenever we went on location we always made sure we had a lot of fun. It was a very light-hearted film. There was a very good camaraderie between Arnold and Pamela, the woman who played his female cop counterpart. We had a lot of fun working on that film. It wasn't an action picture, so it wasn't as physically grueling as lot of the stuff we had done before that. So, it was just one of those kinds of movies where it's nice to have some time to where you're actually working, but at the same time, especially me, I'm not out there getting the shit beaten out of me every day.

Astoria is a little town with great food and great sights to see. In fact, that town is where – and nobody really knows this story – Arnold saw a Hummer. He has many Hummers now. In fact, they named a wing after him in the factory. We were driving by the Army base, I think it's Camp Kirby, or something like that, or Reilly, I'm not sure which. Anyway, we saw the Hummers coming out of the base, and Arnold said to me, "Jeez, those look cool. I wonder what those are." And I was reading a magazine, a *Car and Driver* magazine, on set a couple of days later in my spare time. And there was an article in there on how AM General had one of their Hummers driven across Mongolia and China by a private citizen to test the vehicle out. So, I said, "Arnold, this is what this thing is." So I wrote away for him to AM General, and they sent us a video tape and a huge press package for the vehicle and it was then when he ordered one. So, basically I was the one responsible for Hummer being in the private sector, out of the military and into the private sector. I don't have one. Maybe if I hadn't written that letter to AM General and not got the press package, he may have just not paid much attention to it and it might have just gone by. But that wasn't to be.

In 1992, when Arnold purchased his first Hummer, it kicked off a nationwide craze for the gas-guzzling behemoths. He went on to acquire a fleet of seven, thought to be worth around $950,000, before getting rid of his fleet to highlight his environmental concerns. He kept one and reportedly spent $21,000 to get one converted to burn hydrogen. Protecting the environment did not require one to be against large SUVs or trucks, he explained when he was the governor – instead, we should develop technology to cut down greenhouse gas emissions. His collection of prestige cars have included a Ferrari 360 Spider, a jet-black Bentley Continental Supersports, a vintage Mercedes Excalibur and a Porsche 911 turbo.

Brian Grazier, the producer of *Kindergarten Cop*, says Arnold was the dream star for a producer and a studio. Unlike many big stars who are above such concerns as marketing and promotion, Arnold was willing to do all the promotion and converse with the press to promote a movie. And all the smiling you could want, the producer stated. *Kindergarten Cop* was a role intended to show the action man's light side, and he pulled it off flawlessly. In preparing for his role, Arnold paid a visit to a real kindergarten accompanied by Ivan Reitman to get the feel and atmosphere of how the children would interact. "The first time I went in there with a hundred of them," Arnold recalled, "I was sweating. You say, 'Hi!' and they look at you strangely. You say, 'How are you today?' and they look at each other like you were talking Russian."

One critic described *Kindergarten Cop* as being violent and offensive. *Entertainment Weekly* stated, "The idea of the extremely big (Arnold Schwarzenegger, whose upper arms are larger than the average person's thighs) in comic collision with the very small (a kindergarten class) is rich in possibilities. But *Kindergarten Cop*, in which America's favorite hunk goes undercover as a teacher in Oregon to retrieve big drug money, is, above all, offensive and violent. Conan the Teacher turns the tots into something resembling Hitler Youth with the kids (obviously too old for kindergarten) goose-stepping their way toward obedience and responding to boot-camp commands." Despite the critics, it didn't stop the film from being a huge success grossing over $200 million, with a reported budget which was around $26 million.

**Q: What was Arnold's relationship like with the stunt guys and the crew in general, and was his appreciation of the hard work which went into stunts, which merits our attention, visible?**
Peter Kent: Always good. The stunt guys would always kind of

hang out together. The reputation John Wayne had with hanging out with the stunt guys, and I think Arnold was pretty much on the same level. He always liked to hang out with the guys and smoke a cigar. I was always to be found in his trailer. I had my own little room. So, whenever they were looking for me on set, they would always go to Arnold's trailer, or Arnold had a radio in his trailer so they would call for me there. I was generally in there, we were eating, smoking a cigar or drinking coffee or playing cards or reading a magazine or rehearsing dialog or something.

He always appreciated his crew and would take a moment to say hi to everybody. He always appreciated them. When we did *True Lies*, when we were in Florida a couple of guys got hurt really badly, and he showed a lot of concern. When we shot *Total Recall* in Mexico, one of the stunt guys, Joel Kramer, doubled him on a scene where he was supposed to get shot on the planet when the reactor explodes. I was working on the other side of the set, working with a different camera team, and so they said, "Joe, get into the clothes, we want you to go down on the slide and shoot on the planet." And something went wrong, and Joe ended up shooting about 30 feet above the air and coming down on his tailbone on the stage floor and almost broke his back.

And Arnold made sure . . . In fact, Sven Thorsen and I went to the hospital and went in and stole Joel Kramer from the Mexican hospital, took him down to a car, took him to the airport and put him on Arnold's private jet. The doctors were chasing us down the hall, trying to get us to let go and leave him, but we didn't want to leave him there because we didn't believe in the care of the Mexican hospital. So we actually just went in there and stole him out of there and put him on Arnold's plane and sent him back to Los Angeles.

**Q: Premieres in Hollywood. Did you go to the *True Lies* party?**
Peter Kent: I also work as an actor and was working on a TV series at that time. Between my stunt career I had actually started out as an actor. So many times after I finished doing the film with Arnold, I would go do my acting job. At that point, I didn't go to

the *True Lies* premiere party. I did, however, go to the *Total Recall* premiere party, which was held on Sunset Boulevard at one of the nightclubs. That was a big, big party. I think by the time, a week later, it had generated many millions of dollars, so it was quite a big party. Everybody hangs out in their kind of groups together. Arnold never had a tendency to stay very long at a premiere party. He would come in, have a drink, have a cigar, walk around, say hi to a few people, do some photos and then usually leave. He wasn't the kind of guy to spend the entire night there.

**Q: What is one of the most thought-provoking conversations you ever had with Arnold. Firstly, pertaining to work, secondly, to life in general?**

Peter Kent: My acting coach used to be a woman named Zena Provendie, who was the head coach at MGM for twenty-six years. I had started to do Shakespeare before I even went to Los Angeles. Arnold used to call me the 'Shakespearean stuntman'. I was also a dialog coach for him. I worked with him many times rehearsing his dialog scenes for his movies, almost for all of his movies, especially later on. And I don't know if I would call it thought-provoking, but I just remember many times sitting with him up till three o' clock in the morning sometimes, working on the scenes trying to make them better. It's funny because we did one scene in *Eraser*. We worked so hard on that scene and when I saw him shoot it after we had spent hours polishing it, we shot it the next day in New York City, it was one of the best scenes I had ever seen him do acting wise. And unfortunately, it was deleted because the producers wanted to see more action in the story. In the final cut of the film, it's chopped off, which I was really sad about because I was really proud the way he did that scene.

**Q: Can you tell me about the stunts involved in *Eraser*, and also about working with James Caan, Vanessa Williams and, of course, Arnold?**

Peter Kent: Well, there was a lot of work on *Eraser*. I was getting blown up running through fire. In the end, of course, I think you may have seen there's a scene where they're on the big shipping container. I ended up getting my top ribs broken and nearly getting killed. In fact, I got hit by that container, 100 feet in the air, and it went badly wrong. The container that was supposed to fall we had a wire on our backs, which would pull us away when the container would smash on the ground. It didn't. So now you have a three-ton shipping container spinning round and round, and it smashed into me. I ended up in hospital and was out of work for a while because of the injuries. We were all pretty lucky. There was myself, the girl who was doubling Vanessa Williams and the guy who was doubling James Caan. I think I sustained the worst of the injuries, but we were all pretty beaten up from that.

They were great to work with. I didn't get much time to talk to Vanessa very much, but I spent quite a bit of time hanging out with James Caan. In fact, in Vancouver not that long ago I was in a bar downtown having a drink with some friends, and someone slapped me on my back really hard. When I turned around, it was Jimmy Caan. He was in town working on a film here. But I hadn't seen him for quite a few years, so it was very nice. They (Arnold and James Caan) got along very well. Jimmy Caan was always trying to get the last word in a scene, they were always joking around. The director would say cut and they would still keep on acting, trying to add another line in there. He is a real joker and a lot of fun to work with.

**Q: Let's talk about the stunts in *Terminator II*, which were a lot more sophisticated with intricacy attached to them compared to the first one.**

Peter Kent: I was the first guy ever in the history of stuntmen to wear sort of a Mission Impossible type mask made out of latex and glued to my face, so I looked more like Arnold. In fact, if you look at the motorcycle jump coming off the bridge, you could see it's not him, you can tell it's not Arnold's face one hundred percent, but it looks like him. That's me wearing a mask, which I wore for sixty-six days on that movie. It was hell. Every day I went in, there was a four-and-a-half-hour application every morning, and I wore it for twelve, sometimes eighteen hours a day. It was very, very hard on the skin. Usually, now all of that stuff can be done with computers, but it was pretty tough back then. And there was a lot of work on that show. I think I worked sixty-six days. Arnold only worked forty-two or something.

I remember James Cameron coming over to me one morning, when we were shooting in the steel mill in Fontana, shaking me awake in a chair and looking at me and going, "I have beaten on some stunt guys in my career, but I have never beaten on anybody like I have beaten on you." He said, "Go back to the hotel and go to sleep." It was just relentless on that. I was working on three different units sometimes. I would work on the main unit, and then I would have to jump in my car when I finished on there and makeup and go across town or to the other side of Los Angeles for another shot and then back somewhere else.

**Q: How would you define James Cameron and Arnold's relationship working on *Terminator II*?**
Peter Kent: James Cameron, they say he can be a difficult guy to work with. I've always gotten along with him because we're both Canadians. I know Arnold and James had a good rapport. I think James is a very exacting director and knows what he wants, and he's not going to play around or fool around in getting that. And some actors have thin skin, so they are taken by that or they get offended by that and then they don't want to work with him because they say he's difficult. I don't think that at all. I think James Cameron is very exacting and he's a brilliant director. I think if he feels he's got you on the run so to speak then he'll work on that. I never had a problem with him. He would give me shot sometimes and I would go right back at him, you know, and say, "Fuck you, Jim," and we'd just laugh at each other and carry on. I think Arnold and Jim had the same kind of relationship. They would make jokes. Everybody worked hard on that movie – everybody! From the craft services to the driver, it was really an intense six-month shoot.

**Q: Did Arnold suggest certain things and collaborate with the director or did he merely do what he was told?**
Peter Kent: He would say, "I think we should try this," or "I would like to try this." And always they would do it. He would be accommodated. And they would look at it later on in the edit suite and see if it, in fact, worked or if it didn't work.

**Q: What was the most grueling movie Arnold and you worked on, which really demanded a lot of physicality?**
Peter Kent: It would have to be *Terminator II*, for me, anyway. I know for him as well it was very difficult because in the scenes in the steel mill he had a very, very bad cold, and he was sick quite a bit. But he never quit, never stopped, never took a day off because we knew we had to get it finished. Between him being sick and tired, falling asleep in the chair coughing and stuff but still getting up and doing the shots in that freezing cold. It's in a steel mill, it looks like it was molten metal and you would assume it was hot, but it's not. None of that metal is real. It's all done by lighting. The place is actually like a giant refrigerator, it was freezing cold in there. It was a tough shoot, and six months of it relentlessly.

**Q: Can you tell me about any conversation you had with Arnold regarding bodybuilding and working out on the set?**
Peter Kent: Yes. I had many conversations about bodybuilding with him because I had to look like him. Once I started working with him after *Commando*, I started training hard with him. I would meet him every morning at World Gym in Venice, California, and we would have our morning workout and go for breakfast. That was pretty much a ritual every day. Then, of course, on set he would always have his gym with him – he had a mobile gym – which would be set up somewhere, whether it was a big trailer, like a big truck trailer, or whether it would be in a convention hall in the hotel. But always we were working out. Many times I would be very tired from having taken a beating all day long doing stunts.

Then Arnold would say, "Peter, are we going to the gym now?" I'm like, "Are you fucking kidding me? I can barely drag my ass across the room to get into a car to go home, and you want me to go train?" There were times when I would actually sneak off the set when they were wrapping. I would take off because I knew if he saw me he would try to drag me into the gym. I was too exhausted to go there.

**Q: Anything you would like to share working out with Arnold at World Gym in Venice, which is a hub for bodybuilding?**
Peter Kent: Oh, God. I mean, there was always something going on. There were always some tricks being played on each other, the bodybuilder guys, a lot more so when he was competing. Basically, he would come in the morning and we would do the workout, ride the bikes and then take off and go for breakfast or lunch. Sometimes there weren't a lot of shenanigans going on, not like in the bodybuilding days. Back then there were all kinds of stuff going on. You read all about that in the bodybuilding magazines, I'm sure.

**Q: Did you converse with him about anything else other than work and training? Would you say Arnold is the epitome of hard work?**
Peter Kent: I think all you can say about him is, whatever he puts his mind to he does. That's all you need to say about him. It was usually work-related or fun-related or something like that. I never really had conversations about life, no.

**Q: How did you end up working as the stunt double of Arnold on *Raw Deal*, what recollections do you have about working with Arnold on this movie?**
Peter Kent: I just became part of his deal. He would just request me and I was part of his package. I was there all the time. *Raw Deal* was a fun shoot. We were in North Carolina, Dino De Laurentiis, who has passed away, was there, too, at the studios in Wilmington,

North Carolina. I remember when we first got there, and Dino wanted to show Arnold his brand new boat that he had just got made, custom-made – beautiful mahogany boat. So we all came down to the dock, me and one of the other stunt guys and Sven Thorsen. Dino was standing on the dock with his friend, and he's, like, in his Italian accent, "Arnold, see my new boat." Arnold's, like, "Nice, Dino. Let's see the keys." He took the keys from Dino and we all jumped in and we roared away from the dock. We were gone for the whole day waterskiing in Dino's new boat. We came back five o' clock at night, Dino was still sitting there on the dock looking quiet. Arnold just tossed the keys to him, "Very nice boat, Dino. Thank you." And we just walked away.

Dino De Laurentiis had given Arnold his first major role in *Conan the Barbarian*, the film that propelled the bodybuilder-turned-actor into the forefront of the public's imagination. When the Italian producer passed away in 2011, Arnold was among the many personalities at his funeral. At the funeral, which was attended by a long list of Hollywood names, Arnold talked about how the producer had inspired him. And he stated that he had unbelievable memories of the producer. Arnold also expressed that De Laurentiis had also taught him to be courageous. "He never feared failure," said Arnold of his friend. "And this is the only way you can be successful in life."

**Q: Making movies means living a compressed life. Were Arnold and the crew accustomed to traveling on shoots staying away from home, and can you elucidate on Arnold working on *Raw Deal* and how he spent his time away from the set?**

Peter Kent: There was a little bit of everything there, the driving stuff. I remember Arnold tearing the transmission out of two of the cars from the driving scenes, which was a good laugh for everybody. There was a lot of work on that show, but not so much for his character, but a lot of the other characters. His character had some fights, etc, a bit of driving, but there was a lot of work for the other characters. You get used to it, that's why you kind of become good friends because you know each other. You work together. You've known each other for a long time. You trained together. When we finished working, we would go back to the hotel and we would work out in the hotel gym. Then we would go have a shower and get cleaned up. Then we would go out and have dinner. And then maybe go back and read the script a little bit, go to bed. And do it again. That was basically the extent of it, you know. Every night you just tried to get out and do a little something, just to keep your sanity; not just sitting in the hotel room staring at the walls. We always hung out with each other. I would cook for him many times. My mother ran a boarding house when I was a kid, so I learned how to cook at a young age. So, Arnold always appreciated a home-cooked meal, and a lot of times if we had access to food. I'd make him my famous spaghetti sauce, which he used to love.

**Q: What do you remember about Arnold as far as his lighter side on the set?**
Peter Kent: Arnold had a scene in *Raw Deal* where he had to come down the stairs in his suit. And he lights a cigar in front of the camera and looks really cool and walks toward the lamp. We waited until he rehearsed it. Then we went to the box of cigars they had and we put an explosive in the cigar. So, we waited when they rolled the camera. He comes down the stairs looking very swell like Cary Grant. And he pauses there and sticks his lighter out straight up the cigar and takes a puff on it. He takes two steps toward the lamp and brings it up to take another puff, and the cigar exploded in his face. The director knew straightaway who it was, the director was John Irvin. And in his English accent, he shouted "Peter!!! Where are you!!!" yelling for me, I took off, ran and hid. It was really funny. The cigar just disintegrated on camera. He didn't keep that in the outtake.

Always on the forefront when it came to the action scenes, Arnold said, "One of the things that you, as a main actor, have to do is to be able to trust the special effects department. And, of course, what that basically means is, when he comes to you and says, 'Arnold, I would like you to do the scene although 10 inches away from your face glass would explode.' Then you say, 'Wait a minute, glass would explode in my face?' He says, 'No, the way its set up it will explode away from your face.' And you look at the guy and say, 'Sure,' looking at him unconvincingly." It was Arnold's belief that if you were an action star, the most imperative thing you do is to make sure the action is believable and that the audience got to see your face. Unlike most other action stars, he advocated the need for the action star to do most of the action himself. Of course, he was willing to use a stunt double on things that he couldn't do.

**Q: You worked with Arnold on *Jingle All the Way*, which was another comedy movie. What can you recall as far as spending time with Arnold on location on this movie?**

Peter Kent: I did. I didn't do a whole lot on that. I think I did about four or five things. At that point, I was starting to work myself away from doing stunts. I was getting ready to go back to Canada at that time because I had been injured previously on *Eraser*. I went to Minnesota with Arnold and worked a little bit on that film. He wanted me to come and do dialog rehearsals with him because there was quite a bit of dialog in that film, and it was more of an acting role than an action role. I had been hurt on *Eraser*, so at that point I kind of had decided I wasn't going to do much more in the stunt business. But Arnold came and – I was rehearsing with him at home, anyway – he said, "Look, I'd like you to come on the road with me to Minneapolis." There were some minor stunts, photo doubling stunts where I didn't need to hit the ground so hard. I had been still sore from the damage I had received from *Eraser*. So I was mostly there working on the dialog with him.

I stayed in the hotel with him and rehearsed dialog with him for the whole time. Every night we would sit in his room, and we would go over the dialog and I would rehearse with him. Basically, that's what I was really there for. As far as the movie itself goes, it was fun working with the cast again – some great people. It's always fun when you go out of town to work, you're out of Los Angeles. We were some place where there was snow. There was a lot of snow. It was a nice change as opposed to being in Los Angeles where the sun is shining all the time. For me especially, I'm Canadian-born and I love the snow. An Austrian guy named Danial Donai came in who was doubling Arnold, most of the flying stuff in the flying suit.

**Q: What are your recollections about *The Running Man*, which is set in a totalitarian society?**
Peter Kent: *The Running Man* was a tough one, too. The only thing I can really remember is it was a lot of night shoots – a lot of late days. I do remember that I really enjoyed working with some of the cast on that. Paul Michael Glaser, who played Starsky in *Starsky and Hutch*, was the director on *The Running Man*. I really like Paul Michael Glaser. He's a nice guy.

**Q: Did conversations with Arnold ever lean toward expressing his desire of becoming the biggest action movie star?**
Peter Kent: I don't think we ever had a conversation along those lines, but it was evident what was going on for both of us. I watched him. I learned a great deal working with the man, put it that way. Not only on set but being with him every day in his trailer for fifteen years, I saw a lot of things going on, how to manipulate . . . No. I wouldn't use the word 'manipulate', just how to make the business work to your best advantage and how to do it, really. I learned by watching him. We never really had any conversations about what direction he was taking because that was self-evident.

**Q: Did Arnold tell you what his favorite movie was?**
Peter Kent: I think *Terminator II* by far.

**Q: What was the toughest stunt you did on an Arnold movie?**

Peter Kent: I think one of the bigger ones was getting on the truck in *Terminator II*, climbing out of the little truck, running across and jumping onto the big rig. Climbing up and shooting the windshield out and turning the rig over to the side, which was all done in one take. And we were traveling, it was very dangerous because if I had slipped and fallen off the truck, I would've been run over by the big rig – all eighteen wheels – at least nine of them on one side. So it was one of those things where we rehearsed it a few times until we found the right speed. Because the truck was shaking so badly by being pushed by the big rig that I couldn't even get across the back first.

When we finally got it, we were going for lunch. Everybody was, like, OK, break for lunch. It was two o' clock in the morning. I said, "You know, Jim, I'm not hungry. My stomach is in a knot right now, I'm so psyched. Can we just shoot this?" And Jim turned to the crew and said to everybody, "The man wants to go now." Everybody was going to lunch. "We're going to shoot this right now." I think that was really awesome of him because he could've put me off by saying let's just wait and let everybody eat. I wasn't being selfish by wanting to do it. I really, really wanted to get it done. I felt, in my own mind, I had it right. I was ready to go and I didn't want to wait any longer. I just wanted to make sure we got the shot right, and we did! We got it in one take.

**Q: Did you visit Arnold at his residence, what was he like away from the cameras and work?**

Peter Kent: I went to his house many times, many, many times. And he would come to mine for dinner sometimes, or he would come over and we would rehearse the script. In fact, I would work out with him. Some mornings instead of going to the gym in Venice, we would just train at his house because he had a full gym set up there. So we would train in his gym and then have some breakfast out on the patio, and maybe sit in the Jacuzzi for a while, then rehearse the script. Like I said, I worked with him on the dialog level as well. I had been an actor long before I became a stuntman. He was never – with me, anyway – a much different guy on the set or off set. We always got along the same. I can't really say there was much of a comparison there. I think everybody's a lot more relaxed in their own environment at home. He would just be in a pair of shorts most of the time, or even a swimming suit, and we'd be out on the porch eating, having a coffee or smoking a cigar or sitting in the Jacuzzi.

**Q: What was your most memorable or happiest moment with Arnold?**
Peter Kent: I think one of my happiest moments was being finished in *Terminator II*. I was so exhausted and so tired. I had to go have water drained, my elbows from landing on the ground, even though I had elbow pads on, landing on my elbows on the decking in the steel mill. I was just so happy for that movie to be over. I was so exhausted that I think I slept for almost a week straight because I was so tired. So, I think that's probably one of my happiest moments, finishing *T2*.

**Q: Did you both frequently talk on the phone after you finished working on the movies?**
Peter Kent: I was in a film with Hulk Hogan, *Mr Nanny*, I played the bad guy. I played the German character Wolfgang. I remember calling him up because I needed some German (words) that I could say, which wasn't very, very bad language, but something I could direct to the kids because it was a family movie. I remember asking him some questions about some stuff – what to say to a child, what I could say to him in German which would work, but not be telling him to fuck off. Arnold called me back giving me a list of things I could use. It was good. I pretty much was with him every day for almost fifteen years. Sometimes we would do two films a year – each film was either three or six months. So you can imagine that's nine months in the whole year working with the guy and rehearsing and training with him. So I spent a lot of time with the man and learned a lot from him.

We became really good friends, and we're still friends. We talk quite a bit. He congratulated me with the birth of my boys and sent some photos up and signed them for the boys. It was really a great time. It was one of those things in everyone's life where you sort of take a look back and say, *OK, that was then*, and use what you've learned and move on and keep going in life. I learned a great deal from working with him, from every angle, from how to be behind the camera. I worked with some of the best directors in the world: Walter Hill, James Cameron, Ivan Reitman, some great directors. So I've learned a great deal about the business, not only from a business standpoint and Arnold's standpoint, but I've learned a great deal from a filming standpoint, and the directorial and editorial standpoint, and a screenwriting standpoint – all the aspects of movie making. Because I worked with him close to fifteen years, I was privy to some really great artists in the industry. And it's all really, really helped me a lot in what I do now. So I'm grateful for that.

## TIA CARRERE

An American actress, singer and former model, Tia Carrere came into prominence with her appearance in the comedy *Wayne's World*. She also appeared in *Showdown in Little Tokyo* and has co-starred in many movies. In 1994, the Hawaiian-born actress was cast in *True Lies*.

**Q: How would you adumbratively define Arnold's and your own character in *True Lies*?**

Tia Carrere: Let's see. *True Lies* was a huge film. It was just an honor to be part of. I played Juno Skinner, a rather shady art dealer of ancient antiquities, who is really a threat for terrorist activity. I guess that's the only way to put it. I'm also sort of a terror for Arnold's character, Harry Tasker; unbeknown to his wife, Jamie Lee Curtis, he's a spy, and unbeknownst to me as well. I'm basically trying to buy and sell arms for terrorists, funded by my art dealership. I don't think of myself as a villain – people characterized me as a villain. I think more of myself as a very dubious businesswoman with rather questionable morals. But I am basically a businesswoman, not necessarily a villain per se. I think it was fantastic in that he didn't have to play like just one side of the tough cyborg or the tough soldier. In this role, he got to show charm and humor – and self-effacing humor. And I thought it really humanized him. Because he's such a larger than life, powerful figure, in this film he was able to be a little more vulnerable, funny, charming and a little softer. It was a perfect balance between the two.

**Q: The plot was similar to a James Bond movie, wasn't it? Arnold is a big James Bond fan and finally got to play a formidable superspy.**

Tia Carrere: Jim Cameron wrote the script. I mean, it's very Bond. People come up to me all the time and say, "Aren't you a Bond girl?" And I say, "No, you're probably thinking of *True Lies*," which is very Bond in its storyline because he wears a tuxedo and he has a hidden camera, the crew and the van following him around. So it's very much like James Bond.

In 1992, when Arnold and James Cameron were having breakfast at Arnold's Schatzi restaurant in Santa Monica, Arnold brought the concept for *True Lies* – originally based on the French film *La Totale* – to the attention of the director. Arnold, who liked the script, later explained, "I loved the Bond movies. I think the Bond movies really set the base for all the other action movies because they had everything." A staunch Bond fan, Arnold hoped to play a role that echoed the heyday of Ian Fleming's character. "I'd say the beginning Bond movies, the later ones were not that great anymore, but the beginning ones with Sean Connery, and also the other one, Roger Moore, there were some really good ones." Among the elements that invokes Arnold's interest in the Bond movies was great humor, great action and always larger than life things. Arnold felt there were a lot of things that could be taken from these action franchise.

**Q: What was it like working with Arnold on the movie?**
Tia Carrere: I love working with Arnold Schwarzenegger. He and Jim Cameron both have such a work ethic. They're on the set eighteen hours a day. So you really can't slack off around them because they are there. And a lot of movie stars go hiding in the trailers or whatever, but no, he and Jim Cameron were around the set 24-7. They're just wonderful people to work with. Arnold and his crew of stunt guys that he worked with all the time are great friends. And it's really nice to see someone so loyal to their friends.

**Q: Can you relate any hilarious incidents on the set concerning Arnold?**
Tia Carrere: Oh, yeah. It was funny learning to do the tango with him because he's a guy who can't do the tango. But I think he did a wonderful job. It's necessary for him to have strong shoulders and a

very straight back. He's got that natural posture, anyway. So he was a wonderful tango dancer. But I made a mistake once – and only once – doing my lesson in my bare feet, until Arnold stepped on my feet, and that was it. I was like, "No! Oh, God." Another time, everybody would be sitting on the cast chairs on the set, his crew of stunt guys that he worked with all the time. They'd be sitting there talking and then one of them would sneak up behind the other one and do some sort of a prank. Once somebody lit a fire underneath the bum whilst they were sitting there. And you see the seat's slowly heating up, until you see them jumping for their lives. That was very funny. Just like child pranks. But it was two o' clock in the morning.

**Q: Did you and Arnold find any obstacles whilst shooting any of the sophisticated scenes, which required meticulous planning?**
Tia Carrere: The hardest scene was the scene with the helicopter. I had just taken Jamie Lee hostage into my limousine and my driver drives away and the helicopter lands exactly where the car was. So, we rehearsed it and all the stuff. But during the take, and everything's going off, huge, huge scene, and the car wouldn't start. The limo wouldn't start. It was really dangerous because the helicopter was going lower and lower. Me and Jamie Lee jumped into each other's laps, and I picked up the walkie-talkie and said, "Stop! Stop! The car doesn't start! The car doesn't start! Lift the helicopter!" So that was quite a frightening moment.

**Q: Every Arnold film has action. Can you tell me more about the action-packed scenes?**
Tia Carrere: Yeah. The most amazing one that I saw, which took us days to shoot, was the scene where, it's like every single explosion has to go off in tandem one after the other. The factory blows up then Arnold jumps into the water to save himself. That was a very complicated thing. They set up for that. It wasn't going right, so they had to do it again and again.

**Q: What did you learn about Arnold's personality?**

Tia Carrere: I would say he's a great student of life. I never went to college; I learned everything from traveling the world and speaking to people. If something interested me, I would read up on it. What strikes me about Arnold is, he has a lot of that. I think he's got natural curiosity. He's a perfect example of the American Dream. He has achieved what is possible to achieve in America if you work hard and apply yourself, and I really admire that about him. My favorite conversations were about working out. I went to his sixtieth birthday and he was in amazing shape. On the set he had his workout trailer. He said, "Hey, go, you can use it if you want to work out." And this is important. It's the basis and the foundation to everything else, and that work ethic that carries him through.

**Q: Arnold, who has been known for being primarily an action man, was he able to evince the caliber of his acting skills?**

Tia Carrere: I think he was terrific in *True Lies*. Mostly because he and Jim Cameron have a great relationship and they have shorthand to their work. So, you know, Jim would know what to say to Arnold to get the response out of him. Arnold's work in the film was terrific. I think he got the tone of the comedy perfectly. It's, like, he's in on the joke. He has a very sort of an impish nudge and a wink to his performance. I think it's great. But I think definitely Jim Cameron is a great director. And they have a great relationship, so he's able to get that. Arnold's got a very fun-loving personality. You can see it through *Kindergarten Cop* to *Twins* and every number of things. He likes to have fun. He's got a little nudge, nudge, wink, wink, sort of aspect to him that is just delightful.

I think the performance in *True Lies* was a combination of the fun-loving characteristic to his personality, as well as Jim Cameron's direction right in the right spots. He's a wonderful director. I loved working with Jim Cameron. He empowered every actor on the set. For me, I'm like fifth on the call sheet. I'm not Arnold or Jamie Lee. But he would ask me, "What did you think of that performance?"

He would show it to me and I would watch it back. He took the time. I would say, "You know what, may I try this different thing?" He would say, "Yeah, that sounds great, do it." He's very collaborative and open with his actors, and I think that's why I think he gets such great performances.

**Q: Arnold got on well with Jamie Lee Curtis, but when she was being cast he wasn't too sure about her being casted. Can you tell me more about Arnold working with her?**
Tia Carrere: I never saw any divisiveness whatsoever. I just saw them getting along great. So I've never heard that before. I never heard that story, so I can't speak on that, I don't know. I think Jamie Lee is a great broad, like in the old movies you see Bette Davis and Joan Crawford. These are broads. They are tough, strong female characters. Jamie Lee is a very strong woman who's playing a great role in this film. It was great to hang out with her because I like it how she's a broad. You know, it's cool. She can hang with the guys and hold her own, let's put it that way.

James Cameron wasn't sure whether Jamie Lee Curtis and Arnold would bond. Moreover, Arnold was doubtful about having her play the role, too, and was vocal about this to the director. Arnold had a way of 'testing' people when he first meets them. As it happens a chemistry cultivated between them as far as working together. Tom Arnold, who played Albert Gibson, cultivated a close friendship with the star on and off set. "It was great, because I had great chemistry with Arnold off camera and so we just carried that on to the camera and then it turned out good," he explains. "We just had that kind of a relationship where I'm giving him a hard time. He's giving me a hard time. And, you know, we just played that out there." Tom liked his co-star and the character Tom played also likes him, too.

**Q: Can you tell me about shooting the scene where you have taken Arnold and Jamie Lee Curtis hostage?**

Tia Carrere: That was fantastic, the scene was something else. That scene, the torture room scene where Arnold and Jamie Lee are locked in the room, was the craziest day of shooting ever because it was the day after the huge Northridge earthquake in Los Angeles. It was a huge earthquake, buildings had collapsed. I mean, apartment buildings, it was a big deal. The day after we were shooting in this huge warehouse about three miles from the epicenter of that earthquake. And, of course, the only thing that matters is what's on film because no one else in the world knows that that's happened three miles away from where we're shooting. And everybody's freaked out, and every few seconds the whole building would go du, du, du, du, rumble with aftershock all day long. And who had all the dialog? Me! It was quite something. I had all these monologs talking about the torture to Jamie Lee and Arnold.

But that really tested my focus as an actress. It was frightening. I mean, the ground wasn't really still most of the day. The only thing that mattered was, you keep your eye on the ball and you do your work. No one in the world knows that this is the day after one of the hugest earthquakes in California we ever saw. We shot right by the epicenter of this earthquake. And actually, after I had completed my scene that day, they evacuated the area because of a fear of a gas leak. So it was quite a day, everybody was freaked out. But the show must go on and you just keep your concentration and you keep doing it. I've not told this story before. That was one of my favorite scenes of all the films I did, which was kind of funny.

When *True Lies* was released by 20th Century Fox, the studio stumbled upon a problem. Arab-American advocacy groups led protests in various major cities around the country. The film depicted Arabs as anti-American zealots, which many members of the Islamic community found repugnant. Tired of Hollywood portraying them as terrorists and criminals, some Muslim spokesmen were indignant at what they saw as a lack of depth in the movie's Arab characters – while Arnold was unrepentant. "The film is a work of fiction and does not represent the actions or beliefs of a particular culture or religion," said a spokesman from the studio at the time. *True Lies* would certainly be viewed differently in light of more recent events.

**Q: Did you attend any parties with Arnold, or were you invited to any parties which Arnold often threw at his home?**
Tia Carrere: Going to the premiere was just amazing. It was. All the publicity and the personal appearances we did after that, it was just a huge wonderful film to be a part of. I can't remember anything specific about parties or anything. I went to a birthday party at one of his residences. It wasn't like tons of people. One thing that struck me, and always has, about Arnold is that they're all about family and friends. They could've had thousands of people, but it was a very intimate gathering and people you see time and again in his life. He's always a very loyal friend to the people who are in his crew, and that's what strikes me – a good solid family man that keeps his friends and loved ones close to him. You saw that at tributes over and over again.

# ANDREW G. VAJNA

One of the leading Hollywood executive producers, Andrew G. Vajna has produced a plethora of movies such as *Red Heat*, *Total Recall*, *Basic Instinct II*, *Terminator III*, *Die Hard*, *Nixon*, *Evita*, *Escape to Victory* and the *Rambo* franchise.

**Q: The first movie you produced with Arnold was *Red Heat*. How did the concept manifest itself into a reality?**
Andrew Vajna: It was an idea that was developed by Walter Hill, the director. He came to us with a concept: a Russian cop and an American cop working together to solve a case. Arnold could be the Russian cop, and we'd see who the American cop could be. He said, "What do you think?" We loved the idea. We talked to Arnold and he loved the idea. So we went forward and had the script written. Walter wrote the script and we went on to make the movie with Arnold and James Belushi.

**Q: Were there any obstacles when making this movie? Obviously, on a big-budget movie you're going to encounter hurdles and pursue to overcome them. What were your hurdles?**
Andrew Vajna: I think the biggest obstacle was that we never really got permission to film in Russia. We wanted very much to have an authentic background, with the Kremlin and everything else, to say that this is Russia. The obstacle was: how do we get there? We had written to the government agencies to allow us to shoot there, but we couldn't get any answers. So we finally took it upon ourselves, and through a friend of ours who was supervising bands – music bands – told him to come play in Russia. He said, "OK. I'll organize it for you." We went with him without any official permits or official papers.

We flew to Russia and in three days did all the shooting and then left Russia. We got it, so that was fantastic. That was our biggest obstacle except for the weather. In Hungary, while we were shooting the snow sequences, because in Russia it was snowing so we had to match everything else in the movie, we had to manufacture snow everywhere. Then as we were getting toward spring, everything was melting and we had to keep moving further and further to the west. Because originally, we were going to shoot the snow fight sequences in Hungary, then we moved to Austria. And then we moved further into Austria, then finally we went on top of the hill where we were able to find some snow. The weather and the political relationships were the two issues.

**Q: What was your viewpoint of the final product?**
Andrew Vajna: We thought it was great. We liked it very much. It did very well all over the world so we were happy with it. We felt it might have been a little bit funnier, could've been, but the director felt that he wanted to have a serious angle, so we had less of the comedy. So, we said fine and we let it go.

**Q: You were involved with the *Rambo* movies and produced them. Stallone was a big star, so was Arnold, in the 1980s. Did you have any conversations with Stallone or Arnold about their rivalry, a rivalry that became well-publicized?**
Andrew Vajna: Sure. I mean, there was constant rivalry between Arnold and Sly in those days. They weren't really friendly as they are today. In those days, Sly was already an established star after *Rocky*, and Arnold was still on the edge of stardom not quite being there after *Pumping Iron*. Stallone was way ahead of him. And he picked Stallone as his sort of running mate, or as his example and tried to sort of catch up with him and surpass him. And I think he certainly caught up with him. He was able to maximize his popularity with the bodybuilding and with the movies he was doing, that he was able to catch up with Sly.

So that contest, I think, kept him on the edge all the time, and to be better and try to compete. So the two of them were definitely rivals in those days. I'm sure we talked about it, but it was always with good intensions, joking. I don't remember what the conversations were because it's more than twenty-plus years ago. Working with Sly was great! I mean, Sly is a very talented person. People don't give him enough credit for his writing and directing ability. I think he's a really talented writer and he's a very, very talented director. He sometimes gets a little lazy as a writer, but he needs sometimes to focus on the paper and he comes out with something viable. But when he does do it, he becomes a real success. And he's a very well-liked actor. I think he's got everything going for him.

It's no secret that for years Arnold and Stallone were competing for the number-one spot as the ultimate action hero, as well as the most valuable slot at the box office. However, it's interesting to note what a member of Stallone's entourage in the 1980s told Ian Halperin, author of *The Governator*, when questioned about the legendary 'feud'. "That was all bullshit," his source told him. According to the source, Arnold and Stallone were friends and were both in on the gag. He said whenever Arnold and Stallone got together they'd be ragging on each other and insulting one another. It also happened at public events, he claims. But then they'd laugh about it. One thing is for sure: both men are friends and eventually even collaborated together on several movies.

In 1990, Wendy Leigh released the sensationalized biography *Arnold*, an unflattering portrait focusing on his father's unsavory past, Arnold's inappropriate behavior and claims that he used steroids during his illustrious sporting career. There were attempts to stop the publication of the biography. Harry Poltnick, who was the publisher at Contemporary Books, recalled, "The caller suggested that Arnold would do a joint book with me if I quietly dropped the biography, retained the rights and paid the author off. In the other case, the caller, who was also very close to Schwarzenegger, said I would be reimbursed for what I paid the author, plus something extra, if I didn't publish the book." Nonetheless, Poltnick refused to accept the offers and the publication of the book went ahead. In 2011, Brigitte Nielsen's revelations of her liaisons with Arnold when they were filming *Red Sonja* were divulged in her autobiography.

In the early 1990s, Stallone's movies *The Specialist*, *Judge Dredd* and *Assassins*, one by one, stumbled or sank at the box office somewhat putting an end to the megastar's run at the top of the industry. In 1996, Stallone expressed his disappointment with his agent at ICM. He felt it was time to move on and redeem his start status so he left them for another agency, William Morris, piqued somewhat by his former agent's failure to procure the coveted role of Mr. Freeze in Warner Brothers' *Batman and Robin* – a role which went to Arnold. Arnold told a magazine once in the mid-1980s, "I think Stallone, as far as I knew him, is extremely intense all the time – even when it comes to the gym." It was continuous competition for the *Rambo* star, claimed Arnold. "If you're doing 120-pound curls, he will say, 'I can do 130.' He's obsessed. And that carries through in the way he dresses, how hard he tries to belong to a charity organization." Stallone himself says, "There are always goals. If you don't have a mountain, build one and then climb it. And after you climb it, build another one. Otherwise you start to flatline in your life." He also possesses a drive uncommon to most, always striving to reach new heights. "People think retiring is fun. Well, maybe, but if you have a certain kind of fire inside, there is no end in sight," Stallone says.

**Q: Interestingly, you knew Bruce Lee. Before he passed away, he received movie offers from a Hungarian producer, was this producer yourself?**
Andrew Vajna: Yes, that's me. I was actually a friend of Bruce Lee's in the 1970s in Hong Kong, when he made his first three movies, and, in fact, I had a deal with him to do his next movie. Unfortunately he passed away before that came to be, but I was a friend. We were working on a picture together that we were going to do. Actually, he bought my house in Hong Kong. I was living in Hong Kong at the time, and we actually made a deal where he just bought my house as part of the deal he was going to do the next film. Unfortunately he passed away. So we're all very unhappy about that.

**Q:** *Total Recall* **was a science fiction movie, some critics saw as imprudent to glorification of violence, which was one of Arnold's most successful ones. Can you tell me how the concept materialized?**

Andrew Vajna: This was based on a short story that we had acquired. And the script, I think Dino De Laurentiis owned it at the time. He wasn't going to make it because he wasn't quite sure how to. We acquired the script from him. We got Paul Verhoeven involved in reworking the script and we gave it to Arnold. And the rest is history. It was a huge hit. We shot the movie in Mexico. I think that one was pretty smooth going. I mean, the director and we had some difficulties in making sure we could keep the budget in control because Paul likes to spend a lot of money. But I think ultimately, he was on his best behavior as far as this movie is concerned. We were able to bring it on budget, and Arnold's performance was great, you know. We built a star – Sharon Stone – in later movies. So it worked out pretty well for us.

I can remember the party afterward, it was a private club which used to be a Japanese restaurant, that's where we celebrated the – not the premiere – $200 million mark that *Total Recall* reached. And the party with Maria and Arnold and all the people that participated in the film, it was just a celebration, you know. I think it was very good. I don't remember the exact numbers now because it was so many years ago. Arnold is a great salesman, he's brilliant. I remember one particular thing when we were doing, I think, *Total Recall* and we brought him to Cannes to promote the movie. We were a young company so didn't have a lot of money. So we didn't put a lot of posters all around the place. He said, "How do you expect to sell the movie? There's no marketing. You came here and you should be the most visible picture in Cannes. And here I come and there's nothing." And he was right! He's a good salesman, and he went out there and met up with all the distributors. He hyped the movie and he was very supportive in whatever he did. That was a great asset because a lot of movie stars are not that way.

243

Critics were harsh and didn't hold back. *New York Times*' Janet Maslin wrote: "Fifty million dollars worth of exploding glass, blazing bullets, ears splitting noises and sometimes clever, sometimes gut-wrenching special effects say that Mr. Schwarzenegger is no figment of anyone's imagination except, possibly, his own. *Total Recall* is a thunderous tribute to its star's determination to create, out of the unlikeliest raw materials, a patently synthetic yet surprisingly affable leading man. Melding the ever-more-workable Schwarzenegger mystique with a better-than-average science-fiction premise, the director Paul Verhoeven has come up with a vigorous, super violent interplanetary thriller that packs in wallops with metronomic regularity." Fans, however, didn't seem to want him to. *Total Recall*, released in America in June 1990, which had a budget of $65 million, took in over $260 million worldwide resulting in one of Arnold's biggest blockbusters.

**Q: Arnold initially refused to do *Terminator III* because James Cameron wasn't going to direct it. But Arnold was compelled to star, once again, in this third installment of the classic series. Can you please shed some light on this?**

Andrew Vajna: Yes, that's correct. We bought the rights to *Terminator III* from an auction when they were selling off the assets. I guess Jim Cameron was also interested in having Fox buy it for him, but Fox never stepped up to the line, and we ended up getting the rights. Our intention was always to go to Jim to direct it, but he felt that we had stolen his baby. Even though we're the ones who made *Terminator III*, and made it such a big hit, together with him, we felt that it was kind of the same family. But I guess he felt differently about it. He was very upset that we didn't let him know ahead of time that we were doing this. We, on the other hand, thought it was a great thing that we would buy it and have him direct it. And we would form some kind of a partnership that would make sense for everyone. But he was definitely against it.

Then Arnold said he's very close friends with Jim so he doesn't want to do anything against Jim's wishes. If Jim didn't want to make the movie, then he wasn't going to make the film. So we said OK, we are going to have to pare down and see what happens. In the long run, we decided to develop a screenplay. And we felt if Arnold read the script that he really liked, then he'll do the role because it was an important role for him in his career. And, in fact, that's what happened. He read the screenplay. He said I understand Jim doesn't want to do it, and he talked to Jim and Jim said sure, you should do the movie. Then we got together and made number three.

Arnold had approached his friend James Cameron in relation to directing *Terminator III* because Cameron had been overlooked to direct it, according to some sources, when he was approached by the producers. Arnold says, "I'm always optimistic when talking to directors. But it was very clear he could not commit to a certain time." The director was involved in other things and wanted to pursue and explore other ideas. "James Cameron is not a director, so to speak, but much more of an explorer. And there is another dimension to his directing. I'm the last person to say, 'Hey, Schmuck, you really let me down,' because I want people to move on." *Terminator III* was originally slated to film in Canada. At the time, a lot of films were being shot there because of the great incentives for filming, but Arnold was adamant that production should take place in California. The producers told him that it would cost $8 million more if the movie was shot in California. Arnold, always a man with the solution, suggested that they sit down and negotiate. Arnold remembers, "So we sat down and negotiated. I put in, out of my personal salary, some money. They said, 'OK, the producer should put some money in,' and they put some money in. 'It was a collective effort to bring the budget down, and then the various different departments cut down some of the fees. And in the end the production company saved $8 million." To this end, it created five hundred jobs in Los Angeles. Fittingly, the movie would be released a few months before he became the Governor of California.


**Q: Arnold's Terminator character burned its way into the American consciousness, moreover, the world's consciousness. Why do you think the *Terminator* movies caught the public's imagination, it is a hugely successful franchise globally?**

Andrew Vajna: It became a brand name. There are very few movies where you have a line 'I'll be back', or 'make my day', or 'show me the money'. There's maybe three or four or five movies in the world that have a tagline that everybody in the world identifies with. And *Terminator* had one of those lines. Two of those lines were 'Hasta la vista, baby' and 'I'll be back'. Those are very simple things, but they totally identified with Arnold and the movies. So it became a real big hit and it became a brand name, a brand name kids identified with and enjoyed as a character.


**Q: In your opinion, what were the marked differences between the first and the third *Terminator* movie, in terms of production values and box office receipts?**

Andrew Vajna: I didn't do the first one. The first one was done by John Daley. I thought that the first movie set the groundwork really well for that character. For some reason John Daley didn't want to continue it. Then we at Carolco started bidding for the rights and got them, paid a fortune for them. Then Mario (Kassar) and I separated. He went over to make the sequel number two, which was a big breakthrough in character and special effects for a sequel as a whole. Then, of course, we went out to take that one step further for number three.


**Q: Out of all the movies you did with Arnold, which was the most gratifying experience?**

Andrew Vajna: I think in the *Terminator* series. The movies we've done with him, I think *Terminator II* is the most liked movie.

As far as which one is my favorite, that's also my favorite. I liked *Terminator II* a lot, but I think *Total Recall* was very interesting. So it's very difficult for me to choose from between those. I think all three of them were special movies in his career.

**Q: Having worked with and known Arnold for many years, can you tell me about the immense drive he has to succeed and his ability to reach a higher plane?**
Andrew Vajna: I think he's totally dedicated to his passion. His passion was bodybuilding and he became the best at it. Then his passion was to become a personality in the motion picture field, where it's most difficult to make it. And he mastered that and became one of the most sought-after movie stars. So, I think it's his passion that drives him. I think he's totally dedicated to what he's trying to be successful at, and he would not allow himself to deviate from that for a moment.

**Q: Arnold developed this colossal persona, which was projected on the screen. How would you define his off-screen personality having socialized and worked with the man?**
Andrew Vajna: I think he's got a great sense of humor, always the practical joker. He loves a laugh and he's a very good friend. He will be there to help you when you're in need and he'll reach out. So I would say those are the characteristics of a very positive personality. Planet Hollywood, they were huge fun parties and events. Hollywood was able to be present at a local diner. And it was a great combination of fun and happiness and just outgoing personalities that you don't get to see every day were there. Each opening was like a movie premiere.

**Q: Were there any movie projects you were pursuing with Arnold, which didn't materialize? Was it hard to negotiate a deal with him and induce him?**
Andrew Vajna: I was there for the beginning of it, then I left the company. But *Crusade* was the movie Paul Verhoeven and

047 re

Arnold were going to do. Unfortunately the financing didn't come together. The budget was out of control. And they couldn't bring it down so the movie got canceled. He's tough. He knows what he wants and he usually gets it. I know it was always very difficult. He always knew what he wanted. He often didn't use his attorneys to get there; he often did it himself. He said, "Listen, don't worry about it. It might be a lot of money, but I will give it back to you in promotional value of the film. I will go out there and promote it." He always did that, and we were always happy with the result.

**Q: Can you tell me about your climb on the ladder of success?**
Andrew Vajna: It's the same kind of thing as Arnold. My partner Mario had a tremendous drive and we had tremendous passion for the material for the films that we were doing. So we were dedicated day and night for years to make it happen. When you are putting that kind of dedication into it, hopefully if you choose well, the results will be there, too. We were fortunate enough that we chose well and the results came.

**Q: In your opinion, how much of an impact did Arnold have on Hollywood and pop culture as an action hero?**
Andrew Vajna: I think tremendous. I think people love him all over the world because of the Terminator character, as well as some of the other things that he's created – *Conan*, *Predator*. I mean, those were characters he mastered and people loved him for it.

# MARIO KASSAR

Born in Lebanon, Mario Kassar is known for his collaborations with the Hollywood executive Andrew G. Vajna. He is the executive producer of *Basic Instinct I* and *II*, *Total Recall*, *Terminator II*, producer of T*erminator III*, the *Rambo* movies and *Red Heat* to name a few.

**Q: Mario, can we talk about *Terminator II*, how did you obtain the script? And what were the hurdles that were in the way of getting the film into production?**

Mario Kassar: I was running Carolco and I had a good relationship with James Cameron. I wanted to do *Terminator I* with him, but he was under contract. I think if I recall, in those days it was Orion. I read the script and I really liked it. I said to him that, if by any chance it doesn't go well with those guys, if it falls apart, you can come back here and we can do it here. But, obviously, that didn't happen and it was done over there. Then I went to the screening and when I saw it I thought, *Oh, my God! Whatever you want to do next, just call me.* And then, as all sequels, it was a very complicated one because of the rights. When he divorced his wife Gail Anne Hurd, following the divorce he gave her, as a settlement, 50 percent of the sequel rights. He had the other half. Everybody tried to do it, but it was very, very complicated. We tried to get Arnold, tried to get James, tried to get all the writers together and tried to do it.

And the budget, obviously, would have been very high because it was a very big idea. We're talking many, many years ago, not like now. Anyway, I got involved and made the deal basically with Cameron and Arnold. Then I had to go and make a deal with the wife of Cameron, Gail Anne Hurd, who basically gave me only the rights to one sequel for quite a substantial amount of money. But I had to take it because it was the only way. Then with Carolco, I made it. In those days, it was above $100 million movie. Of course, it was all over the place. But that's how expensive it was and that's how I was running the company into . . . whatever. Of course, everybody saw the movie and we know what it did, everybody loved it. And the rest is history about *Terminator II*. It wasn't an easy thing to put together because it took about a year and a half to put it together before shooting and everything else.

**Q: Of course, *Terminator II* was much more sophisticated than the first one and it did huge business. Can you reveal to me the budget issues surrounding *Terminator II* because it was the most expensive film ever made at that point?**
Mario Kassar: Yeah. In fact, it was a little bit above the hundred million mark. I think it was hundred and eight or hundred and ten – something like that. We had sets in those days worth $17 million, which was enormous. We're talking twenty-something years ago. Those were sets that James invented and created. We tested them and we saw a lot of them before we spent money on them to make them. Then, the rights were expensive. Cameron is not cheap and Arnold is not cheap. Then when James shoots, he shoots for perfection – everything has to be perfect. So it was a very expensive movie in those days, and as I told you before, I got a lot of heat from the media and everybody the fact that I was doing such an expensive movie. Then the movie was done and the results, of course, were great.

**Q: The absolute peak of Arnold's popularity came when *Terminator II* was released. Do you believe *Terminator II*, which did more business than the others in the series, is renowned as far as a cult classic compared to the others?**
Mario Kassar: Yes, everybody talks a lot about *Terminator II* because it was a pioneer, and the story was great and everything fits together perfectly. But it's always very difficult to please people. But we tried and we succeeded a little bit in *Terminator III*. And then on the fourth, unfortunately, we sold the franchise. And whatever they've done, it didn't really work out somehow.

**Q: Can you recount any conversation you had with Arnold when *Terminator II* came out, which reflected the movie's success?**

Mario Kassar: The good thing about Arnold is he knows exactly what he wants, and he sees it. When he works with the director, in production, or whatever he's doing, he's one hundred percent committed. He always has amazing faith in the whole combination, between us, and mainly the director. He talked to James to do it. We all knew James did a great job. I mean, this was his baby. He did the first one. He knew what he wanted to do in the second one. I mean, you could see he already had it all plotted in his head – design storyboards and the effects ready. It was only a question of time and money. He was always upbeat about it, and when we went to the first screening – not the final cut but the first screening – you could see the smile on Arnold's face. He knew he had a big success on his hands. Everything was always very positive and nothing really at all . . . except on our point of view: we kept on seeing the budget a little higher than we originally had thought. The money situation was a little high, but we were expecting it. If you think about it now, it was cheap compared to the movies they are making now.

**Q: You were one of the people in the industry who pioneered the foreign market. When *Terminator II* was unleashed upon the world in the summer of 1991, can you tell me about going around the world with Arnold promoting this film?**

Mario Kassar: We went and we promoted the movie. The guy's a publicity machine. He knows exactly how to handle the media. He knows exactly where to go, what to do and what to say. He's a magnet. I mean, he's nice to everybody. And actually, from all the actors I've worked with, he's probably one of the most who leans toward promotion that I've ever met. He is very good at promoting movies and he loves to do it. He knows at the that end of the day, by promoting the movie he's also promoting himself, which is good for everybody. And he does do what he says he will. Because sometimes you get actors who tell you they'll do this, or they'll do that, but they really don't do everything, or they become a little

251

more difficult, or they get tired after a year of shooting, or they cut the schedule short. Arnold does it from A to Z and if he could do more he would do more.

**Q: What was wrong with *Terminator IV* compared to the original *Terminator* movies, was it devoid of the substance that was integral to the first three movies?**
Mario Kassar: Well, we sold the franchise and we have seen that they somewhat gravitated toward something different. I think maybe there weren't so many . . . When you're not involved, I wasn't really involved, we were far from it. So there are new producers, new actors and new people than when you were in the business. I don't know, maybe the actor wanted to do something (different). I heard there were revised shootings, but I can't really confirm because I wasn't there. I had nothing to do with it. I'm sure they tried their best to make it a good movie – nobody wants to make a bad movie. But somehow, it's not maybe so bad, but it is not to the level of the first three and definitely not to the level of the second.

**Q: When you made *Terminator III*, did Arnold advise you to buy the rights from Dino De Laurentiis, which were worth $7 million, but he said to you to bid $3 million for them?**
Mario Kassar: No. I don't remember that at all. My recollection is we paid for half of the rights, $7 million from the bankruptcy of Carolco. And that was only for half of the rights. And the other half were still with, as I told you, James Cameron's ex-wife. So we took a big risk by just buying the half. Then we approached Arnold. He said, "I don't want to do it. I'll only do it if Mr. Cameron will direct." But James felt we had taken it away from him. I don't know if he was offended or something, but we said we got it (the script) and we want you to direct it. But he didn't want to direct it. He said no. He didn't want to do it. Then we went ahead and told Arnold, "Look, I don't think James wants to do it." I guess when Gail heard that James wasn't doing it, and maybe Arnold wasn't going to do it, she said, "You know, I'll sell my 50 percent now."

And the minute she said yes, we went and bought her 50 percent and secured the whole rights. Then we said, you know, James and Arnold, we believe in the franchise and we're going to make the screenplay. We made it and we got Jonathan Mustow to direct it. We ended up with a good screenplay. At that stage, I wanted to have a woman Terminator in the movie, which we did. And we took it to Arnold to see and he liked it and he was on board. With the new director things started progressing, and we put the finance together. And those are the days when they had the German Tax Fund available. German-owned movie financier Intermedia Films invested with us, and we did it. And we made a deal with Sony and Warner and a couple of other territories that we sold to independently, and the movie came out and did OK.

**Q: Some people found James Cameron hard to get on with, does this reflect the fact he's a perfectionist and extremely devoted to bringing the best out of people?**

Mario Kassar: Yeah, he's definitely a perfectionist – only if you try to interfere in his business. I mean, I go hire him because he's very good at what he does. If you're going to come and tell him what to do, then I don't understand why you hired him. I mean, he's been proving film after film that he knows exactly what he's doing. He gets exactly what he wants and he does deliver it. If you try to put your fingers everywhere in what he's doing, then he's not a happy camper. He's kind of the king of the set. He runs the show. He's the captain. And he should be. I'm sure he's got his ups and downs, had some bad days and good days. At the end of the day, he's such a perfectionist that he wants everything to be perfect. When you look at the end result of the movie, you forget whether it was twelve months, six months or two months of making it. You forget all the dramas and the little stories because you just look at the result and you forget about anything else that happened. You only see the good stuff. He is absolutely a perfectionist. His movies, they talk for themselves.

**Q: How did the concept of *Crusade* come about, which was going to star Arnold and be directed by the same director who directed *Total Recall*, Paul Verhoeven?**

Mario Kassar: Paul Verhoeven was in my office one day. I've always been affected by these (historical) kinds of stories, and Paul came up with the idea of doing a movie about *Crusade*. We got a writer – I don't remember his name now, but he was a writer – to write us a screenplay. And Arnold was on board. We had a very good screenplay, we met Arnold and we met Paul. We were scouting in Morocco to shoot. We were almost there, but unfortunately it didn't materialize due to technical and budget reasons. And the company, at that time, wasn't really in the best financial situation and I had another movie I was preparing for the company. But I could not really get a budget that I could maintain a certain amount that was agreeable to all parties, so unfortunately I had to stop it.

It probably was the wrong decision, but you know when you cannot financially do all of those things at the same time, and when you're not certain of how much the budget could be. Because sometimes they can go over budget, they always do, whether it's 10 percent, 20 percent or 50 percent. I really had no clear idea the way things would progress, for many technical reasons and whatever reasons. I don't remember them now well. I could not put my finger on the exact amount that I could predict for the budget. So I said I'll cut my losses now. I had to stop.

**Q: What exactly was Arnold going to play in this movie, which was touted as being the bloodiest historical epic ever made by some critics, and what was the core concept? You had meetings with Arnold pertaining to this project, what were his sentiments?**

Mario Kassar: He was a kind of a happy-go-lucky kind of thief running around in this area who, by mistake, ends up with the Crusade and becomes what he becomes. He was not a Crusader, nor part of any faction or political group. He just happens to be there doing something and he's caught in the middle of all of this. And, of course, he makes the best out of it. We didn't know how the people would react. It's hard to believe that Arnold with that accent would be in that area (Middle East). Arnold was all for it. In fact, he owned the rights for a while. I don't know whether he still owns them or not. He was a big, big believer in the movie and so was I. I wanted to do it very badly.

Of course, there were also the studios with their own worry on how you handle the Crusade because of the religion factor. You've got the Christians, you've got the Muslims and you've got Jews. It's very difficult to always be politically correct in things like this. So the studios were scared to touch it. They were really scared to release it. But in my mind, it didn't matter. If I was doing this then I would have enough advice, so I wasn't worried about that. After Carolco, I was looking if I could do it again with Arnold. But I think Arnold and Paul tried unsuccessfully to go to the studios to do it. But somehow it didn't work out, whether it was because of the budget or whatever.

**Q: What's the most intriguing or compelling conversation you had with Arnold?**
Mario Kassar: The only kind that always stays in my head is when we were doing *Total Recall*. He wanted to get to a certain amount for acting. He called me very early in the morning – about six, seven or eight o' clock in the morning – and he said, "Mario, I want you to give me more than that. I want you to give me this amount of money and I promise you I'll promote the hell out of the movie. If you have to go and pay for promotions, it'll cost you anyway, that amount of money. I'm trying to establish myself at a certain amount of salary." I thought about it for a second because he keeps his word all the time.

It's usually against the rules in Hollywood to increase and put the salary up for an actor. Let's say he's worth $8 million or $9 million, and they all agree to pay more unless he comes out with a $300 million movie. And it becomes ten million, and they all agree to pay that amount. They don't compete on each other to pay more money – the studios to an actor. You know what I'm saying? When he called me, I thought about it for a second. I said, "OK, I'll give you nine (million dollars) and you promote the movie all the way as much as you can." Which, for me, was like money in the bank because promotion is so important for a movie. I did that and he was very happy. I kept my word. And believe me he kept his word because he promoted *Total Recall* like there's no tomorrow when he went on a tour.

**Q: Arnold became a commercial commodity. What was his agent Lou Pitt like to deal with?**
Mario Kassar: When I dealt with him, his agent was a very nice guy and he was very helpful. But at the end of the day, Arnold makes his own decisions. But his agent is a, I don't know if I would call him a typical Hollywood agent. I mean, there was nothing special – he's kind of open. But he is a very nice man, a man of his word and he never played any games with us. He was cool, very nice guy.

**Q: After much introspection, Arnold no doubt clearly was able to ascertain the formula of success. What strikes you the most about Arnold?**
Mario Kassar: Mostly his character. He's got an amazing character. I think when the guy comes to a meeting, he's always so prepared. He's done his homework, so he doesn't sit in the meeting and act like he doesn't know. I mean, he knows and he always asks the right questions to get the right answers. On the set, he knows everything. He's ready before, during and after and ready to do more. One thing about him is his persistence. When he wants to get something he will get it. He will go and do anything humanly possible to get it, and he does succeed at the end of the day. So, I mean, he has an amazing will of discipline. I mean, he's Austrian so he's got that discipline and the persistency and the enthusiasm. For him, it's like nothing is impossible. Obviously, nothing is impossible. You can see where he's come from and where he is now. Oh, my God, he's come a long way, hasn't he?

# CHUCK RUSSELL

The director of Arnold's *Eraser*, Chuck Russell's credits as a director and producer include *The Mask* with Jim Carrey, *A Nightmare on Elm Street III*, and *The Scorpion King*, with Dwayne Johnson. More recently he produced Tom Cruise's *Collateral*. He lives in Los Angeles.

**Q: When the concept of the *Eraser* movie came up, were you actually working with Arnold at the time on something else, and did you discuss the minutia of the *Eraser* script?**
Chuck Russell: I was working on a pirate movie. It was a remake of *Captain Blood* that Arnold was interested in doing for Warner Brothers. And Arnold persuaded me he had a script called *Eraser*. We discovered that the film *Captain Blood* was in studio development, so it was going to take a long time. This was all before *Pirates of the Caribbean*. And the studio wasn't sure about a big action version of a pirate movie. Arnold had come across this script called *Eraser*. I was very pleasantly surprised that it had everything at the time that I felt an action movie should be, and something that was very tailor-made for Arnold.

The pirate film may have been a more difficult fit. So, we immediately began final script polishes and working out what was a very good production plan. Even then it was still a year before shooting. It takes time when you're dealing with films of that level of production. But I was quite pleasantly surprised. It's something you learn in this business: to develop films through. I've been very lucky in that I've never done a film that I haven't been very excited about. But to collaborate and work with a star, at that time Arnold was at the top of his game, but he wanted to have one more big hit, and that was another goal. He wanted to have one more commercial success in an action film that still had some fresh exciting ideas in it. I think what helped make that film successful was casting Vanessa Williams. It was a bit of a surprise for the audience – a good surprise. She was a good match for Arnold. She was an actress with a real grip of heart to her as well.

**Q: In this movie, the plotline was inclined toward more reality based. Because a lot of the movies Arnold did, science fiction was subsumed into the manuscript.**

Chuck Russell: This was a little more reality based, it was broad action. You have to have some fun in an Arnold Schwarzenegger movie. And at that point of his career, I wanted to have some sense of humor along with the action. Arnold was a United States Marshal in a witness protection program, who had to work on his own. In the story there's a mole within the United States Marshals. I think it was a great idea for a character. He's so good at relocating his witnesses and creating new identities for them that he's one of the erasers. He literally erases people from the records in this modern day in every computer everywhere. And seeing him work as a rogue agent, it was the fun of the movie. There was a plotline that involved real guns, which was something that we researched and had found which was being developed. Which were magnetic powderless weapons and the most powerful. It's something on a large scale. The storyline was to keep that technology from falling into the wrong hands. This was really part of the story.

**Q: Can you tell me about some of the locations – New York, Washington DC, Warner Brothers Studios in Burbank – that you filmed at?**

Chuck Russell: We set up in New York, which was really great fun as a filmmaker. We have Arnold trashing through the gates of the New York City Zoo that we actually built the front of in Central Park. It was quite spectacular having Warner Brothers' full corporation on this kind of scale of production. We also blew up a small house, which was built on a set, which was ready for demolition. It was the opening sequence where Arnold saves a mobster who had to disappear and goes into a witness protection program. They were great, great fun. We had cooperation from New York. I think it really helped keep the film on a great scale. It's great about seeing Schwarzenegger crossing the street in front of the FBI building. We shot this in Washington to kind of give the film authenticity and create a setting that this kind of character would be familiar with. I just think it helps make the film kind of classy, gives it a classy setting. In a way, I wanted to do some honor to the United States Marshals, and even the FBI and CIA and the police agencies that do a great job. They're often the bad guys in the movies. So it was nice to make the United States Marshal a good guy.

**Q: Would I be right in saying that the majority of the film was shot at Warner Brothers Studios in Burbank?**
Chuck Russell: It was. One of the sequences, which is very well known from that film, which I think helps distinguish it, is when Arnold escapes from a 747. James Caan plays the villain, a mole within the United States Marshals, and has Arnold at gunpoint. It was the kind of a scene I always wanted to do. And I've seen it done since. There have been some scenes in other action films, with the hero making that kind of escape. In that sequence, Arnold turns a seat into the jet engine, which puts the plain off-course. And he falls chasing a parachute. He has to catch a parachute. It was actually one of the best experiences I've had from the storyboard, from that point of concept this was not in the original script.

I knew we had a lot of Schwarzenegger movies to live up to at that point of his career, and we needed one or two big action set pieces that I felt the audience had never seen before. That's the 747 that I had to campaign the studios for. They ended up being very happy about it. Basically, that was the trailer of the film when the film was done. It involved some of the most spectacular stunt work an actor had done at the time. And Arnold, who was already in his late forties, did a jump on what was a new rig at the time – and a stuntman dropping almost full velocity on a cord, which has a very sophisticated braking system. We went to the biggest stage at Warner Brothers. And on the door section of the 747 set piece Arnold did five takes where he dropped off to get this right. It was quite the pro at the time, only seven of them had used that rig. But he was going for it. We got a very good sequence.

**Q: What was Arnold like to work with, was he easy-going or malcontent?**
Chuck Russell: Arnold, you, know, he's a very bright and competitive guy. He evolved a long way from the guy we all saw in *Pumping Iron*. Actually, after that experience I was not surprised. Everyone else was very surprised when he went into politics because he kept very quiet about that. He had an interest in political affairs. But people were quite shocked when he went into politics here in California. He was really almost like a producer on the show. He was smart enough about the system, how to work with the studio. He was always very good about our need for bringing in the proper experts and getting the scenes done correctly. I could totally depend on him. You're working with someone who already is an icon, and I was prepared to take him through to another hit. But I was surprised that he was so bright. He was really very strong on the teamwork that it takes to make a movie of that caliber.

So, when he went into politics, I already knew he had a talent for working with a team of people. I actually thought he would do quite a good job. Arnold enjoys himself, again, entertaining the crew if we're held up waiting for the lights or waiting for special effects. Arnold cares about everybody, right down to the guy sweeping the stage. I've seen him entertain the whole crew when we've been stuck, at night waiting for an explosion to take place. We had a shot where we had to pop under the floor because of the gun blazing, which was very difficult because of the awkward angle. He had to pop up breaking through the floorboards like a jack in the box. I can recall it was two o' clock in the morning, and we were still trying to get the shot done. He's just a tough guy. He's ready to do what's required. While we definitely used a stunt double, you can count on him. Arnold appreciated that I cared about his safety as much as I did. I think he's worked with people who imagine he is the Terminator. He's just a human being and maybe has sore knees at two o' clock in the morning, but that's part of my job: to make sure and keep an eye on him.

**Q: Were you an executive producer on this movie as well?**

Chuck Russell: I was. It's because of the development of the film. It's something that I started as a producer and putting the pieces together where you get the proper budget and get a script through to completion. I was working very closely with Arnold Kopelson, who was a producer on the film, getting that picture in front of the camera. Problems with filming at studios can arise because there are many films in development and you want to get your film into production. It was actually fairly quick. It took us a year, which is actually quick in films, to take it from the original script to a final polish in front of the cameras.

**Q: What was the most challenging decision you and Arnold had to make when making *Eraser*?**

Chuck Russell: There were various production decisions, but I think this was actually fun and great to make. It's hard work but it's what I love. So I'm very inspired to do it. The most difficult thing is safety. When you're doing this many physical stunts, that was still before a lot of the CGI was available, but we still did more of the stunts physically at that time. So, for me it's really running a safe set when you're doing the explosions and this much action. The filmmaking is fun. And when you tie it in with the special effects, it's the hard part to make sure they're safe and less dangerous as possible. And Arnold appreciated that. It's something where you don't want to break a finger, or something you have to be careful about.

**Q: Can you tell me about working with Arnold's two main co-stars, James Caan and Vanessa Williams?**

Chuck Russell: Vanessa is a very charismatic lady, and in casting there are only certain actresses you want to see with Arnold. Jamie Lee Curtis was with him in *True Lies*. Vanessa, I felt, was another actress with a heroic sense about her as well. I think it's one of the things that captured the audience's attention. They were a very good pairing. There's a shot of Vanessa stealing Schwarzenegger's cigar at the premiere that was circulated in all the papers. That kind of captured their relationship as we publicized it in the film as well. When you make a film, it's one of the important things. I really do believe in old style chemistry between the stars, and James Caan was part of that. It was really all three of them.

James was so great in *The Godfather* and movies like *Gone with the West*. He hadn't really been working for a little while, and I just thought, *What has happened to this terrific actor?* I talked him into doing the role and he had a great time. In a way, it renewed his career at the time. He went on to do a number of films and a very successful television series, *Las Vegas*. James Caan was just a big character, a great actor, a prankster and a guy with a good sense of humor on the set. A tough guy – an old real tough guy. And it was fun. He's now in *Entourage* and in *Hawaii Five-O*, too. His son is a terrific actor now. I still bumped into Arnold when he was the governor. I just saw him at one or two functions and bumped into him by accident almost, and he always takes a moment. This is what's great about Schwarzenegger. You asked me about him earlier – one of the things that I think really sets him apart – it's true of Tom Cruise, too, both Arnold and Tom are really very personable guys. They're high energy guys. It's something I noticed similar with both of them.

I did the publicity junket with Schwarzenegger. We did seven countries in eleven days. I've never done anything like that. It's all about Arnold's level of energy, and how hard he's willing to work for films or projects he believes in. So, his people had planned that junket. Tom Cruise almost invented this style of international publicity. Both of those guys have a work ethic and a kind of personal charisma. They'll take the time with the media, and they'll take the time with their many friends in their personal lives, with all the demands of being a lead in a movie. That is something, ultimately, the public realizes. It's just the energy level it takes. Arnold's a tough guy, and you gotta' come to the table knowing what you're doing, so it's not easy. But I enjoyed it because of that element. He cares, and he cares about everything he does and every film he makes.

When Vanessa Williams' agent first brought to her attention that there was an invitation for her to read for the new Arnold Schwarzenegger film *Eraser* she was set to go on a tour, so initially said she wouldn't be able to read the script. However, there were financial problems with the tour, so she wasted no time in calling her agent back and asked whether the invitation was still open. It was. "I flew myself out for the audition, read for Arnold Kopelson and the director Chuck Russell," says Williams. "Then they called me back the next day and wanted me to meet Arnold and read with him. I flew back. Then that Friday, they called me back out to do a screen test. By the following Monday, I had gotten the part. I didn't realize that nobody wanted me." In fact, Arnold's wife Maria had suggested Williams to the producers, but everyone else had their reservations because she didn't have the profile of a feature film actress. "Maria said, 'Vanessa might be a good idea,'" Williams recalled. Kopelson wasn't familiar with Williams as a feature film actress, and Arnold knew of her as a recording artist, while Russell wasn't familiar with her at all. "These were the people that I had to convince," continues Williams. "I had to go in there and basically kick ass in my audition." Williams fought for the part and was able to convince the executives at Warner Brothers that she was right for the part. And they also probably didn't want her to gravitate toward doing a single like Whitney Houston did for *Bodyguard*. In the end, Williams' role was a huge success – and the script was rewritten to end with the pair in a relationship.

**Q: Chuck, can you tell me of anything you talked about that signifies his persona?**
Chuck Russell: So many things. I think just that Arnold used to kid about Stallone. There was an old- standing competition I think

from the 1980s between them both. Arnold always used to kid about what Stallone is doing down the street. I think Arnold is a real man's man, and I enjoyed that. I'm from the Midwest of America, Chicago, and it's a little more of a tough guy city than California. So I enjoyed Arnold's big manliness, attitude about sports, working out, kind of the brotherhood of Arnold. The Cigar Club was the most fun: hanging out with Arnold at the Cigar Club. We often had support from James Cameron, who came in and gave us his thoughts on the script and was very supportive in general. So that's another Arnold connection from me. It's been interesting to see how great a filmmaker Cameron has turned out to be. Arnold has a habit where he'll test people. He doesn't mind testing. And he's got a great sense of humor. He knows his reputation in his film as a tough guy. I've seen him test people when he first meets other people at the Cigar Club, in a very friendly, charming way. You have to kind of prove yourself to Schwarzenegger if you're going to sit down and have a cigar with him.

**Q: What was the filming routine like from morning to night?**
Chuck Russell: We start early and do rehearsals and if there was action things involved, we'd lay out exactly where the explosions rigs would go. I'd explain everything to Arnold for bigger scenes and I'd show him exactly what was expected of him – how we're going to design the stunt. He cared about the performance. I wanted a little bit more heart from him in some scenes. His relationship with Vanessa as well, there is a sense of protectiveness in actuality. I honestly think he was trying a little more in the acting side than he had done in some other roles where it was really about 'I'll be back'. So we spent a lot of time on that as well. He was going to do rehearsals, and things that I think he hadn't done too much of before.

**Q: That brings me to the next question: Arnold was and is known as an action man, some critics have the tendency to refer to his acting performances as 'wooden'. How did you perceive him in**

**the dialog scenes and acting, coming from the perspective of a director such as yourself?**

Chuck Russell: I expected him to have limitations, but I think when you're working with somebody who is already established with this kind of personality with the audience, you want to present him in his best light and give the audience what they expect. And he, like I said, spent a little more time in rehearsals and tried to come across a human being as well as an action star. I think he did achieve that – he and Vanessa in particular. I had to allow time for him to work out with his weights. He had a truck with his weightlifting kit on it. He was determined to keep in shape, so he's got to put a couple of hours into that each day as well. So one of the things I had to make sure was that he had a break. If I was going to have an hour for the lighting to be set up, I would make sure to let him know it's his time to work out. That's one of the things with people like Arnold Schwarzenegger, where you have to give them a balance as an actor and an athlete.

**Q: The film grossed more than $234 million worldwide. After this movie, his movies at the box office started to decline as if the studios were no longer prescient. Can you tell me more about the premiere?**

Chuck Russell: The premiere was at the Mann's Chinese Theater. I think the studio was holding their breath because it had cost a little more than they thought it would originally. The original script had a lot of gun play. The 747 scene and the crocodile scene, which was shot in a zoo set, I knew I needed something more. Those were the two scenes that were unique. And it played so well at the screening at the studio and the premiere. Premiere audiences are actually not that easy, it's stocked full of Hollywood people that are very critical. But the film has a lot of interest, old fashioned heroism, and the audience really responded to that and responded to the humor in the film. Robert Pastorelli, who has since passed away sadly, did a fantastic job for the comedy. Robert was a very, very skilled actor, almost underrated but a brilliant comedian. He had just the right touch, like a New York tough guy, mobster Arnold had embraced, who was sort of stuck onboard for the adventure. Pastorelli just did a spectacular job. He always fed Arnold the lines, real plus to the show and a great personality. The big moment at the premiere, though, was Vanessa and Arnold. Just the humor, the friendship and the camaraderie they had really played well on the screen.

**Q: Any after-party moments?**
Chuck Russell: This is how you can judge a film premiere: how many people come to your after-party. The film was a real crowd pleaser so everybody was at the party. And Arnold was, of course, the center of attention. He knows how to play that. So, you know, this is what we set out to do. Arnold was at a certain point of his career where he hadn't had a hit in a couple of years, and the goal was to make that $100 million-plus hit. He knew then, he knew right at the premiere, that was when he first knew that it was a success. We could tell he had the crowd.

One of the big thrills of filmmaking is you can plan, you can have a big budget and you could have a star, whatever, but you don't really know how it will do. The crowd decides, the audience decides. Critics tend to underrate action films and comedies. I don't know why. They assume they're easy, but they're not. Action acting is a very stylized kind of acting. It's very interesting to see which actors can pull it off. It's just not that easy. Arnold is Arnold because of his style. He actually is a brave guy. He actually is that disciplined of an athlete that it comes across that well on the screen – you can't fake it. It's very hard to double these guys. It's just as hard to double Schwarzenegger. Dwayne Johnson, 6ft 3, I found it very difficult to double him in *The Scorpion King*. Nobody could swing the sword like Dwayne. We had a 20-pound sword and this other tough guy couldn't move it. So these are macho pictures and it takes a lot of heart to pull off those roles. I think the critics sometimes think they're review proof, but really it's about pleasing the audience. It's about pleasing the audience internationally, which is something I bear in mind. The story has to make sense, even when it's translated.

## BRIAN LEVANT

After starting his career as a writer for *The Jeffersons*, Brian Levant went on to direct the films *Beethoven*, *The Flintstones*, *Are We There Yet* and Jackie Chan's *The Spy Next Door*. He directed Arnold's *Jingle All The Way*, one of Arnold's least well-received films.

**Q: Can you tell me how you got together with Arnold to make *Jingle All the Way*?**
Brian Levant: Arnold (after leaving the governor's office) told his agents that he was ready to accept roles again. He said that after seven years of CAA (Creative Artists Agency) asking him, "When can we put you back out on the market?" He said go ahead after his time in the office finished. Let's go back a little bit. The film was originally developed to star someone like Danny Stern from *Home Alone*. And somewhere along the way, someone at ICM – Arnold's old agency – read the script and thought it would be a good vehicle, a third comedy vehicle, for Arnold and Danny DeVito. Arnold read it and he liked it very much. Danny DeVito was directing a movie so he couldn't do it. So we got Sinbad.

I was sent the script by Peter Sherman, who was then the head of the Fox movie division. I had worked with him in the television department there. I went over to San Francisco and I met up with Chris Columbus, who produced the film and was the director of the *Home Alone* movies and the *Harry Potter* films. We had a wonderful meeting. Then I went to the set of *Eraser* I think. No, the one with apocalyptic turn of the century, what was that one called? Peter Hyams film (*The 6th Day*). He was shooting that. We sat down and talked. We had a good meeting and I told him how dedicated I was to family comedy and that I wanted to make this big epic slapstick film. He was gung ho, he responded to my energy and he listened very carefully. He's a very, very smart man. I don't think he gets the credit he deserves in that respect, you know. His mind is as well developed as his biceps. He finished over seven years of being the governor of the state.

His agent, who later became my agent, Lou Pitt and all of us said, "OK, let's do it." Basically, when I came on we had a release date before we had a script. So we jumped in on the script and started solving innumerable production issues that needed to be resolved. I mean, in the film, in the world of CGI technology 1995 was a long time ago, so we had to do so much of that more practical, a lot of wirework, a lot of costume design for the opening and for the Turboman set. We set in Minneapolis for a month and had to scout there. We had eighty-two days to shoot. The longest by far I've ever had. And on the back lot of Universal in July, we had one thousand two hundred extras who dressed for a Minneapolis winter in one hundred degrees in Los Angeles summer. But we had a wonderful time.

Arnold, it's interesting, you know – Jackie (Chan), too. Peter Morgan, the guy who wrote the last Clint Eastwood film and Ron Howard's *Nixon*, said an interesting thing about Clint. Ron Howard said that they were like sailors from a century who came to port now and again but lived on the ship. Their lives were on the set. They move from place to place, movie to movie. And that's really what their lives are about. Both Arnold and Jackie fit that description very well, too. That this is where they spend undoubtedly so much of their time, surrounded by close associates and the people who help construct all their stunts, protect them and work with them and provide a fun environment around them. And this film was a prime example of that. Arnold comes alive on the set and behind the scenes of the camera, that was his terrain and he occupied it beautifully. I don't think he's ever gotten credit enough for his comedy work in the film.

We asked him to do a great deal more comedy wise, to wield many more comedic weapons than he had before. And things like *Twins*, where his silence and his glare, the things that we've come to know so well and ferocious in action films and comedies became comedic. We asked him to play, really for the first time in his career, an unexceptional man, a normal stubborn dad. I believe he was very successful in carrying the story from scene to scene, in propelling the scenes, in playing a straight man, applying comedy and playing the action helping to find the balance between action and comedy, which is a very delicate thing to do. You want to keep it at a certain level because it's a PG film – it's for kids. We had one big set piece after another. The man is so professional. The first day of work, he not only knew his lines in the entire script, but every character's lines in the script. He memorized the script before the first day of shooting.

**Q: Can you tell me about Arnold's and Sinbad's collaboration?**
Brian Levant: We let Sinbad loose many times! And we let him run, and we wanted to. I felt Arnold was very adept at, we'd do things and shape them and edit them a little bit on the set. And Arnold was great about that. Despite the fact he memorized every line, he said, "OK, we're going to do this and that." He was great about that, "Yes! Yes! Then I can do that." We'd say, "Good! OK! Here we go, let's try it!" So it was a very collaborative film. Chris Columbus, the producer, always had great ideas and everybody pitched in and we had fun. I think on the first day of the movie, we shot a scene with Sinbad and Arnold on the street and it went really well. There was a lot of improvising stuff, and it looked terrific and it had a real nice feel about it. The only time during the whole process of the film that I got a call from the head of the studio, he said, "Hey, that was great! Saw the dailies. Can't wait to see the whole movie!" I don't know if he felt like that in the end, but it was great at the time.

**Q: What would you say was your most memorable moment working with Arnold on the movie?**
Brian Levant: When you're out with Arnold – and the same with Jackie – in public shooting outside in the streets, you see how excited people are just to be in a block with him. How magnetic the personalities are and how they respond so positively to the crowd and the recognition. You never see Arnold and Jackie Chan brush off anybody. They're gracious to everyone. Everywhere I go I

sometimes hear, "You know, I met Arnold, boy was he nice." You know they're a big star, but when you go out in the world and you see the reverence that they command, that's fun. That's really fun. We had many, many good days on the film. It's hard work working with animals, working with kids, working on wires, things that test your patience. Arnold was always in great spirits and very positive of the whole experience.

Brian Levant directed Jackie Chan in the spoof *The Spy Next Door*, one of Chan's breakthrough Western roles after many years of being the number-one action star in South East Asia. Meanwhile, Arnold had a cameo role in Chan's *Around the World in Eighty Days*, which also starred Steve Coogan. Chan remembers trying to communicate with the Austrian actor who never lost his accent, "I've known him (Arnold) for a long time, from being partners in Planet Hollywood. I met him at a party and we talked, but not really deep talking, always just, 'Hi, Jackie. Nice to meet you,' and then we sit down and talk about the business. The next time I saw him again, we were sitting in the bathtub and he said some jokes, but I didn't understand what he was talking about. And probably when I say something, he doesn't understand. He's a pretty nice guy."

**Q: Did you get a chance to socialize with Arnold whilst shooting the movie?**
Brian Levant: We went out. When you're directing a movie, just because you stop shooting it doesn't mean you stop working. So, yes, we did go out a couple of times for dinner and have some lunch in his trailer. And we'd work on things and talk. You know, it's a big job. Sometimes he had his family there and he needed to spend time with them. But we had a great time, we really did. I'm very heartened by the film's growing reputation. It wasn't a blockbuster by far when it came out, but since, it's proven to be tremendously endurable and a popular holiday film. I did a college

speaking tour and the only movie anybody ever asked me to sign for them was *Jingle All the Way*. Everywhere I went the kids had it. They said, "We watch it every Christmas. We love it. I grew up on it." It's surprising and gratifying and shows the enduring popularity of Arnold. I think the world was going to be excited to see him on the big screen again.

**Q: He's an intellectual person, what conversations did you have with him that he exuded his intellectual side?**
Brian Levant: Yes. I enjoyed talking politics with him. At the time, he was starting to become immersed in political thoughts. You could see it was on his mind already. We enjoyed discussing issues. And once again, I don't think people give him credit for developing his mind as much as the biceps.

**Q: Do you think Arnold became recognized and accepted beyond the confines of the action movie genre because of the success of his comedy films?**
Brian Levant: I think he was very lucky to team up with Ivan Reitman, who I did *Beethoven* for. That is a very, very smart man and knows how to get the best out of performances. What he found with Arnold was that he could tap into people's expectations, of Arnold's behavior and your expectations of comic effect. All he has to do sometimes is look at somebody and raise an eyebrow, and people would laugh knowing what's behind those reactions. And the simplicity of many of the things he did for *Twins*, the goofy look he has on his face after he has sex with that cute girl, you know. It's very simple and very unfettered. It's very clean and simple and makes great use of Arnold's personality and his natural charm. So, he was very lucky to team up with Ivan. Then he had a comic in Danny DeVito, who's an expert comic actor. And they did have wonderful chemistry and it was an unusual team. A team like Laurel and Hardy.

## JOEL SCHUMACHER

*Batman and Robin* director Joel Schumacher was already friends with Arnold before he took the role of Mr. Freeze in the 1997 film, which was critically panned by critics and fans. Schumacher's other directorial credits include *Batman Forever*, *Phone Booth* and *The Phantom of the Opera*, alongside two episodes of *House of Cards*.

**Q: Can you tell me when you first started to work with Arnold, was it when you collaborated on the *Batman and Robin* film?**
Joel Schumacher: It's the first time we worked together, but we'd known each other for a long time before that. We had coffees and had talked to each other about working together. We just never had the right opportunity.

Joel Schumacher was a key motivating force for Arnold's decision to get involved in the most infamous comic-book movie of all time. Arnold explains, "Although I'd seen all the other Batman movies, and I have enjoyed them thoroughly and was always interested in, of course, playing the ultimate villain in one of those movies, I didn't really think much about it until Joel Schumacher came to me and said that he would like me to play Mr. Freeze." It invoked Arnold's interest and he thought it was intriguing. However, Arnold told Schumacher that he'd think about it because the character was very interesting. The director made it clear to Arnold that if Arnold decided not to come on board, then Schumacher would not be directing the movie because he felt he could only direct this movie if Arnold played Mr. Freeze. "He made me feel I would make this whole thing fall apart if I'm not a part of it," Arnold recalls. "So he made me feel like King Kong. So I called him up the next day, and I said, 'You know something, Joel, I'm going to do Mr. Freeze.'" Schumacher's second choice to play Mr. Freeze had been Anthony Hopkins – and his third was Hulk Hogan. Those might have been very different films…

**Q: What was your vision for *Batman and Robin*, did you feel Arnold's international fan base would propel the movie in terms of box office success? Arnold said it was very wise for Warner Brothers to have him in the movie from a marketing point of view.**
Joel Schumacher: *Batman Forever* was my first Batman movie, and my job was to sort of refresh the franchise. So we made a much younger and sexier Batman with Val Kilmer, and Nicole Kidman. Jim Carrey, Tommy Lee Jones and Drew Barrymore, there were a lot of terrific stars in the movie. And then *Batman and Robin* was just, you know . . . a sequel made for one reason: to make money. I was expected to make another one. So we were trying to make a bigger, better one and I think the fans were disappointed. I think the first one, *Batman Forever*, was the biggest box office in the United States. That was in 1995. I think Arnold has fans everywhere.

**Q: Can you describe his character, although known for being an action man he seemed to have been able to integrate humor into some of the characters he played during the course of his career?**
Joel Schumacher: Arnold, even in his most serious action movies, usually has lines that are ironic, or comedy, you know. He's a very funny man. I think he's always taken his characters and has used them with a couple of famous lines that seem like, you know, that he gets the joke.

**Q: What was the working relationship between Arnold and George Clooney like?**
Joel Schumacher: They're two of the greatest guys in the world. You couldn't be working with anyone who is more fun, kind-hearted individuals. The whole cast got along great because we had a lot of terrific people in the movie. I think it was a very complex character. It had humor in there and also in his lines. It was a mixture of many things together to make that character so that it had, you know, even though it's still a comic book you try to give it humanity. I think Arnold did. I think like a lot of villains he's misunderstood.

**Q: What would you say were his strong attributes having had observed and worked with him?**

Joel Schumacher: Well, he's so prepared and he's so professional. People that worked with him, some people are an asset in the business. He's very dedicated. He's never late and he helps the other actors. He brings a wonderful camaraderie. He's very jovial on the set and he makes work fun. But none of this surprises me because I know him as a man, and that's the way he is.

**Q: Someone like Nicolas Cage and Nicole Kidman, with whom you worked on *Batman Forever*, can play versatile characters. How would you define Arnold, he seemed to be a one-sided actor, would you agree?**

Joel Schumacher: I don't know, you can't ever put Arnold in a square box. I mean, you never know what Arnold's going to do next. So I'd put nothing past him. I think Nic Cage is like all great character actors, he could play the best of the best or the worst of the worst. I think Nicole Kidman could do that, too. Because they're character actors, they're not just actors. I'm convinced Nicole could do Lady Macbeth if she wants to, or she could play the sweetest human being that ever lived.

**Q: Arnold played a villain in some of his movies and a hero in most. Can you tell me what you detected in Arnold when working with him in terms of the joy in making a movie?**

Joel Schumacher: I think Arnold loves making movies and he's so good at it. So, I think he brings a lot of joy to it and he drives himself into the part. I don't think Arnold does anything halfway; I think he's an all or nothing guy. So, he brings a lot of energy and a lot of focus.

**Q: You also have known him on a social level.**

Joel Schumacher: We're friends and I'm friends with his wife Maria. Arnold and I traveled all over the world promoting the movie, and we had a lot of fun together, night life. I went to his birthday party.

I went to his fiftieth birthday party and his sixtieth. We're friends. He's the best advertiser in the world. He's a great marketer and he goes into each territory and really sells the movie.

**Q: Were there any projects you or Arnold wanted to work on after completing *Batman and Robin*?**
Joel Schumacher: He became governor. It was very late in the 1990s when I was doing different kinds of movies, so we didn't have any plans to work together at the time. Obviously, he had other plans, which I'm not sure what they were.

Critics panned *Batman and Robin*. The *Time Out Film Guide* wrote, "The fourth Bat-flick finds this juvenile franchise running on empty. Oozing insincerity and perplexed paternalism, Clooney plays Batman as an irrelevant bystander. Screenwriter Akiva Goldman sets up a 'revenge of nature' theme, with Schwarzenegger's lumpen Mr. Freeze croaking interminable 'cool' puns ('chill')." Undeniably the studio wanted to continue to capitalize on the *Batman* franchise, keep merchandise on the shelves and churn out sequel after sequel. Despite the fact the movie received negative criticism from reviewers and the audience, it was not enough to stop the movie becoming profitable, earning $238 million worldwide. With a budget of $125 million, all wasn't lost.

## ADAM GREENBERG

Noted for his work both in Israel and America, Adam Greenberg worked with Arnold on the first two *Terminator* movies, *Junior*, *Eraser* and *Collateral Damage*. His other credits include *First Night*, *Rush Hour* and *Snakes on a Plane*. He was nominated for the Academy Award for Best Cinematography in 1992, for his work on *Terminator II: Judgment Day*. He is now retired.

**Q: Can you tell me of your experience working with Arnold on *The Terminator*?**
Adam Greenberg: Arnold and me, we met on the set of the movie. We became very good friends from the very beginning. We had things in common: it was difficult to understand both of us because of our accents. It was difficult to understand him, and it was difficult to understand me. And we were the two foreigners on the movie set. We are friends to this day.

**Q: Arnold's character and script called for nonstop action throughout. He played a bad guy character, which became emblematic, and this made him the star of *The Terminator*.**
Adam Greenberg: Yeah, the first movie, it is what it is: a guy coming from a different place and a futuristic idea. There was a difference between his character in the first and the second movie. I didn't do the third and fourth; I only did the first and the second one. The first one was done without money, very low-budget movie. It was very difficult to shoot the movie at that time. The Union was very strong and they didn't permit you to do movies like this. But it worked out very well, the movie was accepted very well and I expected it would open a lot of doors for me. I became very popular at the time, everybody approached me to do exploitation movies. I didn't do them. I tried to stay away from it, always choosing movies with different subjects.

I tried to make him powerful. I tried to give him the visual look he had and I wanted to shoot him for that. I shot with the camera kind of being on the ground, very widening lens – 80mm lens.

Arnold's not too tall, he's wide but shorter. I wanted to make him big and strong, therefore I built a special type of equipment, very primitive but it works well. You are able to put the camera on the floor and actually not look at the camera, but look and operate this way. He liked it very much. And movies that he shot later, with other cameramen, he always asked them to do the lighting my way. Because he looked good like that, his cheekbones are very strong. I think his head looked very powerful. I showed him a few times and he was very happy with it.

**Q: Did you get to converse with Arnold regularly on the set?**
Adam Greenberg: I don't remember what I discussed with Arnold. To be honest with you, when we shot Arnold in the first movie, way back there was no equipment that we have today where you can see the playback. I don't remember us doing that in the first movie because it didn't exist back then. I never discussed with him how to do certain things. To be honest with you, the way I work is I have my idea set up ahead of time – the way I want the movie to look and I stick to this, you know. I never discussed with the director the script or things like that. I tried a few times, but the directors are mostly involved in reading and actors reading the script. I tried a few times, but very soon you immediately end up with very cold feelings from them, which means they don't think much about the visual. But with my experience with the visual, I'm into the visual – my job involves the visual side.

I'm a filmmaker. I come with an idea for the movie that would be a great look for the movie. I always work this way. I come very prepared for the movie. With Arnold, you know, he's a great guy, he liked what I did. He always liked what I did and complimented me. Later, in *Terminator II* and other movies, we had the instant playback. So he would come and look at it, and he could like it or not like it. He understood very well. He was always very cooperative with me. He understood what I was doing: to make him look like what he was supposed to look like – his character. He was always cooperative and understanding and patient. He's very disciplined.

**Q: Can you tell me about Arnold working with his co-star Linda Hamilton on the first movie?**

Adam Greenberg: Yeah. Linda Hamilton. I think it was *Terminator II* when he's in the garage gas station. In his movies he doesn't speak much, but in that scene the boy's standing and Linda was there. But he had about one page of dialog, which we did many times, maybe thirty-five takes. He had the piece of paper in front of him to read the lines. He said I'm a bodybuilder, not an actor. That's what he said. He knew his weak area, but he's a great guy and had a great sense of humor. I remember him and Linda, both of them, being very cooperative, but they worked opposite ways. She was with Michael, the other Terminator, in the first one. I don't remember any incident or complaint between Arnold and Linda. But both of them were very cooperative. In the second *Terminator*, when he dies he's melting down, there was no tension between them that I can remember.

**Q: Linda Hamilton said after the movie came out, Arnold didn't mention her name in all the press interviews he did. Do you feel Arnold wanted to be the center of attention and ostentatiously endeavored to do this?**

Adam Greenberg: Could be, could be. But I'll be surprised because he's not that kind of a guy, you know. To mention names, it shouldn't come from him; it's the advertising and the producer's responsibility. Obviously, it could be that they pushed Arnold, the studio and the advertising, they want to make him the hero, they want to 'punch' stronger because he's the star of the movie. She does have a big part, she's on the screen. Naturally, he's the hero. He's the guy they're building up and advertising around him. So naturally they would lift him up and push him to build him up and promote him more than her. But I don't think Arnold is that kind of a guy.

**Q: Were there any unusual incidents at break times that you can recall?**

Adam Greenberg: He's a great guy. Arnold is very smart. He has his feet on the ground, a great guy, smart and very friendly. He's like one of the guys talking to everybody and he tried to help everybody. Sometimes later on, when he became a big star – not in the first or second one (*Terminator*) – you had to wait for him maybe half an hour or forty-five minutes until he finished his chess game. If you interfered in his chess, he would not come on the set. You had to wait for him. Fifty people would wait for him on the set because he's playing chess. Later on, he had a lot of power as an actor. Eventually, the studio gives a lot of power.

**Q: When the first *Terminator* came out, was Arnold incredulously surprised by the success of this low-budget movie?**
Adam Greenberg: All of us were surprised. You have to understand that all of the people involved, I have to justify for myself, I think maybe myself, when I came to do the movie I had already behind me maybe thirty or forty feature films. Not television but feature films. I was all ready to go. But all the others, including Arnold, I think Arnold did one movie and the *Conan* films. Jim hadn't done anything, the producer, Gail Anne Hurd, had done nothing. She had invested the money. She financed Jim. She gave Jim $500 a week to keep him up – she financed him. But all the other people involved in this, they had previous experience.

When it came out everybody was astonished. And the people in town – Hollywood people – were astonished. Don't forget the movie was done for only $6.5 million. Two million out of the six and a half would go to Arnold. So really the movie was done with not enough money. I think looking back, there was a lot of drive, including myself, everybody wanted to prove themselves. And on top of this Arnold and the director, Jim Cameron. It was something new. Even visually it was something new. I remember I was looking to get a new metallic kind of look for the movie. This was a pleasure to work closely with and we came up with a different look. Today, every second movie is like this, with a metallic look. But at that time, it was something that I think had never been seen before, before any of these digital things, all that you see today. I think everybody was astonished, and everybody's careers built up from the result of this movie, there's no question about it.

Reflecting on the initial success of *The Terminator*, Arnold explained, "He's indestructible, no emotions, no feelings, can just eliminate anything that's in front of him. I think this is why the film became such a success. Because I think everyone has a dream to just maybe for one day to be a Terminator. I think that's why it became so successful. Because everyone wants to just be a Terminator one day and take care of the 'job'. You know, the payback against whoever did them harm, those sorts of things. So I think that's what really is the fantasy in everyone." Arnold's friends had advised him not to pursue playing a villain, the conventional wisdom being that it would be bad for his career. However, Arnold believed he would give it a shot, partly because he found the script well written and the director was very enthusiastic and determined – two qualities he himself possessed. It was a gamble that paid off handsomely.

**Q: Do you feel the character Arnold played in *Junior* put a dent in his image at the time? You have said, "Why is he doing this movie like this?" But the producers and Arnold seemed to be enthusiastic, they thought it would do well. What did he think about playing such a role?**

Adam Greenberg: Yeah. He did *Junior* with Ivan Reitman. I didn't talk to him about it, but the same director, Ivan Reitman, had done a movie with Arnold and Danny DeVito called *Twins*. It's a very funny movie. And if you put an actor like Arnold playing the hero, obviously, in a pregnant situation, it already becomes controversial with people and something which is unexpected, something shocking. Arnold was willing to shoot it and he enjoyed it. I could tell he enjoyed it. I didn't discuss it with him asking him why he was doing that kind of movie. The director was a comedy director, and I think the previous experience between Arnold and Danny

DeVito in *Twins* worked out very well, and so the contrast and difference between them two was like black and white.

Emma Thompson was in the movie, too. They liked each other very much, and, obviously, Emma Thompson's a great actress. I like her very much. I remember she was a great actress and lady. I still have memories of her today. She liked Arnold and respected him very much. You see, Arnold is very likable – you cannot not like him. You may not agree with him, but he has a good sense of humor and he's one of those guys who's nice to be around. In situations with Arnold whenever you go to a party, always there's a group of people around Arnold. He's a funny guy, nice to be around and people enjoy to be around him. I always go to parties for the movies I've shot. I'm not a party guy but I do go to them.

His wife Maria would come on the set. I don't remember his kids coming but Maria did. And the movie we did in Mexico, *Collateral Damage*, which was a distant location, she would come there, too. They had a private plane and she would come on the plane. But *Junior* was done here in town (Los Angeles). But she was always on the set. We stayed in Mexico in a very isolated place. I can tell you that ahead of time, the company Warner Brothers sent a lot of equipment to Mexico before the production crew arrived, before we all arrived. I think film negatives and many printers and faxes, a lot of stuff, they had an entire truck loaded, a big truck at the airport by air. They were supposed to take the equipment to the location, but it was robbed. Some guys with guns came and told the driver to step down from the truck and they took over and drove away the truck with all the equipment and the negatives – everything disappeared. Then I came to Arnold, and I told him, "Arnold, I think you should think about it. They might kidnap you over there. You should have protection. Think about it."

I told him they could kidnap you for money, because he's from a very rich family. He was very thankful to me and eventually they hired an international protection team of guards in Mexico for the entire shooting. He was coming to the set with one jeep with guns ahead of him and another car in the middle and one behind him.

They were guarding him 24 hours. In these places you disappear, they kidnap you. He's a very valuable man they can take him and ask for anything they want. But she (Maria) would come on set. I don't remember their kids coming on the set, but the wife, yes. She was very friendly, but she was also busy. They have four kids. She's an independent woman.

Although Arnold's tough guy rep had prevailed through his comedic roles in box office hits *Twins* and *Kindergarten Cop*, the role he undertook in *Junior* was, perhaps, the most challenging to his image. "The great thing about it is you're so . . . you can't afford to play a woman or let the sensitive side to come out because that is tougher to do than to play in an action movie and play a tough guy – that's easy," he said. He continues, "But I mean, to play the opposite of that, people always ask me – and the show asked me when I did the press junket – 'How can you do that?' You need to be secure with your masculinity to play a woman, or someone who gets pregnant." Arnold has always believed with great conviction that the only way you know how far you can go is to take risks. "So I cannot blame any actor or any athlete or any businessman for taking risks," Arnold said. "The chances are you can fail." Arnold said that he wasn't trying to be a woman being pregnant, but was trying to act as a man being pregnant, basing his behavior on how he'd seen his own pregnant wife behave. Maria, reportedly, laughed all the way through the movie.

**Q: Can you tell me of the obstacles encountered during the course of filming *Collateral Damage* in 2001 in the jungle?**
Adam Greenberg: Working with a foreign crew is one issue. In Mexico they have a very strong organization, and my point of view is when you ask for four, you get the whole. For example, on this movie we had a hundred and twenty drivers. Technically other than the distance and location, you prepare yourself well, snakes and

bugs and being bitten by mosquitoes. You have to prepare yourself well and have a special cream. The mosquitoes were a big issue.

**Q: Arnold would play chess in the jungle, is this correct?**
Adam Greenberg: Yeah, he always played chess. He had an assistant and he taught him to play chess. He would be locked in his trailer playing chess, until there was a certain situation in the game where he could win. Once I took on his assistant, to try to see how good he was. I think in three or four moves, I gave it back to him. I beat him. So the story spread on the set about me beating his assistant.

**Q: Can you recall Arnold's working relationship with the director, Andrew Davis, who indicated that Arnold played a more reality-based character in this movie, compared to his previous movies where he seemed to play a mythical action hero?**
Adam Greenberg: Arnold is very disciplined and would do anything the director asked him to do. He's very accurate. He discussed his ideas and he came with his own stuntmen and his assistant. For example, the first *Terminator* until *Eraser*, there were many scenes he shot with his assistant who was his double. He had a double in the first movie who looks like him. But with Andy it was pretty simple. Arnold's a hardworking guy. I think the bad luck with this movie came because it came out on 9/11. Let me tell you, I was in Hollywood and they were processing the film. I came that day to see the first print, to approve the first print. I came to the studio. This was the day 9/11 happened. They said not to release it yet. The timing was so accurate, opening for the movie for a long time. Then when it opened, I don't think the movie did very well.

**Q: When *Collateral Damage* was released in February 2002, there were complaints from some Arab and Muslim organizations because of the sensitivity of the subject – terrorism!**
Adam Greenberg: I'm not really aware of this. There might have been. When we shot it I don't think anybody came to the movie set

to advise us the proper way to make the characters and the best way to shoot. All of us tried to do the best job we could.

**Q: In your opinion, what are the manifold attributes of Arnold as a person and actor which reflected the primal life force that may have been apparent?**

Adam Greenberg: On a private level, he is very loyal to his friends. You can rely on him. He's very smart and a businessman. He's very approachable. Even though he is a big guy, the governor, or a big star and a very wealthy man, you know, he's very approachable. At least to his friends. Me and him go a long way back together, from the beginning from *The Terminator* and till he went on to become the governor. Obviously, he didn't work on any more movies (when he was in office) and I slowed down, too, but we stayed very good friends. He's very loyal to his friends, all of his friends. He invited me to Sacramento and we flew together on his private plane. He took me with him all day to San Francisco where he made a speech in front of four hundred and fifty people. I asked on the jet, "Could you believe one time you'd be the governor of this big state?" Because California is a big state. He said no. He's a very accessible guy, very good guy. He's speaking much more and he got coached in English. Arnold played well as long as he doesn't have too much dialog. He's better now since he became the governor.

**Q: As an actor, he's not a dialog actor. Can you recall any scenes he was having problems with dialog, was he just content with being an action star?**

Adam Greenberg: Before I mentioned what happened on the second *Terminator* movie, where he said I'm a bodybuilder not an actor, laughingly. But when he shot movies, he never had much dialog, you know. For some takes, he would prepare himself ahead of time and he used a coach. The difference between him and other big star actors I've worked with, I've seen experienced big star actors, who sometimes took $30 million for a movie, taking a long time on the set doing thirty-five takes on a scene. And they're Americans, it's their own language, but they couldn't do the proper delivery of the dialog because they didn't prepare themselves. But Arnold's a hardworking guy and with a coach he would come ready. Again, if you look at his movies he doesn't have much dialog.

He's better now because he's speaking more. He's very pleasant to be around and a very good guy. He's a figure. He will not be in any Shakespeare part. He is what he is, you know. I don't think he's a great actor. In certain situations his presence is good, but I don't think somebody will be shocked at his great acting. He will never be and he doesn't intend to be. He didn't aim to be a great actor; he's a personality. He comes there, you know, he can say two lines, I don't think he'll be the best actor.

**Q: Did you socialize outside of the confines of the studio and set?**
Adam Greenberg: In his trailer I would come to check his makeup, etc, and when we flew to location sometimes I flew in his jet. He took me with him in his jet. I don't want to talk about it. I don't feel comfortable talking about it.

**Q: Were there any complications involving filming scenes for *Collateral Damage*?**
Adam Greenberg: Acting wise, the interior was shot in the jungle there in Mexico, but whatever we could bring home onstage, we did it here. But still to make it look direct continuation from the jungle to here, he needed to make the acting. In acting he did very well. He has some scenes running with explosions all around. You never put the actor in some dangerous scenes, always do it with a double. In *Eraser* he's hanging on the plane on the wing and jumps with the parachute. We did that on the set. In the second *Terminator*, all the chases and everything's done and every time you have the actor doing such scenes you use protection. Before the green screen was used in those days, it's done onstage.

**Q: Arnold's relish and fervor pertinent to making movies seemingly was apparent. Just how much did he enjoy making movies?**

Adam Greenberg: Very much so. He got involved and had much interest all the way from throughout the shoot, so the end product will be the best possible. I remember on Eraser we had some problem with the director, and we had a meeting in his house here in Santa Monica on a weekend. We went to his house with one of the head of the studios of Warner Brothers to talk about the movie. We discussed what should be done and how it should be done. He was close to it right to the very end, to ensure he was very close to the project.

When somebody does very good, he expresses himself very well and congratulates you. I remember we did a scene in *Collateral Damage* or *Eraser*, I don't remember which film, but we had fire in the building. It was in *Collateral Damage*, where he plays a fireman in New York. It's the very beginning. He appears as a fireman trying to put out the fire in the building. We did all this control fire on the stage, very small stage, but it was looking great and he came to me and said, "Adam, this is good." He stayed close to everything that was done, paying attention and interest. Some actors don't have so much interest in what is done, or how it's done, but he does.

## KEVIN POLLAK

Actor, comedian, impressionist and game show host Kevin Pollak has appeared in more than 80 films, including *A Few Good Men*, *Casino* and *The Usual Suspects*. He played Bobby Chicago in *End of Days*, directed by Peter Hyams.

**Q: Kevin, you worked on *End of Days* with Arnold. Did you know him before working with him or was this the first time you both met?**
Kevin Pollak: It was the first time I met him on the set. He was pretty wonderful, open and approachable completely, very gregarious and outgoing with all the crew members and cast members. He was very social and had an open-door policy on his trailer where you could stop by and say hello. He was very friendly.

"For me, it was very important because I hadn't done a movie for a while to come back with the right film," Arnold said. "And so the right film, meaning a suspense thriller, something that is big, something that has a lot of production value on the screen, something that has a lot of stunts, a lot of action, a lot of suspense and all those things."

Arnold hadn't been on the screen for two years and really wanted to return by getting involved in another big hit, which would redeem him as a box-office draw. It was a partial success: although the Peter Hyams movie received mostly negative reviews, Arnold, once again, brought home a victory with strong international box office receipts. With a budget between $80 and $100 million and taking in $211 million worldwide, financially it was successful because of strong international numbers and DVD sales. Arnold pocketed $25 million for his efforts, matching what he received for *Batman and Robin* two years earlier.

**Q: You're a comedian yourself, with a great sense of humor. Was Arnold able to resonate with this?**

Kevin Pollak: Well, there were moments, for example, when I would pass by his trailer – he had a separate trailer with workout equipment in it – and I would pass by it and see him working out. And I would make a point by showing him the big slobby cheesecake I was carrying back to my trailer from the catering service. I would make sure that he would see I was eating it whilst he was working out. There was playful nature like that between us.

But I will tell you one thing I did notice about him, not necessarily funny, but how politically savvy he was, and not just about American politics. I remember being in a conversation with him one day on the set, and a crew member came up to us and said, "Hello, I have my cousin visiting me from Tel Aviv and she wanted to meet you." Arnold smiled and reached out to shake the hand of the relative from Tel Aviv, and he said, "Oh, yeah, Tel Aviv, you just had your mayor elected," and then proceeded to tell this person from Tel Aviv the three different candidates that were running and why the two lost that did lose and why the one who won did, in fact, win. And I remember thinking, *First of all, who else do I know that even knew there was a mayor raised in Tel Aviv last month? Second of all, of those people that I know that may know that, how many could name one candidate let alone all three? And have I ever met anyone who could then have told you why the candidates lost and what was wrong with their candidacy and their positions on certain issues that caused them to lose?*

He wasn't showing off, he wasn't trying to impress this person from Tel Aviv; he was merely engaging them in a conversation as if he was talking about a local restaurant in Tel Aviv that he had once eaten at. It was a way of his relating to this person. And I found it beyond sort of impressive, rather this is clearly a hugely important part of his life that may be a hobby to someone, which is to be politically aware on a world scale. It was beyond a hobby for him; it was a passion. It was one of the things I, of course, instantly remembered when I heard that he was running in California for the governor.

**Q: What would you say was the most memorable scene in the movie to work on with Arnold?**

Kevin Pollak: Well, to work on it would be when we were actually in the helicopter flying over downtown Los Angeles with huge open-side doors that one can easily fall out of. This helicopter was making maneuvers, and Arnold was extremely comfortable while I was not. I remember he enjoyed my lack of being comfortable. I need to say that I'm not an action hero. And I made that clear to everyone when we were maneuvering a mile above downtown Los Angeles, so it seemed. Arnold has a tremendous sense of humor. So he thoroughly enjoyed the opportunity to suggest I was being a wimp and, you know, a girlie man.

**Q: What did you find the most intriguing aspect to Arnold?**

Kevin Pollak: Just the generosity, you know. He had myself and my wife over to his house a few times, and we became friends. He was very open and generous and kind, that's what I remember. I think he was living in Brentwood.

**Q: Were there actually two endings filmed for *End of Days*?**

Kevin Pollak: You're absolutely right, there were two endings. I don't remember the context. I kind of remember in one ending Arnold lives, and in the other he dies. That might be the difference between the two.

**Q: Gabriel Byrne was, of course, one of the co-stars. Was the filming schedule really hectic for the stars?**

Kevin Pollak: Not hectic, it was a very big production so it was a long shoot – three or four months. But it was a very well-organized production. I knew Gabriel Byrne from working with him previously on *Usual Suspects*, so we had a camaraderie and friendship before. So I enjoyed working with him again. It was great fun to be part of such a giant-budget action movie with Arnold, and he really was a tremendous host on the set. Like I said, he made everyone feel like they were part of the winning team. He has a great sense of competitiveness in him, which comes from being an athlete. He would always try to engage people in a game of chess in his trailer. And, you know, like I said, doing the action sequences with him, I just remember being teased a lot. I either couldn't run fast enough, or climb fast enough, even the way I held a gun he would make fun of me. So he had quite a sense of humor during the shooting.

**Q: How did you perceive Arnold off set, you mentioned you went to his house a number of times for dinners?**
Kevin Pollak: I would say he was a classic sort of patriotic character. They have several children, also with the gatherings at his house there would be a lot of children and families. To some people, he seems like a patriotic character, Father Christmas, depending on your perspective there's a bigness about him that goes beyond his physical attributes in sort of a gregarious personality. Again, it wasn't a surprise for me when I heard he was running for governor because he's a leader by nature. To me, to be honest, it was also a sense of being in the presence of almost a superhero like Superman. He's the closest thing to a live action superhero that I've ever experienced, quite frankly, that didn't seem like an actor but more like the real thing. And I think having been an award-winning and widely celebrated athlete himself this had something to do with that. Also, being a self-made businessman. He made his fortune as an athlete long before he was in the movies, and he was buying and selling real estate. And he's a great businessman, way before he got into the movie business. All of that was wildly impressive and inspiring to be around.

**Q: Do you feel he was able to ameliorate as an actor because he was more like a John Wayne and Clint Eastwood playing one type of a character?**
Kevin Pollak: Well, I think you just did. He always has been pretty much one-dimensional like a John Wayne, where John Wayne eventually won an Academy Award for *True Grit*, I'm not sure Arnold's going to. He represented I think a time and a certain genre

of film that appears to be a young man's game, although Stallone suggested otherwise with *The Expendables*.

**Q: Do you feel age was a factor when he made *End of Days*, and some of the movies at the time that weren't as successful as some of his other movies he did, was this the decline of Arnold?**

Kevin Pollak: You could make that argument, but I would argue that there's another flow. If you're that big of a movie star, there's always an even flow throughout the course during one's career, be it a Bruce Willis, a Stallone. If you get to that level, it's just a natural order of things that there will be highs and lows from decade to decade. You could say, well, he had a heyday in the 1980s and early '90s because there was a certain sensibility to that kind of film. Can he reinvent himself yet again? I have no question in my mind that he is a one-of-a-kind personality on screen, and in the right vehicle . . .

**Q: After working with Arnold in *End of Days*, for which he reportedly banked $25 million, did you see him and keep in touch?**

Kevin Pollak: Yes. He invited me to a couple of dinners at their home. Also, I have been invited to a couple of fundraisers for various causes, which he was helping with. Also, he called me when he became governor to say hello and to let me know how much he was enjoying the job. I'd say we've stayed in contact over the years.

**Q: What are some of the charities he was and is involved in?**

Kevin Pollak: I'm not quite as comfortable in talking about his charitable efforts. I feel I wouldn't do them justice in describing them in detail because I know they're very, very important to him and without all the details in front of me, I'd do it a disservice.

**Q: What would you say was Arnold's ultimate attribute on a professional level?**

Kevin Pollak: From a professional level, I think he's a one-of-a-kind unique personality, and in the right vehicle I think people will always come and see a film starring Arnold Schwarzenegger. Because he represents a certain feeling that premade in most people, not only are you coming to have a good time, but there's going to be a sense of raw energy and action that he promises to deliver. And I think that's why when you mentioned some of the films that didn't do well, I think it was just a period that the consensus of the audience had drifted from that style, the same way a Western is a genre that comes and goes. Now you have the Coen brothers doing *True Grit*, and getting all these awards and nominations, when some people might have made the suggestions that the Western had gone on the waste side. I think the same is the truth. And I mentioned Stallone bringing back tremendous success with an action film with *The Expendables*. It was just a tremendous joy and a thrill to work with Arnold on *End of Days*. I would be equally if not more thrilled if I had another opportunity.

## KRISTANNA LOKEN

Kristanna Loken, born October 8, 1979, in New York of German and Norwegian descent is best known for her role as the cyborg T-X in *Terminator III*. A former fashion model, she also starred in *Mortal Combat: Conquest* in 1998. Loken continues to act – including appearances in the *Lethal Weapon* TV series – and has recently ventured into producing.

**Q: The *Terminator II* director said you had the physicality required to take on Arnold in this movie. When did you meet Arnold?**
Kristanna Loken: I believe it was on the set for the first time. I think there was a large and long series of auditions. I probably had to do different auditions before I actually got the job. I think it was my physicality, like Jonathan Mustow said. I'm tall, I'm 5ft 11, and I've always been athletic and I love the outdoors. Then from there on, I did the extensive training and I actually put on 15 pounds of muscle mass, you know, getting bigger and stronger for the role. I had always been a fan of Robert Patrick's performance in *Terminator II*, and he was a real inspiration to me when I was doing all the auditions.

**Q: What did you and the cast and crew see in Arnold, which caught your imagination on the set working with him?**
Kristanna Loken: Well, I think a couple of things. Definitely, I learned a lot by working with him and watching him do the action because he's such a pro at it. So by watching him I was able to glean a lot of experience. And also he's very, very gracious with his fans. He's very giving. And I think that's been one of the big things to his success. Because the fans are the ones that keep you going and go to see your movie. So, I could tell that it was very important to him.

**Q: Any intricate and sophisticated scenes you and Arnold filmed, which come to mind that required meticulous planning?**
Kristanna Loken: Sure. I would say the final action sequence in the bathroom, and then when we fell through the floor. That was

really interesting to shoot because Jonathan Mustow really wanted us to be like two bulldozers going at it. So it was just pure power and strength. I thought that was a very creative approach and a new approach for the characters. The bathroom sequence was quite something. I mean, obviously, there are a lot of CGI shots in there, going through the different things in the bathroom and throwing me into the toilet and various things, it was quite creative.

One of the biggest challenges for Arnold in this installment of *The Terminator* was convincingly battling a woman. It helped that Loken was in great shape. "What was challenging about doing it with a woman were the fight scenes," Arnold recalled. "I had no training of how you grab a woman. How you throw her against a wall. How hard can you really pick her up and throw her. How hard can you hit her." Ultimately he had to rely on his co-star to tell him that you can go harder, you can grab rougher. It took about half a dozen takes to get up to that level of rough handling of Loken because initially Arnold felt uncomfortable. Loken, for her part, didn't mind taking some bruises to ensure the fight scenes were as realistic as possible. She put a lot of energy and effort into making the scenes visually believable. She trained well with the stunt coordinators and proved she could handle the pressure – and the results are clear on screen. The team effort paid off in the end.

**Q: Regarding Arnold's collaboration with the new director, what input did Arnold have and did he and you make any suggestions to the director?**
Kristanna Loken: Frankly, their relationship – from what I can ascertain – they got along quite well. But I'm not really that privy of the ins and outs of what was said between them. But from what I could see, they collaborated very nicely together. As far as I'm concerned, for me Jonathan had a lot of faith in the choices I was making for the character, as far as my movements, and he really

gave me free rein to do and create what I wanted and what I felt was appropriate for the character. So, he would usually say, "Go on, go ahead and do your thing." He really had great belief in me.

**Q: Can you tell me some of the locations used for *Terminator III*?**
Kristanna Loken: We shot the movie in Los Angeles. The set was built on a soundstage. Part of the huge chase scene with the crane, they filmed part of that on an airplane hangar. And they really demolished it. They really destroyed it. So a lot of what you see when those buildings are coming down, that really happened.

**Q: Was Arnold in any way intimidating to work with?**
Kristanna Loken: He was a very professional person overall, I would say. He definitely was also a practical joker on the set. He likes to make practical jokes, which were fun and funny. He really enjoyed and loved to play chess. And with his stand-in between the scenes, he would play chess. I didn't really find him intimidating in that sense. Of course, I have a lot of respect for him as a fellow human being and with all his success. I think that I had done a lot of training and was ready for the job, so I gave it my all.

**Q: Arnold grew up in a small village and you grew up on a farm in the New York area. Did you exchange stories about growing up?**
Kristanna Loken: Not really. He didn't really talk much about his past. I did, of course, spend some time with his family, his wife and his children, especially when we were doing the press tour all over the world. They came along for that. So it was nice to meet his family. But he didn't speak much about where he grew up.

**Q: What were the most challenging aspects of working with Arnold on the movie?**
Kristanna Loken: Keeping up the very strict workouts routine and diet that I had set for the film. It was tailor-made for me. I worked with a nutritionist and it was very, very specific, including the three, four months prior to the shooting, then the eight months

of actually shooting. It was a good year of having a very, very strict diet and workout regime. So it was a good physical challenge.

Arnold went back to the drawing board for his third outing as the Terminator, getting himself in peak physical condition to play his most iconic role again. "It was very important to really prove that it is the same Terminator," he explained. "So therefore my body, I had to build up again to the size the way I was in the first *Terminator* and the second *Terminator*." Because, again, the Terminator arrives from the future in a similar fashion, which is naked. To this end, Arnold dedicated himself to bodybuilding, working out for up to two-and-a-half hours every day. His desire was to get in the same kind of shape he was in the first two *Terminator* films.

"That was a key thing for me – you have to get into that kind of shape so it's more believable that it's the same character," Arnold said. "It's difficult. You have to have a lot of will and a lot of motivation." As in previous installments, Arnold has a nude scene. After so many years away from the franchise, his feelings on the scene were, "Anytime you take your clothes off and do a nude scene, it's embarrassing . . . That's why it was important to train hard. I went into the mode of training as if I'm preparing for a competition again." Arnold also gave co-star Nick Stahl an invitation to his gym – something he would often do for his main co-stars – telling him he could use his 20-foot gym trailer. But after one look at the gym equipment, Stahl reportedly declined the generous offer and went outside for a cigarette instead.

**Q: You have said he'd open up in the makeup trailer, in terms of conversing, any conversations you both would engage in?**
Kristanna Loken: Not that I can think of, off the top of my head. Mainly, like I said, he liked to do practical jokes and he was very friendly. He enjoyed his cigars. He's a real cigar aficionado. All round he was a very relaxed and a likable person.

**Q: When you did the press and the publicity around the world, where did you go with Arnold to publicize the movie?**
Kristanna Loken: We went all over the world. I mean, we went to Tokyo, we were all over Europe, in the United Kingdom and numerous countries. We publicized on the Formula One race cars outside of London. We had a big premiere of the film in Cannes during the festival. And we had several premieres, like I said, all over Europe and Asia. It was really an incredible experience.

**Q: *The Terminator* trilogy made Arnold a household name. By the time he filmed *Terminator III*, he was a lot older. Does the third *Terminator* surpass the second one, in your opinion?**
Kristanna Loken: Oh, for sure. I think the *Terminator* franchise is huge and continues today. I mean, people love the *Terminator* franchise around the world. I mean, I constantly get fan mail from every corner of the world about *Terminator*. They have the kind of mystique and there's a real sense of the history and the complexity of the characters. And I think it will live on in people's memories for a long time to come. Well, of course, my opinion is a little biased. I was in *Terminator III*. I think he got himself in incredible shape for this film. Obviously, when I worked with him we had a great cast. I really enjoyed working with Nick Stahl and Claire Danes – I've always been a fan of hers. I ironically ran into Nick on a plane. I hadn't seen him, I don't think, since we did the film and he was sitting right in front of me, which was ironic. I think Arnold has his muscle memory from all the years of bodybuilding and training. Of course, it's much easier for someone who's done all that work already to get into shape than a random person off the street. I thought he really looked amazing.

**Q: What was the most memorable moment?**
Kristanna Loken: I think one of the things that stays with me is we had a huge premiere for the film in Tokyo in Japan. I just remember him complimenting me on the job well done, which was really nice to hear coming from him. He said I'd have a great career and this

was the beginning of launching it in a very large global way. I think it was the biggest premiere we had. It was huge. They had it in a large stadium that was filled to capacity with people. I remember that they had a couple of Special Olympics children there, who came up on the stage with us, because Arnold's a big advocate for the Special Olympics. The fans were crazy outside. I'll never forget that experience, it was like, you know, being a rock star onstage. It was huge.

## DOLPH LUNDGREN

Swedish-born actor Dolph Lundgren is perhaps best known for his breakout role in *Rocky IV* in 1985. He went on to co-star with Jean Claude Van Damme in *Universal Soldier* and became part of a wave of actors known for their impressive physiques in the 1980s and early 90s. He worked with Arnold in *The Expendables* series.

**Q: Arnold made cameo appearances in a series of movies you co-starred in, *The Expendables*. When did your paths actually cross?**

Dolph Lundgren: I met him actually on the set of the second *Conan* movie. I was a karate fighter and I hadn't done movies yet. I was going out with Grace Jones, who was in the movie with Arnold. I met him on the set of that movie and we got on well. Basically, he just looked at me as an athlete, you know, a young Swedish kid who was this karate fighter. Then when I was doing the *Rocky* picture, I remember Grace had a party at my house that I was renting. I was in the guesthouse trying to get some sleep because I had to get up and train with Sly in the morning. There was a knock on the door at midnight. I woke up and I said, "Who is it?" And I heard this voice outside, "It's your trainer. I'm here to check you out." It was Arnold. He's a funny guy and we got on well. I didn't do any scenes with him in the first installment of *The Expendables*.

**Q: That's interesting, that you had met Arnold on the set of the second *Conan* movie. Do you think Arnold, the epitome of bodybuilding, was able to have an impact on Hollywood making the transition from a sportsman to the movie screen?**

Dolph Lundgren: Yeah, huge impact! I think I moved here (California) before he got very famous. But yes, he did. I think it was *Pumping Iron*, the documentary that he was in which brought bodybuilding into the mainstream, and, of course, he was the figurehead of the whole movement. Bodybuilding in the 1980s became very well known, and he was the figurehead of it. So, sure, he is, obviously, the most famous bodybuilder ever and probably will be forever. I think it will be hard to beat him. He was the first guy in the 1980s who came from a sports background and made it in Hollywood. Then there's a bunch of guys. I mean, there's him, Van Damme, Seagal, myself, to some extent Chuck Norris. For some reason, in the 1980s you had real athletes who became action stars and actors. And, of course, he's done extremely well in other walks of life – he became the governor and so forth. He had a huge impact on bodybuilding. Of course, he's a truly charismatic bodybuilder. I guess the guy before him was Steve Reeves in the 1950s, who did the same thing. Arnold is certainly one of the greats of both bodybuilding and cinema.

**Q: Anything interesting on the set of the second *Conan* movie, did you converse with him about training?**
Dolph Lundgren: I was not doing a lot of lifting in those days; I was just fighting. I was actually thinking of becoming a professional fighter. A boxer actually, as well, so I was training boxing and also doing a lot of running, things of that nature. He was doing more weights. But, I mean, he was hanging out with his buddies, Sven Thorsen, who's a Danish powerlifter, and a couple of other guys. I think we just got along. Like I said, he looked at me as an athlete. But I remember watching him and I was impressed with his physique and by his personality and charisma. I met Maria Shriver on the set, who was visiting who became his wife, obviously, later. That was a good experience.

**Q: Did you both ever venture to work together, or was this something that was never brought up?**
Dolph Lundgren: I think for *The Running Man* I was up for a role. That was one of the films he made. I think I was up for a role on that. Apart from that, no, we really haven't. He's kind of a step ahead of me all the time. Basically, by the time I appeared in big movies, he was already thinking about his political career. So, no, we haven't.

**Q: Would I be right in saying you also were asked to pursue politics in your native country Sweden?**

Dolph Lundgren: Yes. In Sweden they asked me to run for office for parliament for MP – the Green Party. It was a very flattering offer, but I couldn't do it because it would mean moving back to Sweden. And I don't feel like doing that right now. But in the future I will do something like that, who knows.

**Q: Being in the Hollywood fraternity working with action stars, how would you define Arnold as an action hero? You came from the same generation – 1980s and 1990s. And you both came from Europe to find fame and fortune in America.**

Dolph Lundgren: I think he's very charismatic. He's a very smart man, a businessman. He kind of was very, very clever in how he pursued his career. He does have a lot of charisma and charm as a person and he's done very, very well, better than most of the other people in the business. So I think he's certainly somebody that everyone could look up to as a role model when it comes to pursuing a career in this town.

Arnold, who had always promised his audience that he'd be back, took a day off his duties as governor to film a scene for *The Expendables*, the first time Arnold would be appearing on-screen with his friend and former rival Sylvester Stallone, as well as former Planet Hollywood collaborator Bruce Willis. Arnold and Willis appear for a very short time on-screen in their cameo roles, but Arnold still brought his trademark intensity to the role. "Arnold was relentless, like this perfect machine," Stallone later remarked. "People asked if I could have played the Terminator. Are you kidding? Not a chance. I never could have played the Terminator." Stallone says he saw Arnold's eyes light up in front of the camera. It's one thing to run a state, but another thing to get back to what you're really known for.

**Q: Did you extensively socialize with Arnold over the years, and did you get to know him well?**

Dolph Lundgren: I'm close to Stallone, I guess, as a person. I spent more time with him than with Arnold. Arnold, we're just acquaintances so we really didn't get into more personal conversations. He's a funny guy, basically. I remember at the opening of *The Expendables*, they pulled me out of my seat. We were flying out getting on a plane for Europe. Some guy pulled me through the Mann's Chinese Theater here in Hollywood, and I felt a big hand grab me. I looked up and there was the Governator, with his wife, and he's going, "Congratulations, you look great." He takes everything with a sense of humor. He doesn't take it all seriously, which I think is something you can learn from Arnold. He has this sense of humor about life and about business, which is important sometimes, you know.

# PETER BART

A journalist and film producer, Peter Bart is widely known for his lengthy tenure as the editor of the entertainment-trade magazine *Variety*, a position he held for twenty years. He also worked at Paramount Pictures as an executive.

**Q: When did Arnold become prominent in the Hollywood community for the major media to take serious notice?**
Peter Bart: It was quite some time ago. I don't have a list of the dates of his released pictures in front of me, but he has been a star a long time. *Last Action Hero*, which was done in the early 1990s, was the beginning of not his downfall but it was his biggest flop. But he's been around for generations. He was also brilliant at self-promotion. I remember running into him in the 1980s at the Cannes Film Festival, and he took me to the side and he was very boastful. He said, "I'm going to do fifty interviews." Some stars complain; they don't want to work as hard. He said, "I can just churn out the interviews. You watch, I'll do fifty." You know, he was just an absolute frenzy of promotion and he loved doing it. I always felt that he was very much a very sharp marketing person. Now in Hollywood, everyone talks about brands. Long before everyone talked about brands, Arnold had an idea who his brand was and what it was. When you really think about it, he was a pioneer in managing his own brand.

**Q: His competitor was Sylvester Stallone in the 1980s and 1990s. Do you have any intriguing stories when both stars went head to head to compete and churn out blockbusters?**
Peter Bart: Yes. Stallone was amazing in that first he had the *Rocky* franchise, then the *Rambo* franchise. He was remarkable in being able to reinvent himself in different franchises, whilst Arnold was never quite that lucky or smart – he was always the 'Arnold' franchise. And he had sort of, every picture he started from scratch, it wasn't, like, he had a series of sequels. I never discussed it with

him, but I expect he was jealous of the fact he never could get into the sequels business.

**Q: You interviewed Arnold on numerous occasions. What was he like to interview?**

Peter Bart: Yes, many times. The thing about Arnold is he was always very accessible, very good natured. He was very anxious to sustain a good relationship with the press, and if you were fair and quoted him right then he was very good. I never like to do interviews on movie sets because I always found that there's a lot of trouble getting there, and then you have to wait there a long time for the set ups. I always prefer to talk to people when they are not working. So I guess most of the interviews with Arnold were at the Cannes Festival, or when he was promoting a picture. We would be in a restaurant or something like that. I remember one time, he owned a restaurant in Los Angeles, Santa Monica. Sometimes I would go out to that restaurant, which I rather liked, actually, called Schatzi. It was very congenial, had German food I happen to like, good beer which I happen to love, and it would be fun to go out there. So, you could talk to him and he could smoke his cigar.

**Q: What was one of the most intriguing interviews you did?**

Peter Bart: Well, I think it was some years ago. I began to feel like talking to him about political events that I felt more and more he was caught in the middle of because he really was a Republican. On the other hand, his position on many issues was not a conservative one. I mean, he understood the danger of global warming and he was very much in favor of healthcare. So in many ways, he was more liberal than he was conservative. And that's why I think he became isolated in California because the Republican Party is so far to the right that he was just not conforming to their policies.

**Q: What is your take as to why *Last Action Hero* was a flop?**

Peter Bart: I felt the basic concept of the movie was more like a comic book. It was before the era of the video games. But it was like a video game in a way, and I just didn't think . . . I felt it was the wrong concept. I visited the set, not to interview him, but my friend Peter Gruber was the CEO of the company at that time so I went and had lunch with Peter Gruber and then I walked over to the set. I just felt something that just struck me of simply being wrong. I mean, conceptually wrong. What happened was, the studio ended up nervous about the picture and decided to spend more money on marketing than less. They shouldn't have doubled it. It lost money. It was better overseas than in the United States. The critics hated it, the audience just didn't buy it and it was really an embarrassing picture.

When you hired Arnold for a movie, as Columbia Pictures did for *Last Action Hero*, the industry's working assumption was that you were guaranteed a minimum of $75 million at the box office, one Sony executive said. And it wouldn't be unusual if the same amount would flow in from overseas receipts and the video market at the time, making hiring Schwarzenegger a worthwhile investment despite his hefty price tag. For Mark Canton, then – one of the executives who convinced Arnold to take on the role of Jack Slater – the movie became the costliest of blunders, and one of Arnold's biggest flops.

When Arnold was in politics, he said, "Maria was always by my side, and always was participating in all decision-making – in my movie career, in my business, and now also in politics. We are partners. That's why I got married: to have a great partner." Maria played an integral role in advising her husband pertaining to decision-making when it came to his movie career, often accompanying him to important meetings with executives. She would often steer him toward what she felt was right – whether that meant taking certain roles or reading scripts – and was never reluctant to give her criticism. Often when they attended rough cuts of a movie, Maria would go the extra mile and contentiously make notes and had a long list of comments to the director.

According to Arnold himself, the *Last Action Hero* script was one of the best scripts he'd ever read. The movie seemingly alienated Schwarzenegger's action fans. With its violence softened to ensure a PG-13 rating, the film, said a source close to the production, "Landed between the cracks too old for kids and too young for adults." The best thing about Arnold was he was tough and mean, and with the studio bending over backward to sanitize the movie, they took out its primary appeal. It cost the studio around $120 million to make and market, and for Columbia Pictures, reaching even the minimum threshold looked dicey. To make things worse, when it opened up, Steven Spielberg's *Jurassic Park* had also been released and was chewing through the box office, eventually taking over $500 million worldwide. Eventually, however, the studio was able to recoup their money – coming close to breaking even.

**Q: Generally, Arnold's movies did really well overseas, particularly in Europe. That became an integral part of his success – the European marketplace.**
Peter Bart: That's true. Just like Tom Cruise really worked very hard around the world to promote his pictures, so did Arnold. And it paid off. Arnold had such a good sense of humor, he made some good comedies in his later years and he enjoyed those. He was a very Austrian person, he does like to kid around. He loved making comedies to show he could do other things beside kill people. I'll give you an example of an actor who really grew as a person and became more thoughtful and much more sophisticated. There are some actors who shrink with celebrity and they isolate themselves. Arnold, I always respected him because he kept growing, read a lot and didn't become isolated. He was a very social person.

**Q: How was Arnold's relationship with his agents, who are the key people making decisions for their clients?**
Peter Bart: I honestly do not know. I always had the feeling he had a strong say in what he was doing, and that he wasn't controlled by

an agent. But I don't know. I wasn't that privy to his business life.

**Q: The decline at the box office came mid- and late 1990s with such movies as *End of Days* and *Collateral Damage*. It's open to conjecture if a combination of age, fading novelty and diminishing prudence was the cause of this.**
Peter Bart: Yes, exactly. That most definitely marked the decline. But he was also not lucky. He had a hot streak and he had a cold streak. I think he is a totally driven person. Very few people I've met are totally focused and ambitious like him, every career step was really life or death to him. I mean, he was not somebody who fooled around, and for that kind of ambition you have to have respect, and also can be intimidating.

**Q: Did you go to the premieres?**
Peter Bart: You know, I hate to say but I don't like premieres. Because movies are supposed to start at eight o' clock, but you sit around and barely start at 9.15. I hate going to premieres. At parties he's always very jovial, always shaking hands. He doesn't hide in the corner like some stars; he's out there chatting. There's an extra version to him.

**Q: Can you tell me about your background in the movie business and were you an executive at Paramount?**
Peter Bart: Yes, I was. I spent seventeen years as an executive at Paramount and MGM, and then more and more productions.

**Q: What made him succeed and become a major star when he wasn't really the best actor in the pure sense of the word?**
Peter Bart: He could never lose his accent. I was talking to Mark Wahlberg one time, and he has a big Boston accent and he got trained to lose the accent. Arnold still has his Austrian accent. He never lost it.

## ALEX BEN BLOCK

Alex Ben Block is an award-winning Hollywood entertainment industry journalist, show business historian and author. A senior editor for *The Hollywood Reporter*, he has also been the associate editor of *Forbes* magazine and an editor at the *Los Angeles Herald Examiner*.

**Q: You're a veteran Hollywood journalist, who interviewed the icon Bruce Lee when he was at the brink of achieving global fame. Do you feel Bruce and Arnold, who both developed a physical persona, which countless men could resonate with, shared a commonality in a sense they had to overcome certain obstacles in achieving the American Dream?**
Alex Ben Block: Well, Arnold Schwarzenegger, of course, took a different path to Bruce Lee. He was a bodybuilder and got great recognition in that area. When he came to the United States, he was already known in certain circles among the bodybuilders. And his first movie roles and documentaries and movies related to his roles as a bodybuilder. He showed a great ability in business and building himself in business early on and started creating companies and selling products relating to his bodybuilding at first. So he got recognition that way. Then, of course, because of his huge physique he was cast in the early sandal flicks – the *Conan* movies and so forth – that gave him a ticket to become known. And despite the accent and the unusual physique, he found unlikely stardom.

You have to remember, what happened to Bruce Lee was, he had lived in America and he was born in America, then he came back after his eighteenth birthday and lived many years here. He studied martial arts and went to the University of Washington. Then when he finally came to Los Angeles and wanted to be an actor, he found great prejudice. He was told he was too 'Chinese' to play Chinese. There were no roles for Chinese, Asians and minorities in those days. So he had to go back to Hong Kong and make a couple of movies, which became successful. And after *Enter the Dragon*, he was accepted outside of China. And tragically, of course, he died before he could capitalize on that success. Whereas Arnold has lived a long life, and has been able to make very different kinds of movies, building his businesses and becoming very wealthy and then move into politics.

So they took very different roads. What I remember about the interview I did with Bruce Lee is that I was surprised he was so smart about philosophy, and how intelligent he was about what was going on in the world. How self-aware he was about what he had to do to have a career, and how charming he was. But most of all he wasn't just about muscle, he wasn't just about money. He was about putting together philosophy and ideas along with culture in the muscle and all of that to create a very unique persona, and to become the first Asian American movie star to break through on a global basis.

**Q: How much impact and contribution did Arnold's PR have in his meteoric rise to fame? Was it easy to have access to him through Charlotte Parker, who was his publicist? She ensured that the media coverage of her client was tightly controlled and was able to utilize the ever-intertwining tendrils of media conglomeration to her client's benefit.**

Alex Ben Block: I know Charlotte very well and actually first met Arnold through Charlotte. When he had something to promote, when he had a movie or product or he was in a business, he got attention. The bigger the movie, the more attention he got. So, the first problem was to get him interviews. Then the problem was to not get interviews because the job of the publicist becomes to control the gate more than it is to try get people to come in once you become a big star. Arnold is a very personable guy. He speaks very well. He's very boisterous in public. He's very animated and he's got a way of being very charismatic in front of the crowd.

So, I think maybe very early on it was a problem to get publicity even when he got publicity because of his relationship with the bodybuilding magazines. He got a lot of publicity in that area. So he wasn't an unknown quantity. Then once he became a hit in the movies, it wasn't just Charlotte Parker that was helping him; he had De Laurentiis' PR department and the studio PR department and other staff who worked on his behalf. When he started appearing with stars, he was part of the overall junket of the publicity machines of his movies. He did a lot of publicity. In the end, both the movies had to deliver and Arnold had to have the personality to be interesting enough so that they want to interview him – and he had both. So, it was quite natural for him to get more and more publicity.

**Q: Sylvester Stallone was big box office, and there seemed to be an element of competitiveness going on. How did Hollywood perceive this?**

Alex Ben Block: Well, Sylvester Stallone, again, took a very different path. In 1976, it was *Rocky* that became a big hit and an Academy Award winner. He had a very different career and path. There is room in Hollywood and the world for more than one action star at a time. So, while they were competitors, each had plenty of their own things to do. Stallone's problem was very different. Stallone's problem became: how to manage his fame and how to choose the right vehicles, having to use his talent not just as an actor but as a producer, director and writer and an entrepreneur to further his career. He made some good choices and he made some not very good choices – that hurt him a lot more than any competitor ever hurt him. Stallone also played a lot of different kind of roles. He tried comedies. He tried dramas as well as action roles. He wasn't as successful in those as he became known for Rambo, but he tried different things. I think maybe there was some professional jealousy, but that I'm not really aware of, but it really was more each of them had their own path. You can have two successful action movies in the same summer. There's room for everybody.

**Q: Arnold and Stallone, along with Bruce Willis, went on to pursue business ventures together and became the faces of**

**Planet Hollywood, which was one of the most celebrated business venture of Arnold's career. Can you tell me more about the Planet Hollywood venture, please?**

Alex Ben Block: Well, there was a man who was an entrepreneur who brought these stars in together to be investors. First, it looked like a very good idea. They could use the memorabilia and things to open the restaurant. And it worked. Most of the restaurants were opened in places where there were tourists. So in the beginning the restaurants were very successful because of the association with famous people, and they were created to be a fun place. The restaurants failed not because of the celebrities, they failed because the food wasn't good and the service wasn't great. And after a while, it wasn't just enough to have just tourists; you also had to have repeat customers from the community. These restaurants offered greasy food with high prices. And if you've seen the memorabilia on the wall and gone a few times, the lure disappears very quickly. So, I think the celebrities were mostly just investors. They didn't play any big role beyond showing up and doing PR. It was a flawed concept. Eventually, the restaurant has to be a good restaurant, but they weren't very good restaurants.

Planet Hollywood was originated by Keith Barish, an entrepreneur and film producer (*The Fugitive, The Running Man*). It was the brainchild of Robert Earl, former president and CEO of Hard Rock Cafe and an entrepreneur, who also owned Everton soccer club. One of the global investors included Saudi Arabia's Prince Alwaleed Bin Talal. The first branch opened in New York on October 22, 1991. Arnold, along with fellow stars Sylvester Stallone, Bruce Willis and Demi Moore, was the public face of Planet Hollywood. Stallone expressed, "Planet Hollywood's a success really because it's pure escapism. It's eating wonderful food around extraordinary surroundings, it's like being in a museum, but a light-hearted one." He, of course, said he'd recommend it for everyone. Arnold, who had always made great effort to provide his input to those with whom he collaborated, claimed that he was involved in everything from having a hand in scouting sites and whatever else he strongly felt could be done to make the venture bigger and better. Moreover, he allegedly played somewhat a role on the financial side of the scale: how much money would be spent. According to Arnold, the investing stars were involved together in literally every business decision. But this was disputed by Stallone's mother.

When the London branch of Planet Hollywood opened in May 1993, in Piccadilly, Arnold, Stallone and Willis, as well as an array of celebrities, were present on the glitzy opening night. Arnold, always the ebullient star, said, "So many people out there, it was amazing. I mean, we have done a lot of openings before and we have seen a lot of people before when we go to the Academy Awards, or when we go to the movie premiere openings, or Planet Hollywood openings, but this was absolutely amazing. It was much bigger than ever before."

Arnold enthusiastically added, "Originally, when we started out with the Planet Hollywood concept, we didn't really know that we had such a great winning formula together – you never know when you start any business." He said that when the first ever branch opened up in New York, the assumption was that around a thousand people would pay a visit to eat and spend their hard-earned cash on memorabilia. But it was claimed that between two and four thousand people a day were visiting. So the business venture became a monster hit with the public. Subsequently it led to the investors tapping into the overseas market. The long-term vision was to open Planet Hollywood in European capital cities such as Paris, Rome and Moscow, and literally to open them up all over the world.

The formidable restaurateur Peter Morton and Hard Rock Cafe investors in Chicago and Orange County filed lawsuits against Planet Hollywood alleging that it ripped off the Rock 'n' Roll concept of Hard Rock and converted it into a movie theme. Despite success and backing from megastars, and the ambience and glittering facade, the chain suffered from declining sales at many locations. Merchandise and t-shirt sales, which accounted for a quarter of revenue, also fell drastically.

Consequently, in January 2000, merely four days after the troubled chain emerged from bankruptcy with new investors, Arnold announced he was terminating his five-year contract with Planet Hollywood. He said, "It was lots of fun and very challenging to come up with and develop the celebrity restaurant concept on an international level. Of course I'm disappointed that the company did not continue with the success I had expected and hoped for." He wished Planet Hollywood well and was focusing on new American and global business ventures as well as his movie career. The Orlando-based company, which at the time had almost eighty branches worldwide, had assets of $392.2 million and debts of $359.1 million.

**Q: Can you tell me about some of the Arnold movie premieres you attended?**
Alex Ben Block: I attended premieres of his movies in the United States and in Cannes. I attended the *Twins* premiere, which starred him and Danny DeVito. In fact, by then they were already big stars and they had a big studio behind them. In that case, they had a big production team behind them as well. Like I said, Arnold is very good with crowds. I was once at a movie exhibitor's convention and he came and spoke to the group. He was very well received because he told jokes and he related to what they were doing. He was actually very fun to watch up on the platform speaking to everybody. So, for the same reasons he became a successful politician. He's very people oriented, very charismatic, very magnetic when he's in a crowd. So it was a natural thing for him when he had a premiere or a public event and the media use his strong personality and his self-confidence. When he had something interesting, people would be interested to further his career, and he did this very well.

Let me say, I don't have any great friendship with Arnold Schwarzenegger. I met him on a professional capacity over the years, and I've observed him at a distance. I live in the state where he was the governor. I think he's successful. As a young man he had the hunger to become a bodybuilder, to be self-disciplined, then to become a movie star and then to marry into the Kennedy family and make a lot of money. He's obviously a very ambitious man, and he's succeeded in those ambitions.

**Q: When Arnold became a top star in Hollywood, did this place him in a despotic position and just how much power did he have as far as studio executives are concerned?**

Alex Ben Block: When you become an A-list star, you have many, many choices. You also have a team of agents, managers, publicists and hangers-on and business people around you. He certainly had his. He also had a powerful wife. So within reason, he had a lot of choice. He could do what he wanted. He was able to use that power, not just limited to action roles, but also to do all these other things he wanted to try from comedy to playing romantic roles and branch out into another area and do a lot of business deals. He's an entrepreneur with real estate and he owned restaurants and all these other things. So, in his world in that era, he was a very powerful voice and he was able to make the choices he wanted to make, whether they were good choices or not, we can debate. He called his own shots.

**Q: In the beginning, do you feel he was cognizant of the fact he might be typecast because of his accent and play a German role? Also what are your sentiments on his flops?**

Alex Ben Block: I don't know if 'typecasting' is the right word. I'd say 'limited'. In the beginning, it seemed like he was limited to certain roles because of the accent. But he was able to use it to his advantage by choosing roles and characters and developing scripts to challenge his capabilities and his accent. He became a big star despite his accent. He's a very talented performer. Some of the movies he was in were not successful, but it's rare you get anybody who had every movie successful. He reached a plateau of his career

– it was more in his head than in his career. He got tired of doing the things he was doing. He continued to make movies, while some of them didn't work a lot of them did. His career didn't stop until he went into politics because he was, let's say, Ronald Reagan's career was over by the time he went into politics. In this case, he took the opportunity and got involved in a special election in California to make a career and life decision to move in a different direction. And while he had some flops, he could've continued to be an A-list star for years to come.

**Q: Whenever you interviewed him, what significant element did you detect as far as the depth of his character?**
Alex Ben Block: I did a couple of times over the years, and I certainly heard him interviewed. He's very self-confident. Whether he was talking about his movies, his business or his politics, he was very assertive. He had a strong point of view. What I remember about him most was the strength of the man, his character and his personality.

**Q: He no doubt developed a reputation within the circles for his voracious appetite for promoting. For example, someone had him logged for twenty interviews, but he'd say he wanted to do forty.**
Alex Ben Block: Well, the greatest movie stars, often they're able to use their magnetic personality for promotion. They can turn it on and off. And Arnold had that ability as a movie star. When he chose to, he was very charismatic. People wanted to talk to him, people wanted to be around him and he delivered. He told you stories and he had a personality. He was a lot of fun and he spoke his mind. So he was an easy person to be interested in. I saw him at conventions or a premiere. I remember seeing him at Cannes and covering him at Cannes. He'd sweep in with his bodyguards and his entourage and at premieres do his thing. Once again, he was a great promoter and he had a great sense of awareness of what made him famous and he used it.

**Q: What was he like with the press?**
Alex Ben Block: He could light up the room. He had a great personality and he loved to talk, smoke a cigar and hold court and people were fascinated.

**Q: Do you feel he still has goals to achieve?**
Alex Ben Block: I waited and thought about what he'd do after he'd stop being the governor. I felt he had many opportunities from going back to the movie business, or he could go into private business, or he could go to Washington in public service.

**Q: Do you feel Arnold had his fair share of critics during his movie career in the 1980s and 1990s?**
Alex Ben Block: Of course. The critics like you or they don't like you. It's not based on who you are, but based on your work. And he always made the kind of movies the critics liked. There were times when the critics were bad, but that wasn't important. What was important was the public loved movies and they went to his movies. And if they were the right kind of movies, people turned out for him. *Terminator I* was kind of an accident. I mean, in *Terminator I* he played a villain. It's only from *Terminator II* that his character became heroic, and that became a huge worldwide success. They were very successful. With the movie, the merchandise and the markets, it was very successful.

**Q: Do you feel he was bigger than action movie stars such as Stallone, Van Damme and Seagal?**
Alex Ben Block: I don't know if bigger. He was bigger than a lot of these stars. He was bigger than Bruce Willis. In his days, he was an A-list star, whereas Van Damme was never really an A-list star; he was always a B-list star. Arnold had a much greater body of work and a much more powerful career.

**Q: What was one of the biggest Arnold news stories in Hollywood?**
Alex Ben Block: When he ran for the governor of California – that

was a big story. It was a big surprise at the time. I think during his career, he became a phenomenon and he was an A-list star and he got a lot of publicity and a lot of attention. He was able to resonate with the public because he made very entertaining movies. He had a great magnetic presence on the screen and it was a lot of fun to watch great action movies, and that's why the public loved him. He became one of these unique characters and his image became iconic. He knew who he was and what he was all about and it was exciting. And if you're into movies, you want to know more about him. Not so many people have achieved that level.

**Q: Last words on Arnold?**
Alex Ben Block: I want to tell you, I liked him much better as a movie star than I liked him as a governor. Hopefully, in the future he will stick to the movies and stay out of politics. It's not about the years, the question was: what is he going to do with them? If he is going back to the movies, he's going to have to pick his roles very carefully. He's not going to be the young action hero. It's not going to happen. I felt he'd find the right kind of vehicle just like Bruce Willis, it becomes harder and harder to find the kind of (action) roles as you get older.

**Q: Do you think he might have turned to directing and producing, when he left the political platform?**
Alex Ben Block: He's certainly capable of it. He directed *Christmas in Connecticut* and he produced some movies. If he chooses to go in that direction, he's certainly capable. But I don't think he's going to. He's got business interests. He's been in politics now and he's seen by the public in a different way. I'll be a little surprised if he wanted to go back to that, but we'll wait and see.

Speculation was beginning to mount as to whether Arnold would return to Hollywood after he left his political post. After he left the governor's office, Arnold claimed he was inundated with offers – receiving fifteen offers from the film industry including remakes of *Predator* and *The Running Man*, and, of course, a new *Terminator* movie – but now he faced a new challenge, in the form of his advancing years. Extreme fight scenes, explained the former governor, would not be possible anymore. One new project based on a comic book character was briefly announced, which Arnold planned on promoting at the Cannes Film Festival, but he withdrew venturing there to take care of personal issues. Hollywood was still keen to embrace one of its all-time greats, however, anticipating fresh box office success despite Arnold's new roles. Arnold returned churning out a number of movies with varying degree of success at the box office. In 2015, Arnold returned to the franchise that made him famous in *Terminator Genisys*, a reboot of the series co-starring Emilia Clarke, famous from *Game of Thrones*, as Sarah Connor. *Terminator Genisys* grossed over $440 million worldwide, making it the second-highest-grossing film of the series, and of Schwarzenegger's career, behind *Terminator II*.

## ERIC WATSON

Hollywood producer and director Eric Watson collaborated with Arnold Schwarzenegger on *Aftermath*. A committed environmental activist, Watson had a good relationship with Arnold while working on the film. His credits include classic films *Pi* and *The Fountain*.

**Q: How did you come to work with Arnold on *Aftermath*?**
Eric Watson: I got a phone call from a friend, Darren Oronofsky who said he was making this movie with Arnold and director Elliot Lester. And then I met with Elliot and Arnold at Arnold's house here in Los Angeles, and we talked about what we wanted to do. And we did it.

**Q: What is Arnold like to collaborate with?**
Eric Watson: Arnold is an icon and a legend in the world. And he had been living at that house for a while. We pulled up at the driveway, there's the Hummer. We walked up to the front door and he's there waiting. He greeted us. He was very friendly. We walked out to the back yard and sat down. The meeting took place out on his patio where he had the script. And he read the script and he's really intelligent and he knows what he wants and the process. He wanted our ideas and had his ideas and he's very collaborative. He's a professional. He loves his job and he loves acting. Loves what he does and he's very good at it. He really applies himself a hundred percent at what he does.

**Q: Arnold had been out of the movie business because of being involved in politics. Did he talk to you about this and if he was nervous to be back in the movie business?**
Eric Watson: Yes, he did. He enjoys making movies more than he enjoyed being a governor. And he talked about that. He said when he became the governor all he did was meetings, meetings, meetings. He did meetings, speeches, meetings, speeches. And he told us it is a lot more fun making movies. Although he did enjoy

being the governor – I think he did his best as the governor here in California – his true love was to make movies.

**Q: While shooting *Aftermath* can you tell me anything compelling?**

Eric Watson: Yes. We made the movie in Columbus, Ohio. It turns out that Arnold had been doing the Arnold Classic, the fitness and bodybuilding show for almost thirty years there. So he had been involved with that for a very long time. So, when we got there, we realized that he was like a local hero there. Right in front of our hotel there was a very large statue of Arnold Schwarzenegger. And so when we all got out of our car, we all laughed because right in front of our hotel there's a statue of Arnold. We joked around with him about that. We took pictures in front of the statue with him and it was very fun. Then every day before we go to the set I would go to the gym in the hotel to work out. And every day he would be at the gym too to work out. And one day I was sitting there in the gym – I wasn't as big as Arnold, I'm still not – I was working out, and he said, "Eric, Eric, come here, come here." I stopped and went over. And he said, "You're doing this wrong!" And he started to show me how to lift weights. He said, "Tomorrow we go to the real gym. Six o' clock meet me!" I said, "Six a.m.?" So, he took me to the gym down the road and he started training me how to lift weights. That was a really amazing thing because whenever you work with a master of anything, you're learning more than anything you've learned because they've gone to a place where they're a master at transmitting something beyond what they're actually teaching you. I was very privileged to learn something from this master of the sport. And he also really likes to tease you when you work out with him. That was a real pleasure for me. On set in the shooting of the movie, he was a real professional. He was very generous with the crew. He was always on time and he brought good energy to the set with him. That made a difference every day he was there. It was a joy to work with him. Arnold really brought his whole self no matter what was going on. And because it wasn't a big budget movie relative to some of the movies he made, we couldn't do all the fancy things that you want to do on a big budget movie. Nevertheless, it didn't matter to him because he was all about what he was doing with his role and his passion. He knew all the crew members' names and what they did and he talked to them. He was just very inspiring to work with.

**Q: Arnold has been known for action movies. Do you think he's not finished yet in terms of making movies?**
Eric Watson: He loves making movies, and also you have to look at when stars like Arnold get this far in their careers they have to look at their legacies: what have they done and what have they not done yet? I think, and he didn't say this, but looking at himself he thinks, *OK, what is the part of my acting career that I can grow and work on that I can be recognized for that I wasn't when I was younger?* And I think that he's been taken seriously as an actor. I think that's why he chose to do *Aftermath* because he wanted to show that you can see his skills as an actor beyond just being an action hero with one-liners. I think he has a desire to expand and grow as an artist.

**Q: *Terminator: Dark Fate*, did he talk to you about continuing the franchise? It failed at the box-office.**
Eric Watson: Yeah. Certainly for myself, Arnold is the Terminator. It's hard to imagine a *Terminator* film without Arnold. He defined the role going back to the original movie. When I was a teenager growing up in the 1980s, I watched the movies that Arnold made from *Terminator, Raw Deal.* And I would watch them again and again, maybe some others didn't watch them like I did. Definitely *Terminator* and *Predator* were very iconic movies for my friends and me growing up. So, I think for Arnold he understands the importance to the fans of stepping into the role and doing his best to bring back that joy from the character of the Terminator. I know that at one point – a couple of years ago – there was some talk of him doing a *Conan* movie again. Those iconic characters live forever. But we don't keep on living forever. But if you continue

that legacy and bring back that joy to the fans, I think it's a great thing and he understands that. He cares about his fans.

**Q: What is the most compelling conversation you had while making the movie with Arnold?**
Eric Watson: There was one morning we went to breakfast after we made the movie – it was soon after Donald Trump was elected – and Arnold was sitting there with his phone and they were tweeting about each other. They were making fun of each other. Then Arnold said to me, "Hey Eric, watch this." He was on his phone tweeting something about Donald Trump, and he said, "Five minutes he'll respond, watch this." And that's exactly what happened. He just laughed. It was really funny to just watch him sitting at breakfast, the way we perceive social media. They're just sitting at breakfast with a phone in their hand. And it was blowing out of proportion because he was just having fun. But I think the president was taking it really seriously; he didn't understand that there was fun involved. Arnold said that if someone takes teasing seriously, then it's somebody we have to be careful about. If you take teasing seriously and get angry there's no flexibility there. You can't function properly. I think he was showing me and showing the world: I'm just teasing this guy, but he's taking it really serious, that's something to pay attention to.

As a larger-than-life personality with interests in politics and real estate, Arnold has had several encounters with Donald Trump over the pair's shared decades in public life, but the latter's presidential ambitions brought their differences to the fore. In 2017, Arnold replaced Trump as the host of *Celebrity Apprentice* and the ratings promptly dropped – something that the president was quick to point out to the former actor. Arnold, for his part, said that he was disappointed in Trump's inability to shift from personality to president, something he himself had struggled with during his days as governor. He was also vocal in his criticisms of the way Trump conducted himself in office. "I don't think he's happy in his own skin," he told interviewers. "I think he wants to be me. He wants to be a great, studly guy that looks good and is muscular, doesn't have a gut sticking out – all of those things." A long-term opponent of political gerrymandering, he continues to campaign against it in 2020.

**Q: What do you think his future holds?**
Eric Watson: Honestly, I think the most important thing for him is his family. He is just wanting to have good relationship with his children, it's his priority. He wants to love and be loved by his children. Any mistakes that he may have made in the past, he just wants his children to be happy.

In 2019, Arnold would once again return to the *Terminator* series, this time reuniting with his *T2* co-star Linda Hamilton after 28 years. *Dark Fate* once again rebooted the series, this time pitching itself as a direct sequel to *Terminator II*, based on a story by James Cameron that ignored the other sequels. Though some reviewers praised the film as something of a return to form, others found the plot confusing, and the film performed poorly at the box office, especially considering its production budget of around $190 million.

# FOUR

## POLITICAL FRATERNITY

## IN PURSUIT OF POLITICS

Arnold Schwarzenegger was not the first Hollywood star to have political ambitions. One of the most prominent actor-turned-politicians, of course, was Ronald Reagan, a man Arnold admired. To Arnold, President Reagan symbolized what America signified: hope, opportunity and freedom. Further, Arnold said that he embraced something else significant from his hero: in America the greatest power is not derived from privilege, but from the people. Reagan represented a role model, he believed, for those who have been granted the public's trust as elected leaders.

Arnold could trace back his political aspirations to his days as a young man living in obscurity in his native Austria. There, people he was growing up with were associated with political and public affairs. So, he had already somewhat had a taste of this world. After moving to America, the young man was freshly intrigued. He was also drawn to the Republican Party, as he explained, "I came first of all from a socialistic country, which is Austria. And when I came over here in 1968, with the presidential elections coming up in November – I came over in October – I heard a lot of the press conferences from both of the candidates – Humphrey and Nixon. And Humphrey was talking about more government is the solution, protectionism, and everything he said about government involvement sounded to me more like Social Democratic Party of Austrian socialism."

It's clear that Arnold was already looking beyond the sporting sphere when he first arrived in America. "When I heard Nixon talk about it, he said open up the borders, the consumers should be represented there ultimately, and strengthen the military and get the government off our backs. I said to myself, *What is this guy's party affiliation?* I didn't know anything at that point." Arnold asked his friend what party was Nixon affiliated with. His friend told him that he was a Republican. "And I said, 'I am a Republican,'" Arnold recalls. "That's how I became a Republican."

In 1986, Arnold had married into a political family. The Kennedys – more accurately, the Shrivers – were hugely influential in pushing Arnold toward public service and politics, and his mother-in-law, Eunice Shriver, had an indelible impact on his decision to run for governor. She encouraged him, prodded him and kept close to him throughout his time in office. In her first public campaign appearance in San Jose, the lifelong Democrat and sister of the late President John F. Kennedy, told reporters, "I think he'd be a very good governor. He's been committed to people all his life. Since the day he first arrived here, he's been a success with people."

Arnold's wife Maria's greatest role in his political career was steering her husband to the right people – as she had done previously with his movie career – getting him the best political advisors who could take control of the chaos that ensued after he announced that he would be running for office in August 2003. Shriver found Mike Murphy, who brought some stability to the Schwarzenegger campaign, and helped make sure Arnold was getting good advice from the right advisers. Arnold's rolodex was vast, so he could really call anybody he wanted to – but this was no guarantee of a smooth campaign. *Los Angeles Times* political reporter Robert Salladay recalls, "It was by far the most intense and strangest election I've covered. There were a hundred and thirty-five candidates on the ballot, including Lt. Governor Cruz Bustamante and Arianna Huffington."

Others included porn publisher Larry Flynt and the late Gary Coleman, star of the 1970s sitcom *Diff'rent Strokes*. The prerequisite for running for office was merely $3,500 and sixty-five signatures, but Arnold was the frontrunner based on name recognition alone.

Arnold was obsessed with politics and enjoyed and embraced new challenges, the latter two things that are crucial for any successful politician. Just as he had done in the entertainment world, Arnold had met a lot of people in the profession he found to be pretty interesting. I think all of those things, to some measure, contributed in Arnold's quest to pursue politics. He was convinced that the State of California was in a bad way, and that he was someone independent enough to have a better chance than most making the change. Moreover, realizing his personal dream. Ultimately, Arnold's improbable rise to political power played out before a captivating global audience. Campaigning as an outsider borrowing a line from the movie *Network* to tell charged-up supporters that, "We're mad as hell and we're not going to take it anymore!"

Once Arnold was elected, his problems were far from over. California's supermajority system makes it almost impossible to get the Democrats and the Republicans together to agree and form a consensus, which was one of Arnold's fundamental challenges. The governor tried to solve it in many different ways, very pragmatic, but in the process he came close to proving that the California system doesn't work. Robert Salladay explains, "Arnold is in the communication business. He understands that it doesn't matter what policies you enact; you have to sell it to the public. There is no greater salesman in the political arena – he's a salesman." Arnold knew little about California public policy. So his team produced briefing books for him and the action star studied them, absorbing as much as he plausibly could. He apparently was a quick learner.

# BRUCE E. CAIN

Bruce E. Cain is a professor of political science at UN Berkeley. He has served as a consultant to the *Los Angeles Times* and a polling consultant for state and Senate races. He is currently working on state regulatory processes in the areas of water, energy and the environment.

**Q: Can you tell me the magnitude of influence the Kennedy family had on Arnold, when he initially pursued politics, and the effect Eunice Shriver had on him?**
Bruce Cain: I would say it helps in America to be tied to a political family, in particular an entertainer, because it gives you connections and networks. And it also kind of marks you as a serious person – this isn't just a random whim that you can get into politics. So, I think Schwarzenegger has had that effect that it made him part of a political family. It also helped him to signal that he was open to ties with the Democrats, so that when he put himself forward as a moderate Republican it was plausible. Because his wife was a Democrat and his family came from a very prominent Democratic family. He didn't really need the money that they were associated with because he had his own personal wealth.

So, I would say that it was mainly that some level of credibility and a connection to the Democrats would soften his image as a Republican. I really don't know what effect Eunice Shriver had on Schwarzenegger. So that's something I'm not versed on. To be honest, I think that Arnold probably didn't need a lot of encouragement. I think he may well have been interested in and attracted to politics for quite a while. He may have got advice from her, but I don't think it was an idea that was put in his head by anybody. But, again, I don't know the relationship with Eunice. That's something that's been written about a lot in newspapers, maybe it is in some of the biographies on Schwarzenegger, but it's not something that's come up a lot in the last eight years.

**Q: Maria's greatest concern was that Arnold would be consumed by a political life. What role did Maria play when Arnold pursued a career in politics, and how did she support him?**

Bruce Cain: Yeah. I think, particularly in the beginning, she put aside her own political career. She took on various causes in California. She's media savvy so she no doubt helped him think about that. In the end, I don't know how much influence she had over his ideas because he fluctuated all over the map so much. There were years when he came across as a Bush Republican. And then there were years it looked like maybe he would head back to a more moderate Republican direction. And I know at various times he made comments to the effect that he had disastrous elections. For example, in 2005 in which he took a very conservative agenda to the electorate, and I remember that he very visibly said something after about how he should've listened to his wife, or she told him this was not going to work.

But interestingly enough, I think he took a woman named Susan Kennedy as an advisor and she made possible that Maria Shriver was not directly but indirectly the source of that. That he was getting advice essentially from a moderate to conservative Democrat as opposed to a diehard Republican. When Susan Kennedy was put in there, it was a very controversial thing. If she had any connection to that, that's possible. But at any rate, Arnold felt comfortable taking advice from a strong moderate Democratic woman, and it may well subconsciously have been a reason Susan Kennedy was chosen.

**Q: In the early years, Arnold had a problem being accepted by some of the Kennedys. Maria has said that everybody had a problem with Arnold, that she didn't know a person who thought it was a good idea for them to get married. Do you think Arnold had a lot to prove for acceptance?**

Bruce Cain: I'm sure that's true. Arnold Schwarzenegger is a very unconventional actor; he's an action hero type of a person. I think the Kennedys had the same reaction that everybody else would've had, *Is this person really serious?* The kind of issues you need to be governor. But as a family, when you marry a Hollywood type, somebody who's had a bit of a reputation as a womanizer, as we recall that was a big issue in the 2003 election, I'm sure there was a lot of skepticism. As you say, he proved people wrong. He became a dutiful husband. He seemed to have blended in the family pretty well. So, I think he's just not a person you can easily forget.

**Q: Arnold once said I wish I could experience the feeling President Kennedy had, speaking to fifty thousand people at one time and having them scream and be in agreement with him. Arnold seemed to have a penchant for leaders who were great speakers.**
Bruce Cain: Yeah. I think that's part of his concept of leadership. And I think that's right, he was probably very much attracted to the Kennedy family because there's no figure in Europe who's more revered, more admired than President Kennedy. Arnold is a good speaker, and many of his finest moments were prepared speeches that he gave. I think he did draw inspiration from that. I think saying the way he thought of being governor, which is that he could inspire with his rhetoric and salesmanship, people to follow him and agree with him.

I think probably one of the great disappointments with him, or maybe it was a surprise, that good rhetoric doesn't get you that far in terms of getting people to being inspired into following you, at least in the modern era it's a lot harder to do than when Kennedy was president. You have a much more partisan electorate, much more vehement meteorite on the other side than you had in the 1960s. It's all kinds of evidence, which put science the matter of fact the temperatures are just a lot warmer in contemporary politics than forty years ago. I think that was probably a dream he had, that he could also inspire people with speeches with his ability to persuade. And it worked for a certain moment. Most of the time it didn't work, just like it doesn't work for Obama. People are going to look at the policies, or look at the budget and realize what the problems are and work out who's going to lead them out of the rigid situation.

**Q: Arnold was elected in a controversial recall election in November 2003. What was so controversial about this?**
Bruce Cain: First, we did not have much experience in California at state level with recalls; we had a lot of experience at local government level. City Council called out of office, but we did not have much experience in the state recall. And secondly, it was, shall we say, a 'freakish' kind of a show because it was so easy to get on the ballot. We had dozens and dozens of candidates. Some of them like Gary Coleman were actors, like Arnold. Some of them were porn queens. Some of them were just average deluded citizens who thought they could run. Some of them were celebrities like Arianna Huffington. It was just a mad zoo! And the procedures, we never did fix them. They made it very easy for anybody just to file and put their name to run for governor. So it was controversial for that reason. And it was controversial, thirdly, because the Democrats had one governorship under Gray Davis, and to many this looked like hijacking the process by the Republicans, initially when the recall started. Then, of course, Arnold had his own money. There was a lot of confusion and anger on the Democrats side.

Out of all that, Arnold did win and it was probably the easiest way to win. I think he would have had a hard time in a regular election, getting nominated for the Republican Party as their candidate for governor. Because the Republican nomination rule at the time was basically for semi-closed primaries, meaning only hardcore Republicans and state Republican first round. And most experts believe that if Arnold tried to run outside the recall election, he had to go through this process where the most conservative Republicans had to choose, he wouldn't have gotten through the first round. So it was really a stroke of luck that opened up this much easier path for him and everything fell into place. It's not clear that if those things had happened, he would have been able to do this.

**Q: Democrat Dianne Feinstein bowed out of the race in early August, do you feel she was a primary threat to Arnold in some respects, which would have sent him in the depths of despair if she had run for office?**

Bruce Cain: Yeah, if she had run I think it would have been very hard for Arnold. It would have been much, much closer. Cruz Bustamante, who was the Lt. Governor at the time, just doesn't have the same electorate. Dianne Feinstein is perhaps, in terms of public opinion, the most popular state official that California has. And that's been true for almost all the time she's been in the office in the 1990s. So it would've been a much tougher race. But fortunately for him, Dianne Feinstein flirts with the idea of running for governor, but often walks away from it. She's got a nice job as senator, and I think her husband's past would have been dragged out and scrutinized in the press. I think she didn't want to go through that again.

**Q: Can you shed some light on who was part of Arnold's integral campaign team? It included Mike Murphy and David Crane.**

Bruce Cain: I think, as you say, Schutzman, basically I would characterize them as sort of the young turks, the younger Republican operatives. You had the older group of political operatives such as Wilson. So, you had Wilson, who I believe was involved in the campaign, you also had a lot of younger people that were like the next generation of political consultants. So, this was a real opening and opportunity because many of them were looking at the fact that 2002 was very dismal for the Republicans because they weren't winning anything. They lost the governorship and it just looked like there wasn't going to be much business. So, for many of them, and this may seem a little harsh but it's true, having a celebrity who had already had recognition and had an unlimited bank account was like a Christmas present. Because if you're consulting, you worry about whether you are going to get paid or not, particularly if somebody loses. If you're business people that nobody knows, you have to spend a lot of money introducing yourself or introducing this candidate. So to have a celebrity with a lot of money was a big deal for all of these guys.

And, of course, once they had that success with Schwarzenegger, that became their formula and they started to look for new millionaires that they could work for. That's, of course, what happened with Goodman. It's kind of, in my opinion, the lazy way out that the Republic consultants had taken. They wanted to make sure they got paid. And instead of looking for somebody who had paid their dues and worked their way up, they go out and find themselves a celebrity millionaire and latch onto that. And if they lose it's no big deal because they'll get paid. Arnold was a success and a formula. I think what happened in the last election made him even surpass the whole formula.

**Q: Who were the most instrumental of his advisors when he stood for the first or second time, and were there any who were relinquished from their duties?**
Bruce Cain: Most of that period I was in DC, I was not actually in Sacramento. So I didn't observe that sort of air and inner workings of his office. I think Susan Kennedy was a major figure. David Crane was a major figure. It seemed to me he dropped a lot of people, he had a bunch of people from the Wilson era that worked with him up until 2005. He had Tom Campbell in there and a bunch of other people. He got rid of the Wilson people for the most part and switched over to Susan Kennedy and David Crane and people like that.

**Q: Arnold bemoaned the failure of Gray Davis, expressing to talk show host Jay Leno, "The man that is failing the people more than anyone is Gray Davis." Can you please tell me about some of the obstacles Arnold had to overcome facing Davis in the first election?**
Bruce Cain: Gray Davis had been in California government since the early 1970s. He had served as chief of staff to Jerry Brown in the '70s. He had been an Assembly man. He'd been the controller,

Lt. Governor. He had worked his way up. He was not and is not a charismatic guy. We had a whole bunch of non-charismatic governors. We had Pete Wilson who was non-charismatic. We had George Deukmejian who was non-charismatic. To many people, it looked as though California was destined to . . . You need to have these solid non-charismatic people governors because it just looked like if anybody had a strong personality they were going to get hit with lots of negative ads. Gray Davis was good at raising money. He was a Democrat. He won in 1998 and he won in 2002. He knew a lot more about what was going on in the state.

So, on the face of it, here you had a rookie who knew very little about issues taking on a governor who was very experienced. Of course, he had the energy crisis he was dealing with and we were in the middle of a recession. Democrats were divided between liberals and moderates and were angry with Davis. So he was in a weakened position when Arnold ran against him in 2003. Voters were unhappy with the motor vehicle license fee, which had been raised. And, of course, the way the formula . . . There were a lot of people who were angry at the governor and wanted to get rid of him. Arnold was on the top of the list.

**Q: Davis vacuously made a remark, "Someone who can't pronounce California should not be the governor." Did Arnold make any derogatory comments which may have offended Davis?**

Bruce Cain: My memory was, Arnold didn't get involved in a lot of that. What I remember is that he was very focused on increasing the motor vehicle license fee, and Arnold was full of promises about reinventing government and making it more efficient and low in taxes. I don't recall there was, in Californian standards, a time that he took a very personal attack on Gray Davis. Again, that's partly because of the very unique nature of the recall election where you were basically asked whether or not you wanted to retain the governor. But everybody was unhappy with the governor and said no. Then all Arnold had to do was focus on the question of:

would he be better than everybody else who was on the ticket on the second part of the ballot?

**Q: Arnold accused the Davis camp of playing dirty. What were some of the more controversial and scurrilous stories that came under close scrutiny, and to what extent did these influence the voters?**
Bruce Cain: Well, in the end they didn't very much. But we didn't know that at the time, particularly there was some question about the *Los Angeles Times* investigation into sexual harassment claims and whether the Davis people had any role in it. In the end, I think if it had been a normal election, in which there was concern about the economy and the energy cost and the motor vehicle license fee, the issue of sexual harassment might have played more. But in the context of everything else, I don't think it did.

When Arnold was considering seriously pursuing a career in politics by standing for governor in the 2002 election in California, Gary South, a political consultant for Arnold's opponent Gray Davis, brought a *Premiere* magazine article to countless journalists' attention containing derogatory allegations intended to tar Arnold's reputation. Peter Jennings of ABC took the opportunity to ask Arnold about this in an interview, he said, "It cannot be easy to spend the last few days of this campaign having to deal constantly with being called a serial groper or a serial abuser of women. Is that tough?" Arnold replied, "I get upset about it. But I knew that before I got into this campaign, that this is going to be that kind of a situation where people will throw everything at me at the last minute and the last week. And it is going to become a dirty campaign, sleaze campaign. And, you know, down to the gutter." People around Arnold had even warned him about potential pitfalls that could lead to disaster. He added, "People, political leaders from both parties said, 'You know, Arnold, I don't know if you want to do that. Because let me tell you, I've campaigned. I've run for office and all this, and the last week they throw things at you that is embarrassing many times. It's terrible for your family." Some of those around him told him to contemplate because no matter what it is something would surface.

One such friend was Jesse Ventura, co-star of *Predator*, former professional wrestling star and former governor of Minnesota, who shared his own opinions on his co-star's conduct in *Time* magazine. "Arnold, what the heck are you doing? You're getting out of Hollywood to go into politics? Well, then forget agents and studio bosses. Now you're dealing with real predators." Ventura advised Arnold if he didn't know the answers to any questions then he should be upfront and admit to the gaps in his knowledge. Ventura himself, he explained, had fed the people 'pre-canned bullshit'. "Plenty of the old Republican gang will come around and want to be your new best friend," Ventura wrote in *Time* magazine.

Later, when full-blown scandals broke relating to Arnold's behavior, his wife stood by his side supporting him. In 2003, on the *Oprah Winfrey Show* Maria sought to put down reports that her husband was a womanizer. "I know the man that I'm married to," she told the host.

In May 2011, Arnold and Maria separated. Mildred Baena, who was employed by the Schwarzeneggers for twenty years as a housekeeper, had given birth to a boy named Joseph. Arnold went public to confirm that he had fathered a child out of wedlock, born in 1997. In his statement, he said, "I understand and deserve the feelings of anger and disappointment among my friends and family. There are no excuses and I take full responsibility for the hurt I have caused. I have apologized to Maria, my children and my family. I am truly sorry. I ask that the media respect my wife and children through this extremely difficult time. While I deserve your attention and criticism, my family does not." The tabloid media frenzy continued.

Allegedly Joseph's grandmother sat him down a year before the scandal broke and revealed to the young boy that Arnold was his father, to which he replied, "Cool!" Maria began to have her own suspicions after she started hearing whispers pertaining to the pair's resemblance. One day Maria asked Baena point blank. Baena told *Hello* magazine, "She (Maria) was so strong. She cried with me and told me to get off of my knees. We held each other and I told her it wasn't Arnie's fault, that it takes two."

Of course, Arnold is a human being and has made mistakes just like anyone else. But because of him being a public figure, the press seemingly took every opportunity to bring him down. Had it been any other person off the street, who may have committed a serious crime, nobody would have taken much notice. Unfortunately, the media more often than not focuses on and gravitate toward the negative, deviating from projecting the celebrity's more palatable side when they can instead make sensational headlines. Someone's personal life is personal, and the media respecting the individual's and their family's privacy is something that may never manifest into a reality. But in the media frenzy world in which we live, the more sensationalist the material the more the public wants to know about it.

Arnold's popularity tumbled in America following revelations he had fathered a child out of wedlock. A new poll revealed his popularity had plummeted to its lowest level, which showed the disdain from the public was reasonably rife. Even celebrities joined in voicing their vilification. "I was really, really disappointed at him for being so horribly disrespectful and deceitful to do that in your own home," Sharon Osbourne told an entertainment source. "He can do whatever he wants in hotels on the road, whatever, knock yourself out, but you don't disrespect your family by doing it in your own home. To me it's just unthinkable." She continued, "I would have chopped his private part off. Arnie's private part would have been down the disposal unit spinning around. That's where it'd be. And I'd make her (Baena) clean it up. That mop would have been wrapped around her head."

In June 2011, Prince William and Kate Middleton, according to sources, were to meet the former governor at the British Consulate-General's residence in Los Angeles, but this was canceled. However, a spokesman for the former governor insisted that no such meeting was ever scheduled for Arnold with the royals.

**Q: Arnold's people seemed to have shielded him from the media journalists, in case he was put on the spot on intricate issues he lacked knowledge of, which may have been convoluted. What were Arnold's weak areas, at the time of running for the first time, and how was he able to elude these?**

Bruce Cain: I think he just didn't know the issues as well as Gray Davis and Cruz Bustamante and the other people who were in California government. He had been involved in initiative campaign, so he wasn't ignorant. But you just couldn't compare the level of knowledge he had. And this is, of course, the way the Republicans deal with their novice candidate, if they try to shield them long enough so that these people can get up to speed and not get torn apart by the press. That's what they tried to do with Arnold.

**Q: In September 2003, Arnold did not participate in the debate where five of the other prime candidates, including Tom McClintock and Cruz Bustamante, would be confronting one another for the first time. Do you feel other candidates were much more cognizant of issues and policies which needed addressing in front of the California public?**

Bruce Cain: Some of them were. Tom McClintock certainly was. Cruz Bustamante certainly was. Not all of them were. There were others who were on there but were not, who like Arnold did not know as much. In some circumstances that can be fatal, not knowing enough about government. But in this particular election, people were so angry that they were willing to try for an outsider who didn't know as much because that person shared their anger basically. Tom McClintock had been the legislator for many years and was an articulate spokesperson, almost a libertarian, i.e., minimal government issues. So he was probably the most visible small government candidate in the race. He could be counted on to get a lot of support from the more conservative Republicans in the electorate. But in a sense, he made Arnold look like a moderate.

People could look at him and then look at Arnold, and if you were an independent or a Democrat you could say, "Yeah, I'd much prefer to have Arnold over McClintock." Cruz Bustamante was a conservative Democrat Latino from Central Valley. Soft-spoken, but I wouldn't say he's a dynamic guy – not the showman that Arnold was. As far as Latino goes, he was considered more conservative than most so he had some crossover appeal. He had been a speaker at the Assembly, and it's very hard to go from being a speaker in Assembly to having a state position. There are a few examples: Willie Brown became the mayor of San Francisco. But they don't generally go any further than that because it's kind of an image of being an insider's politician as opposed to being the kind of salesman a politician like a governor can be.

**Q: When Arnold was whisked into office, just how big of a responsibility did he have on his hands?**
Bruce Cain: He came in at a very hard time and there were a lot of issues pressing, most particularly what we call the 'structural deficit'. Meaning that the state had committed to programs like reducing classroom size, standard healthcare for children. We simply didn't have the revenues for when the stock market took a tank. So, I think Arnold recognized that. He recognized there had to be a way to bring the structural deficit. And he tried to do that by establishing a commission, which would look at the possibilities of efficiencies, closing down some of these commissions and boards that were very controversial.

But in the end, after a year of kind of study and serious recommendations, he backed off. He cut the vehicle motor license fee, which took money and revenue away from government. And that made the structural deficit worse because he didn't cut programs. So, I think Arnold found himself in a very difficult situation, but he was able to do some things that were very important such as signing the greenhouse gas bill. He managed to persuade the voters to pass some bond measures. It would finance projects that could no longer be funded under the general budget. But in the end, he was never really able to solve the structural deficit problem, and that's what Jerry Brown inherited in his third term now as governor.

**Q: Arnold ran for re-election against Phil Angelides in November 2006. Can you tell me about some of the prominent people involved in this, and how much support did Arnold receive?**
Bruce Cain: I think by that time, he had got rid of the Wilson people. He was pretty much using these younger Republican consultants and he was working with Susan Kennedy. He had had a very disastrous year in 2005, when he tried to pass a whole bunch of Republican measures. And the voters had rejected him in the special election. So he turned to the last so to speak and signed the global agreement, the greenhouse gas bill, with the Democrats. And for a period of time, the economy recovered from the dotcom bust and started to look again largely on the housing, the appreciation of housing. So, Arnold was flush with resources, and timing in politics is everything. Phil Angelides was looking at the structural deficit, saying we really have to adjust and increase the taxes. And that is something the voters didn't want to hear. Once Phil said that, basically Arnold just jumped over at that issue, all over it, and got himself re-elected. He also put himself in the box, meaning he couldn't find any permanent solution to the structural deficit, but it was enough to get him re-elected in 2006.

**Q: Can you tell me about the collaboration between Susan Kennedy and Arnold?**
Bruce Cain: As far as we can tell, she really became his most important adviser. She had had a very important role with Gray Davis, advising him as cabinet secretary. She's very business oriented. She's a lesbian but, of course, that doesn't bother Arnold – he comes from the Hollywood world. I think they tried very hard to maintain a kind of a moderate agenda, not cutting social services

and state by too much. But at the same time, Arnold was holding the line on taxes. So, on the one hand it took Arnold too far to the right, and on the other hand I think the fact he was trying to have it both ways to please the Democrats by not taking huge deficit programs but not please the Republicans by raising taxes. I think it was a middle-over-the-road strategy, which I'm sure Susan Kennedy had a lot to do with, which was what got him re-elected in 2006. But it didn't help solve the problems the state was confronted with.

**Q: When he stood for the second time, what promises did Arnold make this time to the people, not circumventing, and what were their thoughts in terms of whether these would materialize?**

Bruce Cain: To be honest, I don't remember other than . . . I can't recall he had a major theme; it was more that they jumped on top of Phil Angelides for his tax increases. My impression is: he was largely running on his success, by that time he had become a sort of an environmental spokesman. He was going to implement the greenhouse gas law. So he was really running as a kind of a worldwide figure, a sort of Republican who cared about going green and carbon emissions. He was riding that image pretty heavily. But I don't recall that any of the other proposals were really important in that election. I'd have to go back and take a look.

**Q: Would I be right in saying that sometimes he was far from being a hyper-partisan politician? What were the hurdles and obstacles for Arnold to overcome in the 2006 re-election?**

Bruce Cain: For the 2006 election, I don't think he had any. I think the problem was that Phil Angelides was going to raise his own money because he had his own wealth. And at that point, it looked as though – the state is predominantly Democratic – and many of the Republicans were very unhappy with Arnold. In fact, going into the 2006 elections his biggest challenge was that there were some Republicans that wanted to run a primary opponent against him because they felt he was too moderate, that he was almost a Democrat in drag if you like. So, his real problem on that side, in terms of the Democrats, he had a very good relationship with the speaker at the time when they cut the deal on the global warming bill and various other things. He basically was able to split the Democratic Party. So, I think his major obstacle was the fact he didn't have the united backing of the Republicans, and they basically thought, *Well, it's better to have Arnold even though he's half Republican – not a real Republican – it's better to have him than a Democrat.* He was able to prevail, even though there was a lot of discontent within his party.

**Q: Can you differentiate between the contrast between state politics and national politics in America – did Arnold influence national politics?**

Bruce Cain: Well, I think that Arnold was able to do international politics by virtue of his climate change law. So he got to play an international role. I don't think he had much impact with the national side because he was basically looking for the national government to give the state more money, and they were not interested in helping bail out the state of California. So, even though he campaigned for Bush in 2004, in the end he really didn't have a good relationship with Bush. And in his travels to DC, aside from the fact that they were a bunch of political figures who wanted to have their picture taken with him, he was never really able to get anything out of the Republican Congress. So, he never really became a leading figure in a Republican Party. He was pretty much abandoned in 2006 as being way too liberal. And it was the best that California could produce. But it was clearly not going anywhere in the Republican Party.

So even if he had been a citizen of the USA, he would have had a hard time at a national level getting a presidential bid going. Because I don't think the southern Republicans would have liked the fact his social views were so liberal, and that his politics had been cooperative with the Democrats. So he would have had a hard time parlaying that into a presidential bid. But it definitely got the possibility that, if Arnold is healthy enough he might run for one of the Senates in a few years. I think it's fair to say that he has some big wins and some big losses. His big wins were in the area of green, carbon emissions and the environmental issues. I think his big loss will be in the area of the budget and his inability to really bring structural deficit in control. I think his legacy includes having some big achievements, like the global and greenhouse gases. I think this will be an enduring legacy.

Arnold had experienced life under communism first hand. When he was growing up, the Soviets occupied part of Austria. "I saw their tanks in the streets. I saw Communism with my own eyes," Arnold remembers. "I remember the fear we had when we had to cross into the Soviet sector. Growing up we were told, don't look the soldiers in the eye; just look straight ahead. It was common belief that the Soviet soldiers can take a man out of his own car and ship him back to the Soviet Union as slave labor." Arnold's family didn't have a car, but one night his family and Arnold, when he was a little boy, were in Arnold's uncle's car. They were stopped at the Soviet checkpoint. Arnold was scared and feared that the soldiers could pull his father and uncle out of the car and take them away, and he would never see his family again. His family and so many others lived in fear of the Soviet boot. "Today," Arnold remarked many decades later, "the world no longer fears the Soviet Union, and it is because of the United States of America."

In October 2010, the governor flew to the United Kingdom and joined David Cameron, the British Prime Minister, on a visit to Wellington Barracks near Buckingham Palace. There he met and spoke in front of three hundred troops. Addressing the troops, he said, "I get hailed a lot of times when I travel around the world as being the action hero. But I know the difference between a movie action hero who is make-believe and the true action heroes. You all are the true action heroes because you are risking your life. You are risking your life every day when you go out to the front. So I say thank you, thank you, thank you for the great work that you are doing." The governor stated he's always interested to spend time with heroes.

He also managed to visit the barracks gym where he watched the troops work out. He added in his speech, "First of all, I was amazed when I saw you guys pumping up in the gym with those deltoids and those biceps and the six-packs. Wow, you guys are really in great shape." He said that he was in contact with President Obama. "We are absolutely united in making sure we make Afghanistan safe from terror and that will make us safe from terror." The governor praised the troops for their outstanding work for keeping democracy. "It's because you, for hundreds of years, have fought for the freedom to keep these countries free and to keep these countries strong and to have the freedom of speech. Many countries in the world don't have that." Mr. Cameron, who seemed to somewhat enjoy rubbing shoulders with celebrities, was able to strike up a relationship with Arnold when he visited the governor in California to discuss green policies back in 2007.

# MIKE GENEST

Mike Genest served for four years as Governor Arnold Schwarzenegger's chief financial policy advisor. Prior to that, Genest was the director of the California Senate Republican Fiscal office. He is currently married with two sons and works as a consultant.

**Q: When Arnold became the governor, what were the core issues surrounding the budget that required immediate attention with great prudence?**

Mike Genest: The major issue was: the budget he inherited had a massive unfunded debt. They had simply spent more money than they could take in. And they had proposed to borrow $9 billion, and this is on a budget that was approximately seventy-six billion. So, that's a heck of a lot to borrow to finance a nine billion budget. There was no real good legal way to borrow. Probably the most urgent matter he faced upon taking office was how to finance the borrowing that had been assumed in the budget he had inherited, but that wasn't really a good thing to do. He did that.

The second biggest problem was that the trajectory of spending was to borrow more than any projections of our revenues could've supported it. So his second big task was to try to cut spending, not only in the year he took office, but more importantly the next year and the following years. He absolutely had to cut spending. Now, it's not clear exactly how much he had to cut, but it was quite a bit. Probably about at least 10 percent, or something like that, the budget needed to be cut in order to be more affordable. And then I guess the last big budget challenge beyond that was that the previous governor had raised the vehicle licensing fee dramatically, and Arnold Schwarzenegger felt that was both illegal and wrong. So, when he came in he reversed that action, and by doing so restored the vehicle licensing fee to a much lower previous level. When he did that, he created even more need to cut money out of the budget. So in some sense, he made his budget problem worse by doing that. He felt it was a promise to the people and had to be done.

**Q: Some of the cuts and spending that were integral to the budget, what cuts was he proposing and was he being pragmatic?**
Mike Genest: Initially, when he first issued his budget, which was about six weeks after he took office, he took a wide range of cuts. He proposed to cut nearly everything. He proposed to cut education substantially. He proposed to cut welfare and certain types of health services. He proposed a variety of cuts. One of the cuts he proposed was a program that provides a very rich mix treatment of care to children that are born with developmental disabilities. He proposed to cut that as well. That was startling to a lot of people, that he would be so hard-pressed as to have to cut that. But even before the legislator began threatening him for not doing what he was proposing, he relented on that particular cut. And he changed his mind and said I will not propose to make that cut. But he did stick with proposed cuts in a wider range of state services – nearly all of them.

Some things couldn't be cut. He couldn't cut the debt service on our outstanding bonds. That would have been a default. He couldn't do that. He could not cut union salaries that had already been negotiated by his predecessor. At least he couldn't do it without the help of the legislator. And there was no hope of getting that. There's a variety of things, retirement payments – he had no power to even propose the cut. Things that were legally feasible to cut, most of them he did propose to reduce substantially.

**Q: Arnold capitulated signing a bill to increase the state's minimum wage, a move once he opposed. Why did he pursue this?**
Mike Genest: Well, I really don't know why he did that. It's not something I, as a budget person, had a direct immediate impact on the budget. It cost us a little money because we had some people whose salary was paid by the state who were getting minimum wage. But that's a pretty small number of folks that are in that category, so it didn't really cost us a lot. So, I didn't really follow his logic on that.

**Q: Arnold laid out to the Democratic legislators his California Recovery Plan, what did this encompass?**

Mike Genest: Yes. He pointed out that California infrastructure was designed and built, for the most part, in the 1960s and 1970s. And at the time, our population was something, like, twelve million – you'll have to look it up, I don't remember, but it was small. By the time he took office, the population was more than thirty million. And our infrastructure simply had not kept up. We had massive needs for more prisons because our prisons were overcrowded. We had a massive need to improve our highway system because they had been neglected. Our water delivery system was in severe trouble, especially during drought years. Even our parks needed some help. Our schools, we needed to build schools both at higher education university schools as well as other schools. So we had a lot of infrastructure needs that just had not kept up with the really substantial growth of our population.

So, he said, "Look, even though we're in a budget crisis, where we cannot afford to pay for services that we're required to provide by law, we can't ignore our infrastructure needs because that's our hope for the future. If we don't take care of our infrastructure, then our economic growth in the future will be severely impaired." He said we need to borrow a great deal of money to finance a significant expansion or improvement of our infrastructure throughout the state. Then he was successful in convincing them that it needed to be done. Even in the face of the difficult budget situation that the state struggled with.

**Q: Arnold had advisors advising him. Professor Edward Leamar advised him that he needed a three-year plan. Can you tell me about any meetings you were involved in with him and any assertions he complied with?**

Mike Genest: I was involved in the initial Arnold Schwarzenegger team before he became governor. I had been working for the Senate with the Republicans at the time on the budget. I worked with a man named Professor John Cogan at the Hoover Institute at the

Stamford University. It's a conservative . . . it includes the likes of George Shultz and other conservative economists, and Cogan is one of those. Cogan and I worked out a good deal of the governor's proposed budget before he was even governor, and it was based on a situation that we had inherited. We knew there was just no way to cut enough spending to survive the debt that we had inherited, and the higher rate of spending that we had inherited. So we thought it would be wise to develop a workout plan as if it were a bankruptcy, where you have a bankruptcy you mark down your payments and take certain amount of time to work back into solvency. Well, we can't really declare bankruptcy as a state. In the United States, no state has the power to use the bankruptcy courts to solve its problems.

We had to come up with our own workout plans. And it was simply to borrow some money to pay off the debt, and to help survive for the first few years. Then he would freeze spending and substantially reduce the rate of growth in spending. So that over time, the revenue growth in the economy we expected to continue improving, would bring our revenues up to the point we could not only pay off the borrowing, but also get to a point where we wouldn't have to do any cutting. There was a plan that could've worked, but it wasn't fully implemented.

**Q: When Arnold became the governor, he proposed a comprehensive plan to deal with health insurance. What was he planning on doing, was this plausible and what was actually achieved?**
Mike Genest: His health insurance plan was somewhat similar to the time recently adapted by the Congress, what we ultimately refer to as Obamacare. Meaning it's President Obama's vision of how to address healthcare in the United States. It's not the law of the land, but I guess there are two central features to it. One is: it's a requirement under law that every person in the United States must purchase health insurance – that was in Governor Schwarzenegger's plan as well. And the other piece of that is: using government

resources, tax money and a variety of other mechanisms to provide insurance to people who can't afford it, or to subsidize insurance for people who can maybe afford a portion of it but not all of the costs of buying the mandatory healthcare. There were a lot more provisions than that, but I think those are the central features of his plan.

**Q: Arnold, himself an entrepreneur, was no doubt able to resonate with business owners in California. Can you tell me how businesses benefited, what did Arnold propose to help businesses in California?**

Mike Genest: I think he did two really important things – at least in his first term. One important thing was that he took a massive and unprecedented reform of workers' compensation plan. This is the plan for workers who are hurt on the job. So, when you're hurt on the job there's a separate type of insurance that your employer in California, and most states in the United States, must by law purchase for you. The employer must have insurance to cover the eventualities of workers getting hurt whilst on the job. And that insurance covers time off work, it pays pain and suffering and it covers the necessary health costs. The governor reformed that insurance dramatically by things that would keep the costs of healthcare down by reducing the amount of pain and suffering damages that people could get, and by preventing fraud and abuse in the system.

By doing that one reform, the governor saved employers in the state of California billions and billions of dollars every year after the reform was active. It was probably the largest single benefit to businesses that's ever happened in the state from a reform of a government program. It was massive. The other thing that he did was he did not raise taxes. There was a great deal of pressure to raise taxes. Ultimately, in his second to the last year in office, recession forced him into a position where in addition to cutting things he had to raise taxes. But his initial years in office were very helpful to the business communities of our state because he resisted the call to raise taxes.

**Q: Do you think Arnold had the capacity to turn the budget around, or was it almost kind of an impossible task?**

Mike Genest: Well, he tried very, very hard and he made some progress. But he didn't actually solve the state's budget problem. It turned out to be a bigger and a harder problem that even he could solve. And he solved some big things. He made some big differences but he didn't completely solve the problem. My personal opinion is that it was simply too difficult of a problem. When I say this, I don't mean to suggest the arithmetic was beyond him – not at all. He completely understood the arithmetic. He had no problem with figuring out how he would solve the budget problem. The problem was entirely political: how do you get politicians, especially more liberal politicians, to agree to solve a budget problem of that magnitude when they can instead find gimmicks and tricks and temporary measures to avoid having to do the tough things that are required that we have not yet been able to convince our legislator to do?

Now our new governor – Governor Brown – even though he is a Democrat from the liberal wing of the party, he is proposing massive cuts. Because I think we're finally getting to a point where the numbers are just so hard to address that the people are having to relapse logical boundaries somewhat. And because of that maybe now the problem can be solved, and maybe Governor Schwarzenegger gets a great deal of credit, should get a great deal of credit, for pushing on it for all these years. And between his efforts, and the fact that the situation has gotten progressively worse next to the recession, I think we may have some breakthroughs and actually start rolling possibly. But I think unfortunately we'll also have to raise taxes.

**Q: In 2009, to close the staggering $26.3 billion deficit, he demanded even deeper cuts that Democrats said will shred the social safety net.**

Mike Genest: That claim was always made. By the way, there is a great deal of merit to that claim. The social safety net was simply more expensive than the state of California could afford to maintain. So the cuts that were necessary would have, in fact, dramatically altered the landscape of what our state provides its most vulnerable citizens. But I think we're going to end up doing it, anyway. And, in fact, the Democrats who made those statements are now completely in control of the budget here and they're acknowledging – including the new governor – that we're going to have to change what we provide our citizens. And we're not going to be able to maintain the safety net at the levels that we've always for many, many decades have come to expect.

An example is, we have a very rich program for taking care of older and disabled people in their own homes, so they don't have to go into an institution. But we have extended that program to appoint the people's relatives, their mothers, their daughters, their fathers and so forth can actually get paid to take care of them. So we're paying people to take care of their own relatives. Because it's gotten so big, and that is one of the reasons it's gotten so big. There have been many proposals to cut that program back dramatically. Arnold Schwarzenegger made some proposals that would have cut the number of hours of care that those people would have received. There were people who claim that by making that cut those people would be forced into a nursing home and an institution, or that they might even die. But he had no real choice but to propose those cuts. He got some of those cuts accepted, but not all. Some of the ones that he proposed that the Democrats objected to most vehemently, now the new governor, the Democrat, liberal governor, has come right back and proposed those very same cuts. I think that indicates Governor Schwarzenegger wasn't being mean-spirited when he proposed these cuts. As tough as they were, he was just trying to be realistic.

**Q: What was Arnold like in terms of taking advice from his advisors and to collaborate with?**
Mike Genest: He was certainly a very polite and respectful man. He was fun to be around, a great sense of humor, very engaging and a really gracious boss on an interpersonal level. You could not

say that about all bosses, but it is perfectly accurate to say this about Governor Schwarzenegger. I think, however, he took advice from far more people than bureaucrats like myself. He took advice from private people and people from outside of government. Sometimes some of us inside the government felt that he was not getting the best advice. I think he could've been more successful if he had played the budget game much harder and cut more things and been unrelenting on more things. But perhaps it's easy to understand why it wasn't because he's also a human being and cares about people. He listened to a lot of advisors, including Mrs. Schwarzenegger, who could not go along easily with the idea of such cuts in our budget. So often times, despite the physical numbers that he needed, he would either not make them or withdraw the cuts. And I think that made it hard for him to balance the budget.

**Q: What was the most compelling conversation that you ever had with Arnold, whilst you were working with him on a professional or social level?**

Mike Genest: As the director of finance you are in a very delicate situation because the governor has to know that you will never reveal his private thoughts or illuminations. But I can tell you without getting specific that talking to him was a revelation, and listening to him talk about what was going on in the rest of the world. I often had the opportunity to fly on his private plane, and sometimes it was just he and I. Whether it was his observations about fatherhood, he expressed a very good philosophy about being a father. And from everything I could tell he was a great father. He cares greatly about his children. So, either listening to him talk about fatherhood or about some head of state he was going to meet and so forth, or just guy talk sitting around waiting for the plane to land, he was always a fascinating person to be around. It was a great opportunity in my life to be able to speak with him privately and listen to some of his great stories about the movie industry, or sports career. But I don't think it's appropriate for me to reveal any of the substance of that.

# DANIEL WEINTRAUB

Veteran political reporter Daniel Weintraub began his career in journalism writing for the *Los Angeles Times*, and followed Arnold Schwarzenegger's political career from the beginning to end. Weintraub is a columnist for *The Sacramento Bee* and the author of *Party of One*.

**Q: When Arnold decided to run for office in 2003, in your opinion, what motivated him to pursue politics? He had already reached monumental heights in the sport of bodybuilding and the motion picture industry. He also said he would like to be the president one day, was this some unattainable dream or would this be plausible?**

Daniel Weintraub: I think it was some of the same impulses that drove him in his early years in his careers. He likes to be the center of attention. He likes to be the center of the action. Here's a chance for power and glory. And I think he enjoys a challenge. So, the idea that he could come in from the outside and as the person with no experience in government and try to fix these problems that the state has, I think this appealed to him. Sure, if he was allowed to run for president I'm sure he would have wanted to. I think he just loves to be the center of attention. He likes power. He's got a big ego and he thinks he can do big things.

But, you see, the self-serving or serving the public in order to feed the ego, either way he likes to be in the center of the action. And either getting attention or exercising power to change the world, whether it's the world of bodybuilding, world of acting or the world of politics, he wants to tackle the biggest problems with the biggest challenges that people can throw at him. And he thinks he can find a solution. I think the biggest influence on him were the parents of his wife Maria Shriver. Eunice Kennedy, who was the sister of JFK, and her husband Sergeant Shriver, who was involved with the Kennedy Administration, I think influenced Schwarzenegger when he was a young man. As I said before, he had this philosophy which was kind of: every man for himself.

I think the Kennedy-Shriver family sort of took him around the world and showed him the way other people lived, and the way many people who are poor and have less going for them lived. They were born into that situation and find it very difficult to escape it without some outside help. I think their influence on him as a person really changed the way he viewed the world and society. I don't think any of the other Kennedys had a huge effect on him. Bobby Kennedy Jr., who is Robert F. Kennedy's son, is a very strong environmental activist. And at the time, Schwarzenegger was starting to explore formal emissions on environmental issues. I think Robert Kennedy Jr. did have some influence on him. Also, Ted Kennedy was more of a friendly rival. Ted Kennedy is a Democrat, but I think Schwarzenegger respectively rejected much of what Ted Kennedy had to say, even though they had a very friendly relationship on a personal level.

**Q: Before he stood for the race, what links did Arnold have to politicians? Obviously, he was a friend of the first President Bush and also admired Ronald Reagan. Can you elaborate on his links to politicians in the 1980s and 1990s?**

Daniel Weintraub: He was definitely considered much more conservative back in those days. He was almost a libertarian, an anti-government advocate. He was a friend of the first President Bush and admired Reagan. He was a big fan of the American economist, Milton Friedman, who was also an advocate of a limited government and individual rights and responsibility. Arnold was a big supporter of a measure in California that changed the state's Constitution to limit the property taxes, which is always a controversial issue here. He was on the side of keeping that in place and keeping taxes low.

So, he contributed a small amount of money to some politicians. But his role was more behind the scenes, and appearing occasionally at political fundraisers. He wasn't very much involved in state politics; he was more interested in national affairs and economic issues. His first real high-profile connection to state politics was in

2002, just before the recall election, when he advocated a measure that went on the ballot of California. We had direct democracy where the voters get to have the say in setting state policy by voting on measures of the ballot, and Schwarzenegger proposed and supported the measures to get more funding to after-school programs, which was one of the issues he had developed on his own with his own private foundation. So, he brought that to the state political scene and successfully passed the measure to set some money on the side each year to expand after-school programs for the kids.

No one modeled their political career more on Ronald Reagan than Arnold Schwarzenegger apparently. Arnold and Reagan both ventured into Hollywood before making the transition to politics. Both men were charming, ebullient and outspoken. "Reagan was a hero to me," Arnold – who became a citizen of the United States when Reagan was in office – said. "And he is the first president I voted for as an American citizen. He inspired me and made me even prouder to be a new American." Arnold developed a penchant for delivering one-liners with self-assurance, just as his political hero had resorted to in his prime. Reagan had a rational streak that defies his followers among the current crop of Republicans.

Arnold remembers how Reagan used to sometimes talk about the letter he received from a man who wrote, "You can go and live in Turkey, but you can't become Turkish. You can go and live in Japan, but you can't become Japanese. You can go to live in Germany or France, but you can't become German or French." But the man said that anyone from any corner of the globe could come to America – the Land of Opportunity – and be embraced and become an American. Arnold expressed, "When I heard President Reagan tell that story, I said to myself, 'Arnold, you Austrian immigrant, he is talking to you. He is saying that you will fit in here. You will be a real American, able to follow your dreams.'" Interestingly, another trait which Arnold seemingly inherited from his political hero was, whenever Reagan wanted to refrain from answering a specific question from the press, he'd pretend he couldn't hear the question. It became apparent to observers that the same strategy was being implemented by Arnold, as he moved into the political game.

**Q: As a political journalist, can you tell me some of the obstacles he had to overcome when he ran for governor for the first time?**

Daniel Weintraub: I think the biggest obstacle was just to be taken seriously. I don't think people at first believed that an action movie star and former bodybuilder could run a state government as large as California, or that he really knew anything about state politics or government. So, at first he had a lot of support just from movie fans and bodybuilding fans who had heard of him. He was certainly one of the best-known people on the planet. So he had a significant base of support, but he really was not an immediate favorite to win the job. But he stayed in there and his people managed the campaign really well because they sort of kept him under wraps and kept the expectations low. There was one debate among all the candidates in which he participated in, and he came into that well-prepared. He was able to do a good enough job that people who watched the debate and the journalists who watched commented that he seemed to have a grasp of the issues. Then when he was talking and once that debate happened, it really changed the tide of the campaign and people started taking him more seriously and saying that maybe he could do this job. From that point on, he went on to win the race.

**Q: For his first press conference as a politician, which took place outside the Burbank Studios of the *Jay Leno Show*, the world press was present. Was there anything significant in his speech that had substance, which would resonate with the political journalists who were present?**

Daniel Weintraub: Well, there was a point at the press conference when most of the press reporters had moved on because they were interested in the celebrity politics and the Hollywood connection. He started to talk about how he sort of had this middle ground economic philosophy, where he wanted to bolster the state's economy to create more jobs, which would create more revenue for the state's government, which he then wanted to use to expand programs for people who needed them. So, he was espousing this sort of fusion, political message that started with a Republican idea, or a Conservative idea, of expanding the economy and creating jobs. And it ended with a liberal idea. In American politics we call it 'liberal', but expanding government with more revenue. He really combined those two things into a single philosophy, which made him unique in Californian politics.

**Q: He made improving vocational education a big priority, can you elucidate further and just how imperative was this issue for Arnold to address?**

Daniel Weintraub: Yeah. He came from Europe, where vocational education is much more popular and sort of regimented and organized than it is in the United States where kids are pretty much on their own to do that sort of thing. I think he came into it with a respect and admiration for parts of that European system. He doesn't like the part of the European system, as a German and Austrian system. His was sort of overly controlling of what individuals could do. But he did like the way they teach kids and young adults. So he committed to expanding that in California. And did several initiatives to expand the state's offering of job training and skill training, as opposed to just try to teach every kid the academics they would need to go on to university. He knew from his own experience that many kids will either not go on to university, or if they do they'll eventually drop out. So he wanted to give more kids a chance and economic ability, by giving them a skill or trade that they could use if they didn't go on to college.

**Q: Can you highlight the issues on how he pursued healthcare?**

Daniel Weintraub: Sure. Well, he didn't do much on healthcare in his first term. But in his second term in 2007, he proposed a comprehensive expansion and reordering of the healthcare system in California, which eventually more or less became the model for what President Obama did in 2010. It was a hybrid system of private and public care for people who could not afford private insurance and they were covered, almost all legal residents of California. He was not able to get that through. In part it was because not a single member of his own party was supportive because they didn't like the bigger role for government that he was proposing. Then the Democrats got into it, into party squabbles among the Democratic factions legislator and programs they normally would have embraced, and Democrats nationally embraced this year when President Obama was proposing it. The Democrats in California would not give Schwarzenegger the votes he needed to pass that in 2007. But he definitely helped blaze the trail for what came later on a national level.

**Q: Can you shed light on Arnold's take on environmental protection, which became epochal in his political career?**
Daniel Weintraub: I mean, with the environment issue Schwarzenegger tried to find middle ground, although on the biggest issues he tended to actually lean with the opposing party, the Democrats. His most famous action was in supporting and signing legislation that put California in the lead in limiting greenhouse gases to fight global warming – that law is about to take full effect. It will require the state to limit the emission of greenhouse gases to the levels they were in 1990 by 2020.

So by the year 2020, California law will be emitting about 30 percent less greenhouse gases than otherwise would have been if things had been allowed to take their course. That's going to result in very stringent regulations of many different industries, the oil refineries, the power utilities, cement factories, standing out into the automobile manufacture even though California cannot directly regulate what automobile companies do across the country. California is such a big marker that regulations put in place eventually affect cars all across the country. So, that was a very controversial law because global warming by definition is a worldwide phenomenon. And I think what any single state can do is going to affect that very much. But California adapted what Schwarzenegger supported as a way to lead the discussion and set an example that they hope eventually the world would follow, even if there was no direct environmental benefits to California. That probably is his most noteworthy environmental accomplishment. He also had been a big advocate of defending the oceans – his policy to control and regulate activity along the coast in order to preserve marine life. Those are probably two of his biggest environmental issues.

Arnold's stance on environmental issues continues to be unapologetic. "Global warming is one of those things, not like an earthquake where there's a big bang and you say, 'Oh, my God, this has really hit us,'" he explained. "It creeps up on you. Half a degree temperature difference from one year to the next. A little bit of rise of the ocean. A little bit of melting of the glaciers. And then all of a sudden it is too late to do something about it." He said that we'd seen the photographs of the glaciers melting and the water rising, and that we are aware of the fact that we are polluting the world. All of this is a reality, he stated. "I'm an optimist. I don't look at this as if the world is coming to an end," the governor once declared. Arnold perceived this as an opportunity to clean up the mess, further adding, "We're grownups, we aren't children. And we can do it. That's why we like to be out front in California. That's power."

In June 2007, the governor visited Downing Street to meet Tony Blair, then the British Prime Minister. The year before, both politicians had agreed a deal which agreed on a commitment from California and the United Kingdom to cultivate low-carbon economies. Mr. Blair explained at a joint press conference that there was no way this thing is going to work unless there is a deal with not just America but the developed world in it. He added that inaction would eventually cost hundreds of billions of dollars. "So it is better to create the action, and Mr. Blair is the action hero," exclaimed the governor, to warm applause. The media, gathered at Downing Street, asked the governor what job he would like to see Mr. Blair in after his exit from Downing Street, to which Arnold replied he would 'feel good' if Mr. Blair became an envoy to the Middle East.

Arnold was the Prime Minister's last official guest at 10 Downing Street, and clearly valued Blair's advice. In 2011, in Redondo Beach, California, Arnold met up with the former Prime Minister to discuss and seek advice for his new role on the world stage after he exited the governor's office. The same year, he visited London, this time to discuss environmental issues with current Prime Minister Boris Johnson, back then the mayor of London. This included the Barclays Cycle Hire scheme, which allows cyclists to hire a bike for a fee at docking stations to get around the busy polluted city. It was a surprisingly amicable meeting, considering four years earlier Arnold had been heard saying to aides, "This guy's fumbling all over the place," as he listened to a Johnson speech via video link. Johnson later responded by dismissing the governor as a 'monosyllabic Austrian cyborg'. Nonetheless, both men buried the hatchet, looking forward to a brighter future as they discussed environmental issues. The mayor joined Arnold as he spoke to the press. "I made it clear to the mayor that we are very much aware in California of all the great work that has been going on in England," said Arnold. "If it has to do with the six thousand bicycles that are being made available to the public to ride around, which makes everyone get fit, and also it cuts down on greenhouse gases and pollution, the great work the mayor is doing here . . . Also, making the buildings more energy efficient . . ." Arnold said that great work was being done.

**Q: What was he going to do to tackle immigration, which is a sensitive issue, and what exactly did he pursue and accomplish?**

**Furthermore, did this mollify immigrants or have the opposite effect on them?**

Daniel Weintraub: There's not a whole lot a state governor can do on immigration issues because it's a national and federal matter. But Schwarzenegger talked about it. He also sent his National Guard, which is a state-controlled reserve unit that's part of the US Army. But when they're on reserve duty, they're controlled by the governor of the state. He sent his National Guard reserves to the border to bolster patrols there. But mostly he talked about the issue and not always in the most effective terms. He had a kind of an additional view of it, being an immigrant himself and one that really embraced America and American culture that preceded him.

He has a bias toward believing that immigrants should pretty much fold themselves into the existing American culture. And with our large Latin American population, there are large communities where that hasn't really been happening. They maintain the ways of the old country. And the language is in their own media and food and culture and everything else they do, which has been the pattern of immigration in America for a couple of centuries now. The first generation immigrants tend to identify still with their own country, but as they have children, the second generation starts to mix into the existing society. But Schwarzenegger spoke out a couple of times about the Latin American population. And his views that they were not moving quickly enough to sort of become Americanized got him into some hot water with Latin American and Mexican American advocates and actors in California.

**Q: Do you feel a lot of people were able to resonate with Arnold because of his celebrity status?**

Daniel Weintraub: Yeah. I think he didn't have any political career (when he first stood for office). But I think people felt like they knew him because they had seen him on the movie screen so many times. And he was a pretty visible public figure and, you know, he was on television and at public events a lot. So he really was someone that people felt familiar with and comfortable with, even though he had no record of politics. That definitely gave him a huge boost in office.

**Q: You have expressed that Arnold often used contradictory third-way politics. Can you tell me exactly what you mean by this? Were there any oblique political maneuvers implemented?**
Daniel Weintraub: United States and California, especially where we have a very polarized political system, we have a two-part system. And in that system, there are winners and losers, and they tend to gravitate toward the extremes in each party. The Democrats are on the left, the Republicans are on the right. Conservatives and the parties tend to quit. That's California politics. Candidates who are either very part of the right or very part of the left – there's just not much room in the middle. Most candidates who are moderate do not get in the office because of the system we have. Schwarzenegger defied that and stood in the middle, not always, as a compromise between both sides. Sometimes he could be very conservative on some issues, such as economic and business issues. And he could be very liberal on other issues on environmental and some social issues. So, at the time he did try to bridge the gap between the two. So he really stood off in our state political system alone because there were just no other politicians that worked that way. They were either all in the part of the left or part of the right. That's where we got the title of my book *Party of One*. Officially, he was a Republican, but he really was acting as an independent and he was out there by himself.

**Q: The budget was one of his biggest obstacles when he became the governor. Thus Arnold had been elected to office to resolve the budget crisis and return California's financial insolvency.**
Daniel Weintraub: Definitely! It has been from the beginning to the end. As he wrapped up his time in office, there's no difference. Yeah, when he ran for office the state had a huge budget deficit, and he promised to erase it. I think he thought that was going to be a very simple exercise, but later found out it was going to be a

lot more complicated than he knew coming in. He really was never able to get control of it for a few years. In the middle of his term, he came close to balancing the budget as the economy improved and some of the measures he was able to take came into effect. But before he could ever achieve that goal, we had a great financial market catastrophe in 2008. California saw its tax revenue decline, income decline, and the budget deficit completely got out of control again. There's a projection of a twenty-five billion shortfall over two years, which is pretty much as bad as what he inherited when he first took office.

**Q: At the election in 2006, when he was re-elected, what did Arnold have to do to gain trust to be voted in and did he exude altruistic qualities?**

Daniel Weintraub: Well, it really started the year before because in 2005, he took full measures to voters in a special election he called. There was no scheduled election that year, but he wanted to go around the legislature and get some things done. So he took full measures to voters, but they were all rejected by almost two-to-one or two-thirds margin. Sixty percent on average voters rejected his proposals. And in late 2005, just a year before he was going for the election, they had given him a huge vote of no confidence and well under the majority of voters said that they thought he deserved another term. So, that was the biggest obstacle. It was just winning back the voters' trust and confidence. He did that by really admitting that he had made a mistake in taking those measures to the voters without trying harder to get them through the legislator, and taking more time to prepare the groundwork for them.

I think he kind of escaped disaster by doing something most political officials almost never do. And that is: admit he was wrong and apologize to the voters for what he had done. Once he did that, he really turned around public opinion. And by the time the election came, he was back in command. He also worked that year with the Democrats on the global warming bill. And with both parties on a huge package of public bond to rebuild and expand the state infrastructure for flood control, education, highways, he built a pretty solid record of accomplishment in that year. So by the time he faced the voters at the end of 2006, they were admiring him again. The economy was booming again and he had a record of accomplishment in office that he could point to. So he easily won the re-election as a Republican in what was a real big year for the Democrats. He definitely went against the tide.

**Q: Would I be right in saying he became arguably the nation's most successful Republican politician?**
Daniel Weintraub: Certainly for a time he was at the height of his career as governor, from 2006 and 2007. At the time, the Democrats were ascending, which eventually lead to the election of President Obama. Schwarzenegger was one of the few Republicans in the country who continued to do well against that Democratic tide. So, yeah, that would be accurate.

**Q: There were a lot of controversial stories and headlines, which surfaced when he first pursued his political career which caused Arnold discomfiture. As a political journalist, do you feel some of them were to be dismissed as mere conjecture, and what stories do you feel had a profound impact on the voters if any?**
Daniel Weintraub: I guess there were a lot of stories that came out of his career in Hollywood – very sensational. One of them was that his father was a Nazi in Germany. And that Schwarzenegger had somehow said something favorable toward Hitler, or his methods of governing, marshalling public opinion. So that was one issue that was used against him. And another was the more recent case about a story about him with a young woman – and on the movie sets – and that story appeared just days before the election. This could have damaged him pretty significantly, but he was able to successfully turn that into a story about the media being out to get him. So, he very joyfully turned that story around and survived it quite easily.

**Q: You interviewed Arnold on several occasions. From a personal perspective, how would you define Arnold?**

Daniel Weintraub: He's amazingly well-grounded. I mean, here's a superstar athlete, superstar actor. Finally, superstar politician expecting to be kind of a prima donna and not in touch with kind of regular people, but he's actually grounded in a way that he has interests outside of politics. Most of the people who are elected the governor of the state of California, who have dedicated their entire lives to the political worlds, they don't really have very many interests outside that. Schwarzenegger has led such a varied life. His upbringing, which was in another country, was barely middle class. It was even a little bit on the poor side. And so he had a lot of experiences that put him in touch with regular people all his life, and that really shows up when you talk to him. He's a good conversationalist. He listens and he doesn't always need to be the center of the conversation. He's himself. He talks. He's curious. He tries to ask questions and listen to what other people have to say. So, on a personal level, I'd say he's very charming.

**Q: What's the most intriguing speech or conversation you had with him which you found to be thought-provoking?**

Daniel Weintraub: I'm not sure you can pick a single speech he's given that really would rise to that level. Certainly some of the things he said about the environment and trying to use environment protection to actually expand the economy and create jobs. But he's really not known for his speech-making. I guess just combining those two things. I think the most intriguing thing he said was when he was describing his transformation from a person who really believed in individual rights and personal freedom. And was against any role for government into the more moderate person he has become. He talked about how he once believed that everybody like him could pull themselves up by their bootstraps. And later, he came to realize that not everyone has boots. So, it was just his way of describing how he modified his own ideology and political views from kind of an "every man for himself" to the idea "the community did need to step up" and help some people.

**Q: You have said, "I have been disappointed often by Schwarzenegger's performance," in your summation of Arnold's political career, do you feel he could have done more in certain areas?**
Daniel Weintraub: Yes, definitely. He really wasted the first couple of years he was in office. He came in with that celebrity power, and being elected in such an unusual election when the sitting governor was thrown out in the middle of his term. He really had a mandate to fundamentally change the state government structure and the way it worked and the political system. Instead he tried to master the existing system, rather than changing it, rather than overturning it. It was really what his mandate was. He just tried to become better at it than the people who had preceded him. But as he later found out, it kind of was bigger than he was and the system ultimately defeated him, kind of chewed him up and spat him out. So, it took him a few years to realize that before he could try to move out on his own and take a different approach. But he never really advocated a fundamental overthrow of the system that he inherited. I think that was his biggest failure.

**Q: What legacy has Arnold Schwarzenegger left as far as American politics is concerned?**
Daniel Weintraub: I think in the short term, people are going to remember him as pretty much a failure because he was not able to fix the broken budget system and turn the state's economy around. But I think in the long term, he has undertaken several reforms that will change politics and government in California for many years now. A couple of them involved the way we elect our political leaders. He was able to change the way the political districts are drawn, taking that job away from the politicians and giving it to an independent commission. Most people believe that's going to lead to the election of more moderate legislators because the old system

was gained by the politicians who favor, again, the most extreme members of each party. The new system will avoid that.

Also, change the way your political primaries work. In California and the United States, historically each party chooses its nominees. And those nominees fight it out in the second round of the elections. And under the new system that Schwarzenegger supported, everyone who wants to run for office will be on the ballot together. And the top two finishers will move to the second round regardless of their party. That kind of allows members of the other party to vote at any point in the process for the opposing party if they prefer that candidate, and allow independent voters to choose from either party if they want. Again, the effect of that is going to probably lead to more moderate politicians being elected. So, in the next five to ten years, you could see California change and more into a system that elects far more people who are like Schwarzenegger – people who have views that cross party lines and are willing to work with the opposing party to get something done. That's probably going to be his biggest legacy.

# CARLA MARINUCCI

Award-winning journalist Carla Marinucci is a political reporter for the *San Francisco Chronicle*, specializing in California State gubernatorial politics and national politics. Marinucci covered Arnold's political career and broke numerous national news stories.

**Q: Carla, Arnold's critics argued that he had a historic opportunity to change the nature of California politics. Can you shed some light on this, what is your conviction on this?**

Carla Marinucci: Yeah. Well, Arnold Schwarzenegger was a politician like California and the United States had never seen before. A man who was, of course, the world's number-one action hero who, just a few years before, was in movies and killing bad guys with a sword in *Conan the Barbarian*. Then when he ran for office, it was a shock and a surprise for everybody. In the face of ninety days, he went from an action hero to being the head of the world's eighth largest economy. And the recall campaign, which I covered from the beginning to the end, really showed how he had an enormous goodwill. He had the hopes of a lot of people and voters in California. They really believed that, you know, just like Conan could perform amazing feats, that Schwarzenegger could lift California out of an economic decline and a political decline.

Arnold had a tremendous charisma, and still does. He had the outsider's resume. Someone said he could clean up Sacramento, sweep it clean from special interests and bring a business outlook to California, which is the nation's most populous state. He charged into the governor's office and did things that we'd never seen before. He put up a smoking tent. He gave up the salary. He did things that no other politician had done in California. And a lot of people felt that he had the opportunity because of that goodwill, because of the unusual nature of the recall in which he was elected, to use political capital and to get things done, to knock it together, as he did with *Conan* and *The Terminator*. But the Terminator wasn't able to terminate a political culture in Sacramento that is just extremely difficult to crack. And a lot of people thought, as an actor and entertainer you have to be liked. And Arnold wanted to be liked. In politics sometimes you have to do things that are very difficult and very unlikable.

Many people thought that was his ultimate weakness: he didn't use the political capital that he had. It was enormous when he first came to office to do the tough things, to knock the heads together and let the opportunities go by which were really lost forever in terms of trying to turn around California's political culture. But that said, he did accomplish some things as well. Part of the issue was that the many promises he made coming into the office, he promised to blow up the boxes of state government, cut up the credit card, bring California to sanity. But by the time he left office, California had $25 billion in deficit. He wasn't able to deliver on those huge promises. And the promises, it turned out, were even too huge for an action hero of his stature.

**Q: He broached that he was going to be different to all the other politicians and was going to fix the mess in California. In what way did he endeavor to do things differently?**
Carla Marinucci: You know, on style nobody could compete with Arnold Schwarzenegger. And they often had to, say in terms of his sunny nepotism, the leadership, he still has a charisma, I think, that we haven't ever seen in California governors. I mean, he was somebody who could attract huge crowds. I mean, as I said, he put up a smoking tent. He had his name in gold in the hallways. He rode his own Gulfstream jet to events. He set up his residence in a hotel penthouse across the street from the Capitol, you know. He was a governor who made headlines once by saving somebody's life who was drowning on a beach in Hawaii when on vacation. That doesn't often happen. I went with him on several occasions to the annual Arnold Classic in Columbus, which is a huge bodybuilding event you probably know about where you have a hundred thousand people who just worship him. And to walk through that event as the governor of California, to walk through that event with him it was kind of like being with The Beatles at the height of their fame.

You just don't see that kind of turnout or adulation of any political figure anywhere. So, in that respect Arnold Schwarzenegger brought attention to the office of California and because of that he was able to get attention to some important issues such as trade and import.

I went with him to China and Mexico on trade missions. And there's no question that when Arnold Schwarzenegger was doing an event in China, talking about California products and how Chinese should buy more California strawberries, he would get dozens and dozens of TV cameras and herds and herds of autograph seekers and people who would turn out. This was the kind of turnout no governor could get. It's something only a head of state could get – that kind of attention in a foreign country. So, he got attention for California issues in Mexico, China and everywhere he traveled. He traveled around the world. Only a movie action hero could do that. So, in that respect Schwarzenegger was able to get attention for California issues on a world stage and get the kind of attention only a world leader could get.

He was very instrumental in passing climate change legislation here. The bill was called AB30. A landmark bill that to this day is considered sort of at the forefront of climate change legislation around the world. That sort of will be his legacy, when it comes to his long-term accomplishments, I think. On the other hand, he had some very big setbacks. He took issues before the voters because he really believed he could sell anything to the California public. He was a great salesman coming into office, but he found himself really bruised and defeated some expensive campaigns and expensive unions came up against him. And he wasn't able to beat them. But in the big issue, I mean, some people say that the climate change regulations and issues like trade and imports in Southern California from abroad is what Schwarzenegger will be remembered for.

Because he did a lot of things for the infrastructure of the state. He put money into growth and in infrastructure issues. He got money passed for prison upgrading. He did a lot of projects when it came to growth and looking to the future of California. He worked with Mayor Bloomberg in New York on that. Infrastructure was a very big deal for him, as was the environment. And he supported the environment. So there are positive things that Schwarzenegger will be remembered for. And, of course, his wife Maria Shriver – the first lady of California – did huge work on women's issues and created an enormous body of work on those issues. So, between them, Schwarzenegger and his wife went to an awful lot of effort. The California governor's office, that was a lot of muscle. That was only what a bodybuilder could do. He brought a lot of attention to issues like no sort of regular governor could've got. So there are some positives, absolutely.

**Q: Arnold said, "We build more prisons or we release prisoners," because local jails and state prisons were overcrowded and criminals were being released early. What steps did Arnold take pertaining to crime prevention and the state's sprawling prison system?**

Carla Marinucci: Well, this is a huge issue and an ongoing issue in California. The prison system is enormous. California Prison Guards is a powerful union. The cost of crime prevention is huge in California. California has the largest cost of any state in the nation when it comes to housing undocumented immigrants. Prison has always been an issue, and Schwarzenegger always tried to argue that California was not getting the fair share of money from the federal government for doing that for housing undocumented immigrants. He promised to be the collector and went back to Washington to get some of that money back. He wasn't able to do that.

But the bottom line is: the prison population is growing here in part because of the three strikes law. That says that to increase the number of inmates, the number of prisons need to be built. It's a costly issue in California. Prisons are very overcrowded, the courts have stepped in and have said California must do something on that. But the state's in a huge financial crunch, and to this day Schwarzenegger was never able to solve. At some point, he said – and other legislators have said – we're going to have to let out the lower priority prisoners, some of those who have, for instance, committed non-violent crimes and they're taking up space that California just does not have. So, California is the most populous state and it has the biggest problem on this. This is a problem that Schwarzenegger had and now the current government is wrestling with. He was just not able to solve it.

**Q: In 2005, a federal judge in San Francisco took over the prison healthcare, declaring that the medical healthcare the state was providing did not meet the minimum standard required by the Constitution. How big of an issue was this?**

Carla Marinucci: Well, yeah, the entire prison system in California and all the issues surrounding the healthcare have been massive. I mean, the federal judge basically said that Schwarzenegger was just moving too slow on giving prisoners adequate healthcare. The prison healthcare is enormously expensive. It's something that, as I said, California still struggles with today. Some critics have called it a 'gold-plated healthcare system', which means that the prisoners have been getting better healthcare than many average Californians. On the other hand, the federal judge, federal appeal court, said this system must be improved. There is a multibillion-dollar plan to rebuild the state prison healthcare system. But back then in 2005, the US district judge rejected the state's attempt to regain control of the healthcare system. It's continual and an on going issue. Schwarzenegger continued to wrestle with the prison system, its cost, its union and the high end of pay that they get, many different aspects of the prison system. They continued to be a huge problem and challenge in California government. He just was not able to get a handle on it.

**Q: In 2010, the family of Luis Santos filed a lawsuit. Arnold had the right to commute the prison sentence of a political friend's son, but violated victim rights guaranteed under a water-approval measure. Can you elucidate further, please?**

Carla Marinucci: This was a controversy that came in the very last day, I believe, of his term in office. Schwarzenegger really kicked off a huge controversy. It was his final night before he left office. He commuted the prison sentence of the son of a very powerful former speaker of Assembly, Fabian Nunez. The young man had been sentenced to sixteen years in prison for a death stabbing. He didn't actually kill the victim, but he had a role in it. Schwarzenegger commuted the boy's sentence and reduced his sentence dramatically. The boy's father was a very powerful Democrat who was close to the governor. Fred Santos, who was the father of Luis Santos, was completely outraged. He's the victim of the man who was murdered. He was totally outraged.

He (Fabian Nunez) said to the governor to wait until the end of the last day to commute this – to do it undercover on the night. This was unjust and the family wasn't warned about it. The governor didn't have the courtesy to notify them. I believe he said by law the victim's family have to be notified, and they then challenged that in court. This is sort of a mark on Schwarzenegger. He waited till the last night when he would be leaving office to do that. He knew he was going to get a lot of political heat for it. And many people thought if he truly believed that this young man's sentence was fair and justice commuted, then he just should've done it and stood up and taken the heat for it and explained it to the people. Instead he went in on the last minute. It is a mark I think on him and his final hours in office.

**Q: Hollywood actor Alec Baldwin expressed, I quote, "I am certainly not a supporter of Arnold Schwarzenegger. I think he was unqualified for his current job when he ran in the bogus recall election." Did Arnold have any particular supporters in the Hollywood community and what are your sentiments on this?**
Carla Marinucci: He certainly got a lot of support from Hollywood while he was governor because he supported Hollywood himself. He pushed for California to make it easier for filmmakers to make films in California. He was a big supporter of the Hollywood community, and he often appeared at the major awards events – Academy Awards and the Golden Globe Awards. So he's

remained close to the movie community throughout. But he was a Republican and the recall was . . . Many of the Hollywood big stars are Democrats, or more liberal in their politics, and many of them did not support the recall election. The Democrat, Gray Davis, had the support, even for the fundraising section, from a lot of folks from Hollywood.

So the actual recall election was not very popular with the Hollywood community, the liberal community and the Democratic community, and is very liberal. I think many people in Hollywood probably did not like Schwarzenegger's politics, particularly his more conservative Republican politics. Although a lot of Republicans were angry at him for being too liberal. So, he was a moderate Republican moderating on social issues than more conservative on physical issues. So, when it came to the Hollywood community, they liked Arnold for what he did for movies and for Hollywood – for moviemaking in California, for supporting acting and the filmmaking industry. But many of them did not particularly like his politics.

**Q: In 2004, a judge ruled Arnold had violated campaign laws and would have to pay $4.5 million from his own pockets. Can you elucidate on this, please?**
Carla Marinucci: Schwarzenegger, his problem was when he came into power, he was saying he was going to sweep Sacramento clean, and the special interest in political gamesmanship. And he always said that he had enough money and that he would be owned by no special interest. But he did create sort of a special campaign organization. In this case the judge ruled that he violated campaign plans with a loan of $4.5 million. Schwarzenegger basically had, even though he said he was untouched by special interests, Schwarzenegger was a very, very good fundraiser as a governor. He raised millions of dollars from cooperative interest. In this case the judge said the governor violated campaign laws – the law that required disclosure to voters of all contributions in the excess of $100. There's no question, as much as he said he was completely apart from special interests, it was clear

he was raising money for both the ballot measures and his travel abroad and other things. So he did get a lot of backing from the cooperative interests in California. He wasn't as removed from that as he promised that he would be.

**Q: Arnold Schwarzenegger is a supporter of the Simon Wiesenthal Center, and has been for many years.**
Carla Marinucci: Simon Wiesenthal Center is a renowned center that investigates Nazi activity, and Simon Wiesenthal is a renowned Nazi hunter. His center looks into similar issues, it funds the very famous Museum of Tolerance in Los Angeles. It's an extremely respected center that talks about educating people about the history of the Holocaust and the history of Nazi Germany. It's a hugely respected group, and Schwarzenegger had a great relationship with this group. He often visited them at the Museum of Tolerance. He appeared often with Rabbi Marvin Hier of the center. And that's also part of his support for the Holocaust education. He said he came from Austria where, obviously, the history of the Holocaust is quite relevant.

**Q: It's no secret that when he was running for office, the media linked him to Nazi connections and pursued to probe into his past. Do you think there was an element of spuriousness that was blown out of proportion when it was claimed Arnold was an admirer of Hitler? As I understand, Arnold had a penchant for great leaders, but he did not admire what Hitler did.**
Carla Marinucci: The whole issue of Schwarzenegger . . . I mean, I don't know about it being blown out of proportion. Schwarzenegger sometimes made comments. It's from some outtake from *Pumping Iron*. Let me say it this way: when it comes to *Pumping Iron* and how that sort of related to his political career, Schwarzenegger, by the way, denied many times that he admired Hitler. But *Pumping Iron* had a lot of scenes in it that really sort of dramatized Arnold Schwarzenegger's crazy wild past. I mean, whether it's a scene of him taking marijuana, there's all kinds of statements he's making

about women. It's the kind of activities that are not the norm for most politicians in political office. It really kind of shows how he cut a lot of flak by the public. They personally liked him and he was able to say that he was a changed man. But that didn't stop newspapers from looking into his past.

One of his biggest controversies was the groping incidents, and whether he was inappropriate with women as a bodybuilder and a movie star. But basically he did make many of the controversial comments, and many of his most controversial activities. He apologized publicly for many of those. He said that he never admired Hitler. And he denied that he ever admired Hitler. But just to recap, *Pumping Iron* contained many scenes and incidents that showed the wilder days of Schwarzenegger. And that was just one example of how he really was able to overcome a path that most politicians could not have overcome because many people thought of him as such a likable character.

Arnold vehemently denied any allegations that he had any sympathy towards Hitler or the National Socialist movement. "I have always despised anything and everything that Hitler stands for," he said. "I have from the time that I was a young kid fought against anyone that has protested for Nazis, or had any kind of Nazi sympathies, or anything like this." Arnold campaigned against that and when he moved to the United States he continued. He was very sensitive about the whole thing because he came from a country where there's a history of the whole Nazi thing. "You know, people came up to me many times when I came over here with the Heil Hitler signs, and then say the boys from Brazil are coming and all those kind of derogatory things, which I understood," Arnold added. "But, I'm sensitive about that. So I've sued the tabloids when they've said anything about me being a Nazi, and I've won the lawsuits." When Arnold was growing up, reportedly, his family never brought up the subject of his father's past – and so it's entirely plausible that he didn't have any knowledge of his father's Nazi membership.

Arnold's policies and personal views certainly back up his stated beliefs. Take the example of Jorg Haider, whose notoriety far exceeded his influence on national events, as an Austrian right-wing politician who made the headlines for the wrong reasons. Haider's parents were active Nazis in the Second World War. Haider praised the policies of Nazi Germany and the SS, which prompted widespread international concern. In 2000, Arnold expressed his deep anger at his anti-immigration policies.

"As an immigrant myself, I am offended by anyone who makes anti-immigrant statements," said Arnold in a pre-prepared announcement. "And it is my opinion that someone who makes statements like Haider's has no place in government. I have never supported him in the past and do not now. I am hopeful that Austria will find a way through this. As an Austrian-born, I am so saddened that with all the progress we have made working for an open and tolerant society, one man's statements can taint world opinion of an entire country. I know that there are many tolerant people in Austria. It is my hope that their voices can and will be heard." The far-right leader was killed in a car accident in 2008.

The year Arnold and Maria got married, Kurt Waldheim, the erudite diplomat, was running for president in Austria. Waldheim was a close friend of the Schwarzeneggers, who Arnold invited to their wedding. It eventually came to light this widely esteemed former secretary general of the United Nations had participated in Nazi atrocities in the Second World War. He had risen to the pinnacle of international diplomacy, but eventually his dark past caught up with him when he was running for president. Consequently the United States Justice Department put him on its watch list, which may have left Arnold in a quandary. "My friends don't want me to mention Kurt's name because of all the recent Nazi stuff and the U.N. controversy," Arnold said in a statement at his wedding. "But I love him and Maria does, too. And so thank you, Kurt." Waldheim did not make it to the wedding.

European historian Martin Lee told Amy Goodman in 2003,

"For Schwarzenegger to have made (the wedding toast to Kurt Waldheim) at that time after these revelations surfaced is really quite shocking. It shows, at the very least, insensitivity to the victims of Nazism and anti-Semitism...." She said that the point is not that Arnold is a Nazi, but rather the fact it raises character issues, which reflect that he's not qualified to be in public office.

**Q: Other than economic reform, no issue is more important to the future of California than a public education system. Can you shed light on the path Arnold pursued as far as teachers and education? He wanted merit pay for teachers.**

Carla Marinucci: Yes, he did. He tried to push merit pay. He tried to push reforms. He tried to push sweeping education reforms to shape the school system. But he also got a lot of push backs from the teachers' union who said that he was unfairly putting, in particularly, inner-city schools at a huge disadvantage. He got a lot of praise, Arne Duncan, the US education secretary, praised him as being courageous and saying that some of his reforms could be national reforms.

He wanted things like some school districts to shut down, the lowest performing schools. He wanted to abolish the cap on charter schools. Some of these reforms have been fought and continue to be fought by the California Teachers Union – a very powerful and very large union. So, I think he gets credit for education, which was a very big issue for Schwarzenegger. But the funding for education was also a huge problem, where the tuitions for the University of California and the community colleges were not funded because of the deficit. At the same time, he did put out some ideas and proposals that are continuing to resonate today. He had very big ambitions for California's education system and always put it on top of his agenda. But once again, he fell short of accomplishing them because of the political and financial realities of California.

**Q: Carla, regarding the immigration issue involving giving driving licenses to illegal immigrants, can you shed some light on this issue which happened to also make the headlines?**

Carla Marinucci: The driver licenses for undocumented immigrants is a huge issue to the Latino community in California. Latinos are the fastest-growing voting community in California. They're 50 percent of the voters here. Many of them support the idea of giving driving licenses to undocumented individuals. Because they say it's just safer that people who have to pass a test and have an actual identification document are more likely to report crimes, and are more likely to not be unafraid of coming forward as a witness to a crime, as well as public safety. The immigration issue is another big issue, which Schwarzenegger had wrestled with. And on this one he did not have the support of the Latino community because they were opposed to driver licenses for undocumented people. It's another issue which remains today in California.

**Q: When Arnold left the governor's office, he said he had a loss of earnings of $200 million. In other words, he could've made $200 million in the span of eight years making movies. What's your opinion, do you feel it was worth it for him to pursue a political career and become the governor?**

Carla Marinucci: It's a question of whether he could've continued to earn $20 million a film after *Terminator III*. But that said, there's no question that he took a financial hit, whether it was $200 million, it's debatable. But he did not take a salary; he did at his own expense travel up and down California and around the States and the world on his own Gulfstream jet. He did take a hit. But was it worth it for him? I think time will tell. I mean, being the head of the world's eighth largest economy is a position that no question is going to shape his future. And it has given him access to world leaders, the world's greatest innovators, the world's greatest capitalists, the kind of people that any savvy businessman could parlay into great earnings in the future. And if we know one thing about Arnold Schwarzenegger, it's that he's a very savvy business guy.

He said he gave up $200 million, but he also had an opportunity and time and direct connection with people. And that's certainly going to help him also. I'm not sure how to calculate the cost. I don't think it's a losing position for him in the final because Arnold Schwarzenegger's always been able to turn straw into gold in his life. I'm sure he's going to continue to do that.

When Arnold's time in office was terminated, his ambitions to aid in public life continued. "I have made it very clear with the Obama Administration in any way they need my help, if it's in environmental things or with other issues, and they feel I can utilize or they can utilize my talent, my personality, my star power and all of those things, I'm more than happy to help in any way possible," he told reporters. He added that it wasn't necessary for him to be in the administration to do that. Further reminding the reporter that his mother-in-law, who started Special Olympics, was never in any administration and she created Special Olympics in one hundred and one different nations, where they have now equality for people with disabilities or intellectually challenged people. "I still have the same interest in show business and movies – if it is as a producer, director or actor," Arnold said, referencing his Hollywood career. "As I have always said, I'm not going to go and look for my next job while I sit here . . ." Arnold also made it clear that he didn't have to worry about money – or at least that it was no longer necessarily his key motivation to get out of bed in the morning. He said he had made enough money for the rest of his life. "I had made a lot of money doing it, but I would've done it for no money in the end," he told an interviewer in front of an audience in 2015 at a film festival. "Because everything I've done it was very passionate and I loved doing it. It would've been also my hobby at the same time." Arnold, after his political career came to an end, once said he never has to go out and look for a job or look for something. Arnold has always enjoyed keeping busy and involved with the things that he is profoundly passionate about. He says, "I will be busy till the day I die."

# EPILOG

Few men aspire to the success Arnold Schwarzenegger has found in several areas of his life, let alone achieve it. For that reason alone, his biography merits study. I have long held the belief that if one is passionate enough, ambitious, cultivates a strong desire in whatever one wants and stands firm in the pursuit of a dream, then the chances of prevailing are high. Most people relegate themselves to being mundane and languish in their progress because they lack this drive, and Arnold stands as a reminder to those people of what is possible if they'll just push a little harder. Whatever else you think of the man, the example he sets is near unprecedented.

Arnold once said, "Most people are too close to what they're doing that they can't see themselves anymore. But I always step back and laugh at myself because you can't take it seriously, the whole thing, you know, you can't. It's something I believe we have to do, certain things, in order to keep us going and motivated. And pick little goals and go after them and stuff like that."

As much as his behavior was deliberately almost obsessive at times, Arnold was also cognizant that it is possible to suffer from an obsession too seriously pursued. For those who tend to be too critical of themselves, Arnold's demeanor in *Pumping Iron* or his media appearances is instructive – a man who's never been too proud to make fun of himself, his ability to mock his own image at times has undoubtedly made him the beloved figure he is today.

After Arnold's departure from the Hollywood scene when he was in the midst of pursuing his political ambitions, a new breed of action man emerged – a more serious, everyman figure with an everyday physique, typified by Keanu Reeves or Matt Damon. But Arnold's appeal has endured, and the success of *The Expendables* series, I think, exemplifies the kind of hero a large proportion of the public wants to see: brash, loud, and larger than life. With Dwayne 'The Rock' Johnson to some extent taking up the Governator's mantle, the man himself has reinvented himself yet again as a champion of the climate and animal welfare, trying to change the future in a way that the T-800 might respect.

Ultimately, Arnold became the biggest movie star in Hollywood and achieved global fame. The sport of bodybuilding enjoys its platform on the global stage in sports because of him. He is likely to be remembered as the greatest the sport produced, if not in physique then in popularity. He changed the rules of successful filmmaking with his career, and then changed them again after his run as governor. I have no doubt that he will keep pushing until his body no longer allows it. As the man himself once said, "My whole life I wanted to come to America. I came over here with empty pockets but full of dreams, full of desire. I had this fire in my belly, and I knew that the United States was where I could really succeed. The possibilities here are endless. I wanted to live the American Dream." Arnold Schwarzenegger is the living embodiment of the American Dream, and you need to look no further if you have aspirations to succeed.

# APPENDIX I

# BODYBUILDING TITLES

1965, Germany, Junior Mr. Europe
1966, Germany, Best Built Man of Europe
1966, Germany, Mr. Europe
1966, Germany, International Powerlifting Championship
1967, London, England, NABBA Mr. Universe, Amateur
1968, London, England, NABBA Mr. Universe, Professional
1968, Germany, German Powerlifting Championship
1968, Mexico, IFBB Mr. International
1969, New York, IFBB Mr. Universe, Amateur
1969, London, England, NABBA Mr. Universe, Professional
1970, London, England, NABBA Mr. Universe, Professional
1970, Ohio, Mr. World
1970, New York, IFBB Mr. Olympia
1971, Paris, France, IFBB Mr. Olympia
1972, Essen, Germany, IFBB Mr. Olympia
1973, New York, IFBB Mr. Olympia
1974, New York, IFBB Mr. Olympia
1975, Pretoria, South Africa, IFBB Mr. Olympia
1980, Sydney, Australia, IFBB Mr. Olympia

# APPENDIX II

# FILMS

1970, *Hercules in New York*

1973, *The Long Goodbye*

1976, *Stay Hungry*

1977, *Pumping Iron*

1980, *The Jayne Mansfield Story*

1982, *Conan the Barbarian*

1984, *Conan the Destroyer*

1984, *The Terminator*

1985, *Red Sonja*

1985, *Commando*

1986, *Raw Deal*

1987, *Predator*

1987, *The Running Man*

1988, *Red Heat*

1988, *Twins*

1990, *Total Recall*

1990, *Kindergarten Cop*

1991, *Terminator II: Judgment Day*

1993, *Last Action Hero*

1994, *True Lies*

1994, *Junior*

1996, *Eraser*

1996, *Jingle All the Way*

1997, *Batman and Robin*

1999, *End of Days*

2000, *The Sixth Day*

2002, *Collateral Damage*

2003, *Terminator III: Rise of the Machines*

2004, *Around the World in 80 Days*

2010, *The Expendables*

2012, *The Expendables II*

2013, *Escape Plan*

2013, *The Last Stand*

2014, *Sabotage*

2015, *Maggie*

2015, *Terminator Genisys*

2017, *Aftermath*

2017, *Killing Gunther*

2019, *The Mystery of Dragon Seal*

2019, *Terminator: Dark Fate*

# NOTES

## WORKS CITED

\*Franco Columbu Section:
(Commentary txt 1)
1. Peter McGough. *FLEX* (Weider Publishing), interview with Albert Busek, 2005.
2. Pete Manso, *OUI*, (Playboy Enterprises), interview with Arnold Schwarzenegger, August 1977.
(Commentary txt 2)
3. Daily Motion, interview with Franco Columbu, 2003.
4. The Tim Ferris Show, episode 60, Tim Ferris interview with Arnold Schwarzenegger, February 2015.
(Commentary txt 3)
5. *Total Rebuild* (AKA *The Comeback*) documentary, Polygram, 1980/1988).
6. Arnold Schwarzenegger, *Muscle Builder/Power* (Weider Publishing).

\*Ricky Wayne Section:
(Commentary txt 1)
7. Peter McGough. *FLEX* (Weider Publishing) interview with Albert Busek, 2005.
(Commentary txt 2)
8. *Sports Illustrated*, October 1975.
(Commentary txt 3)
9. Arnold Schwarzenegger, *Education of a Modern Bodybuilder*, Simon & Schuster, 1977.
(Commentary txt 4)
10. Arnold Schwarzenegger, *Education of a Modern Bodybuilder*, Simon & Schuster, 1977.
11. *Globe & Mail*, Karen Howlett, Schwarzenegger Reconnects with His

Bodybuilding Mentor, 31 May 2007.

*Mike Katz Section:
(Commentary txt 1)
12. Brian Johnston, In Conversation with Sergio Oliva, October 2009.
13. *Raw Iron: The Making of Pumping Iron*, (Incue), interview with Arnold Schwarzenegger, 2002.

*Bill Dobbins Section:
(Commentary txt 1)
14. *Playboy*, (Playboy Enterprises) Interview with Arnold Schwarzenegger, January1988.

*George Butler Section:
(Commentary txt 1)
15. *Iron Age*, interview with George Butler, 1987.
16. Nigel Andrews, *True Myths* (Citadel Press) 1998.
17. *New York Times*, Richard Eder, 19 January 1977.
(Commentary txt 2)
18. *Late Night with David Letterman*, interview with Arnold Schwarzenegger, 1991.
(Commentary txt 3)
19. *Raw Iron: The Making of Pumping Iron* (Pumping Iron America Inc), interview with Arnold Schwarzenegger, 2002.

*Barbara Outland Baker Section:
(Commentary txt 1)
20. *Education of a Bodybuilder*, Arnold Schwarzenegger, (Simon & Schuster), 1977.

*Jim Lorimer Section:
(Commentary txt 1)
21. The Mindset of a Champion, Chispa Motivation, You Tube.
(Commentary txt 2)
22. ShowTime Sports, interview with Arnold Schwarzenegger, 2011.
(Commentary txt 3)
23. *Esquire*, Mike Sager interview with Arnold Schwarzenegger, February 2011.

*Joe Lewis Section:
(Commentary txt 1)
24. Brian Johnston, In Conversation with Sergio Oliva, October 2009.
25. *Late Night with David Letterman*, interview with Arnold Schwarzenegger, 1987.

(Commentary txt 2)

26. *Time Out*, interview by Anne Billson with Arnold Schwarzenegger, February 1986.

27. *Cigar Aficionado*, David Shaw, June 1996.

*Eric Morris Section:

(Commentary txt 1)

28. Christopher Heard interview with Arnold Schwarzenegger, 2000.

*Sven-Ole Thorsen Section:

(Commentary txt 1)

29. *Premiere*, John Connolly, March 2001.

30. *Chicago Tribune*, 1982.

31. *Guardian*, 2010, Ben Child, 16 November 2010.

32. *Prevue 48*, James Steranko. 1982/2001.

33. *New York Times*, Vincent Canby, 15 May 1982.

34. *Variety*, staff, 31 December 1981.

35. *Arnold: An Unauthorized Biography*, Wendy Leigh, Congdon & Weed, 1990.

(Commentary txt 2)

36. NBC, Bobbie Wygant interview with Arnold Schwarzenegger, 1987.

37. Ric Drasin article 'Adventures with Arnold', bodybuilding.com, 3 March 2014.

*Mark Lester Section:

(Commentary txt 1)

38. *Time Out*, interview by Anne Billson with Arnold Schwarzenegger, February 1986.

39. Gary Schultz, Film monthly.com interview with Franco Columbu, 2003.

*Bill Duke Section:

(Commentary txt 1)

40. *New York Daily News*, 1986.

41. *Arnold: The Unauthorized Biography*, (Congdon & Weed), Wendy Leigh, 1990.

(Commentary txt 2)

42. *Late Night with David Letterman*, interview with Arnold Schwarzenegger, 1987.

*Vic Armstrong Section:

(Commentary txt 1)

43. *Entertainment Tonight*, interview with Arnold Schwarzenegger, 1984.

(Commentary txt 2)

44. *Entertainment Tonight*, interview with Arnold Schwarzenegger, 1984.

45. *The Tonight Show with Joan Rivers*, Grace Jones interview, 1984.

*Peter Kent Section:
(Commentary txt 1)
46. *Starlog*, Thomas Cleaver, December 1984.
47. *LA Times*, Kenneth Turan interview with James Cameron, August 1991.
48. *Fantastic*, Laurence Leamer, (St Martin's Press), 2005.
(Commentary txt 2)
49. *Spiegel*, interview with Arnold Schwarzenegger, March 2007.
50. *Entertainment Weekly*, Lawrence Toolee, issue #69, June 7, 1991.
51. *True Myths*, Nigel Andrews, (Citadel Press), - page 179 - 1998.
52. *Guardian*, 1991.
(Commentary txt 3)
53. *Guardian*, Ben Child, 16 November 2010.
(Commentary txt 4)
54. *Arnold: The Unauthorized Biography*, Wendy Leigh, (Congdon & Weed), 1990.
55. *Behind the Screen: Raw Deal*, interview with Arnold Schwarzenegger, 1986.

*Tia Carrere Section:
(Commentary txt 1)
56. *Aspel & Company*, ITV, Michael Aspel interview with Arnold Schwarzenegger, 1993.
(Commentary txt 2)
57. Jimmy Carter interview with Tom Arnold, 1994.
(Commentary txt 3)
58. *New York Times*, staff, 'Arab Americans Protest', 16 July 1994.

*Andrew Vajna Section:
(Commentary txt 1)
59. *The Governator*, Ian Halperin, William Morrow, 2010.
60. *Chicago Tribune*, 1990.
61. *Variety*, 1995.
62. *True Myths*, Nigel Andrews, Citadel Press, 1998.
63. *Playboy*, Joan Goodman, January 1988.
64. *Time*, 'Ten Questions for Sylvester Stallone' by Sylvester Stallone, 23 August 2010.
(Commentary txt 2)
65. *New York Times*, 1 June 1990, movie review by Janet Maslin.
(Commentary txt 3)
66. BBC, T33 interview by David Michael with Arnold Schwarzenegger, 2003.
67. WABC Radio Sean Hannity interview with Arnold Schwarzenegger, 2003.

*Chuck Russell Section:
(Commentary txt 1)
68. *Sister to Sister*, interview by Jamie Foster Brown with Vanessa Williams, 1996.

*Brian Levant Section:
(Commentary txt 1)
69. BBC, Stella Papamichael interview with Jackie Chan, 2004.

*Joel Schumacher Section:
(Commentary txt 1)
70. *Making of Batman & Robin*, interview with Arnold Schwarzenegger, 1997.
(Commentary txt 2)
71. *Time Out*, Film Guide, 1997.

*Adam Greenberg Section:
(Commentary txt 1)
72. *Premiere*, article by John Richardson, August 1994.
(Commentary txt 2)
73. *Howard Stern Show*, interview by Howard Stern with Arnold Schwarzenegger.
74. Jimmy Carter interview with Arnold Schwarzenegger, 1994.

*Kevin Pollak Section:
(Commentary txt 1)
75. *Raw is War*, Marrisa Mazzola interview with Arnold Schwarzenegger, 15 November 1999.

*Kristanna Loken Section:
(Commentary txt 1)
76. Blackfilm.com, WM interview with Arnold Schwarzenegger, July 2003.
(Commentary txt 2)
77. BBC, T33 interview by David Michael with Arnold Schwarzenegger, 2003.

*Dolph Lundgren Section:
(Commentary txt 1)
78. MTV News interview with Sylvester Stallone, 2010.

*Peter Bart Section:
(Commentary txt 1)
79. *Time*, Kurt Andersen, 'How to Run a Movie Studio', 5 July 1993.
80. *Entertainment Weekly*, Anne Thompson, 'The Lost Action Hero', July 1993.

*Alex Ben Block Section:
(Commentary txt 1)
81. *LA Times*, Greg Hernandez and Paul Lieberman, 18 August 1999.
82. *Entertainment Weekly*, Josh Wolk, January 2000.
83. *Reuters*, Arnold Schwarzenegger statement, 2000.

*Eric Watson Section
(Commentary txt 1)
84. *Daily Telegraph*, Paul Thompson, 27 April 2011.
(Commentary txt 2)
85. Joel Snape, 2019.

*In Pursuit of Politics Section
(Commentary txt 1)
86. MSNBC, Chris Matthews, interview with Arnold Schwarzenegger October 29, 2002.

*Bruce E. Cain Section:
(Commentary txt 1)
87. UPI, Steve Sailor, 'A Unique Aspect of Arnold', 15 August, 2003.
88. ABC News, interview by Peter Jennings with Arnold Schwarzenegger, October 2003.
89. *Time*, article by Jesse Ventura, August 2003.
90. *Hello*, interview with Mildred Baena, 14 June 2011.
(Commentary txt 2)
91. AP archives, 2010.

* Daniel Weintraub Section:
(Commentary txt 1)
92. *Huffington Post*, Joseph A. Palermo, 2003.
93. *USA Today*, Arnold Schwarzenegger, 2004.
94. *The Governator,* Ian Halperin, (William Morrow), 2010.
(Commentary txt 2)
95. World Entertainment News Network, 2007.
96. *Fortune*, Nina Easton interview with Arnold Schwarzenegger, 23 March 2007.
97. *LA Times*, Maeve Reston and Seema Mehta, 'Arnold Schwarzenegger's Plans Terminated? Not Likely,' 18 May 2011.

*Carla Marinucci Section:
(Commentary txt 1)
98. ABC News interview by Peter Jennings with Arnold Schwarzenegger, October 2003.
99. *Slate*, Timothy Noah, 7 August 2003.

100. *LA Times*, Tracy Wilkinson, 15 June 2007.
101. Amy Goodman interview with Martin Lee, Democracy Now, 6 October 2003.
102. *Variety*, Amy Archerd, February 2000.
(Commentary txt 2)
103. KCRA3 News, Kevin Riggs interview with Arnold Schwarzenegger, 2007.

*Epilog Section:
104. *Total Rebuild* (AKA The Comeback) documentary (Polygram), 1980/1988.

Author interviews with all the interviewed people in this publication, with additional author interviews with prominent political journalists Joe Mathews and Robert Salladay.

# ABOUT THE AUTHOR

FIAZ RAFIQ is a professional author and sports and entertainment writer. An acclaimed biographer of some of the most iconic figures in sport and Hollywood, he is the author of two other oral biographies, *Bruce Lee: The Life of a Legend* and *Muhammad Ali: The Life of a Legend*. He co-authored *My Brother, Muhammad Ali: The Definitive Biography* with Muhammad Ali's only sibling, Rahaman Ali, which was 'A *Sunday Times* Book of the Year'. He remains close friends with more than one member of Muhammad Ali's family.

Fiaz is a contributing writer for more than half a dozen prominent national newspapers including *The Sun*. For fifteen years, he was a chief columnist for bestselling combat sports magazine *MAI*, and also contributed to *MMA Uncaged*, *Fighters Only* (the world's biggest MMA magazine), *Men's Fitness*, *Muscle & Fitness* and *Impact: The Global Action Movie Magazine*. His books have been translated into numerous languages. Since 2003 he has interviewed many famous personalities including some of the greatest boxing, UFC and bodybuilding champions, countless Hollywood actors, producers and directors. He contributed to the authorized documentary *How Bruce Lee Changed the World*.